REMAKING HISTORY

The story this book follows begins on August 15, 1947. As the new nation-states of India and Pakistan prepared to negotiate land and power, the citizens of the princely state of Hyderabad experienced the unravelling of an intense political conflict between the union government of India and the local ruler, the Nizam of Hyderabad. The author explores how the state of Hyderabad was struggling to produce its own tools of cultural renaissance and modernity in the background of the union government's deployment of the central army, the Nizam's idea of "Azad Hyderabad," and the Telangana armed struggle fostered by leftist parties. With evidence from the oral histories of various sections—both Muslims and non-Muslims—and a wide variety of written sources and historical documents, this book captures such an intense moment of new politics and cultural discourses.

Afsar Mohammad is an internationally acclaimed and award-winning South Asian scholar working on Hindu–Muslim interactions in India. He also focuses on Muslim writing and Telugu studies. He teaches at the University of Pennsylvania, Philadelphia. His previously published work *The Festival of Pirs: Popular Islam and Shared Devotion in South India* (2013) has received high praise for its contributions to the studies on vernacular Islam.

REMAKING HISTORY

1948 POLICE ACTION AND THE MUSLIMS OF HYDERABAD

AFSAR MOHAMMAD

CAMBRIDGE
UNIVERSITY PRESS

Shaftesbury Road, Cambridge CB2 8EA, United Kingdom

One Liberty Plaza, 20th Floor, New York, NY 10006, USA

477 Williamstown Road, Port Melbourne, VIC 3207, Australia

314–321, 3rd Floor, Plot No. 3, Splendor Forum, Jasola District Centre, New Delhi – 110025, India

103 Penang Road, #05–06/07, Visioncrest Commercial, Singapore 238467

Cambridge University Press is part of Cambridge University Press & Assessment, a department of the University of Cambridge.

We share the University's mission to contribute to society through the pursuit of education, learning and research at the highest international levels of excellence.

www.cambridge.org
Information on this title: www.cambridge.org/9781009339636

First published 2023
Reprint 2024

Printed in India by Avantika Printers Pvt. Ltd.

A catalogue record for this publication is available from the British Library

ISBN 978-1-009-33963-6 Hardback

For my Ammi Munavar Begum (d. 2019)
and
Abbajaan Shamsuddin "Kaumudi" (d. 1997)

for all their life lessons;

more than that, for their commitment to a political ideal

with which they were associated since their teenage years.

CONTENTS

FIGURES

PREFACE

My memory keeps getting in the way of your history.

—Agha Shahid Ali, *The Country without a Post Office*

When I read this line from a poem by Agha Shahid Ali in 1998, it immediately resonated through the restless chambers of my mind. In Hyderabad on September 17 of that same year, I had witnessed a public rally of the right-wing Bharatiya Janata Party (BJP) and listened to India's then home minister Lal Krishna Advani give a provocative speech. Invoking anti-Muslim sentiment in Hyderabad and Telangana states, Advani declared that September 17 should be celebrated as "Telangana Liberation Day." That charged declaration stoked a hundred questions in me about the history of Hyderabad, a history which is already replete with intense memories of Muslim lives and their discourses between the 1930s and 1950s. On that September day, which marked the fiftieth anniversary of the integration of the Hyderabad princely state into the Indian government, the BJP was jubilant about the military action of the Indian government code-named "Operation Polo" or "Police Action." But could we really call it a "celebration" given the violent history that led to the killing of thousands of Muslims and Hindus, and to the global displacement and migration of thousands of Hyderabadis?

Since the demolition of the Babri mosque in 1992, Advani had already been part of the heightened consciousness of the local Muslims. During this period, wherever I went I heard resounding critiques of Advani's statements. However,

September 17, 1998, was different. Like many young Muslims of the 1990s, I too had grown up with anti-Muslim slogans buzzing around me—among them *Musalmaan ke do hi sthan, qabristan ya Pakistan* (A Muslim has only two choices of abode: the graveyard or Pakistan)[1]—and had been called names such as *Babar ke aulad* (the children of Babar, the Mughal emperor), Aurangzeb *vārasulu* (the heirs of Aurangzeb, another Mughal emperor often remembered for his policies on anti-Hindu and Islamic fundamentalism), and "Jihadists."[2] Graffiti and jeers constantly reminded me that my *mulk* (home country) is somewhere in Pakistan. As Advani and his followers explicitly stated several times, I am not a patriot according to their "nationalist" framework.[3] Those intense moments prompted me to write a poem entitled "No Birthplace" remembering the violent experiences of the Partition of 1947 and the rise of Muslim minoritization.

> *Some limbs and organs*
> *under a vacuum head.*
> *Where did I come from?*

> *None of you told me,*
> *So, at 1947 why I blew up*
> *and remained*
> *—broken since then.*[4]

Many writings and oral accounts from Hyderabad and Telangana emphasize that the 1948 Police Action was nothing but an extension of the Partition. Such sentiments once again started playing a central role in the making of a new Muslim identity around 1992—the beginnings of Hindu nationalism. In that kind of political environment, how does one comprehend the consciousness of the new-generation Muslim? Can we gauge it merely through the lens of their faith (*'īmān*) or by identifying their sense of being and belonging with some "foreign" country? I took up these two questions in my previous work, *The Festival of Pīrs*, in which I questioned our normative understanding of the nature of Muslim public rituals in South Asia.[5]

Between 2006 and 2012, during my field research for *The Festival of Pīrs*, I met several Muslim and non-Muslim witnesses of the violence of the 1948 Police Action. It was through them that I started realizing that the response to these two questions should not be limited to faith. We must ask larger questions to investigate this new Muslim consciousness and its multi-layered history. In talking to various groups of Muslims and Hindus in different parts of Hyderabad and Telangana, I heard multiple responses to these questions. Many of my interlocutors recognized that this variety of responses had barely anything to do with faith—at least faith as many contemporary political factors had defined it. Within the modern history of Hyderabad, these political and religious associations are connected to many regional factors and actors, yet the being and belongingness of a Muslim remains central.

This book is a direct result of asking such larger questions. Although it is a close study of the narrativization of the 1948 Police Action in Hyderabad, many of its observations go beyond that specific event. This book recalls a long journey replete with all kinds of hurdles, as we can imagine from the documentation of any violent event, whether it be the Partition or the Holocaust. Several scholars who have focused on those events tell how different forces commingle to silence or marginalize the voices of such events. In addition to these hurdles, what happened between September 13 and 17 regarding the integration of Hyderabad into the Indian government has been endlessly misinterpreted and falsely recounted, largely because of the dominance of ideologies of nationalism, majoritarianism, and religious fundamentalism in the local historiography.[6] In the case of Muslims and Telangana, there has been a constant hegemony of the privileged localism, such as Telugu nationalism, that led to the formation of the Telugu-speaking state of Andhra Pradesh in 1956.

The oral accounts in this book document the deeply expressed concerns of many Hyderabadis, concerns that their story even now remains silenced by the overemphasis on the Telangana rebellion, Telugu nationalism of the same period, and the politics of the nation-state. When I began my archival work, I very soon realized that their pain was no exaggeration. However, it was not easy to get them to speak out about the violence and its aftermath. It also took me longer than I had expected to find any sources—both oral accounts and written materials related to the Police Action. For even the Sunderlal Committee's report was de-classified only in 2012, and I learned from various sources that documents and images related to the Police Action were also deliberately removed and disappeared from most public archives. In such a time of censoring and silencing, I started thinking about Muslim history as a whole around the Police Action and its immediate consequences. The very first challenge I encountered was the absolute silence of the witnesses, who include not only ordinary people but also the socio-political activists who had been extremely active in the late 1940s. I noticed that most of my witnesses were still experiencing trauma from the Police Action, even six decades later. In fact, contemporary Hindutva politics play a particularly prominent role in silencing them; many of these witnesses (as they themselves told me later) "do not want to get into any trouble." Many also noted that "talking about that event is like inviting the trouble on our own." Because of the political pressure put on witnesses, and their consequent reluctance to talk, I had to wait for more than two years for some testimonies. This situation recalls what the anthropologist E. Valentine Daniel termed "the drone of silence."[7]

Nonetheless, I persisted. After all, I have been fascinated by Hyderabad since childhood. When I started reading about Hyderabad during my college days, I also developed an interest in learning more about the long decades from the 1930s to 1950s, particularly about Muslim politics, the Partition, and the Police Action of 1948. Despite several publications on Hyderabad and Telangana, none of the available materials helped me understand the Muslim question. However, I was always surrounded by books and people celebrating the historical Telangana armed rebellion led by the Communist Party (1946–1951),[8] and my own family had been quite engaged in this movement. Both my parents' families were part of its activism, and my father was on several Communist Party committees and a member of its two prominent literary and cultural wings such as the Progressive Writers Association (PWA) and the Indian People's Theater Association (IPTA). When I talked to my grandmother, Fatima Begum, about the changes she witnessed during the 1940s, she said:

> Everything happened so quickly, we could not even understand what was going on. Since my family—including all my sons and daughters—were active members of the Communist party, most of the information was from the Party. When I look back now and try to remember anything about the Police Action, nothing comes to my memory. I just remember many party workers were killed and unfortunately the party had to wind up its activities thereafter.[9]

It took me a while to comprehend that her memory was extremely selective because she was recalling the event through the lens of the Communist Party. Like her testimony here, every conversation about the Police Action with my family ended with a comment along the lines of, "Well, whatever happened, happened! We've come a long way after that bloodshed. We barely remember anything about it now!" Several publications likewise conclude that the Police

Action was the end of all the history related to the Hyderabad princely state and Muslims.[10]

Since 1948, the language employed at a national level too talks about how the Police Action has tended to be deceptive, politically influenced, and utterly devoid of the sentiments articulated by locals. Rather than being grounded in the past, most of it is defined entirely by contemporary politics that are closely entwined with the ideologies of various political parties. As mentioned earlier, the right-wing BJP was extremely jubilant about imposing their narrative as the singular version of the Police Action. Over the intervening decades, the five days of battle between the Indian government and Hyderabad state have been recounted in many ways and retold from many different perspectives. Though several writings and media posts have also tried to reimagine history by mentioning the "tyranny" of the nationalism that led to the destruction of the Hyderabad state, these are still almost always limited either to praising or blaming the Nizam of Hyderabad. In fact, it has been a very black-and-white conversation since 1948, and more so since 1998.

Precisely seventy-three years later, on September 17, 2021, as I was still working on a chapter for this book, there was an outpouring of social media messages, emails, and online posts related to the "integration" (*vilīnaṁ* in Telugu) of Hyderabad state into the newly formed Indian government in 1948. Those comments clearly perceived the "integration" and the end of the Nizam's rule as a "celebration of the liberation of Hyderabad and Telangana." I read that the home minister, Amit Shah, attended the "Telangana Liberation Day celebration" in the town of Nirmal, and I noted his declarations that the BJP would make sure that Telangana could in future celebrate this historic day without fear.[11] He also recounted the "historic efforts" made by the then home minister Sardar Patel. Yet the idea of "celebration" was actually nothing new as this afterlife of the Police Action goes back to the 1998 politics of the right-wing declarations of the "Telangana Liberation Day."[12] Such contemporary politics have made the entire historical memory of the Police Action even more of an ideological battlefield than before, and the pain of the Hyderabadi community continues to be obscured. At this point, I made it my goal to retrieve this pain and its impact on the community, and to do so from the perspective of an ordinary Muslim of Hyderabad. This categorization of an ordinary Muslim definitely includes the larger Hindu community of the state.[13]

As I finished writing this book, I had a strong feeling that this was just another beginning. There are many dimensions of the violence of 1948 that still need to be explored and debated. In light of all the restlessness I experienced

while writing and thinking about this book, I end this preface with one of my
poems on Hyderabad:

people still have that age-old smile
from the last century
that gracefully flows
and spreads through all the spaces.

You're flooded by the words
that barely sound
either Urdu or Telugu,
it's an idiom you and I forgot to inherit.[14]

NOTES

1. This process of stigmatizing and othering Muslims has a long process in
   the history of India. Christophe Jaffrelot provides a detailed analysis of this
   movement in *The Hindu Nationalist Movement in India* (New York: Columbia
   University Press, 1998); for a recent perspective, see Qudsiya Ahmed, "How I
   Got Over That Dark Geographic Shadow Called Pakistan," *The Wire*, April 6,
   2018, https://thewire.in/culture/how-i-got-over-that-dark-geographic-shadow
   -called-pakistan (accessed July 11, 2022). This essay too suggests searching
   multiple associations that go beyond the faith.
2. See Audrey Truschke, *Aurangzeb: The Life and Legacy of India's Most
   Controversial King* (Stanford: Stanford University Press, 2017).
3. Yamini Krishna and Swathi Shivanand, "BJP Made Gains in Hyderabad
   Using History as a Weapon: But How Accurate Is Its Version of the Past?"
   Scroll, January 21, 2021, https://scroll.in/article/983875/bjp-made-gains-in-
   hyderabad-usinghistory-as-a-weapon-but-how-accurate-is-its-version-of-the-
   past (accessed July 21, 2022).
4. Afsar Mohammad, *Evenings with a Sufi* [Collection of poems from Telugu]
   (New Delhi: Red River Press, 2022).
5. Afsar Mohammad, *The Festival of Pīrs: Shared Devotion and Popular Islam in
   South India* (New York: Oxford University Press, 2013).
6. See the Introduction of this book for a detailed discussion: Swami Ramananda
   Tirtha, *Memoirs of the Hyderabad Freedom Struggle* (New Delhi: Popular
   Prakashan, 1967).

7. E. Valentine Daniel, *Charred Lullabies* (Princeton: Princeton University Press, 1996), 150.

8. For a recent debate about the Telangana armed struggle and the Communist Party's local history, see Sunil Purushotham, *From Raj to Republic: Sovereignty, Violence, and Democracy in India* (Stanford: Stanford University Press, 2021), 6–9, 182–224.

9. Conversation with Fathima Begum from my personal journal.

10. See Chapter 4 of this book for an idea of such materials.

11. Sreebaala Vadlapatla, "Will Observe September 17 as Hyderabad Liberation Day with a Chest Full of Pride: Amit Shah," *Times of India*, September 18, 2021, https://timesofindia.indiatimes.com/city/hyderabad/will-observe-september -17-as-hyderabad-liberation-day-with-a-chest-full-of-pride-amit-shah/ articleshow/94261032.cms (accessed September 18, 2022).

12. For more on this debate, see N. Venugopal, *Lechi Nilichina Telangana* [The resurgence of Telangana] (Hyderabad: Swechchaa Saahiti, 2000) in which he invokes the poet and activist Bertolt Brecht's famous words about "Hitler's lies." For an entire debate in the Telugu public sphere, see Vivek Tadakamalla and Sangisetty Srinivas, *17 September 1948: Bhinna Dṛkkōṇālu* [Different perspectives on 17 September 1948] (Hyderabad: Telangana History Society, 2010).

13. Ashokamitran's novel published in Tamil and then also translated into Telugu and English provides evidence of this non-Muslim perception. See Ashokamitran, *Janta Nagarālu* (New Delhi: National Book Trust, 1985); Ashokamitran, *The Eighteenth Parallel*, trans. Gomathi Narayanan (Hyderabad: Orient Blackswan, 1993).

14. Mohammad, *Evenings with a Sufi*.

ACKNOWLEDGMENTS

Most of the people who deserve my gratitude here have slipped into some unknown past. Now, I remember all those who opened their houses and hearts to share their memories of the Police Action and various historical moments between the 1930s and 1950s. When I started talking to them around 2006, they were active, healthy, and cheerful, bursting with an enthusiasm for life. When I started writing these chapters around 2019, and crept through each page, I started losing them either to COVID-19 or to various other sicknesses. Consequently, I found it hard to listen to their wonderful voices on my audio recorder. That pain of loss delayed the process of transcribing them first into Telugu and then into English. During this gloomy journey, I had many questions and therefore often tried calling one or other of my interviewees, seeking answers or simply more details of an event. Their families typically returned my call by saying, *"Anna,* the elderly one (*peddāyana*) is no more! He was asking about you and your book! Many times, he asked us to 'call Afsar *bēṭā* and ask him to finish the book soon!'"

For many of these families, I have become their *bēṭā* (son) or *anna* (brother) over the past fifteen years. I took so much from them to create this book and felt I was giving them next to nothing in return. The last time I met Quddus Sahab before his death around 2017, he said: "Afsar *bēṭā, kitab jaldi likho ... bas ... voh bahut jaroore tarikh hai!*" (My son, finish writing the book soon. It is good enough, and it is very important history!). He had always been fascinated by Muslim *tarikh* (histories)—starting with the battle of Karbala and through to the Telangana separatist movement of the 2000s. The only thing I could give him for his many conversations was a stack of history books about Telangana. The memories and voices of many people like Quddus Sahab in the city of Hyderabad or the various distant villages of Telangana have filled my notebooks and voice recorder. So, my *salaam*s should go to all these people, whom I met early on in my field research.

For more than a decade, I traveled far and wide to the remotest corners of Telangana and the crucial sites of the Deccan, always in search of people who could speak about the intense moments of the history of the Hyderabad princely state. On those travels, I made friends with several generations of folk performers, activists, local historians and—most importantly—very ordinary people, who barely scratched together a living but had an enormous treasure trove of precious memories. I walked with them to their village fields, I sat with them at the local shrines. I ate their food and had their delicious buttermilk or chai. I still recall all their faces. Like some wall of a war memorial, to do them all justice I would need to list at least 150 names, many of them individuals who shared with me stories of ordinary Muslims and Hindus who suffered and survived all manner of hardships during the Police Action and the Telangana rebellion. Even though relatively few of their words appear in this book, many of their stories will stay with me forever.

During the second phase of field research around 2013, I visited many libraries and research centers in my search for archives and printed materials about the Police Action. Yet the most important materials were ones I found in the private libraries of the freedom fighters, social activists, and some readers who had actually started their reading journey in the late 1940s during those violent times. Heeralal Moriya, Kavi Raja Murthy, Saravadevabhatla Viswanatham in my hometown of Khammam, Jeelani Bano, Burgula Narsing Rao, "Maa Bhoomi" Narsinga Rao, Dasarathi Rangacharya, Samala Sadasiva, Abid Ali Khan, Huma Kidwai, Mutyam, Alladi Uma, and M. Sridhar and their families in Hyderabad—all opened their entire libraries to me. There I found old newspapers, literary bulletins, and printed versions of various party documents which had enjoyed wide circulation in the 1940s.

But for me the true archives and living texts were the conversations that I had with these families. And to my surprise, despite their passion for poetry and fictional writings, these families had saved many historical documents. Until her death in 2019, I shared the details of each conversation with my mother (Ammi), Munavar Begum. Due to our family's leftist activism, Ammi knew some of its history or about some of these personalities, and she helped me by adding a few more details to whatever they had recalled. Since Ammi was also a voracious reader of Urdu and Telugu fiction, her reading experiences also enriched my historical understanding of these particular decades of the Deccan. Many members of my extended family have helped me enormously to make connections and flesh out missing information in those personal and public histories.

Despite all their enthusiasm about my topic, my research and writing turned out to be an extremely slow journey. The sheer amount of violence and trauma, and the many sad memories of my interlocutors, were emotionally hard to take on board, and they haunted me like nightmares. Over the years, many friends and scholars encouraged me to continue with my work, hard as it was. Finally, when I was teaching at the University of Texas at Austin in 2012, Syed Akbar Hyder asked me to give a talk about Kavi Raja Murthy's 1949 Urdu novel *Mai Gharīb Hu* for the university's series on Sadat Hasan Manto's literary influences to celebrate his birth centenary. This talk titled "Manto Beyond Urdu" was well received and followed by an intense discussion by one of my favorite Urdu scholars, Shamim Hanafi sahib, along with Donald Davis, Carla Petievich, Kathryn Hansen, Snehal Shinghavi, Kamran Asdar Ali, and the entire team of the Hindi–Urdu flagship program at that school. Even before he died in 2021, Shamim Hanafi sahab called me and asked about my manuscript. He repeatedly said: "We need more of such work beyond Urdu and its vernacular histories."

On the heels of this 2012 talk in Texas, I was invited to speak at several universities and conferences. It was because of those invitations that I started playing with an idea: to study this literary history by connecting it to the larger history of the Hyderabad princely state and the politics between the Indian government and the Nizam with an emphasis on ordinary Muslims and Hindus of the 1940s.

Rejuvenated by this new set of questions, I returned to the field in 2013 to meet political activists and literary personalities in Telangana. At first, I met the Hyderabad-based Urdu writers and their families. Then, I began visiting not only the locations that had been affected by the Police Action but also the centers of the Telangana armed rebellion. Based on some of these materials, in 2016 and 2017 at Emory University and Columbia University respectively, I spoke about Telugu and Urdu language politics and Jeelani Bano's Urdu novel *Aiwan-e-Ghazal* as an example of a gendered Muslim history. During the discussions at Emory, Velcheru Narayana Rao, Joyce Flueckiger, Harshita Mruthinti Kamat, Gautam Reddy, and Jamal Jones shared their critical feedback. At Columbia, Carla Bellamy's question about the political dimension of Jeelani Bano's novel helped me focus my enquiry. The current version of Chapter 3 was actually a result of my discussions with Carla and her colleagues Frances Pritchet, Jack Hawley, and their graduate students.

At a 2017 conference at the University of Pennsylvania on vernacular politics and identities, my wonderful colleagues including Lisa Mitchell, Ramya Srinivasan, and Megan Eaton Robb shared their appreciation and valuable feedback on my presentation that eventually became Chapter 2 in this book. That same year, Raisur Rahman invited me to participate in a conference on Muslim being and belonging at Wake Forest University; there, I presented some materials that are now included in Chapter 1 of this book. That prompted exciting conversations about various dimensions of Muslim identity, urbanity, and modernity, in which Raisur Rahman helpfully pushed me to rethink many aspects of the Muslim question. Bruce Lawrence, Ali Mian, and Razak Khan were in touch with me with helpful comments and encouragement while I was working on this particular chapter. Another segment of this chapter was presented in 2021 at the British Library (my thanks to Priyanka Basu). Benjamin Cohen, Taylor Sherman, and many other scholars participated in the discussion, and of them I particularly thank Benjamin Cohen. Their thoughtful questions helped me think through and write the Introduction and Chapter 1 of this book. In 2019, at the University of Pennsylvania's Annual Telugu studies conference, where I gave a talk about one dimension of the Telugu–Urdu debate, Jangam Chinnaiah, Rama Mantena, and Mallampalli Chandra Sekhar's discussions with me were particularly helpful.

I drew on some of the book's materials in my courses on Indian literature and South Asian Islam at the Universities of Texas and Pennsylvania. I am grateful to my students who read those draft materials and participated in those intense discussions. In fact, their comparative vision made me connect my materials to different phases of minority activism in the USA, including connecting Black Lives Matter to the Citizenship Amendment Act in India. Lisa Mitchell, my wonderful colleague and longtime friend, read and gave me feedback on some parts of this work. Indivar Jonnalagadda has always been there for me ever since we started talking about this project around 2017. He patiently read multiple drafts of the manuscript, and we met several times over coffee or Telugu food to discuss my ideas and the underlying theoretical issues.

In between, I traveled to Hyderabad several times to collect the materials and conduct the interviews. Before the COVID-19 pandemic, I conducted interviews with Burgula Narsing Rao, Jaini Mallayya Gupta, Jeelani Bano, B. Narsinga Rao, and several activists who had been part of the various historical movements during the 1940s and 1950s. In Hyderabad, Sajaya Kakarla, Vommy Ramesh Babu, M. A. Moid, Suneetha Achyuta, Jeevan, Burgula Vijay, the families of Jaini Mallaya Gupta, Jeelani Bano, Sarvadevabhatla, Vivek Tadakamalla,

Alladi Uma, M. Sridhar, Jayadeva Rentala, Safiullah Sahab, Sibghat, and Anant Maringanti were particularly helpful. K. Srinivas, N. Venugopal, and Sangisetti Srinivas were always there to respond to my questions about various historical events and materials related to this project. Venugopal was extremely generous when sharing some books and ideas. Ever since we met virtually in 2013, Mohammed Ayub Ali Khan has been a constant inspiration as I researched and wrote this manuscript. During my many trips to India, Gurram Seetaramulu was always fully present to me for both friendly and scholarly conversations. Pathipaka Mohan and Mehak Hyderabadi shared some images for this book. At the University of Pennsylvania, during several conversations, Davesh Soneji shared his critical feedback and encouraged me to finish this book. Daud Ali, Deven Patel, Suvir Kaul, Ania Loomba, Jamal Elias, and Greg Goulding have always been kind to me and have shown great interest in this work ever since we met in 2016. At Cambridge University Press and Assessment, Qudsiya Ahmed, Sohini Ghosh, Anwesha Rana, Priya Das, and Aniruddha De have shown great interest in this book and inspired me to finish it on time. I am particularly grateful to three anonymous reviewers who read each chapter carefully and shared critical feedback.

Beyond the University of Pennsylvania, Charley Hallisey, Chris Chekuri, Sunil Purushotham, Razak Khan, Yamini Krishna, Kena Chavva, Eric Beverley, Himadeep Muppidi, Torsten Tschacher, Deepra Dandekar, Danielle Wildmann Abraham, Kerry San Chirico, Bala Venkat Mani, Sarah Waheed, Raj Karamchedu, Kathinka Frøystad, and Ravi Verelly have been my support group for this book work. For more than a decade, Ulrike Guthrie has been an efficient and skilful editor, and I appreciate her help throughout my writing journey. Last but not least, my wife Kalpana Rentala and my son Anindu deserve my heartfelt thanks for all their inspiration, personally and professionally. Finishing this manuscript happily means spending more time with the family!

INTRODUCTION

1948 POLICE ACTION

A SILENCED HISTORY OF HYDERABAD

The Police Action was an end of many good beginnings in our lives. We lost not only many friends, our personal careers, and houses, but also and most importantly, the tehzeeb of our shared culture. If someone says it is just about few Muslims, no, not at all. It's a pain about the entire community of the then Hyderabad and Telangana.

—Abdul Quddus Saheb, September 20, 2006.

In September 2006, during the field research for my previous book *The Festival of Pīrs*, I took an early morning bus to Karim Nagar, an urban town famous for the public rituals of Muharram. Almost 200 miles away from the city of Hyderabad, this urban town has a significant Muslim population and was also greatly influenced by the Shi'i Islamic practices of Hyderabad. In Karim Nagar, I met 78-year-old Abdul Quddus Saheb, who began our conversation by talking about the songs of his youth during Muharram, the commemorative event of the martyrdom of the Prophet's family. After a while, he surprisingly took a detour just to talk about the Police Action of 1948. Being a young man of around twenty at the time of this violent event, Quddus Saheb was one of the witnesses of that traumatic era and the consequent divisive politics that partitioned Muslims and Hindus. Many of his memories, as I document here, narrate the story of the new generation of Muslims whose everyday lives and future dreams were brutally shattered by the Police Action of 1948.

According to Quddus Saheb, "It was a nightmare for us, as every Muslim in the Hyderabad state had suddenly become an enemy of the people. We were experiencing the height of every form of hatred and could not even step out of our homes." Growing up in such a hateful environment, Quddus' own story offers a lens through which to glimpse both the external and interior struggles of many Muslims during this period. Before this tragedy, Quddus Saheb was known for his mesmerizing performance of the songs of Muharram, both in Telugu and Urdu. When the Police Action was executed between September 13 and September 17, 1948, along with many other traditions, this narrative performance, according to Quddus Saheb, "started fading out" too.[1] He recalled many memories from this period. During my interview, Quddus said:

> Abdul Quddus Saheb (AQS): In those days I would sing the songs of Muharram both in Urdu and Telugu. I was not even twenty and so enthusiastic about this performance as I strongly believed in its ability to connect Hindus and Muslims. There was no separation between Hindus and Muslims either in daily life, or during these religious events. The people of my town or any village around this place never made any distinctions when it comes to Muharram. I thought that was an ideal setting, and I had also trained several groups of the performers of the songs. It's unfortunate now that I also witnessed a wall of separation and people start using the terms such as "Hindu Muharram," and "Muslim event."

> Afsar Mohammad (AM): Do you remember when exactly this separation happened?

> AQS: In my understanding, it was all either before or after the Police Action, 1948! The violence followed by those five days of invasion shattered our lives—took away the *tehzeeb* of our everyday lives. It was nothing short of any war—the *jung*, *yuddham*. I am not talking just about the Muslims, but the entire community of Muslims and Hindus.

Whereas Quddus Saheb's usage of the terms *jung* and *yuddham*—meaning "battle"—for the Police Action is key for my argument in this book, I was also reflecting on how he was emphasizing the term *tehzeeb*, and towards the end of the conversation, we returned to the same idea:

AM: I want to learn more about the idea of *tehzeeb* in this context. How do you make a connection here?

AQS: The *tehzeeb* of our town's life comes from Muharram and many other devotional practices that we shared. That's where we learn about co-existence and sharing—*milan sār*, "way of life" [*milan sār* in Urdu and *kalupugolu* in Telugu].

Then he suddenly switched to Telugu to say: "idantā ā yākṣan taravāta cediripōvaḍaṁ ṣurū ayindi. jaṁg aṇṭē yuddhaṁ vacciṁdi" (All this had begun to shatter after the Action. The battle had started!). Somewhat prompted by his words, I took on the task of researching the archives of written and oral sources about the Police Action of 1948. These expressions from the oral accounts also compelled me to start meeting different kinds of people from various parts of the city and Telangana. First, I had intended to talk to the primary witnesses of the Police Action—popularly known as "action" in public memory and Pōlīsu Carya in the political writings on the state of Hyderabad. Many interlocutors consider this as another Partition and narrate the stories of violence and trauma that left many Muslims homeless and displaced. Nevertheless, they were also conscious of the politics of remembering and forgetting.[2] Initially I asked myself and these witnesses two apparently simple but actually quite complicated questions: Why and how was such a traumatic event ignored by mainstream historiography? How does the politics of mentioning, forgetting, and remembering play into this negligence, denial, or misinterpretation of this violent event?

Whereas a few studies offer more evidence about the political tensions between the nation-state and the Hyderabad state, this book focuses on how such processes resulted in the making of a new Muslim discourse in the wake of the Police Action.[3] It proposes that this historical event was a commingling of multiple aspects that had begun with the tensions between the making of the new nation and the question of Muslim representation in 1948 and then extended further into the recent debates about the strategic minoritization and isolation of Muslims, particularly those in Hyderabad state. Several studies discuss this formation of the political minority of Muslims as related to the Partition of India and Pakistan.[4]

This book begins by questioning various ways of the mainstream historiography that privileged the master narratives of nationalism, the

Telangana armed rebellion between 1946 and 1951, and the Telugu linguistic state formation of 1956.[5] Those narratives totally ignored the violent event of the Police Action and the Muslim question. Despite many disenchantments and heavy losses, I argue, the Hyderabad and Telangana situation offers a model for how Hindus and Muslims responded and emerged out of a crisis by offering new strategies such as urbanization, Islamic reformism, and Muslim belonging to resolve the conflict between Hindus and Muslims. This model is much needed today in India—a country ridden with increasingly divisive politics and the rhetoric of Islamophobia. Informed by recent studies on diverse Muslim identities, Islamophobia, nationalism, religious conflicts, majoritarianism, and the post-secularist turn along with the related debates in contemporary literary and cultural engagements, I will discuss multiple dimensions of Muslim identity and religious politics as articulated in various literary narratives and oral histories throughout this book.[6] Unlike the dominant historiography, these sources offer evidence for the mutuality of the shifting Muslim discourses and the rise of the Muslim public sphere, including specifically local Telugu and Urdu hybrid aesthetics in post-1940s Hyderabad.[7] In conversation with global Islamic movements and activism, these locally produced aspects define a new framework to understand the complexities of the Hyderabad and Telangana-based Muslim identity.

By focusing on how this specific period also was successful in producing a new set of modern prose writings in Hyderabad city and Telangana, this book argues that the Muslim question has acquired many nuanced features as it journeyed through different phases of the public sphere. This crucial turn was reflected in both oral and written cultures that emerged in rural and urban locations—thus representing a constant flow between the city of Hyderabad to even remote regions of Telangana. Many of these themes from the Police Action are now being revisited and retold against the backdrop of the post-2000 Telangana state movement. In many ways, these connections take on deeper interpretations as the process of retrieval and reconstruction of the historiography of the Hyderabad state and Telangana engenders multi-layered discourses.

By documenting the stories of diverse groups of actors and agents in this historical event, I analyze varied understandings of Muslim contextualization between 1940 and 1950. However, it is quite intriguing to define a "Muslim" context within the literary sphere of Telangana and Hyderabad. Many "Hindu" writers, including Nelluri Kesava Swamy (1920–1984), Bhaskarabhatla Krishna Rao (1918–1966), Kavi Raja Murthy (1926–1985),

Dasarathi Krishnama charya (1925–1987), and Samala Sadasiva (1928–2012) whom we meet in this book, always deliberately located themselves in a liminal space which was neither Hindu nor Muslim. In addition, they were all writing in Telugu and Urdu at once while participating in various literary, cultural, and political organizations that promoted a shared Hindu–Muslim *tehzeeb*. When we read their texts and life stories closely, as I do in this book, we understand that their voices have always been much closer to the idea of Muslimness, thus owning every aspect of Hyderabadi and Telangana Muslim practices. How one non-Muslim individual or writer or social activist could locate himself or herself within this Muslim public sphere remains a key question. In the process, the definition of Muslim belonging within this local cultural and religious milieu complicates any understanding of *the* singular definition of Muslimness by challenging nationalist, secularist, and even leftist readings. Such readings, in fact, have origins in the immediate reports published after the Police Action, as I briefly discuss in the following pages.

FIVE DAYS OF POLITICS AND CONFLICTS: "HAPPY WAR" OR "MILITARY INVASION"?

On August 15, 1947, as the new nations of India and Pakistan prepared to negotiate land and power, their borders were bloodied by the violence of the Partition. But India's territorial disputes were not limited to its western and eastern boundaries: instead, the citizens of the princely south-central state of Hyderabad were experiencing an intense political and religious conflict between the union government of India and the princely state of Hyderabad. A year later in 1948, to control the regional power of the Nizam of Hyderabad and his private army known as the Razakars, the union government of India deployed the central army for a violent intervention under the code named "Operation Polo," popularly known as the "Police Action."[8]

The five-day military invasion of Hyderabad state (Figure I.1) resulted in tragic consequences, although the media projected it as a "happy war." *Time* magazine of London specifically assigned a correspondent to cover this event and published extensive reports. The very first news story on September 20, 1948 began:

> *Time* correspondent Robert Lubar, together with a *Life* reporter and photographer, set out in a hired 1935 Ford to have a look at the war

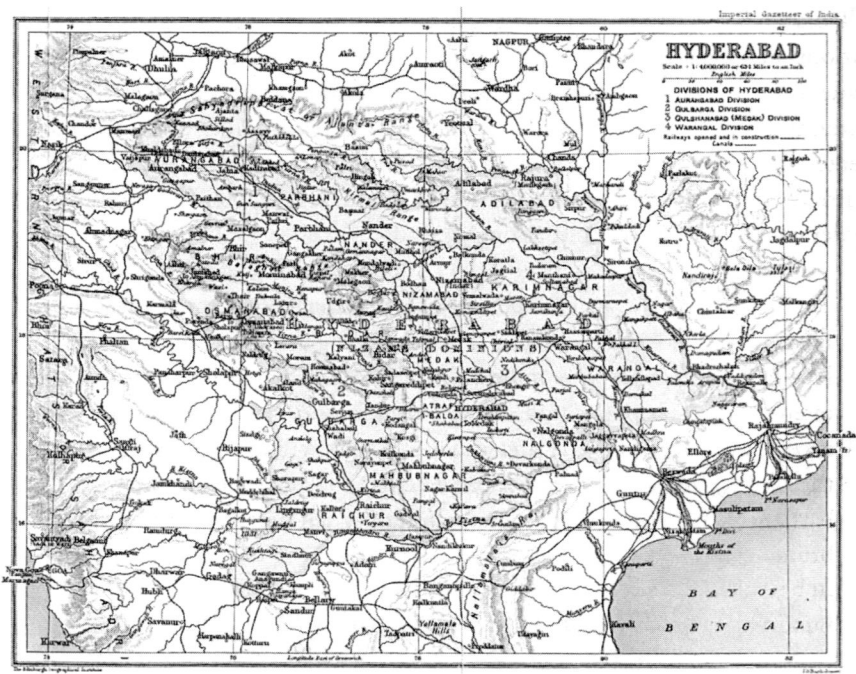

Figure I.1   Hyderabad state from the *Imperial Gazetteer of India,* 1909

Source: Wikimedia commons, https://commons.wikimedia.org/wiki/File:Hyderabad_state_from_
the_Imperial_Gazetteer_of_India,_1909.jpg (accessed May 2, 2023).

between India and Hyderabad. The Indian army had undertaken
a "police action" (which it also called a "mission of mercy") against
Hyderabad where predominantly Hindu population was ruled by a
stubborn Moslem Nizam. The would-be war correspondent sped 180
miles towards the front, found that the war was over by the time they
got there. All in all, it is one of the shortest, happiest wars ever seen.
Cabled Lubar:

"Everyone is satisfied. The aggressive section of Indian public opinion
has been appeased. Hyderabad, which was never really out of India, is
now indisputably part of India. There have been no terrible outbreaks of
communal violence."[9]

Efforts to retrieve the ordinary voices of Muslims against this background
were hindered by the media politics of the late 1940s. In one of the stories,

as I discuss in Chapter 1, Nelluri Kesava Swamy describes how two radio stations—a national station of the Indian government and a local station in Hyderabad—were busy broadcasting their competing versions of the news materials rather than the actual facts. The ambiguity and utter confusion created by the media exacerbated the havoc of this event. The historian Wilfred Cantwell Smith, who witnessed these developments in the city of Hyderabad, described the situation:

> On September 13, 1948, the Indian army, moving on five fronts, invaded Hyderabad; and in less than a week the conquest was complete. The Nizam's army, apparently more of an exhibition than a fighting force, offered negligible opposition. There were relatively few battle casualties except amongst Razakars and other Ittehad civilian volunteers, who threw themselves in as a rather pathetic but devoted resistance. Off the battlefield, however, the Muslim community fell before a massive and brutal blow, the devastation of which left those who did survive reeling in bewildered fear. Thousands upon thousands were slaughtered; many hundreds of thousands uprooted.[10]

According to the Sunderlal Committee, which was appointed by Jawaharlal Nehru, the first prime minister of India, and led by Pundit Sunderlal and Qazi Abdul Ghaffar, "only three of sixteen districts in Hyderabad state were free of communal trouble." Whereas the districts of Osmanabad, Gulburga, Bider, and Nander were the worst affected, Aurangabad, Nalgonda, and Medak had lost 5,000 in each district. The committee reported:

> We can say at a very conservative estimate that in the whole state at least 27 thousand to 40 thousand people lost their lives during and after the police action. We were informed by the authorities that these eight were the worst effected districts and needed most the good offices of our delegation. We, therefore, concentrated on these and succeeded, we might say, to some extent at least, in dispelling the atmosphere of mutual hostility and distrust.[11]

About the extent of the violence and deaths, Taylor Sherman noted:

> It is difficult to elaborate the scale and nature of the violence that occurred. The information available to the historian is incomplete,

both because of the difficulty in capturing such events in historical documents. And because not all of the reports that were drawn up have been opened to public view.[12]

Indeed, for the most part such stories about the violence, migrations, and survivors remain unexamined in the history of Hyderabad. The suppression of the Sunderlal report, as the historian Omar Khalidi noted, was "due no doubt to its adverse comment on the conduct of the Indian army."[13] Despite its first-ever disclosure of such violence during and after the Police Action, the Sunderlal Commission's report remained "classified" until recently as the Indian government considered it to be harmful to "national interest."[14] In his book *Hyderabad: After the Fall*, Khalidi documented several reports and early writings about the Police Action, which he called "[t]he Hyderabad Holocaust."[15]

Sardar Patel, the then home minister, who masterminded and supervised the entire Police Action, even went so far as to insist that there was no such thing as a "Good Will commission" appointed by the government.[16] According to the political scientist Noorani, the government of India also used its media and suppressed the hard facts of the entire action, convincing the authorities that "at times one has to close his (*sic*) eyes in the national interest."[17] Patel's distrust of Muslims and his view of them as "aliens" further complicated the entire issue.[18] There were also reports about how Patel ignored even the warnings of Prime Minister Nehru, who clearly said: "One of the persistent charges made against us is that we intend to kill what is called Muslim culture. Hyderabad is known all over the Middle East as a city of Muslim culture."[19] Nevertheless, the grand narrative of nationalism and Sardar Patel's anti-Muslim ideology buttressed by political authority ended up marginalizing and suppressing the Muslim side of the story. Recent studies by Taylor Sherman and Sunil Purushotham have presented more evidence for various aspects of violence during the Police Action. Purushotham's 2015 essay "Internal Violence: The 'Police Action' in Hyderabad" and the 2021 book *From Raj to Republic* together document and analyze how internal violence became an "important engine of state formation" in post-Independence India.[20] This side of the story of endless violence towards Muslims and the migrations and survival of Muslims is still marginalized in the dominant historiography of Hyderabad. Local newspapers like *Inquilab*, *Zamindar*, and *Ehsan*, as documented by Sunil Purushotham, had extensive coverage of this "Muslim butchering en bloc."

In addition, this particular period also witnessed numerous political and religious transformations related to the Hindu–Muslim question (Figure I.2). The Nizam of Hyderabad and the Razakars had started circulating the idea of Azad Hyderabad (Independent Hyderabad) and a "Muslim State"—some writers used the Telugu term *Mahammadīya rājyaṁ* (literally, "Mohammadan State")—to claim their independent political authority.[21] On the other hand, the leftist parties undertook an armed guerilla movement known as the Telangana armed rebellion (*Telaṅgāṇa sāyudha pōrāṭaṁ* in Telugu) between 1946 and 1951 against the locally dominant feudal system.[22] Between these two modes of political violence and the battlefield of diverse viewpoints, Telangana was struggling to produce its own tools of political transformation

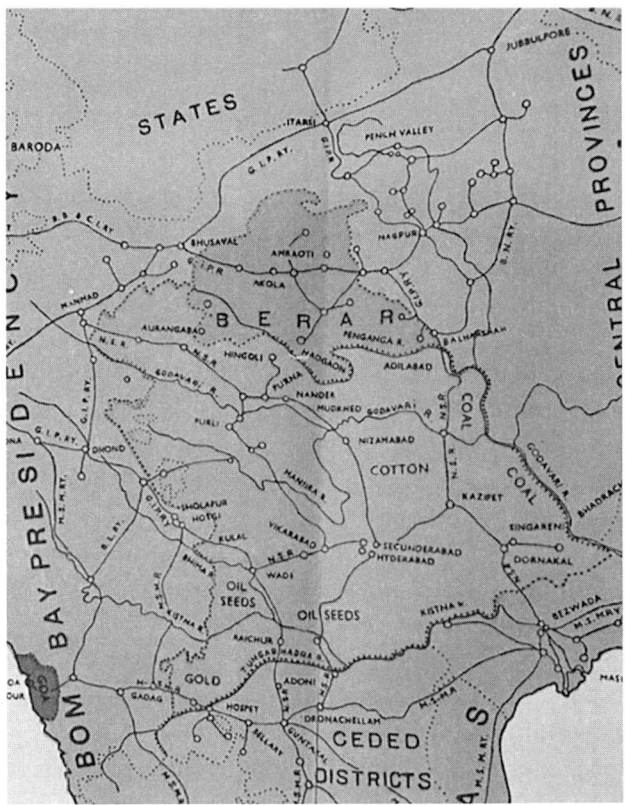

Figure I.2 The map of the Hyderabad state from the document of the appeal made to the United Nations (later published in 1951)

Source: Document on the Hyderabad Question before the United Nations, Karachi, 1951.

and a local version of modernity.[23] Prior to this violent political moment, argues historian Benjamin Cohen, Hyderabad state had envisioned a clear break from the feudal setting to being an era of a "new Hyderabad."[24] From 1908 to 1948, many such developments produced an urban Muslim category, which culminated in the making of a new Muslim identity along with the "new Hyderabad" during the Police Action. Against this complex background, any discussion about Police Action, as I show in this book, was not confined to immediate violence and trauma. Despite its unsettling impact, the political event of the Police Action in many ways resulted in revisiting the Muslim question that includes an urban dimension of Muslimness and the Hindu–Muslim composite culture—otherwise popularly known as the Hyderabadi *tehzeeb*. How do we understand these two dimensions when the very identity of Muslims was in danger during the Police Action?

THE MUSLIM QUESTION, HYDERABAD, AND TELANGANA

Although a wave of anti-Muslim sentiment pervades many of the writings promoted by the nationalists and leftists, the question about Muslim being and belonging remains largely unanswered or buried. The Muslims of Hyderabad did indeed experience intense moments when their belonging was challenged. But the critical moment of the Police Action, which historians such as Omar Khalidi and A. G. Noorani described as the "fall of Hyderabad," created a new dilemma. This led to an unprecedented disenchantment with the nationalist mission of the Indian government along with a fear of majoritarian political authority. Being a Muslim in this political and religious context challenged the individuals' everyday life and survival beginning in 1948. This book emphasizes the urgency of reading this history through the lens of Muslim belonging to understand various political and religious transformations that fashioned the everyday life of Muslims in the long 1930s and 1940s. It proposes that this historical event was a commingling of multiple aspects that had begun with the tensions between the making of the new nation and the question of Muslim representation in postcolonial India, and then extended further into the recent debates about the strategic minoritization and isolation of Muslims, particularly those in Hyderabad state. Several studies discuss this formation of the political minority of Muslims as related to the Partition of India and Pakistan.[25]

Hyderabadi Muslims perceived the idea of *azadi* as, to use the Urdu novelist Jeelani Bano's words, "a broken promise." Most of my interlocutors of the Police Action including several cultural and political activists; both Muslims and Hindus viewed this violence as "nothing but one of the major side effects of the Partition."[26] Indeed, some of them said that this entire event and violence was in aid of an immediate political resolution to the Muslim question, which remains unresolved. Whereas we barely have any studies that focus on the Partition or related violence in south India, many of these oral accounts narrate how the idea of Partition and Pakistan transformed the dynamics of Hindu–Muslim everyday lives locally, even in the remotest parts of Hyderabad state.[27]

According to many interlocutors of the Police Action, the entire Muslim community of Hyderabad state experienced deep trauma and paralysis in their everyday life, even in remote parts of the region. While many families lost their livelihood, thousands of young Muslims migrated to the city seeking refuge from the violence caused by the local police and the union army. As the Indian Civil Service Officer M. K. Vellodi remarked, "the majority of the population had resigned themselves to being alternatively beaten up by the Police, by the Army, or by the Communists."[28] Given this deep trauma, it is understandable that the Hyderabadi community was experiencing a sense of grave loss and even lost hope of receiving any outside help.

The evidence in this book portrays manifold ways of encouraging Muslim agency at different levels of political and cultural discourse with an emphasis on how Islam and Muslimness are defined or interpreted in a local idiom—in this case, the Hyderabadi and Telangana language. Finding a voice and searching for alternative ways of reconstructing their everyday lives had positioned the community differently, rather than merely speaking as victims. In essence, the Muslims of Hyderabad, as portrayed in these oral and written sources, refuse to be depicted as victims. Instead, they rebuilt their everyday lives right from scratch by participating in a wide array of contemporary global and local progressive discourses. Many activists even now believe that Muslim voices in particular were either totally silenced or entirely marginalized by the new language produced by these ideological battles. In such a context, how do we understand the efforts made by various organizations affiliated with the Communist Party of India, and various left-affiliated trade unions and the Progressive Writers Association to restore the resilience of the Hyderabadi community?

Figure I.3 Makhdoom Mohiuddin: A symbol of Urdu–Telugu progressive legacy in the Telugu public sphere of the 1940s

Source: Courtesy of Makhdoom Mohiuddin's family.

Speaking from the perspective of a Muslim belonging, well-known progressive writers and political activists such as Makhdoom Mohiuddin (Figure I.3) also contributed to this dimension of resistance by writing and circulating booklets that discussed the Muslim question even before the Police Action took place. Many of Makhdoom's Urdu writings and speeches were translated into Telugu and made available to the new generation of political and cultural activists during this period. In addition, several fictional writings and non-fictional works including memoirs, personal essays, and autobiographical writings likewise describe Makhdoom's role in the making of the Telugu public sphere. Makhdoom's 1947 essay focused on how the Nizam's rule exploited the country's new resources, mainly industrial and business ones. He also explained what Muslims should do against the Nizam's policies that were bent on promoting local upper-caste landlords.[29] Arguing that the Nizam was nothing but a representative of British colonialism, Makhdoom called for action against the Nizam's autocratic rule. Makhdoom's analysis, published in Telugu, however reveals more about the status of Muslims in the state of Hyderabad and deserves some attention here. Despite his explicit leftist perspective, Makhdoom debates the marginalization of a lower-class/poor Muslim community that, to use his words, "was being exploited by all means." This position is similar to what I will describe in Chapter 2 where the novelists Kavi Raja Murthy and Bhaskarabhatla Krishna Rao portray the life stories of two Muslims. Murthy's novelistic representation of a *garib* (the poor) and Bhaskarabhatla's depiction of a middle-class Muslim shatter the stereotype of the Muslim *navābi* lifestyle. These two novels and Makhdoom's essay published before and after the Police Action conceptualize the idea of the class, thus unpacking the discourse of a subaltern Muslim identity.

The historian Margrit Pernau's recent study on Muslims in nineteenth-century Delhi theorizes about how the idea of class should be revisited. Pernau also points out that the "Muslim workers are hardly studied":[30]

> Since the 1980s and 1990s, Partition has been replaced as the central question by reflections on the origins of fundamentalism and its counter-forces. For all their differences, these studies share a tendency to assume that Muslim identity is primarily informed by religion and that the creation of a community on the basis of religion surpasses and eclipses other forms. This assumption—that the non-religious identities of Muslims are only tenuous or even entirely undeveloped—probably also explains why there are relatively few studies dealing with Muslim women, workers or the Muslim middle classes, despite the flourishing of gender and social historiography in India.[31]

In the case of Hyderabad, Makhdoom's essay and literary narratives including Murthy, Bhaskarabhatla, and Swamy, inform us about how even the economic status of middle-class Muslims had deteriorated essentially to that of the lower class due to a major shift in the power structures, the continuing economic hegemony of non-Muslim landlordism, and the marginalization of Muslims in the postcolonial and post-Independence government sector. These writings demonstrate that even during the Nizam's rule, this particular section of non-Muslim landlords had control over most of the economic resources. These writings explain the process that made Muslims remove themselves from the *navābi*-centered lifestyle and demonstrate the growing levels of poverty among Muslims. In the process, Makhdoom also questions the version of "modernity" that the Nizam had strived to bring to the state of Hyderabad. For Makhdoom, it was nothing but an attempt to mimic Western modernity. He emphasized that this modernity was meant to promote "the economic needs of the north Indian Muslims and their newly created employment opportunities in the city." The establishment of Osmania University, likewise, he thought, was intended to support the educational needs of those non-*mulki* Muslims.[32] In contrast to this debate on the Nizam's modernity, now I turn to another major topic—the creation of a "New Hyderabad"—as a strategic site in the construction of Muslim discourse. However, I argue that this version of Hyderabadi modernity has always been much more nuanced and multi-layered, and that it crosses the boundaries of class.

LOCATING MODERN HYDERABAD BEFORE, DURING, AND AFTER THE POLICE ACTION

Although the very idea of defining modernization has its own implications in the case of Islam and South Asia, the Hyderabad state under the Nizam's rule was successful in adapting and appropriating certain key aspects of modernization. Current scholarship, both in the Western and the Indian context, is now also informed by more local processes rather than Euro-centric modernity.[33] Nevertheless, when it comes to Hyderabad, this global approach acquires multiple dimensions as the Nizams took pride in producing Hyderabad's own version of modernization. According to the historian Bhangya Bhukya, British colonialism tried to project princely states such as Hyderabad as "backward enclaves that kept alive an older feudal polity characterized by autocracy and underdevelopment, while British colonial India moved towards modernity and capitalist development." Such modernity in colonial India, mainly circulated from British-ruled Andhra, is now being critiqued as a strategy of the imperial regime of "imposing British power on the region's natural resources."[34] In the wake of the recent Telangana separatist movement, this critique now emphasizes the modernization project initiated by the eighth Nizam and his prime minister, Salar Jung-I. During the early phase of socio-political, religious, and economic reforms, Hyderabad was being defined as a "new Hyderabad," *kotta/ādhunika haidarābādu* in Telugu, and *nayā haidarābād* in Urdu. What were the components of the idea of the "new Hyderabad" and why it was key against the background of the Police Action? In this section, I argue that envisioning Hyderabad as a modern space encompasses multiple aspects, but the most important for us here is its constant engagement with the making of a Muslim identity, which was disrupted by the violence of the Police Action. The historian Sunil Purushotham effectively sums up the Nizam's efforts to connect with the larger Islamic world:

> The Nizam generously patronized Islamic scholarship and funded the Hajj for hundreds and thousands of Indian Muslims. The Nizams funded Syed Ahmad Khan's Muhammadan Anglo Oriental College at Aligarh almost from its inception, and many Aligarh-educated Muslims from North India found employment in Hyderabad. Hyderabad became a center of Urdu and Islamic scholarship in its own right after the founding of Osmania University in 1918. India's first vernacular university, Osmania served as a symbol of Hyderabad's unique modernity. Osmania enhanced Hyderabad's status as an important center of a trans-regional 'Urdusphere' that connected Muslim intellectuals in India with those as far away as Kabul, Durban, Istanbul, and Cairo. Hyderabad was thus a 'nodal center in the Muslim intellectual world,' linking Muslim thinkers from Aligarh, Deoband, and Lucknow to their counterparts in the eastern Mediterranean.[35]

In the wake of the Nizam's fight for Azad Hyderabad, such efforts were portrayed as attempts to create a "privileged minority." According to the *Time*, "The Indian government's biggest objection to the Nizam is that he has elevated the Moslem minority of the population to a position of power and privilege."[36] Such strategies of labeling the Nizam as a "Muslim" were the result of the communalization of politics even two decades earlier in Hyderabad. Like any region in India, Hyderabad, too, had experienced a phase of Hindu and Muslim revivalisms that indeed transformed the entire picture of everyday life.[37] Nevertheless, such a process of minoritization—as one of my interviewees, Imam Hussain, told me—hit the most vulnerable Muslims the hardest.

> What about ordinary and poor Muslims like me? We never had any *jāgīr* or any piece of land or even enough bread to survive the day. I know hundreds and thousands of Muslim families living in utter poverty. The *ashraf* and *nawabi* families—both from Muslims and Hindus as well— never cared for our daily basic needs of food, water or housing.[38]

Even now, many political activists and writers express similar concerns about the status and fate of ordinary Muslims in the late 1940s. Most believe that the modernization projects in practice benefitted largely and only the upper caste and class, elite communities of local Hindus and non-local Muslims in Hyderabad state. These imbalances in the new economic policies led to an entire movement of *mulki*—calling for "Hyderabad for Hyderabadis"—that sprang up in the era between the Police Action and the formation of the separate Telugu state of Andhra Pradesh (1948–1956).[39] Despite many manifestations of such political and economic marginalization of the "locals," the very idea of *mulki* has been a constant presence in the history of Hyderabad and Telangana since the late 1940s; the Police Action had indeed worsened the economic status of Muslims in the city and state.[40] Within this entire debate, the making of the city (*şahar*), the neighborhoods (*bastī* or *mohallā*), and endless migrations from the rural and semi-urban sites to the city were key in defining the making of a Muslim self after the Police Action. Against this critical background, we need to study the making of Hyderabadi and Telangana literary culture as it emerged in the 1940s.

RECONSTRUCTING HYDERABADI AND TELANGANA LITERARY HISTORY

Many anthologies of Telugu writings published by various literary groups of the coastal Andhra fail to document the contributions made by Telangana- and Hyderabad-based writers.[41] Contemporary literary critics from Telangana state argue that most of these historians and literary anthologists were "blind" to the early phase of creative writings coming from the Hyderabad state.[42] These critics countered the statements made by the coastal Andhra editors and anthologists who continuously projected that there was no significant production of literary writings or cultural refinement in Telangana. Pointing out such statements as "incomplete" and "hasty," Mudiganti Sujatha Reddy described various activities that produced modern prose in the 1940s.[43] In particular, Mudiganti analyzed how writers' associations such as Sādhana (1936), the Nizāṁ Rāṣṭrāndhra Sārasvata Pariṣat (1943), the Andhra Sārasvata Pariṣat (1948), and the Telangāṇa Racayitala Sanghaṁ (Telangana Writers' Association) were instrumental in making space for a wide array of new modern prose genres in Hyderabad state.[44] In 1941, Vattikota Alwaru Swamy (1915–1961) indeed electrified the literary sphere throughout the state by traveling even to remote villages, carrying a box of newly published books

Figure I.4   Vattikota Alwaru Swamy: One of the pioneers of modern Telangana print culture

Source: Courtesy of Sangisetti Srinivas.

and giving talks about them (Figure I.4). In this way, Vattikota's publishing house, namely Dēśōddhāraka Grantha Māla (1941), ushered in a new era of the book market in Telangana.[45]

According to Sujatha Reddy:

> The literary scene between 1940 and 1956 was an embodiment of the modern consciousness.... There was not only a resolute effort from individual writers, the entire activity was solidified by various Hyderabad-based literary organizations, which had humble beginnings and then acquired a broader base throughout Telangana. The initial efforts of this particular period have deeper consequences even in the contemporary politics of the Telangana after 2002.[46]

Of late, the Telangana separatist movement produced a new set of discourses about the reconstruction of the history of the Hyderabad state and early modernity in Telangana. This entire effort began with the popular statement made by Vattikota Alwaru Swamy in 1956:

> In almost all nine districts of the Telangana region, there are large number of works related to history, sculpture, inscriptions, paintings, palm leaf texts, tanks, forts and the related warrior stories. The number of writers and artists is enormous, and they have been leading various social and cultural movements ever since the beginning.[47]

Invoking these words, several historians, writers, and cultural activists gathered in 2006 to institute the "Telangana History Society." For the first time in the recent history of Telangana, the documents published by this society have enabled us to theorize the idea of the reconstruction of Telangana's history. Vivek Tadakamalla's introduction exposes many "misreadings and manipulative citational practices" in the historiography of Andhra Pradesh and invites scholars and creative writers to uncover a new set of tools and practices to document the history of Hyderabad and Telangana. Vivek said:

> It is imperative now to understand our history and reconstruct it in its entirety to assert the regional identity of Telangana. For a long time, we had no information in our text books about our Golconda empire, Qutub Shahis, and the Nizams. Nothing has been documented about our struggles of resistance, the fight for the rights of the ordinary people and about our historical figures. We always hear that the Nizams were dictators and fundamentalists. We just started realizing that many historical aspects of the Nizams have been continually misrepresented. It is now our responsibility to gather all these historical facts and rewrite our own history.[48]

Many essays published in this booklet discover different aspects of the Telangana historiography including the Police Action and the Muslim question. Several scholars in this booklet unequivocally state that literary writings from the Hyderabad state should be excavated to understand the multi-dimensional history of Telangana.[49] Despite many such efforts, however, the Muslim question remains understudied, resulting in an incomplete understanding of the Muslim-related politics and cultures in the Hyderabad state and Telangana.[50]

Methodologically, this book takes particular note of various Muslim portrayals available in the Telugu writings of Telangana around 1948. These Telugu materials speak extensively about Muslims, but also about Hindu–Muslim interactions in detail. The contours of such a narrative realm reach out farther into the distant corners of Telangana. The excavation of these alternative archives, I argue, should begin with another key question: How do we understand such a vibrant portrayal of Muslim life against the context of new directions in Indian literature around the 1940s? The textual and oral historical accounts presented in this book propose a unique realm of Muslim-specific aesthetics that bridge the new discourses in postcolonial Indian history and literary narratives. During its early phase of literary history, this realm was defined by the Progressivist writings (1940–1948), Partition literature (1947 onwards), and then the rise of the identitarian writings including Dalit and Muslim discourses (1992 to the present). Several Telugu and Urdu writers and historians explicitly speak about the impact of progressivist writing beginning with the 1940s as I demonstrate in the following chapters. In Hyderabad, this movement of progressivism had many local manifestations as the progressive writers adapted an entirely new set of locally produced cultural practices, including setting up writer's organizations and cultivating a literary imaginary that privileges Telangana-specific politics and social life. The Hyderabad-based progressivists expanded their activities even to the remotest rural areas in Telangana, launched book reading clubs, and published leftist literature that includes progressive writings from the Urdu language. This activity also includes a broad range of publications related to Marxian theoretical writings and translations from various Russian writers. Many minor publication centers devoted to leftist writings, journals, and readers' clubs were established throughout Telangana.

According to Guduri Seetharam, by the late 1940s different sections of individuals and activists in almost every village in Hyderabad state had established a library, and many writers had migrated to the city to participate actively in progressive politics. In one of our conversations, both Jeelani Bano and Huma Kidwai explained the deep influence of Urdu poets such as Makhdoom Mohiuddin even in rural situations. Most of these activities in many ways had, in the words of Seetharam, "democratized the literary sphere by allowing the writers from the lower sections including Muslims to participate extensively."[51]

Such a process further extended into contemporary Telugu discourses as a new group of Muslim writers emerged in the post-1992 period of Hindu nationalism. More importantly, the religious consequences of the demolition of the Babri mosque had resulted in a definitive historical moment in Muslim writing in India.[52] First, there was a continuous wave of Muslim responses to the 1992 event and the rise of Hindu nationalism; second, several writers also revisited the questions raised by the Partition. In many writings in Telugu, we see a blend of the influence of the Partition and the response to Hindu nationalism, as several of them literally described the post-Babri demolition situation as the "second partition." To describe the literary works of these writers, we can invoke the term "Partition effects."[53] In *Translating Partition*, Ravikant and Tarun Saint pointed out how "the new archives of survivor's memories are being created to supplement the available sources such as autobiographies and biographies, poetry and fictional accounts."[54] Using the term "long partition," the recently edited volume entitled *Revisiting India's Partition* recognizes the importance of studying the regions beyond Punjab and Bengal.[55] Such an excavation of the archives would be incomplete without documenting the oral histories from Telangana with an emphasis on how the Telugu community responded to various historical and political events of the Partition and Police Action.

In addition, following the model provided by various debates on Dalit literature, several studies now offer fresh insights into revising the Indian literary canon and historiography. Based on the Marathi literary corpus, Sharan Kumar Limbale's work *Towards an Aesthetic of Dalit Literature* critiques mainstream literature and aesthetics.[56] Literary historians Judith Mishrahi Barak, K. Satyanarayana, and Nicole Tiara describe it as "sketchy, suggestive and rhetorical."[57] Laura Breuck's recent work on Dalit literature in Hindi provides more tools to understand this new framework and shows how Dalit aesthetics emerge as a "political statement."[58] Such a conceptualization is relevant in engaging with different modes of Muslim writing during historical moments such as the Partition, Police Action, the Babri mosque demolition of 1992, and the recent Gujarat genocide in 2002. In the last few years, studies on progressivist writing and the Partition have offered fresh insights into the question of Muslim belonging, along with Hindu–Muslim interactions.

The historians and cultural critics Mushirul Hasan and Asaduddin, in their anthology of Muslim writings *Image and Representation*, pointed at the rupture among various discourses and noted:

While we share some of the concerns of the traditional and modern interpreters of Islam, we do not necessarily endorse their framework and world-view, especially when it runs contrary to a liberal and secular discourse and reinforces, despite their protestations to the contrary, the popular stereotypes of Islam and its followers. Any discussion based on scriptures or on the corpus of knowledge inherited from the theologians cannot explain how Islam and its tenets (a project that is at any rate pursued relentlessly by theologians of all hues) but to challenge scholarly exertions to 'essentialize' civilizations.[59]

Emphasizing the value of diversity and pluralism in everyday life, Hasan and Asaduddin noted:

the enormous diversities and the variety of beliefs and practices, the multiple levels at which a Muslim relates to the temporal and spiritual world in day to day living, and the currents of change, reform and innovation that have influenced the course and direction of quite a few Muslim societies the world over.[60]

Whereas the everyday lives of Hindus and Muslims actively produced the dynamics of a pluralist notion, the post-1990s era was also a moment when the specificity of a Muslim voice was being debated.[61] Around the same time when Hasan and Asaduddin were discussing many such issues related to the Hindu–Muslim interactions, the Hindi-language monthly *Hans* published a special issue on Muslims writing in Hindi and opened a debate on the role of Muslims in contemporary politics and everyday life.[62] Asghar Vazahat, the editor of this special issue, acknowledged the importance of connecting the current Muslim debate with aesthetics with an emphasis on the progressivist agenda by delving deep into Muslim narrativization in India. Several writings in Telugu, however, offer evidence for a diversity in literary expressions that transcends the limitations of a progressivist agenda. This intense moment in the history of Hyderabad and Telangana literature, I claim, begins with the writings on the Police Action and the Muslim public sphere created during the 1940s.

In *Remembering Partition*, historian Gyanendra Pandey discusses how the violence of Partition created "new subjects and subject positions," in "radically altered settings."[63] Similarly, for most of my interlocutors, the events and results of the Police Action were just as dramatic as the Partition, prompting Hyderabad state and Telangana's metamorphosis after 1948 into an entirely different entity with a new set of political and religious subject positions.

Considering the political history of Telangana, even now, many issues related to the Muslim community's political role in the history of the state are being addressed from the limited perspective of the critique of the Nizam's rule.[64] In the case of my family's history, this perspective was defined by their leftist politics and memories of the party. Even the party documents written and circulated by leftist Muslim poets such as Makhdoom Mohiuddin were thick with party jargon and knowledge structures.[65] Beyond such documents, we also find a mighty wave of poetry and prose works that highlight the Telangana rebellion and the triumphant stories of the movement.[66]

As mentioned before, this book begins by challenging this perspective of selective politics that took many forms after the rise of Hindu nationalism and the growing Islamophobia evident both locally and globally. Undoubtedly, the Police Action and its immediate consequences left the elite and upper class (*ashraf*) Muslims of Hyderabad state helpless and homeless. But what about ordinary Muslims? How did they survive? And what alternatives did they figure out to remake their everyday lives? This book seeks to address these questions by telling the story of an ordinary Muslim in the aftermath of the Police Action's shocking violence and trauma.

Several studies about the political turmoil created by the Nizam's insistence on the independence of Hyderabad (Azad Hyderabad) and the Police Action discuss a variety of issues such as diplomatic matters, defense affairs, political negotiations, colonial and postcolonial implications, the politics of citizenship, and the escalating nationalism. One detail in particular from Sunderlal's report struck me:

> Almost everywhere in the effected (*sic*) areas communal frenzy did not exhaust itself in murder alone in which at some places even women and children were not spared. Rape, abduction of women (sometimes out of the state to Indian towns such as Sholapur and Nagpur) loot, arson, desecretion (*sic*) of mosques, forcible conversions, seizure of houses and lands, followed or accompanied the killing.[67]

Although this report reveals several such facts and figures, when I started my field research in 2006, I had barely any sources to examine this history of the Police Action. In many ways, this book is also a personal journey for me—as a Muslim individual, writer, and scholar. Several dimensions of my personal life and family history matter in this search: my conversations with the people whom I met (including my family), the historical writings that I have been reading since my high school days, and my individual engagements with various political movements, and last but not the least, the bilingual life world of Urdu and Telugu that I inherited from my ancestors. This field research and textual journey have allowed me to re-engage with my own past in several ways while continually reinforcing the questions: How far will you go in search of your Hyderabadi past? What do you expect to find there? And what do you do with what you find there? Besides that, my work also highlights how the present discourses after the Telangana movement and in light of the new political awakening among the activists, writers, and the public sphere have contributed to a critical discourse on the Nizams, Muslims, and Hyderabad.[68] This also led to a critique of the way the Police Action has been remembered and discursively constructed.

Now when I revisit those readings from my early school days from a critical distance, I am better equipped to categorize them as (*a*) oral histories, including my family history; (*b*) popular performative tools consisting of the long folk narratives such as *burra katha*, a popular oral storytelling practice that became a political tool in the 1940s and the play of *Mā Bhūmi*;[69] (*c*) films such as the *Mā Bhūmi* (Our land) (1979) that privilege the Telangana rebellion;[70] and finally, (*d*) literary sources that narrate the story of the pre-modern history of Hyderabad and contemporary Telangana. Most of these materials were a central part both of my childhood memory and the public imagination of Telangana, which were actually retrieved after the 2004 separatist movement. Following extensive field research between 2006 and 2020, I realized that people, including my own family, retell the event in their own ways. In doing so, their politics of memory and reimagination undergo irony and playfulness. Thus, along with documenting the history of the Police Action, this book also tells the story of my unsettling journey with different forms of historical materials and their engagement with contemporary Telangana and the Muslim question—the journey that made me look for an alternative archive, as I describe in the next section.

ALTERNATIVE ARCHIVES: THE JUXTAPOSITION OF LITERARY SOURCES AND ORAL HISTORIES

In fact, I felt that the fiction writers of my times were closer to the dark reality of the day than historians or journalists. If you want to understand what was happening in an ordinary Muslim's life in Hyderabad of my generation, you should read fiction. That's where my generation learned more about all that was happening: the *tarikhu katha*, "historical story." That's where the real history is!

—Vara Lakshmi, 92-year-old reader of the 1940s Telugu literature

In 2014, it was by chance that I met Vara Lakshmi Sarvadevabhatla (1930), the wife of Kavi Raja Murthy (1926–1985), an eminent Urdu-Telugu bilingual writer and Telangana freedom fighter whose writings are one of the primary sources in this book. She is one of the few living witnesses of the Police Action of 1948, and when I asked her about the event, the very first reaction was about their family's pain of losing all their Muslim friends in Hyderabad and Telangana. During our conversations, she recounted several incidents of the brutal killings of Muslims and their forced migrations to Pakistan. Many of my interlocutors, including writers and cultural and political activists, provided the minute details of various historical moments between the 1940s and 1950s along with the vivid portrayals of different leaders and ordinary people of the period. Nevertheless, most of their knowledge about that history comes from the literary writings of their days. For them, the fictional writings of their times were not "just fictional." According to them, the short stories, novels, and autobiographies of this specific period function more like testimonials that narrate contemporary communal strife and Hindu–Muslim lives. That way, Vara Lakshmi's words about history are not exceptional or isolated.

During my field research between 2006 and 2020 in and around various regions in Telangana, I heard from many interlocutors about the idea of *tārīkhu katha*. From these conversations, I gather that they use this term which is a blend of Telugu and Urdu words for what can be called the "historical story." This term is commonly used by the Telangana folk performers for their storytelling of the martyrdom of the Prophet's grandsons, Imam Hussain and Hasan, in the seventh-century historical battle of Karbala. The local performers use this term as a strategy to authenticate their version of the Karbala narrative and explicitly acknowledge that this practice is inclusive of both ideas of "history" and "fiction." Using a similar term in the context of the Telugu narratives of the Police Action, I understand, many witnesses from Muslim and Hindu groups too were trying to acknowledge similar popular performative practices. In this world of storytelling or history-telling, there is no definitive line between the terms "history" and "story." In other ways, using this term also allows them to engage with various historical events in an alternative mode, which by all means contests mainstream historiography of nationalism and the singularization of religious identities.[71]

When I hear such conversations about fiction and history, they reminded me of Vasudha Dalmia's words in her work on Hindi novels: "Through their attention to detail, their minute documentation of shifts in structures of feeling, novels are often a record of social history in ways that social history itself is not."[72] Many sources that I investigate in this book portray similar "shifts in structures of feeling," however, with an emphasis on the Muslim question between 1945 and 1950 in Telangana and the Police Action. In his study on autobiography, testimonio, and the novel in the Chicano and Latino experience, Mario T. Garcia noticed that "a literary writer not only can provide us with historical evidence, but also can provide a personal insight into history that more formal documents cannot."[73]

In a similar mode, another historian, Allan H. Pasco, too raises the question about the legitimacy of using fiction as historical archives. Although his observations were mostly about French history, in the case of this book and my emphasis on finding new resources to "uncover the past," these words are relevant:

> Used carefully—and remembering that reality is never pure, simple, or linear—literature and the arts can bring fresh light to our perception of history. One should not expect literature to be an exact mirror or have a one-to-one relationship with objective reality—the mimetic fallacy—but the historian/critic can find it extraordinarily useful. It is a response to reality, whether by reflection or reaction.[74]

While I totally acknowledge the "necessity of care" in handling such fictional sources, in the case of my work, I learned that we can fill those gaps by juxtaposing these sources with oral histories. However, at this point, we should also note that even written sources are not always objective as many subjective factors intervene in the understanding of an event. The politics of remembering and forgetting, silencing, or marginalizing individual persons, sociocultural institutions and political movements play their role in the triangle of fact, memory, and history.

As mentioned earlier, the earliest phase of this oral history research began with my family from whom I heard many stories about the history of the Hyderabad state, which they called the "Nizam." This usage was a contraction of the political term "Nizam-ul-Mulk," the administrator of the realm; the term "Nizam" became the popular way to signify the rule of the Asaf Jahis (1724–1948).[75] Many of my family's stories about this part of history and politics circle around the power of leftist discourse.[76] By projecting the Telangana rebellion as a central narrative, along with the Communist Party, their generation strongly believed that the Telangana would make their dream of a "socialist state" a reality.[77] Small wonder then that I grew up reading fiction, non-fiction, poetry, and songs related to the Telangana armed rebellion, and that my family history inspired me to read more about that heroic guerilla battle.[78] In this way, my own understanding of the history of Hyderabad and Telangana had certain immediate political and personal implications inherited from my family and their immediate political setting. Since most of my textual and family narratives were fully occupied with these materials, the Police Action of 1948 remained an extremely insignificant event in my memory. Like most of the post-1980s generation of people, I took serious note of the Police Action only when I attended the public meeting of the then Home Minister L. K. Advani in 1998. Questions about "liberation" (*vimōcana*), "integration" (*vilīnaṁ*), and also about the "betrayal" (*vidrōhaṁ*) of the Indian government were hot topics after 1998.[79] Until that moment, I had carried with me only a version of the leftist narrative passed on to me by my family. Later, the identity politics known as *astitva udyamālu* ("identity movements", to put it clearly, the post-Marxist identity movements, as their emphasis on the negligence of the leftist discourse about their identities remain the foci of their argument) in Telugu that focused on women, Dalits, and minorities began to push me to reassess both these historical events and everyday Muslim life in Hyderabad state. This was also the moment when I witnessed an emerging Muslim discourse in the Telugu and Telangana public sphere that forced me towards reconsidering the histories of the Nizams and Hyderabad.[80]

Along with these dynamics of religious identities and ethics, I argue, the political dimension of Telangana and its Persian connections also characterizes Muslim being and belonging. Specifically, my work utilizes the vocabulary provided by historians such as Marshall Hodgson, who emphasized the extended realm of an Islamicate world referring to the hybrid forms in which Islam exists and thrives on the convergence of Muslim and non-Muslim values.[81] For many Telugu writers and literary activists of the 1930s, various concepts and stylistic paradigms of living Islam, popular Sufism, and Urdu literature provided a model for engaging with multiplicity

Figure I.5 The title image of the famous folk narrative (*burra katha*) *Haidarābādupai Pōlīsu Carya: Burra Katha* (The Police Action on Hyderabad) published in 1948 immediately after the Police Action

Source: Sundarayya Vignana Kendram, Hyderabad.

and diversity. This gradually inspired an alternative mode of writing in poetry and prose in the Telugu language in the 1930s and 1940s. The emergence of Telangana journalism and print culture explains this long association between Urdu and Telugu literary spheres. Many Telangana- and Hyderabad-based journalists were trained primarily in various local Urdu newspapers and then started Telugu journals in the 1940s.[82]

How does contemporary politics define such interactions between Urdu and Telugu, particularly after Partition and the Police Action? In the present political narrativization, these historical events function more like metaphors, thus transcending the temporal limits of an event. The historian Shahid Amin in his pioneering work on the event of Chauri Chaura of 1922 describes how the entire event became a metaphor for nationalist historiography, thus connecting past and present:[83] "A singular event eight years in the past had by now come to inform the entire nationalist strategy."[84] Unpacking the historian's dilemma, Amin dissects the entire event and its postcolonial transformations.

Figure I.6 The trio of the performance of *burra katha* arrested in the case popularly known as the "burra katha case of 1946." *From left to right*: Gurrala Venkata Reddy, Pulikonda Picchayachari, and Salar Mohammad (author's maternal grandfather).
Source: Courtesy of Gurrala Siva Reddy.

For me, some of these questions were posed by a folklorish narrative song written by Adluri Ayodhya Rama Kavi. His *Haidarābādupai Pōlīsu Carya: Burra Katha* was published in 1948, in short immediately after the event (Figure I.5). This hybrid genre of poetry and prose *burra katha*—a story told using a single-string instrument with a hollow shell—became a major vehicle of various political ideologies during the late 1940s.[85] Popularized by Shaik Nazar (1920–1997), again a Muslim (*dūdēkula*, the cotton corders sub-caste) storyteller whose *burra katha* performances made this genre a political tool in spreading the leftist agenda.[86] During his career in the times of the Telangana rebellion, Nazar used this genre to retrieve the histories of various heroes who represent the idea of resistance politics.[87] Concerned about the power of such an innovative protest narrative, the government of India and the Nizam, too, issued a ban order which led to the arrest of many *burra katha* performers between 1946 and 1948 (Figure I.6).

Following a similar political and historical narrative strategy, Ayodhya Rama Kavi's *burra katha* too attracted the audience of the late 1940s. The entire text of this narrative song, however, privileges the constant circulation of the hegemonic nationalist argument about the Police Action and undermines many events of the military invasion and the construction of a Muslim minority. Totally subscribing to the nationalist narrative offered by the then prime minister Jawaharlal Nehru and his home minister Sardar Patel, this song valorizes the army and local Congress leaders as heroes.[88] I first heard about this long poem from the freedom fighter and Gandhian

Sarva Devabhatla Viswanatham when I was an undergraduate. At that point, Viswanatham also shared with me a photocopy of this text, as he knew about my interest in learning about the history of Hyderabad. Later, in 2008, when I met him again during my field research, he said: "Ayodhya Ramakavi's poem was actually a chapter of our history. You are not going to find any poetry there. He described every event that led to the Police Action in an extremely careful chronological order."[89] Revisiting this text and Viswanatham's comments made me realize how influential the nationalist agenda promoted by Nehru and his government was during various phases of the local history. Like many nationalists, Viswanatham was specific about the chronology described in this text. Rama Kavi's poem begins with a song of praise to Sardar Patel as a savior of Indian nationalism. The poem immediately takes on a political interpretation with the comparisons between two princely states: Kashmir and the Hyderabad state.

The white rulers were not happy
With the two pieces they made—Pakistan and Hindustan.
Now they also target for partition
The princely states.[90]

Describing the idea of an independent Hyderabad as another partition, Rama Kavi showers praise on Nehru and Patel along with the state Congress party. Hence, the narrative brings together every actor and agent of this nationalist mission. In this story, the entire Hyderabad princely state is portrayed as a dictatorial and anti-national entity. Typical of some of the leftist and nationalist narratives, rather than atrocities committed by the Indian state, he focuses more on the atrocities committed in the name of the Nizam. For Rama Kavi, the history of the Nizam's rule was a black-and-white scenario, and the Police Action was the only resolution to dissolve the conflict. Since the *burra katha* was written and performed in the immediate period of the Police Action, this might have resulted in creating a public opinion that was promoted by nationalists such as Viswanatham.

Being skeptical about the canon that privileges the nationalist and leftist discourses that speak to the power of the dominant, in this book I chose to introduce minor and subversive texts that the mainstream literary and political histories had marginalized. One of the immediate goals of this book is to confront the Telugu literary canon by pointing out its failure to portray the life stories of ordinary Muslims who were indeed waging a battle against state oppression, political authority, and an anti-Muslim environment. Although I discuss well-known writers like Dasarathi Krishanamacharya, Nelluri Kesava Swamy, and Jeelani Bano who were also prominent in leftist and nationalist literature. Nevertheless, I pay particular attention to the texts that were barely mentioned in the literary history of the Hyderabad state and Telangana. By reading these minor works closely and discussing how the personalities of these writers were being shaped by the Police Action and its consequences, this book unsettles the normative history of Hyderabad and Telangana.[91] In many ways, this choice of minor texts also helped me understand how ordinary Muslims mapped their journeys through a deeply traumatic period of their lives.

Methodologically, I begin with and make central to my story the oral accounts of different kinds of people, from ordinary Muslims and Hindus to specialists such as writers and political and religious activists. I show how oral and written sources have been in a conversation since the Police Action. These two key sources, I argue, operate in a dialogical space that constructed a specific sense of Muslim being and belonging in the history of Hyderabad state. This dimension led me to understand the multiple ways in which various scholars have explored the Partition by using literary sources.[92] The oral history accounts in this book offer evidence of the Partition-related violence and the Police Action, which some of my interviewees consider to be "nothing but another Partition when it comes to violence and separation of Muslims and Hindus."[93]

The process of documenting oral histories was also not that simple, as many witnesses of the Police Action were reluctant to speak out. As one of the witnesses said, "it was so painful even to remember those incidents."[94] Most of my interviews were conducted in three ways between 2006 and 2020: first, formal and informal conversations with ordinary Muslims and Hindus who personally witnessed the Police Action; second, unstructured and structured interviews with specialists such as writers and representatives of various literary, cultural, religious, and political organizations that had either a direct or indirect connection with various historical and political events of the 1940s; and, third, everyday conversations of various types of people from Hyderabad and different parts of Telangana state which we can categorize as conversational narratives—as these people were just mentioning some aspects of the Police Action during their informal conversations. While most of the interviews with the witnesses of the Police Action were conducted in the early phase of this work around 2013, several of these conversations took enormous effort on my part as I had to wait for the interviewees to feel sufficiently safe to open up and speak freely. For some interviews, I had to return repeatedly to the interviewee's place as they were not yet ready to speak about the violence, loss, and displacement. Hence, I have been in communication with several of these interviewees for a longer time. Many of these interviewees had lost their families and friends and had migrated to the city to escape the violence of both the government army and the private army of the Razakars. Raziya Begum, one of the witnesses, told me:

> I didn't think at any point of my lifetime I would be able to return to those sad memories of separation and hatred. We suddenly begun to realize that we were actually in the middle of new language—the language of ... hatred. Until then we were happy and our lives were peaceful, or at least, confined to our quiet homes. And, with this violence, we were on the streets fighting with each other—Muslims with Hindus, and Hindus with Muslims. And, we're all surrounded by the troops, troops, and troops! We had never experienced such things before the Police Action.[95]

Several of my interviewees noticed a shift in the idiom of public language, both in Telugu and Urdu. According to Guduri Seetharam:

> It was not only about ordinary people. Even the literary idiom, too, underwent a major change. As Muslims became more conscious about being Muslims, Hindus also became more conscious about their identity. This actually created a new language in the post-Police Action writings. Added to this, the secular language that was being promoted by the nationalists and ... the Congress party was also being questioned. Neither Muslims nor Hindus were owning this secular language propagated by the Congress.[96]

Throughout the field research, I noticed how the perceptions of these language politics were redefined and how the very idea of nationalist-centered secularism was being critiqued by diverse groups of literary activists in the late 1940s.[97] Many literary narratives and memoirs in Telugu demonstrate this shift in idiom that was on par with the language used by Urdu and Hindi writers in their Partition writings. For instance, I heard from the Urdu-Telugu bilingual writer Samala Sadasiva whom we will meet in Chapter 4, that "many writers and poets were passionate about Urdu and moreover, they could not embrace the standardized coastal Andhra Telugu just to convince the literary magazines published by the Andhra editors and publishers."[98] For many of them, this transformation was against the spirit of the Hyderabadi *tehzeeb*—a composite culture widely appreciated for its shared realm of Urdu and Telugu public sphere. At the ground level, this marks the shared religious practices between Hindus and Muslims too. Most interviewees recollect the memories of the establishment of Osmania University as a modern and secular space that produced a new generation of scholars not only in Urdu and Telugu but in multiple languages.[99] I also interviewed the organizers of various literary associations, publishing houses, and the editors of the local newspapers that trace their histories to the 1940s—the key moment of Telangana activism.[100] These oral accounts, as documented in this book, offer evidence for Hyderabad as an alternative literary and cultural field against the mainstream historiography produced by the coastal Andhra historians.[101]

Due to lack of sufficient resources after the Police Action and the formation of the Telugu linguistic state of Andhra Pradesh in 1956, most publications from Hyderabad and its mufassil areas were neglected and barely survived. In several conversations with many activists including Guduri Seetharam, Heeralal Moriya, and Burgula Narasinga Rao from the late 1940s, they told me that many libraries were destroyed by the Indian army during the Police Action. According to them, the union government of India was under the impression that all of Telangana was fast becoming a leftist camp.[102] In the process, they used the Police Action as a pretext to control the alleged communists and destroy their presses and libraries. In this situation, acquiring print materials including journals became an impossible mission. It took me enormous effort to find many Telugu and Urdu texts published between 1946 and 1949. For instance, it took me several years to discover the printed copy of the novel *Mai Garib Hu* by Kavi Raja Murthy, whom I will introduce in Chapter 2. I first heard about this 1949 novel in a conversation with his wife, Vara Lakshmi, and then his contemporaries, who actually made hand-written copies and shared them among those close to them. Lakshmi told me that since Murthy was politically very active, both the Razakars and the police of the Indian government were hunting him and that in the process, they burnt their huge library. Several literary and social activists of the late 1940s told me about various ways in which private libraries were burnt down throughout Telangana. According to Ramanatham, the brother of Kavi Raja Murthy, "it was nothing but another form of gruesome violence—the killing of knowledge produced in Telangana!"[103]

As I continued to review and reflect on the Telugu literary corpus produced between 1948 and 1950, I gradually realized that this corpus is key to deconstructing the historiography that encompasses a wide range of political, literary, and historical discourses. This might be equally important when we critically engage with the oral histories, personal essays, memoirs, and autobiographical texts of these times. After collecting huge amounts of textual materials and documenting several oral histories, I have selected only a few sources that engage with the Muslim question as related to the history of Hyderabad and Telangana. By exploring these alternative archives, this study stresses the need to open a conversation with the postcolonial Muslim trajectory in South Asia and the many versions of nationalism. Most importantly, the literatures and oral accounts of 1948 allow us to examine a locality that blends global political movements and the rise of a new Muslim. Most of the evidence in this book shows that this new Muslim was not a victim but a survivor. This history is not about those political survivors who won the battles and militarized everyday life. In this lifeworld, the real hero is an ordinary Muslim whose sense of belonging and citizenship has always been in danger since the late 1940s. The stories of their everyday lives, as portrayed in these literary works and oral histories, are particularly valuable in our times of growing religious hatred and anti-Muslim discourses. Their stories, however, acquire much nuanced and multi-layered narrativity particularly when non-Muslim writers and activists engage with the idea of Muslimness.

By drawing on the sources provided by these "non-Muslim" writers, my work counters an argument that the identity of a South Asian Muslim is largely defined either by Hinduism or Hindu-centric practices, or Muslim-centered or Islamic dimensions. Various scholarly approaches fail to recognize and attend to the locally produced diversity among South Indian Muslims. In the case of the Tamil Muslims, J. P. B. More's 2004 work *Muslim Identity, Print Culture and the Dravidian Factor in Tamil Nadu* critiques the French sociologist Louis Dumont's argument suggesting that "non-Islamic Hindu values underly Islamic values."[104] More also points out how Muslim scholars such as Imtiaz Ahmad likewise subscribe to similar ideas by stressing "Hindu" elements and separating them from the larger Islamic world.[105] The Tamil Muslim literary scholar Torsten Tschacher also questions various ways in which these vernacular Muslim authors were portrayed as "isolated," and as "grappling with [the] non-Muslim environment."[106] Whereas More and Tschacher focus largely on the Tamil Muslims, my evidence from the Telugu Muslims offers insights into how even non-Muslim writers and political activists during the Police Action were trying to maintain an equivalence of Islam and Hinduism. In addition, these writers from Hyderabad state offer rich evidence for how global Islamic and local Muslim practices from various sources have shaped their personal and cultural activism. This book argues that these "vernacular" (or "local") Islamic narratives from non-Muslim authors participate widely in the larger debates on Islam and the Muslim community in South Asia and beyond. Such an equivalence in the local public sphere becomes more crucial during violent events such as the Police Action in the case of Telugu Muslims.

In a recent work, the Islamic studies scholar Khurram Hussain has stressed the importance of revisiting historical events while undertaking "the long overdue task of excavating the voices of Muslims long dead and buried for their salutary contribution to our conversations in present."[107] In the process of revisiting and re-evaluating the Muslim question, Hussain emphasized the value of re-politicizing the Muslim sense of being and belongingness. By offering evidence from oral and written accounts of Muslim lives during and after the Police Action, this book unpacks the key questions related to the local-specific Muslim dilemma and its ongoing dialogue with the global public sphere. Nevertheless, the rich tradition of Telugu-speaking Muslims and Urdu-speaking Hindus is central to this conversation, which I will discuss in detail in Chapter 4.

In an age of Islamophobia, scholars such as Bruce Lawrence have exposed us to the value of repositioning the debates on the relationship between violence and Islam by using the tools of cosmopolitanism.[108] Drawing attention to multiple manifestations of violence in contemporary Muslim life, Lawrence alerts us to aspects such as structural violence and representational exclusion.[109] During the Police Action and the resulting consequences between the late 1940s and the recent Telangana separatism, the Muslims of Hyderabad and Telangana have been experiencing similar structural violence, marginalization, and representational exclusion. Further complicating this entire dilemma, the political scientist Sanober Umar's critique of secular and religious distinction raises concerns about the invocation of the idea of the Ganga–Jamuna *tehzeeb* between Hindus and Muslims.[110] In the case of Hyderabad and Telangana, the idea of the Ganga–Jamuna *tehzeeb* is often invoked to "secularize" Muslims by underscoring the intensity of routinized violence. My evidence demonstrates how contemporary debates specifically about the Police Action interrupt such notions of secularization.

To sum up what I aim to articulate throughout this book has four mutually connected layers of historical methods:

1. The nationalist/textbook version of history is determined by the nation-state as is seen in how a nascent India emphasized and celebrated the "integration" with an utter disregard for native opinion or the costs people paid associated with the bloody event. All that mattered was that a defiant power was subdued for larger nationalistic purposes. This chimes in with how Kashmir has been subjected, viewed, and "integrated" with India after the rushed manner in which Article 370 was repealed. The dominant narrative quashed what Kashmiris themselves thought and wanted; even their plights went unnoticed.[111]

2. Popular understanding is largely shaped by what exists in circulation. This is what we see in the form of how people understand the Police Action across India as well as folklore, including the reconstructed folk narratives such as Adluri Ayodhya Rama Kavi's *burra katha*. Such popular representations further reinforce the larger narrative peddled by the state.

3. This book attempts to bring in a set of narratives that has not been represented, but is one that is critical to fully understand a historical event in order to foster a balanced understanding of what transpired in Hyderabad before and right after 1948, mostly to its own natives across linguistic divides. My approach is a corrective to 1 and 2 whose overbearance has helped create a "false" or partial understanding of one of India's key events .

4. Lastly, 1948 is an example of state-sponsored nationalism which will enable us to understand better what is going on in our own times in the context of majoritarianism that seeks to impose and broad-brush narratives leaving little or no room for alternative voices.[112]

ORGANIZATION OF THE BOOK

Although the Police Action was a battleground of multiple new ideas and the reconstruction of Hindu–Muslim communities of the Hyderabad state and Telangana, this book focuses on key themes such as the decline of the feudal or any form of authoritative systems and the rise of a new Muslim discourse, political issues such as the debate on Azad Hyderabad, the Razakar militancy and religious conflicts that affected the larger community, and the shifting question of gender in the late 1930s, which had multiple manifestations in various socio-political movements such as the Communist Party, the Telangana armed struggle and the post–Police Action/Partition discourses, and finally the language politics between Urdu and Telugu that defined the Muslim question as well.

Chapter 1, "No Longer a Nawab: The Making of a New Hyderabadi Muslim," analyzes the short fiction works of the Hyderabad-based Telugu writer Nelluri Kesava Swamy and discusses the Muslim sense of belonging and its transformations during the times of the Police Action. Witnessing the shifts in the everyday lives of local Muslims in the city of Hyderabad, Swamy describes how the late 1940s Muslim young men and women used the new tools of education, social institutions, and reformist ideology to contest feudal or any mode of authoritative practices. Swamy's short stories provide evidence for three layers of this transformation: the break from the *ashraf* upper-class mode of Muslim life; the immediate consequences of the Police Action; and a new generation of Muslims who embraced progressive ideology and modernity.

Chapter 2, "All Muslims Are Not the Razakars: The Political Idiom of an Independent Hyderabad," focuses on two novels that characterize the contours of a newly constructed political idiom of the Razakars, the paramilitary force of the Nizam. I begin with Murthy's Urdu-Telugu novel *Mai Garīb Hu* (I am poor!) and then introduce Bhaskarabhatla Krishna Rao's novel *Yuga Sandhi* (Transition). While Murthy's novel introduces us to the political idiom of Azad Hyderabad, Krishna Rao's deals more with the various characters that were the products of Razakar militarism and the idea of a Muslim state. Through these two novels' documentation of two different phases of the Police Action, this chapter discusses the impact of the Razakars on the state of Hyderabad and the extent of its influence on the making of Hindu–Muslim identities.

Chapter 3, "'I Am Going to Fight …': Muslim Women's Politics and Gender Activism," deals with the question of recasting the role of Muslim women as one of the prominent tropes in fictional writings during the Police Action. Various short stories and fictional writings articulate the struggle of the new Muslim woman in addressing the concerns of modernity and Islamic reformism. This chapter asks how this question was further extended and debated in the literary works of Jeelani Bano with a focus on her novel *Aiwan-e-Ghazal* (The palace of Ghazal). In this novel, Bano presents four models of Muslim womanhood who are in dialogue with the new education, reformism, progressivism, and a version of radical feminism. The four Muslim women as narrated in this novel struggle with various aspects of Islam's public roles and represent a tension between multiple layers of Muslim identity as articulated in Hyderabad.

Chapter 4, "For the Love of Urdu: Relocating Urdu in Postcolonial Hyderabad," discusses how language politics play into the narrative of Hindu–Muslim literary space. For many writers during the Police Action, the invocation of Muslim literary cultures (including aesthetic aspects such as the love for Urdu and its literary practices including ghazals) served as a strategic site to counter the separation between Muslims and Hindus. This chapter introduces and analyzes two autobiographical works whose authors have purposely returned to the earlier literary practices of Urdu and its role in the making of the literature of Hyderabad and the current state of Telangana. This chapter also discusses the rise of translation as a major literary activity between Urdu and Telugu from 1940 to 1960. While the literary public sphere of Urdu still functions as one of the major influences on Telugu literature, a new wave of translations between Urdu and Telugu in this era turned into a tool of resistance against the dominant discourses of Telugu linguistic nationalism. Focusing on various translations beginning with poetry and moving to polemic writings, this chapter shows how this new tool of resistance produced a novel hybrid mode of writing in Telugu with a blend of Telugu and Urdu literary practices. This mutual existence of two languages and their hybridity is unique and represents the ethos of the city and Telangana.

In the Conclusion, I discuss how the Muslim community and literary narrative practices during the Police Action have become part of the new debate on the reconstruction of Telangana history with an emphasis on urban transformations in contemporary times. Through different periods in the history of Telangana, contemporary writers in Telangana have begun to revisit the events of the Telangana Armed rebellion, Partition, and the Police Action. I focus on various literary and cultural materials produced between 1980 and 2017 that discuss or describe the formation of Telangana as a separate state and the role of Muslims. In revisiting the question of the role of Muslims in the Police Action, authors and activists have reframed it in terms of their contemporary discourses. In analyzing the connected histories of Telangana as a region and the Muslims of Hyderabad who have been in dialogue with global and local Islams, the Conclusion sums up major themes on how these two histories traveled together.

NOTES

1. Quddus Saheb's words about the "fading out" (*nemmadigā māyamavutunnāyi* in Telugu) of Muharram practices was debatable even when I was talking to him. For a group of three or four young men then immediately questioned him about it and explained how Muharram practices have been gaining new popularity among the younger generations. For more discussion about this, see Afsar Mohammad, *The Festival of Pirs: Popular Islam and Shared Devotion in South India* (New York: Oxford University Press, 2013).

2. Ananya Jahanara Kabir, *Partition's Post-Amnesias: 1947, 1971 and Modern South Asia* (New Delhi: Women Unlimited, 2013; Dhaka: University Press, 2014).

3. V. K. Bawa, *The Last Nizam: The Life and Times of Mir Osman Ali Khan* (New Delhi: Viking Penguin India, 1992); V. K. Bawa, *The Nizam between Mughals and British: Hyderabad under Salar Jung I* (New Delhi: S. Chand, 1986).

4. For more on such implications as related to the Partition, see Vazira Fazila-Yacoobali Zamindar, *The Long Partition and the Making of Modern South Asia: Refugees, Boundaries, Histories* (New York: Columbia University Press, 2007).

5. Suneetha Achyuta argues that "the massive destruction of Muslims lives and livelihoods of Deccani Muslims during this period have been erased from the public memory, official histories, and progressive political discourse in the region due to the historical emergence and the continuing hold of the Telugu linguistic nationalism from the 1950s." See Suneetha Achyuta, "Telugu Nationalism and Police Action against Hyderabad: Notes on History, Historiography and Memory" (Unpublished paper presented at the Berkshire conference on the History of Women, "Histories on the Edge," May 22–25, 2014).

6. Whereas several recent studies are relevant for the debate on the question of Muslim being and belonging, I am particularly indebted to Bruce Lawrence, *Shattering the Myth: Islam beyond Violence* (Princeton, NJ: Princeton University Press, 1998); Nathan Lean, *The Islamophobia Industry:*

How the Right Manufactures Fear of Muslims (London: Pluto Press, 2012); Shahab Ahmed, *What Is Islam? The Importance of Being Islamic* (Princeton, NJ: Princeton University Press, 2016); Peter Gottschalk and Gabriel Greenberg, *Islamophobia: Making Muslims the Enemy* (Maryland: Rowman & Littlefield Publishers, Inc., 2007).

7. For the recent study of the accession of Hyderabad, see T. Uma Joseph, *Accession of Hyderabad: An Inside Story* (Delhi: Sundeep Prakashan, 2006); for a detailed description of propaganda tactics, see Syed Ali Hashmi, *Hyderabad 1948: An Unavoidable Invasion* (New Delhi: Pharos Media and Publishing Private Limited, 2017); Mohammad Mazharuddin, *Zawal-e Hyderabad Aur Police Action* (Hyderabad: Rafeeq Printing Press, 1982).

8. Mike Thomson, "Hyderabad 1948: India's Hidden Massacre," *BBC News*, September 24, 2013, https://www.bbc.com/news/magazine-24159594 (accessed February 20, 2022).

9. "India: The Happy War," *Time*, September 20, 1948, https://content.time.com/time/subscriber/article/0,33009,780030,00.html (accessed May 2, 2022).

10. William Cantwell Smith, "Hyderabad: Muslim Tragedy," in *Hyderabad: After the Fall*, ed. Omar Khalidi (Kansas: Hyderabad Historical Society, 1988), 20–21.

11. For more on the Sunderlal Committee, see A. G. Noorani, *The Destruction of Hyderabad* (New Delhi: Tulika Books, 2013), 362.

12. Taylor C. Sherman, *Muslim Belonging in Secular India: Negotiating Citizenship in Postcolonial Hyderabad* (Cambridge: Cambridge University Press, 2015), 27.

13. Omar Khalidi, ed., *Hyderabad: After the Fall* (Kansas: Hyderabad Historical Society, 1988), xii.

14. A. G. Noorani, "Of a Massacre Untold," *The Frontline*, March 3, 2001.

15. Khalidi, *Hyderabad*, 204.

16. Noorani cites the contents of Patel's letter dated January 4, 1949, in detail here:

> I notice that in your report you mentioned that you were asked by the Government of India to proceed to Hyderabad State on a goodwill mission. At least I am not aware of any such mission having been entrusted to you by the Government of India. As far as I know, you wanted to go there and it was arranged that you should go there at Government expense. There could have been no question of Government of India sending any goodwill mission to Hyderabad State.

I notice that your report is and your activities were, restricted to making inquiries about what happened during and after the police action. There is nothing in it about the extent and consequences of Razakar atrocities. Probably that was out of the terms of reference which you had set for yourselves. At the same time, you have covered in your reports matters which could by no stretch of imagination, have formed the purview of your enquiry. I should also like to say at once that the detailed in queries which have been made by the local administration over a fairly long period as opposed to the roving enquiries which you have made during such a short period show that your estimate and your appreciation of the position lack balance and proportion. Finally you have rushed into a sphere which might have been more appropriately left to be covered by experienced statesmanship and administrative ability. (Noorani, "Of a Massacre Untold")

17. Ibid.
18. Noorani, *Destruction of Hyderabad*, 223.
19. Ibid., 228.
20. Sunil Purushotham, *From Raj to Republic: Sovereignty, Violence, and Democracy in India* (Stanford: Stanford University Press, 2021).
21. Sunil Purushotham's recent work provides political evidence to these claims and argues how the new nation made a deliberate choice to control the idea of Azad Hyderabad. For more about these political debates, see Noorani, *Destruction of Hyderabad*.
22. For more on the Telangana Armed struggle, see Inukonda Thirumali, *Against Dora and Nizam: People's Movement in Telangana* (New Delhi: Kanishka Publishers, 2003).
23. Bhangya Bhukya, *History of Modern Telangana* (Hyderabad: Orient Blackswan, 2017); K. Srinivas, *Telangāṇa Sāhitya Vikāsam, 1900–1940* (Hyderabad: Telangana Prachuranalu, 2015).
24. Benjamin Cohen, "Modernizing the Urban Environment: The Musi River Flood of 1908 in Hyderabad, India," *Environment and History* 17, no. 3 (2011): 409–432.
25. For more on such implications as related to the Partition, see Zamindar, *The Long Partition*.
26. These witnesses were both Muslims and Hindus. This sentence from the conversation of Jaini Mallayya Gupta, a freedom fighter from the

Hyderabad state sums up their agony. Interview with author (originally in Telugu and Urdu), Hyderabad, India, January 30, 2019.

27. For a discussion on Partition and the idea of Pakistan, see Dhulipala Venkat, *Creating a New Medina: State Power, Islam and the Quest of Pakistan in Late Colonial North India* (Delhi: Cambridge University Press, 2015).

28. Vellodi to Menon, April 13, 1950, file no. 17 (I)-H/50, MoS, NAI (cited from Purushotham, *Raj to Republic*); for the Indian government's version of the event, see *Hyderabad Reborn: First Six Months of Freedom (September 18, 1948–March 17, 1949)* (Hyderabad: Director of Information, 1949).

29. Makhdoom Mohiuddin, *Nizāṁlō Dōpiḍi Vidhānaṁ: Muslimla Kartavyaṁ* [Exploitative policies of the Nizam and the Muslim task] (Bejawada: Prajasakthi Prachuranalayam, 1947).

30. Madhurima Chakraborty and Al-Wazedi Umme's 2017 edited volume also points out this lack of "urban poor" in the studies on urbanization. However, Hyderabad is still an understudied city whereas the new market economy and rapid technologization totally marginalize lower-class neighborhoods. Madhurima Chakraborty and Al-Wazedi Umme, ed., *Postcolonial Urban Outcasts: City Margins in South Asian Literature* (New York: Routledge, 2017). Nazia Akhtar's essay in this volume focuses on the three Anglophone novels to discuss Hyderabadi Muslims (Chakraborty and Umme, *Postcolonial Urban Outcasts*, 21–38).

31. Margarit Pernau, *Ashraf into Middle Classes: Muslims in Nineteenth-Century Delhi* (New Delhi: Oxford University Press, 2013), xxxi–xxxii.

32. Mohiuddin, *Nizāṁlō Dōpiḍi Vidhānaṁ*, 24.

33. For more on these debates, see Arjun Appadurai, *Modernity at Large: Cultural Dimensions of Globalization* (Minneapolis: University of Minnesota Press, 1996); Timothy Mitchell, ed., *Questions of Modernity* (Minneapolis: University of Minnesota Press, 2000).

34. Jon Wilson, "How Modernity Arrived to Godavari?" *Modern Asian Studies* 51 (March 2017): 399–431.

35. Sunil Purushotham, "Federating the Raj: Hyderabad, Sovereign Kingship, and Partition," *Modern Asian Studies* 54 (January 2020): 157–198.

36. "India: The Happy War."

37. Taylor Sherman writes:

> However, these manifestations of community and forms of political organization were also weathered by same currents that were battering British India. Over the course of the nineteenth century, Hyderabad,

too, experienced its own Muslim revivalisms, with similar ambitions and effects to those in greater India. Hindu revivalism in Hyderabad, as in the rest of India, not only worked towards creating a sense of unity among Hindus, but heightened their sense of difference from the Muslim minority. In the two decades before the police action a number of parties rose to prominence which ignored the subtleties of the existing power structures and instead equated political loyalty with religious affiliation. Hindu nationalist parties, including the Arya Samaj, had begun to use the state's demographics to make a case against what they called 'Muslim domination' in the territory. (Sherman, *Muslim Belonging*, 6)

38. Interview with author (originally in Urdu), Hyderabad, India, January 29, 2019.

39. For the beginnings of the *mulki* and non-*mulki* debate in the Hyderabad public sphere, see Rama Sundari Mantena, "Publicity, Civil Liberties, and Political Life in Princely Hyderabad," *Modern Asian Studies* 53, no. 4 (2019): 1248–1277, doi:10.1017/S0026749X17000233.

40. Karen Leonard's essay "Hyderabad: The Mulki–Non-Mulki Conflict," demonstrates the three different stages of the *mulki* conflict: (*a*) from 1853 to 1883; (*b*) from 1884 to 1911; and then (*c*) 1911 to 1948. According to Leonard:

> In the third period, from 1911 to 1948, there were three major developments within Hyderabad state. First was the broadening of the Mulki category to include men from the Hyderabad districts, accompanying the extension of effective administration to the rural areas of the state. But the professional, social, and political integration of these district Mulkis was only partial.

See Karen Leonard, *Hyderabad and Hyderabadis* (New Delhi: Manohar, 2014), 47.

41. For an idea of the development of modern Telugu prose and the related institutional efforts, see Gautham Reddy, "An Empire of Literary Telugu: Remaking Language and Community in Colonial South India, 1812–1920" (Unpublished dissertation, University of Chicago, 2020).

42. Throughout their lives, Guduri Seetharam and Sadasiva complained about these partial and incomplete histories of Hyderabad literary culture. During my conversations with them, these two critics literally used the term "blind."

43. Mudiganti Sujatha Reddy, ed., *Telangāṇa Tolitaraṁ Kathalu* (Hyderabad: Rohanam Publications, 2002), xi.

44. K. Jitendra Babu's pioneering work on Telangana political and cultural history demonstrates the rise of a Telangana-specific political consciousness. His edited volumes showcase a detailed history of the 1930s and 1940s events. See Jitendra Babu, *Telangāṇalō Caitanyaṁ Ragilcina Nizāṁ Rāṣṭrāndhra Mahāsabhalu* (Munagala: Sahitee Sadan, 2007).

45. For a detailed analysis of Vattikota's work, see Sangisetti Srinivas, *Vaṭṭikōṭa Āḷvāru Svāmi* [A monograph in Telugu] (New Delhi: Sahitya Academy, 2017).

46. Interview with author, 2014.

47. Vivek Tadakamalla, *Telangāṇa Caritra: Punarnirmāṇaṁ* [The reconstruction of Telangana history] (Hyderabad: Telangana History Society, 2010), 5.

48. Ibid.

49. Himadeep Muppidi also notices the lack of global research about Telangana. See Himadeep Muppidi, *Politics in Emotion: The Song of Telangana* (London; New York: Routledge, 2015).

50. As far as anglophone and Urdu works are concerned, see Nazia Akhtar, "From Nizam to Nizam: The Representation of Partition in Literary Narratives about Hyderabad, Deccan" (Unpublished dissertation, University of Western Ontario, 2013); John Roosa, "The Quandary of Qaum: Indian Nationalism in a Muslim State 1850–1948" (Unpublished dissertation, University of Wisconsin-Madison, 1980).

51. Interview with author, Karim Nagar, India, September 20, 2008.

52. For an immediate outburst of the post-Babri mosque demolition writings in Telugu, see Namadi Sreedhar and Vommy Ramesh Babu, eds., *Kanzira Poetry Bulletin* (Rajamundry: Kanzira Prachuranalu, 1993).

53. Zamindar, *The Long Partition*, 238.

54. Ravikant and Tarun K. Saint, eds., *Translating Partition* (New Delhi: Katha, 2001), xxiii.

55. Amritjit Singh, Nalini Iyer, and Rahul K. Gairola, eds., *Revisiting India's Partition: New Essays on Memory, Culture, and Politics* (New York: Lexington Books, 2016), xviii.

56. Sharan Kumar Limbale, *Towards an Aesthetic of Dalit Literature* (New Delhi: Orient Longman, 2014).

57. Judith Misrahi-Barak, K. Satyanarayana, and Nicole Tiara, eds., *Dalit Text: Aesthetics and Politics Reimagined* (New York: Routledge, 2019), 4.

58. Laura R. Brueck, *Writing Resistance: The Rhetorical Imagination of Hindi Literature* (New York: Columbia University Press, 2014), 11.

59. Mushirul Hasan and Asaduddin, *Image and Representation: Stories of Muslim Lives in India* (New Delhi: Oxford University Press, 2000), 4–5.

60. Ibid.

61. Anna Bigelow, *Sharing the Sacred: Practicing Pluralism in North India* (New York: Oxford University Press, 2010). Particularly, the introduction of this book is extremely relevant about this discussion of pluralism in everyday life.

62. Rajendra Yadav, ed., *Hans*, Hindi Monthly, August 2003.

63. Gyanendra Pandey, *Remembering Partition: Violence, Nationalism, and History in India* (Cambridge: Cambridge University Press, 2010), 15–16.

64. G. D. Adhikari, *What Is Happening in Hyderabad?* (Bombay: V. M. Kaul, 1949).

65. Mohiuddin, *Nizāmlō Dōpiḍī Vidhānaṁ.*

66. For an idea of this mode of leftist writing, see Vara Vara Rao, *Telaṅgāṇa Vimōcanōdyamaṁ: Telugu Navala – Samāja Sāhitya Sambandhālu, Oka Viślēṣaṇa* [The emancipation of Telangana: The novel—The interactions between society and literature, an analysis] (Hyderabad: Sweccha Prachuranalu, 1983).

67. Noorani, *Destruction of Hyderabad*, 362.

68. Anveshi's broadsheet and various articles published in various large-circulation daily newspapers, little magazines, and the new efforts to reconstruct the histories of Telangana together have played a crucial role in the making of an alternative discourse on Muslims and the Nizams. See the Conclusion of this book for more details.

69. "Since Burra katha was a medium to educate people about the political situation, the British government had banned it in Madras, where the art form had gained momentum during colonial times, and the Nizam's government banned the left-leaning folk-art in the princely state of Hyderabad." See Nidhi Dugar Kundalia, *The Lost Generation: Chronicling the Dying Professions* (Gurgaon: Random House Publishing, 2015). *Mā Bhūmi* was a popular play about the Telangana Armed Rebellion and the role of the Communist Party. See Satyanarayana Sunkara and Vasireddi, *Mā Bhūmi: Nāṭakaṁ* (Vijayawada: Visalandhra Publishing House, 1957).

70. Considered to be a pioneer of the new wave movies in Telugu, *Mā Bhūmi* was released in 1979. Directed by Gautam Ghose, this movie was based on the Hindi progressive novelist Krishan Chander's novel, *Jab Khet Jāge* [When the fields were awake!] (Allahabad: Nafees Publication, 1967); for an analysis of the movie *Mā Bhūmi*, see Ashish Rajyadhyaksha, *Indian Cinema*

in the Time of Celluloid: From Bollywood to the Emergency (Bloomington: Indiana University Press, 2009).

71. For more on this idea of local Karbalas and their historiography, see Mohammad, *The Festival of Pirs.*

72. Vasudha Dalmia, *Fiction as History: The Novel and the City in Modern North India* (New Delhi: Permanent Black, 2017), 406.

73. Mario T. Garcia, *Literature as History: Autobiography, Testimonio, and the Novel in the Chicano and Latino Experience* (Tucson: The University of Arizona Press, 2016), 5.

74. Allan H. Pasco, "Literature as Historical Archive," *New Literary History* 35, no. 3 (Summer 2004): 373–439.

75. See Roy S. Fischel, *Local States in an Imperial World: Identity, Society and Politics in the Early Modern Deccan* (Edinburgh: Edinburgh University Press, 2020).

76. Several Communist Party documents and writings highlight the Telangana rebellion, see Chandra Rajeswara Rao, *The Historic Telangana Struggle: Some Useful Lessons from Its Rich Experience* (Delhi: Communist Party of India, 1971); Devulapalli Venkateswara Rao, *Telangana Armed Struggle and the Path of the Indian Revolution* (Calcutta: Proletarian Path Publications, 1974); Arutla Ramachandra Reddy, *Telangana Struggle: Memoirs*, trans. B. Narsing Rao (Delhi: People's Publishing House, 1984); Putchalapalli Sundarayya, *An Autobiography*, ed. and trans. Atlury Murali (Delhi: National Book Trust, 2009).

77. For more on the idea of "socialism" as articulated in local narratives, see Chapters 1 and 4.

78. Many Telugu poets and fiction writers portrayed this side of the story of Hyderabad between 1946 and 1952. For more on such writings, see Vara Vara Rao, *Telaṅgāṇa Vimōcanōdyamaṃ.*

79. Tadakamalla and Srinivas, *17 Septembar 1948.*

80. For an idea of the post-Marxist identity formations, see Volga and Vasanta Kannabiran, eds., *Neeli Meghaalu: Streevaada Kavitwa Sankalanam* [Blue clouds: An anthology of feminist poetry] (Hyderabad: Sweccha Prachuranalu, 1996); Lakshmi Narasayya and Tripuraneni Srinivas, eds., *Chikkanavutunna PaaTa: Dalita Kavitwam* [A deepening song: Anthology of Dalit poetry] (Vijayawada: Kavitwam Prachuranalu, 1995); Skybaba and Shajahana, eds., *Jaljala: Muslim Vaada Kavitwam* [The earthquake: Muslim-ist poetry] (Nalgonda: Neela Giri Sahiti, 1998).

81. Marshall Hodgson, *The Venture of Islam: Conscience and History in a World Civilization*, vol. 1 (Chicago: University of Chicago Press, 1974), 58–59.

82. For more details, see Mandumula Narasinga Rao, *Yābhayi Sam.vatsarāla Haidarābādu* [Fifty years of Hyderabad] (Hyderabad: Mandumula Narasinga Rao Smaraka Samiti, 1977).

83. Shahid Amin, *Event, Memory and Metaphor: Chauri Chaura 1922–1992* (Berkeley: University of California Press, 1995), 192.

84. Ibid.

85. Adluri Ayodhya Rama Kavi, *Haidarābādupai Pōlīsu Carya: Burra Katha* [Police Action of Hyderabad: Burra katha folk narrative] (Secunderabad: Konda Veerayya, 1948).

86. S. A. A. Saheb, "Dudekula Muslims of Andhra Pradesh: An Ethnographic Profile," *Economic and Political Weekly* 38, no. 46 (2003): 4908–4912.

87. For more about Shaik Nazar's life and work, see Sambasiva Rao Kandimalla, *Burra Kathā Pitāmaha Padmaśrī Ṣēk Nājar* [Padmasri Shaik Nazar, the father of burra katha] (Hyderabad: C. P. Brown Academy, 2009); Venkata Ramana Murthy Angadala, *Pinzaari: Mahā Vāggēyakāruḍu Ṣēk Nājar Āṭōbayōgraphī Autobiography* (Hyderabad: Sauda Aruna Literature, 2001).

88. Srinivas, *Telangāṇa Sāhitya Vikāsaṁ*, 486.

89. Interview with the author, Khammam, India, September 20, 2008.

90. Rama Kavi, *Haidarābādupai Pōlīsu Carya*, 3.

91. In the case of modern Urdu prose fiction, Maryam Wasif Khan recognizes the importance of a "radical reconsideration of what constitutes the 'cannon' of Urdu fiction." Maryam Wasif Khan, *Who Is a Muslim? Orientalism and Literary Populisms* (New York: Fordham University Press, 2021), 8.

92. In his 2019 study, Anindya Raychaudhuri emphasized the importance of studying oral history and cultural representation together in the case of the Partition. He asks about the relationship between "the private form of testimony, the oral history narrative, and the public form of cultural representation, literature, cinema, and visual art." See Anindya Raychaudhuri, *Narrating South Asian Partition: Oral History, Literature, Cinema* (New York: Oxford University Press 2019), 4.

93. Many interviewees, both ordinary people and specialists such as writers, political activists, and the representatives of various religious/community organizations, view the Police Action as another manifestation of the Partition.

94. Interview with author, Hyderabad, India, December 20, 2019.

95. For more about this interview with Raziya Begum, see Chapter 2.

96. Interview with author, Karimnagar, India, September 20, 2008.
97. These shifts in the perceptions of the idea of secularism resonate with what Lalita and Deepa Dhanraj also documented in their oral histories after the 2002 communal riots in Gujarat. One of their interviewees, Sophiya Khan, points out how she became more assertive about being a Muslim. She said:

> After 2002 … in NGOs and women's groups, I was now merely seen as a Muslim. Some people wanted to call me to their meetings because I was a Muslim, and some did not want to because I was a Muslim! This was very strange! I felt that, though I had become a feminist, in the end I was only a Muslim. I mean, I was being reminded I am a Muslim.

See K. Lalita and Deepa Dhanraj, *Rupture, Loss and Living: Minority Women Speak about Post-Conflict Life* (Hyderabad: Orient Blackswan, 2016), 8.
98. Interview with author, Adilabad, India, September 20, 2009.
99. For a detailed study of the role of Osmania University, see Kavita Datla, *The Language of Secular Islam: Urdu Nationalism and Colonial India* (Honolulu: University of Hawaii Press, 2013).
100. For an understanding of these new public spheres, see Mantena Rama Sundari, "The Andhra Movement, Hyderabad State, and the Historical Origins of the Telangana Demand: Public Life and Political Aspirations in India, 1900–1956," *India Review* 13, no. 4 (2014): 337–357.
101. As I discuss in Chapter 4, Telangana writers such as Sadasiva were extremely critical about this role of the coastal Andhra historians who denied the share of Telangana in the making of the modern public sphere. However, this became a major complaint after the rise of Separatist Telangana too.
102. D. Anjaneyulu, "Impact of Socialist Ideology on Telugu Literature between the Wars," in *Socialism in India*, ed. B. R. Nanda (New York: Barnes and Noble, 1972), 244–260.
103. Interview with the author. For more on the contributions of the family of the Sarvadevabhatla, see K. Mutyam and Sivalingam, *Kaṣṭāla Kolimi: Tyāgāla Śikharaṁ Sarvadēvabhaṭla Rāmanātham Jīvitaṁ* [The life story of Sarvadevabhatla Ramanatham] (Khammam: Rayala Subhash Chandra Bose Memorial Trust, 2021).
104. Louis Dumont and Homo Hierarchicus, *The Caste System and Its Implications*, 211, quoted in J. P. B. More, *Muslim Identity, Print Culture, and the Dravidian Factor in Tamil Nadu* (Hyderabad: Orient Longman, 2004), xv–xvi.

105. More, *Muslim Identity*, xvii.

106. Torsten Tschacher, "Can 'Om' Be an Islamic Term?" *South Asian History and Culture* 5, no. 2 (April 2014): 195–211.

107. Khurram Hussain, *The Muslim Speaks* (London: Zed Books, 2020), 27.

108. Lawrence, *Shattering the Myth*.

109. For more discussion about these aspects, see Bruce Lawrence and Ali Altaf Mia, *The Bruce Lawrence Reader: Islam Beyond Borders* (Durham, NC: Duke University Press, 2020).

110. For more on urbane Muslims, see Sanober Umar, "City of Tenuous Peace: Reconsidering Ganga–Jamuni Tehzeeb in Lucknow," Hot Spots, *Fieldsights*, March 16, 2021, https://culanth.org/fieldsights/city-of-tenuous-peace-reconsidering-ganga-jamuni-tehzeeb-in-lucknow (accessed March 2, 2022).

111. For more on Kashmir, see Ather Zia, *Resisting Disappearance: Military Occupation and Women's Activism in Kashmir* (Seattle: University of Washington Press, 2019).

112. I am deeply indebted to the feedback from Raisur Rahman for making me realize these aspects.

1

NO LONGER A NAWAB

THE MAKING OF A NEW HYDERABADI MUSLIM

Mother, please do forgive me. I've done two things that would be unacceptable to you. First, I've come far away from the contrived atmosphere of our nawabi families that are steadily in decline. I've come here for good, far removed from loathsome customs and demeaning attitudes. Please don't look for me. I shall not return.

Writing this letter was a defining moment in the life of Sultan, the protagonist in Nelluri Kesava Swamy's short story, "Vimukti" (Liberation).[1] Against the long history of the *nawabi* and *ashraf* practices of his family, this act of writing a letter itself was a groundbreaking move—and signifies his desire to embrace a version of modern Islam and reformism. Whereas this specific period of the 1940s represents several strands of modern and reformist debates in the larger Islamic world, I suggest that the case of Hyderabadi Muslim identity offers us a quite different example—one of an entirely modern Islamicate milieu. The short stories published during and around this period seem to function as a site of tension between the normative expressions of Islam and the shifting paradigms in the everyday life of Muslims in Hyderabad. Basing my discussion on Swamy's stories, I will examine how these two mutually connected concepts deal with gender equality, social justice, and pluralism—the key ingredients that shaped an alternative Muslim identity in the aftermath of the Police Action in Hyderabad. The production and circulation of such an intriguing discourse led to the creation of what we can call a version of the "New Muslim" (*nayē musalmān*) in the history of the

Hyderabad state during the turbulent 1940s. I take this term "New Muslim" from my interlocutors such as the post–Police Action writers and activists, who were specifically mentioning the rise of a new Muslim consciousness in the wake of the Police Action.

For the entire community of Hyderabad state that had suffered either directly or indirectly during and after the Police Action, the Muslim identity was a daily recurring challenge for at least two decades after the event. In one of the conversations, Imam Hussain, an 80-year-old survivor of the Police Action told me:

> In fact, I was not even aware that we had gained Independence from the British rule and that they had already left India forever! When the entire country was joyously celebrating the new *azadi*, we Muslims in Hyderabad were devastated by the Police Action and we were struggling hard to save ourselves on a daily basis.[2]

When the Police Action occurred, and the army was hunting down Muslims, Hussain had to run away from his village to the city to escape the violence triggered by the Razakars and the union army. According to him, the very identity of being a Muslim—or even having a Muslim appearance— itself became a "dangerous matter" (*khatarnāk māmlā*) in many villages. Known as an expert mechanic in his village, when he arrived in the city, he was nobody, and it was hard for him to find even menial jobs. He said: "At that moment, I was just trying to save my skin and escape the public eye. The fear was such that I had hard time even uttering my name." After searching for many days, he settled as a daily wage worker in some cigarette factory in the city. These cigarette factories, according to the Urdu poet and trade unionist Makhdoom Mohiuddin, "had emerged as a developing industry that created a new working class in the Hyderabad state."[3] Published and widely distributed in the Telugu language, Makhdoom's writings related to trade union activism show how these factories resulted in opening a dialogue between the lower class and religious groups of the Muslim community. Referring to these new working-class Muslims in the city, Hussain told me:

> At that point, I was just happy that I had survived! But there was a hope as the trade union leaders such as Makhdoom were in support of us. Yet, being a Muslim during the Action was like ultimate punishment and endless suffering. We lost everything and had no help from anywhere.

Despite the newly gained independence, we remained like orphans of a stepmother. Those who had already migrated to Pakistan, they were lucky enough. Those who remained here, they were like living corpses facing death on a daily basis. Against this situation, there was a ray of hope in the work of these trade union leaders.[4]

One of the major objectives of this book is to retrieve this voice of ordinary Muslims and Hindus from various parts of Hyderabad and Telangana. Along with the lower class and the working class, the category of "ordinary Muslims" also includes the middle class that evolved following the industrialization of the 1940s; the bureaucratization that had started with the modernist reforms initiated by the Nizam, including the post-Independence transformations of the newly created section of salaried employees; and the post-1940s gender discourses. These stories about the resurgence of Hyderabad's Muslims explain much about the socio-political environment that promoted a shift in the public sphere, thus creating "new Muslim" as a category.

At this crucial moment, a few organizations such as the Tāmīr-ē-Millat set off to rehabilitate the community and provide its members with sufficient tools to tackle the difficult situation. According to Syed Jaleel Ahmed, the president of the Tāmīr-ē-Millat, one of the organizations that emerged in the wake of the Police Action:

The dawn that heralded an era of the rule of the people, by the people and for the people also brought in its fold miseries in the lives of thousands of people. The so-called Police Action that is officially known as Operation Polo of the Indian Army unleashed a reign of terror on the Muslims by Hindutva goons in its wake. Tens of thousands of people were massacred, women raped and houses looted and burned down.[5]

Amidst violence and hatred, as many of the volunteers of Tāmīr explained to me, there was a consistent effort to restore the resilience of the Hyderabadi Muslims. Around 1948, Syed Khalilullah Hussaini was a teacher in a local school in Hyderabad who responded to the immediate concerns of Muslims in the city in the aftermath of the Police Action (Figures 1.1–1.2). He gathered a small group of young Muslims and started an organization called Bazme Ahbab (Assembly of Friends), which later became popularly known as Tāmīr-ē-Millat, meaning "The Reconstruction of the Community."[6] According to Zia Uddin Nayyar, who had been taking care of the social and

Figure 1.1   Khalilullah Hussaini was a source of inspiration for new-generation Muslims in the aftermath of the Police Action.

Source: Tāmīr-ē-Millat.

Figure 1.2   Tāmīr-ē-Millat founder Khalilullah Hussaini with Nawab Shah Alam Khan of the Vazeer Sultan Tobacco Industry

Source: Tāmīr-ē-Millat.

cultural activities of the Tāmīr for a few years, the organization's motto was to provide "a voice for the voiceless." For the Tāmīr, this mission of helping others found their voice began by gathering just a few Muslims at first with the primary goal of encouraging them to share their stories of trauma and desolation. Nayyar explained:

> Speaking out and talking about their suffering made these Muslims conscious of their status that had undergone the gradual minoritization of the community. However, it was not merely the pressure [of being] minoritized, as they were also stripped of … all regular benefits an ordinary citizen should be provided. Even in such oppressive conditions, Muslims were not in a position to utter a single word and they were pushed further to an inferior status. Tameer's immediate task was to make them speak out so they could recognize their suffering and look for the possibilities of resolving the conflicts.[7]

To this end, the Tāmīr's instantaneously available tool was the Urdu language and creative writing including personal narratives, short stories, and poetry. In the small-scale gatherings organized by the Tāmīr, the young Muslims of Hyderabad first started sharing their writings about the pain and suffering during and after the Police Action. Nayyar said:

> It was the first ever opportunity for the survivors to voice their concerns and share the bitter reality of their everyday life in the aftermath of the Police Action. With these small sessions of story-telling, poetry recitals, and personal essays, the new generation Muslims had begun to articulate their agency.[8]

According to some of the Tāmīr organizers, this act of speaking about the violence and trauma itself was a radical step. Very soon, the organization expanded its focus to social and cultural activities—the next phase of its efforts. Since its founder Hussaini was a teacher and known for his educational efforts in the old city, he primarily focused on using pedagogy as a tool and made it a mission to teach Urdu to the younger generation. In the process, Hussaini was successful in accomplishing two major tasks: first, retrieving Urdu as a device of Muslim selfhood, and second, encouraging young Muslims to work in the areas of writing stories and poetry that evolved into an imaginative space for articulating their agency.

Imam Hussain, whom I have introduced earlier, noted:

We lost everything, but not the love for our families, friends, and community. Whatever we're undergoing at that point of violence, we travelled many distances, left many friends and families, yet we regained control over our lives. Many Muslim families in many neighborhoods in this city tell you their life stories—not the stories of victimization, but the value of leading a life with a promise. For all of us, we need to remind ourselves on a daily basis that life itself is a promise (*har rōj yeh vādā karnā paḍtā hai kī jimdagī yek vādā hai!*).[9]

Many of these accounts tell of two modes of fulfilling this promise: (*a*) continuous efforts within the Muslim community both at the individual and the organizational level; and (*b*) an extended realm of such an effort beyond the boundaries of the Muslim community to include Hindus and various other non-Muslim organizations. Whereas the efforts within the Muslim community were initiated by the Tāmīr and the *Siyāsat* Urdu daily newspapers, several other organizations, such as the Progressive Writers Association (PWA), had extended similar initiatives to shared spaces. Jaini Mallayya Gupta, a freedom fighter and one of the witnesses of these changes, has shared a detailed personal narrative about the role of the *Siyāsat*, not merely as a newspaper but as a shared site of Hindus and Muslims that rebuilt the community. Like the Tāmīr, this newspaper also focused on the promotion of Urdu but encouraged a wide spectrum of shared discourses between Muslims and Hindus. In addition, the newspaper also began publishing leftist writings extensively, thus helping young Muslims to participate in a progressivist discourse, including by starting reading clubs and forums for socio-political activities. Elaborating on how this newly created "Urdusphere" impacted the Telugu cultural scene, Gupta said:

The most important task that the *Siasat* accomplished was to create a sense of solidarity for Muslim issues and provide a platform to cultivate a shared culture that ... we would call Hyderabadi *tehzeeb*. If there was no *Siasat* at that point, we the young generation of the post-Police Action, would have lost the connection with this distinctive *tehzeeb* and also lost the Urdu language and literature forever. The literary models produced in the late 1940s Urdu literature ... inspired the newly emerging Telangana journalism and literary writings.[10]

While the Tāmīr was still working devotedly for the local Muslims, the *Siyāsat* as a secular site and the progressive movement affiliated with the Communist Party of India produced a distinctive ideological group of progressive Muslims.[11] Explaining how these two different spaces of Hindu–Muslim shared practices—religious and non-religious—collaborated in shaping an entirely new Muslim selfhood, the literary activist Huma Kidwai told me:

> After the late 1940s, the Muslims of the state of Hyderabad had alternative ways to articulate their identity. Due to the new literary activism promoted by the leftist organizations, most importantly the Progressive Writers Association, Muslims found a new voice to speak out. The early generation Progressivist women writers of the city such as Zeenath Sajida and Jeelani Bano had played a key role in inaugurating gender debates too. The interactions between the Progressive Writers Association from the north India were deeply influential and many writers from the north had intimate connections with the city's literary and political sphere.[12]

During this conversation, Kidwai also described how various Hyderabad-based magazines and organizations in the 1940s circulated a discourse about the future of Muslims. Her particular interest and emphasis focused on the interventions of women writers such as Zeenath Sajida and the legendary poet and trade unionist Makhdoom Mohiuddin in constructing an environment that produced a group of progressive Muslims in Hyderabad state.[13]

Many of these efforts were initially aimed at dispelling the fear that affected the participation of Muslims in public spaces and social life, where even wearing Muslim dress was not a neutral decision. As I discuss in the next chapter, Swamy's story "Yugantham" (The end of an era) raises questions related to the politics of dressing. The narrator, who is a close friend of a Muslim character namely Dilawar, warns him against wearing Muslim dress out of fear that doing so might lead to suspicion or even death. Swamy's short story describes the early phase of the politics of hatred, particularly an excessive articulation of anti-Muslim sentiment in the city of Hyderabad between 1948 and the 1950s.[14] Responding to this hostile environment, the early phase of Muslim activism primarily focused on restoring mutual trust and also reinstating confidence in everyday life among the local community (Figure 1.3).

Figure 1.3 Tāmīr-ē-Millat was instrumental in constructing a Muslim agency, particularly among the new-generation Muslims of Hyderabad.
Source: Tāmīr-ē-Millat.

In turn, M. A. Moid's 2008 essay on Muslim responses to the Police Action explains how the Tāmīr-ē-Millat helped the Muslims of Hyderabad to overcome three fears—fear of the government, fear of non-Muslims in society, and fear of destiny.[15] Moid explained:

> *Tāmīr-ē-Millat* initiatives helped in providing a direction to the thinking of Hyderabad Muslims. It provided a new vocabulary along with producing a substantial network. Tameer's method of social activism with a critical approach, using the platform of religion, was influential and successful. Its objective was not just to bring reform in the conventional sense but also to create new possibilities and abilities.[16]

Whereas these organizations promoted Muslim activism on the platform of religion, various nationalist and leftist groups also participated in the discussions on the Muslim question from a wide variety of fields in the public sphere. According to Jeelani Bano, whom I will introduce in Chapter 3, this public sphere was mostly defined by leftist politics or the nationalists, and the rise of Telugu nationalism between 1947 and 1952. Given this situation, any effort to retrieve the story of the Police Action and a Muslim narrative buried under these hegemonic discourses is much more complicated.

As I discuss further in this chapter, this idea of a new Muslim is closely connected to these fresh initiatives within the community. In addition, they became key building blocks in the making of modern Hyderabad, which several interviews described to me in Telugu as *nayā haidarābād* in Urdu or *kotta haidarābāáu, ādhunika haidarābādu* (new Hyderabad).[17] By connecting the imaginary of Swamy's fiction and the reality of these oral accounts, this chapter argues that the idea of a "new Hyderabad" and its composite religious culture, popularly known as Hyderabadi *tehzeeb*, has always been a key component in the rise of a modern and progressive Muslim self after the Police Action. What constitutes this notion of a new Muslim? And how do locally produced or circulated religious factors reinforce such a broader term? How does this refashioning of everyday Muslim life fit into the 1940s search for progressivism? And what aspects of Muslim life in the city of Hyderabad contribute to such a reshaping?

In this chapter, I introduce three of Swamy's stories to show how the definition of this new Muslim characterized by reformism and progressivism was not as fixed as the leftist ideologues suggested in the context of the Telangana armed rebellion.[18] Swamy's characters, both Muslim and Hindu, present a much more nuanced and multi-layered dimension of a Muslim discourse by allowing space for the ongoing changes in the local community premised on the making of a reformist, progressive, and critical Muslim. Swamy's narrative discourse begins this by capturing the fluidity of the early 1940s as represented in the writings of the progressive and modernist writers in Urdu and Telugu. In the wake of the Police Action, many such definitions had undergone major revisions. Besides concepts such as class conflict and economic determinism, various others including religious identity, gender, and everyday pluralism are critical to reading such an evolving social and cultural milieu accurately. Most of the points that Swamy's short fiction portrayed and that critics debated were corroborated by several political and cultural activists of this period, whom I met between 2006 and 2020 in various regions of the Telangana state. Since Swamy's fiction is semi-autobiographical, his own story within this new milieu likewise plays a crucial role in the making of these literary texts. In essence, this chapter methodologically connects a triangle of Swamy's biography, fictional writing, and the oral histories of the witnesses of the

Police Action that define the idea of the new Muslim and a manifestation of the new Hyderabad.

In light of the recent debates about the theorization of progressive and critical Muslims in Islamic and South Asian studies, this evidence from a specific local Muslim community of Hyderabad enriches our understanding of the broader political and religious implications of living Islam and the formation of modern Muslim communities. Various studies on Islamic modernity inform us about the role of social reforms and their contribution to the freedom of the community. Islamic studies scholars Khalid Masud and Salvatore's description of the role of these reforms is apt: "to free from the shackles of a too rigid orthodoxy and, to accomplish reforms that will render it adaptable to modern life and its complex demands."[19] Contemporary Islamic studies scholars including Omid Safi and Adis Duderija have helped us understand the implications of a modern and progressive Muslim.[20] Duderija explains:

> In fact, progressive Muslims have made it their goal to address the moral and ethical gap that exists between Islam as an inherited tradition and whatever its appropriate manifestation ought to be in the present. As such, it is a constructivist agenda. As an endeavor it is bound to be a work-in-progress, an ongoing debate in knowledge and not a finished product.[21]

Many Muslim characters in Swamy's fiction uncover these gaps between tradition and modernity as manifested in everyday life in the crucial turn of the post-1930s developments in Hyderabad. These continually shifting changes show certain similarities with the broader themes in the south Indian literary tradition.[22] Nevertheless, the Muslim question that lies at the center of these narratives remains a specific feature of the Hyderabad-based short fictional writings. Most of the ideas circulated by these Muslim characters, however, demonstrate a lifeworld embedded in the pluralist ethos of the Deccan Islam. Using "multiple critiques" as a methodological base, we can understand how Swamy wrote about religious co-existence, social justice, and gender equality in his fiction following the Police Action. The entire trajectory of these three aspects, both in everyday life and Swamy's fictional world, plays a prominent role in transforming the sense of being and belonging of Muslims and Hindus in the Hyderabad state in the 1940s. Each Muslim and Hindu character in Swamy's work is positioned in a way that they unequivocally challenge a well-established practice of a *nawabi*-centered life in the city of Hyderabad and the stereotypical images of Muslims.

For instance, in the story titled "Vimukti," Sultan, the protagonist of the story, longs for freedom from the brutal authority of the *nawabi* practices that produce social and gender injustices. In many ways, Sultan's story foregrounds a set of progressive and modernist concepts that Swamy further elaborates in his later fiction. Deconstructing each practice of *nawabi* life in the city, Swamy's characters offer a critical lens on that life and use various devices of resistance. In the story "Kevalam Manushulam" (We are just human beings), Bilquis likewise returns to the similar question of class and gender, though in particular Swamy critiques the sectarianism of Sunni and Shi'isms and their unrestrained power over individual freedom—a new concept intensified by the debates on the specific version of "Telangana modernity."[23] The third story, "Yugantham" (The end of an era), portrays how both Dilawar and his friend Swamy explicitly push the boundaries of the newly drawn religious identities of Islam and Hinduism against the background of the rise of religious politics after the 1940s. While uncovering the sites of various inner conflicts within the Muslim community, Swamy (Figure 1.4) also draws attention to the paradigmatic situations in which Muslims remain forever at a loss. Swamy's fiction shows few characters such as Khasim and Ruhi in other stories who were pushed to the ultimate oppression. From these limited examples of Muslim characters, we can see a diverse group of Muslim men and women as they navigate a new reality in the aftermath of the Police Action.

In the process, I argue, Swamy's fictional testimony contests mainstream historiography including those literary writings that focus heavily on the grand narratives of nationalism to privilege the story of the freedom struggle. Similarly, his characters unveil the world of Muslims which was also marginalized by local leftist politics that heavily fixated on the story of the Telangana armed rebellion. On the other hand, Swamy's fiction also pays close attention to the constantly shifting everyday Muslim life, an entangled world of the personal, political, and religious—and, in so doing, invites the reader to rethink the Muslim question in 1940s Hyderabad. Rather than merely portraying the reality of everyday life, Swamy's Muslim characters— both men and women—register their resolute power of resistance and agency. Witnessing a paradigmatic turn in the rise of a new debate on Pakistan, the Muslims of the princely state of Hyderabad, too, underwent a series of transformations in their everyday lives, most importantly the young Muslims of the 1940s. Along with embracing a progressivist and reformist

Figure 1.4 Nelluri Kesava Swamy

Source: Courtesy of Nelluri Kesava Swamy's family.

ideology, these Muslims also began to rethink the boundaries of tradition
and demonstrate a critical approach towards it. Beginning with resistance
to the established structures of the *nawabi*-centered Muslimness, the young
Muslims of Hyderabad were triumphant in initiating the reconstruction of
their community.

In a discussion on the dynamics of Muslim identity before Partition, the
historian Barbara Metcalf observes three major arguments: (*a*) rethinking
the institutional changes and normative practices of organizations such as
Tablighi; (*b*) increasing the political presence and participation in alternative
ways; and (*c*) drawing attention to the image and metaphorization of
Muslimness as articulated in the public imagination.[24] In dialogue with these
changes, the variety of local Islam produced in the state of Hyderabad blends
several aspects of Shi'ism and the Telangana-specific practices of Sufism
too, thus allowing us to debate the value of pluralism which is locally called
Hyderabadi *tehzeeb* meaning the composite culture. This hybrid religious
setting characterizes several aspects of Muslim identity and the interactions
between Muslims and Hindus. In this way, Hyderabad extends the legacy
of its nature as an interreligious city, a term I borrow from Heather Miller

Rubens, Homayara Zaid, and Benjamin Sax.[25] These scholars argue that "the public square should be full of religious idioms and imaginaries that seek to apprehend pain as well as shape ideals and suggest solutions." They emphasize the empowerment of interreligious networks to speak in those idioms, and raise interreligious literacy and invite the texts that "inspire individuals to become engaged citizens in the public square."[26]

Constructing such an idiom and creating an imaginary to represent various Muslim and Hindu characters who uphold the values of inter-religiosity, Swamy's writings create a "public square" that invites the larger debates related to the Muslim question. Despite the limitations of any fictional testimony, the characterization of such an idea of a progressive and critical Muslim is articulated by diverse means in these writings, most importantly through an alternative narrative agency, a forceful individual voice, and a repertoire of recently available tools of resistance in the 1930s and 1940s in Hyderabad. Although these two terms define the contours of the lifeworld of Swamy's work, it is imperative to understand multiple strands of Muslim thought—global and local—that also shaped the everyday and intellectual life of Swamy and his characters. In many ways, Swamy's characters unpack diverse processes of shifting Muslim life as manifested in the city of Hyderabad after the crucial political turn of the 1930s. The discourses about these new ideas were intense and deeper even before the local wing of the PWA conference in Hyderabad in 1944 and the national conference in 1947. The Muslim connection with this movement requires further analysis of the interconnected histories of reformism, nationalism, and a search for modernity, both western and locally defined versions. According to Jaini Mallayya Gupta, a cultural activist of the late 1940s:

> Progressivism (*taraqqī-pasand*) was not a new idea for us at that point. Even before the 1944 conference, we were well familiar with the debates related to this perspective. We were already reading Urdu writings, meeting Progressive writers and participating in the debates about the role of literature in the making of a new socialist system *sāmyavādaṁ*— that we all believed not that far off! Literary writings—the *adab*—was one of the primary sources towards this goal.[27]

Gupta's emphasis on two Urdu terms—*taraqqī-pasand* and *adab*— and the larger idea of socialism is key in this conversation. Throughout our individual meetings in 2019, Gupta was very keen on using Marxian vocabulary, including the term *sāmyavādaṁ* for the socialist system, as was used popularly in Telugu and Urdu writings of his day. He was quite insistent about the use of the specific term *adab* whenever I tried to use the Telugu equivalents during the conversation. Focusing on how *taraqqī-pasand* and *adab* produced an entirely new repository of concepts and practices in the social and political environment of Hyderabad, Gupta narrated his own story that started with the organization called "the Comrades Association." When the Communist Party of India was banned from 1932 to 1942, the progressive movement needed an organizational strategy to continue its activities, and this need resulted in this tentative structure. According to him, most leftist literary and cultural activists of this decade were the direct or indirect products of the Comrades Association "although," as he said, "it was a very temporary alternative," which was solidified much later during the Telangana rebellion after 1946.[28] Not confined to the city, this organization soon established several centers in various Telangana rural and semi-urban areas where they started reading clubs to promote progressive writings along with leftist activism. Gupta was one of the leaders who started such a reading club in his hometown of Nalgonda; however, eventually he had to migrate to the city to escape the persecution of the local police. According to him, "At that point, the city was like a sanctuary—where you can live incognito and escape the repressive regime." He explained further:

> The Comrades Association was in fact started in 1939 during the next phase of progressivism in the Hyderabad state. I would say, the first phase of progressivism was in 1933 when Urdu newspapers such as *payaam* and *rayyat* initially provided a new language of democracy and Marxism. Our generation by early 1940s started reading Urdu progressive journals from Lucknow.[29]

According to Gupta, "not only writers, but even readers and ordinary people were immensely inspired by these new ideas." Growing up in such a milieu, Swamy was likewise motivated partly by similar leftist ideas of progress which were complemented by the debates on reformism and modern Islam. Swamy's fiction captures this intense moment and demonstrates the participation of the new generation Muslims and their shared life world with Hindus within this milieu.

Towards this goal, Swamy's fiction has three major streams of thought: (*a*) the tensions between *nawabi*-centered practices and modern Muslim thought; (*b*) the rise of urbanity and the shifting interpersonal relationships of men and women; and (*c*) the intriguing spaces of Hindu–Muslim inter-religiosity. Through its more nuanced and multi-layered narrativity, Swamy's fictional realm also reveals the internal dynamics of the disruptions and continuities of an ongoing dialogue between Muslims and Hindus. These three aspects show an interconnected history and religious dynamics that indeed resulted in remaking the local religious fabric of the Hyderabad state. Similarly, themes related to social and gender justice blend with the pluralism of everyday life that complete how progressive Muslims were manifested. In the next section, I will introduce three of Swamy's major stories and their religious environment as imagined by various Muslim and Hindu characters. These stories of young Muslims told by Swamy elaborate on how the new generation was engaging with the global and local networks of modern Islam by relating them to their immediate everyday social and religious life in Hyderabad.

THREE STORIES AND THE TRAJECTORY OF MUSLIM DISCOURSE

I begin by introducing Sultan's story, which was placed squarely at the center of this entire new narrative world. His story helps us understand the dilemmas encountered by various other new Muslim characters within this realm. In his direct fight with the *nawabi* system, Sultan was at least partly successful in liberating himself from what he describes as the "contrived atmosphere" of such families. Borrowing extensively from a model created by the Aligarh movement of Sir Sayyid Ahmad Khan (1817–1898) and the religious reformist milieu, Sultan encounters a path that guides him towards modern Islam. For him, the *nawabi* practices were the reason behind what Khan describes as "the darkness of the traditional Muslim mind" in India.[30] Amidst many "loathsome customs" and "demeaning attitudes" of his family, Sultan declares his immediate destination to be Aligarh, the prominent center of modern Islam in South Asia. As Yasmin Saikia and Raisur Rahman noted, "Sayyid Ahmad can be considered as a true historical marker for Muslims in South Asia. Even today, he remains an unchallenged champion of Muslim modernization and community reform."[31] Swamy's literary corpus and his Muslim characters demonstrate how such a process was successful in the vernacular context of the Telugu Muslim public sphere. Along similar lines, Swamy and his imaginary of Muslim men and women persistently ask: When will the real liberation dawn in place of these static, rigid, and "loathsome" *nawabi* ways of life? And what should be the role of Islam (for Swamy and his fictional characters repeatedly return to the concept of modern Islam and new reforms) in this liberated space? Like Sultan, most characters try to define the contours of this liberated space within the locale of Hyderabad, thus drawing thick lines between tradition and modernity. Witnessing the troubled times of religious conflict and the rise of various new discourses of nationalism, liberalism, secularism, and Marxism, Swamy's characters present evidence that responds to the new Muslim question.

Like many of Swamy's stories, the story entitled "Vimukti" (Liberation) was also set in an intensely emotional and private space of a family. Yet this so-called private space was never really or simply a family setting as it was always filled with multiple characters, thus making it a theater of everyday political affairs of the 1940s Hyderabad. Whereas Swamy's fictional work has its own distinctive literary elements that require a separate and detailed study, here I limit my observations to how this fictional realm imagines a new generation of angry young Muslims, like Sultan, who are actively involved in reconstructing a Muslim public sphere that is specifically Hyderabadi and then a global wave of reformism of the 1940s. Portraying the larger social, religious, and political networks, Swamy uses the lens of "individual" to show the thick line between these two categories of Muslims—one confined to traditional authorities of structure who adhere to age-old *nawabi* practices which they read and interpret as "Islamic"; and the other, a progressive Muslim who takes pride in new kinds of education, reformist Islam, and alternative gender discourses.[32] Swamy's entire literary corpus prioritizes this new set of political and personal anxieties, including, but not limited to, the rise of an extremist Razakar mode of politics, a progressive group of Muslims, the migrations from Hyderabad to Pakistan, the systemic dehumanization of Muslim men and women as controlled by different frames of traditionalism. At this point, Pakistan emerged as an embodiment of Muslim identity in general.[33] Indeed, Swamy's characters document the swiftly evolving social, political, and religious networks of this new individual, who blends local and global Islams. In unpacking the complexities of these contemporary networks, Swamy's stories explain how this "new" Muslim self emerges out of the debris of the extreme violence and politics of hate of the late 1940s, and Sultan's portrait functions as a testimony to this emerging discursive space of an alternative Muslim discourse.

Born and raised in an extremely conservative *nawabi* family, Sultan's new education at the Aligarh Muslim University allows him to embrace various new ideas about individual freedom, gender equality, and social justice.[34] This story presents a different set of perspectives by portraying Sultan, on the one hand, as a representative of modernity, and Siraj and Mirza, on the other hand, as representatives of the leftover *nawabi* practices. In a way, Sultan and the other two male characters are positioned at diametrically opposed viewpoints representing the young generation of Muslims in Hyderabad. Juxtaposing these viewpoints from the *ashraf* family provides an opportunity to understand how the upper-class Muslim community was dealing with the modern social thought of the late 1940s. In contrast, Sultan develops his own perception and outlook towards various personal and religious matters too. Despite endless intense arguments with his family, Sultan fails to convince them about his understanding of the age-old feudal practices that he abhors to the core. Through the image of Sultan, Swamy in this story shows the impact of new discourses related to Islam and progressive ideologies as disseminated by institutions such as the Aligarh Muslim University and the locally active progressive movement in Hyderabad. In many ways, Sultan's image represents the key moment of the rise of an angry young Muslim who was utterly disenchanted with a normalized and rigid *nawabi* and *ashraf* Muslim's lifestyle, most importantly their inability to adapt to "modern" modes of life. In the process, Sultan was not only contesting the family's adherence to the age-old practices in the name of "Islam" but also defining a new Muslim identity that champions a modern and progressive social outlook.

Indeed, it was a critical moment not only for Sultan but also for many young Muslims who were witnessing a major shift in the political and religious lives of their community in the aftermath of the Police Action. Although it was limited to a family matter, when Sultan was dealing with these issues he was participating in a public discourse about Islamic reformism that he seemingly adapts from various contemporary sources including Khan's legacy of the Aligarh movement and the local debates about modern social and religious thought in the city of Hyderabad. While locality defines the text and texture of his short story, the entire narrative comes full circle with the thick descriptions of the thought processes of the local Muslim situated historically in late 1940s Hyderabad. Sultan as a character and Swamy as an author both actively participate in this discourse of post-1940s Islam in Hyderabad. Despite his non-Muslim identity, Swamy's representation of Hyderabadi

Muslim life remains phenomenal within the Telangana–Telugu literary culture. His deeper engagements with the city's new generation of Muslims, his work at Deccan Radio as an Urdu scriptwriter, and his participation in the Hyderabadi Urdu cultures made him an insider of the community. Even in terms of representational politics after the 1990s Muslim discourses, namely *Muslim vādam* (Muslimism) in Telugu, Swamy's contributions have gained more legitimacy. Using a short story as a narrative framework, Swamy presents the reader with an opportunity to untangle the freshly emerging socio-political and cultural networks of Hindus and Muslims. By fictionalizing a wide spectrum of private and public dimensions of this debate, he makes his fictional story a historical testimony and an argumentative text at once as his characters function as primary witnesses representing multiple layers of the Hyderabadi Muslimness.

This intense moment arrived in Sultan's family when the Nizam and the Razakars defined Hyderabad as a "Muslim state," and a singular homogeneous Muslimness had become a device of the political authority or the inflexible traditionalism signified in the practices of the *nawabi* families in the case of Hyderabad. In such an intense social context thwarted by communal conflicts and diametrically opposing viewpoints among the Muslim community, Sultan's act triggers an unambiguous resistance, at first against the family and then, from the perspective of his mother and brother, against the "entire Muslim" community in the city. As incidents unfold, we realize Sultan's story reveals many problematic layers of a personal narrative that acquires the value of social concern. Swamy's status as a citizen of the state of Hyderabad and his role in local cultural and social life portrays him as a literary activist too. Both the writer and his characters indeed participate in the same discourse, thus moving beyond their "fictional" or "literary" boundaries.

Sultan, as portrayed in the story "Vimukti," represents a version of urban and modern Muslim premised on new ideas about education. Two additional characters that I introduce now also begin their journey of resistance from two key and yet quite different vantage points: politics and religion. Although these three arenas—education, politics, and religion—have always overlapped in the making of a new Muslim self in Hyderabad and the larger world of South Asian Islam, Swamy's fictional realm chooses to deal with them separately to highlight the intensity and narrow down the focus on each arena. As defined and interpreted in multiple ways in the context of Hyderabad, this triangle of transformation shows how Muslim identity demonstrates a paradigmatic shift in the 1940s. In each story, Swamy develops one such idea and makes it a debatable narrative by presenting multiple dimensions of a similar issue. Swamy clearly identifies the points of rupture and builds his stories around those intense moments, for instance, Dilawar's story in "Yugantham" (The end of an era). Dilawar's extremely ordinary middle-class life turns into a political story with a rupture created by the idea of a "Muslim state" and the two-nation theory—an idea the Razakars strongly support. And, finally, there is the third story, "Kevalam Manushulam" (We are just human beings), in which Bilquis and Kanwal together further this dialogue by resisting divisive Sunni–Shi'i politics in Islam. I begin by introducing Dilwar's story and then turn to the other two stories.

THE END OF AN ERA: EVERYDAY PLURALISM AND THE DIVIDE

The historian Karen Leonard analyzes how everyday life in the city offers evidence of "a successful plural society."[35] Explaining the contours of the pluralist network throughout the city, Leonard shows how this is evident

> not only in the court and administrative culture, but also in the urban culture as well as the Indo-Muslim and Mughlai at the neighborhood and even household levels. All who lived in the city, especially in the neighborhoods of the old walled city, participated in the dominant public culture, regardless of their religious affiliations and private religious observances.

Despite this heavy emphasis on everyday pluralism, the consequences of the Police Action clearly led to the destruction of this mutuality, what Noorani describes as the "destruction of Hyderabad" itself, gradually separating the community into "Hindu" and "Muslim"[36] (Figure 1.5). Swamy's detailed description of this new separated context provides rich evidence of such a destruction of mutuality. This separation has other implications too, such as the anxiety of belonging and dual citizenship—the two phases that led to the minoritized identity of Muslims in the post–Police Action Hyderabad. Swamy's characters, such as Dilawar, portray this tragic irony of the problem of the minority precisely by him locating them in the political setting of Hyderabad.

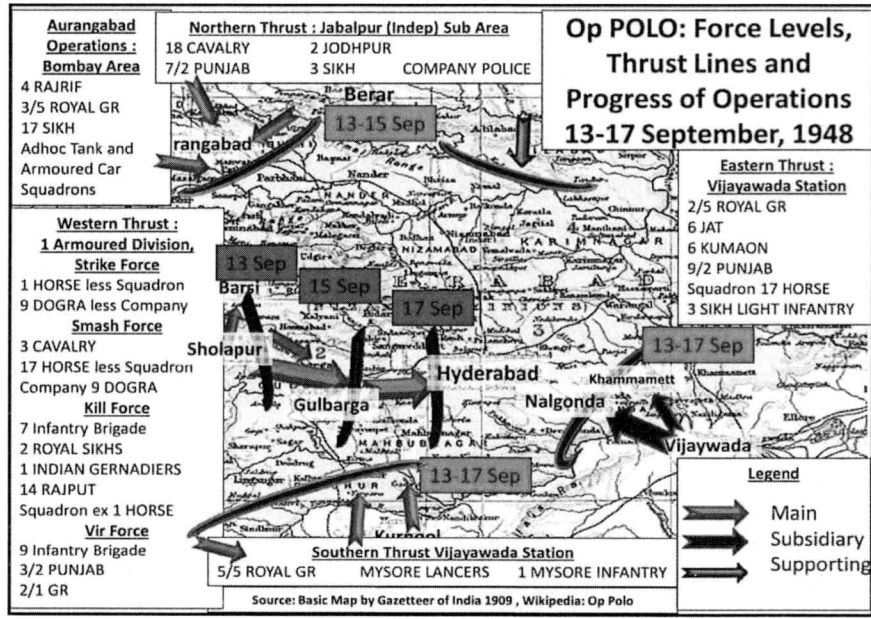

Figure 1.5   The map of the Union military cordoning off the Hyderabad state
Source: Syed Ali Hashmi.

Whereas most writers, particularly in Telugu, are either ambiguous or silent about the events of the Police Action in their fictional accounts, "Yugantham" begins with a precise and particular date:

> September 15th, 1948. It was the third day of the "Police Action." In Hyderabad, we were sitting really close to the All India Radio broadcasts listening attentively. Out of fear, we always lower its volume. The radio says that the Indian army was invading the Hyderabad state, most importantly the troops were arriving faster into the city, now almost fifty miles closer. The city will be soon cordoned off—from the east, meaning Vijayawada and the west, Sholapur. Just today or tomorrow, these troops will enter the city. We're not sure why the troops from the other directions were not fast enough. Hyderabad's exclusive—the Deccan Radio was broadcasting the developing news almost twenty-four hours continually. According to the news, the Hyderabad state army including the Ittehadul Muslimeen Razakars were chasing the Indian army and the radio stations boastfully declared their bravery

with slogans such as "Long Live Qasim Razvi" and "Azad Hyderabad very soon!"[37]

Situating the narrative time and space right at the epicenter of the crisis, Swamy indeed provides a political testimony of the very early days of the Police Action and the problematic phase of the mutual distrust between Hindus and Muslims. Beginning with a description of the everyday climate of those five days that led to "the destruction of Hyderabad," Swamy blends the personal and the political. In the above segment of the story, Swamy also describes the politics of media by referring to the two conflicting news reports that were in circulation—Deccan Radio of the state of Hyderabad and All-India Radio of the union government of India. Being an Urdu scriptwriter at Deccan Radio, Swamy witnessed many historical events that shaped the states of Hyderabad and Telangana. Until the Police Action, Deccan Radio was a center of the multicultural legacy of Hyderabadi pluralism that highlighted the shared practices of Urdu and Telugu. In many ways, this radio encouraged the emerging modernist writers and poets who were part of a pluralist discourse during the 1940s. During the Police Action, however, Deccan Radio confined itself to upholding the political authority of the Nizam.[38]

Very clearly, that was the moment that Nehru described Hyderabad as a place "full of dangerous possibilities."[39] All these "dangerous possibilities" further complicated the making of the public culture, including media and literature. Despite their deep commitments to various ideologies, almost every individual, as portrayed in Swamy's short fiction, was forced to take a side and began articulating their subjective anxieties about the new political climate. Fiction writers, too, were openly subscribing to the state-sponsored narratives, drawing thick lines in the local community to define the boundaries, and in so doing, fixing the categories of "Hindu" and "Muslim." Swamy's characters, too, represent this anxiety though they exist in the same liminality and fluidity of their times. As mentioned before, Urdu writers such as Rasheed Jahan, Sadat Hasan Manto, and Ismath Chughtai were major influences in the making of a post–Police Action writer in Hyderabad state, particularly in the Telugu literary sphere.[40] The story begins with a climate that depicts a wave of the hate politics that engulfed the entire community in Hyderabad. Swamy tries to capture the idiom of such an intense moment of hatred when even a friend appears to be an enemy or suspicious entity.

According to Guduri Seetharam, the editor of the volume of Swamy's short fiction, "the entire community had experienced an unprecedented

tragedy of the dividing lines between Muslims and Hindus by labeling the
community as 'us' (*mēmu*) and 'them' (*vāḷḷu*)." Yet, Swamy's treatment of
various Muslim characters and contexts showcases an exemplary narrative
model as he employs a pluralist lens, defying the idea of "us" and "them." In
the process, he recounts a compelling story of the othering of the Muslims
by unraveling the multilayered psyche of a middle-class Muslim who turned
into a volunteer of the Razakars, the private army led by Qasim Razvi, the
president of the Majlis-e-Ittehad-ul-Muslimeen (MIM) between 1946 and
1948. The protagonist in this story might not be a proper representation of
an ordinary Muslim, yet the way Swamy portrays him helps the reader to
comprehend how the mutuality of Hindus and Muslims had undergone a
key transformation. In addition, he captures the physical and psychological
distancing of Hindus and Muslims by providing a thick ethnography of the
rapidly changing neighborhoods, particularly in the story "Yugantham."
Charting the pathetic journey of the Hindus and Muslims of Hyderabad—
from trust to distrust, friendship to hate, and tolerance to intolerance—this
story is often discussed as a compelling testimony of this growing hatred.[41]
Despite the empathy towards his Muslim friends, the narrator, now filled
with fear and suspicion, laments the separation of Hindus and Muslims using
the explicit categories of "us" and "them."

> Gripped by the fear, the new middle-class employees belonging to
> Hindu families began pretending to be busy, hiding their faces in
> their office files. Most businesses and stores, apparently Hindus, were
> being shut down even before the evening. As the evening arrives, not
> one Hindu venture to walk on the streets, while Muslims go around
> freely. It is true that Muslims were minorities, yet they wander around
> the neighborhoods openly carrying weapons such as knives and hockey
> sticks.

> It's not just about these three days, we had been living under similar
> conditions for almost a year. When India got its independence and the
> Nizam declared the independent status of the state of Hyderabad, it's
> the same story of violence. In many places, the police and the Razakars
> together were attacking the people, mostly Hindus, to sway public
> opinion. From the surrounding villages, we hear all the time about the
> murders, rapes, lootings and the other forms of violence. Relatively, the
> city outwardly appears calm with scattered incidents here and there.

The people who have money and could to do so already left Hyderabad state and migrated to safe places. The helpless ordinary people like us stayed back holding our breath tightly.

Of course, we lived in the Hindu neighborhood. But there was a mosque near our house. There are several Muslim houses around the mosque. They look dangerous like the anthills, the homes of the snakes to us.[42]

Describing the situation from the perspective of a Hindu, Swamy's character here exposes the fear and trauma caused by the very presence of Muslims and the activities of the Razakars too. As the story unfolds, Swamy describes how life in the neighborhood (*basti*) had undergone a massive change physically and then psychologically. The story walks the reader through the narrow lanes of the city which were by then visibly segregated into Muslim and Hindu spaces. Significantly, the descriptions of the workspaces also speak about the partitioning of Hindus and Muslims.

In fact, we used to have more Hindu technical staff than Muslims in our office, yet most of the officers, clerks and attendants were Muslims. We could never open our mouths to talk about politics there. But the Muslim clerks would read the Urdu newspapers with loud voices and debate the politics openly. They particularly read the news articles that attack the Indian government and Sardar Patel. The two engineers who worked with me were Muslims. One of them clearly had the connections with the Razakars. I tried to keep myself away from him. Another Muslim was my classmate and had leftist views. He would always criticize Nizam and his feudalist ways. That way, I was more comfortable speaking to him. We always shared our thoughts openly.[43]

In addition, Swamy makes a clear distinction between an ordinary Muslim and a Razakar by exposing us to the human face of the dilemma throughout the story. He portrays several Muslim characters as the victims of the theory of the two nations and then portrays how their lives were further complicated by the local Nizam's idea of a Muslim state. Although it is not the complete story of how Muslim politics acquired a new dimension around the Police Action, Swamy documents the pain of a community that was being partitioned by new-fangled political ideas such as the Muslim state, the Razakar movement, and the idea of Pakistan that led to the othering of Muslims. Vacillating in the religionized political spaces, the two main characters in the story struggle hard to sustain their friendship in the face of the grim reality of the violence of the Police Action.

Whereas Swamy's other stories depict the socio-cultural consequences of the Police Action, "Yugantham" deals particularly with the consequent shifts in Hyderabadi Muslim politics. At the outset, it is about two dear friends: one a Hindu, named Swamy (note again the autobiographical feature here with the writer giving his own name to the narrator of this story), and the other a Muslim, Dilawar, the protagonist in the story. The narrator of the story and his mother are listening attentively to the news on the two radio stations—All-India Radio of the union government of India, and the other, Deccan Radio of the Nizam. Amidst a turbulent and susceptible situation, and even more, in the middle of the night, Swamy's friend Dilawar drops by. Although Swamy and his mother usually consider Dilawar as family, now, at this midnight hour and particularly after the Police Action, they hesitate to open the door and let him in. A long-time friend now becomes a suspicious entity and a stranger too.

During their conversation at that late hour, they learn about Dilawar's recent metamorphosis into a follower of Qasim Razvi, the leader of the Razakars. While Dilawar had committed several atrocities, of late he had started to feel betrayed ever since the Nizam's surrender to the union government. Dilawar had been anticipating that the Nizam would continue and the Razakars would be successful in creating a Muslim state modeled on Pakistan. The Razakars and the upper-class Muslims who were close to the Nizam strongly believed that a separate nation such as Pakistan could only protect the Muslim community of the Hyderabad state. This belief also led to more divisive politics and the migrations of certain sections of upper-class Muslims to Pakistan after the Police Action. Whereas this idea of Pakistan attained more significance as a political rhetoric, as I show further in this book, the majority of the ordinary Muslims from Hyderabad and other parts of Telangana in fact stayed away from such ideas.

Against this background, after the Nizam's surrender, Dilawar was forced to live incognito because the state police were chasing him. Towards the end of the story, the disenchanted and frustrated Dilawar decides to migrate to Pakistan to escape the state violence further complicated by the hatred of his friends. Before leaving for Pakistan, Dilawar writes a letter to his friend Swamy confessing all his horrendous acts and crimes. While admitting his helplessness in sharing the details of his activities as a Razakar, he also describes various levels of betrayal, ranging from the personal to the political.

Along with the letter, Dilawar also sends in some money and jewelry that he wants his friend to use for himself. Ashamed of using the "bad" money for himself, Swamy hands it over to an officer who heads the local civil team, deployed by the Government of India to protect the people. This officer, like every other member of the civil team, turns out to be corrupt. Later, Swamy learns that he not only lost his friend but all the money and jewelry that his friend believed he would take care of. Nevertheless, there are several "ends" that the writer aims to unveil throughout the story: personal, collective, political, cultural, and most importantly, the end of an everyday pluralist life and mutuality in the Hyderabadi community. Within the narrative framework of the story, Swamy debates the quandary of Hindu–Muslim interactions in the city of Hyderabad, openly using these religious categories and unraveling multiple potential implications involving these categories. Early on, the story describes the narrator's disenchantment with the political power that undermines the safety of ordinary people, both Muslims and Hindus. Being extremely critical about the feudal system promoted by the Nizam, he assumes that the Police Action will put an end to most of these everyday complications, including the political turmoil and uncertainties.

> When I heard that the Police Action had begun, it was a great relief as if some huge burden was removed quickly and there was a sense of elation that guaranteed our liberation from all of these chains. But very soon we're all engulfed in a new fear about how local Muslims would react. They have been quiet and peaceful until now. We're scared that these Muslims unable to stand the attacks from the Indian Army would be forced to wage a battle, like terrified cats caged in a room.[44]

Towards the end of the story, the narrator articulates his disenchantment with the outcome of the Police Action. Parallel to these external violent activities, he describes the inner life of his friend as if he were trying to juxtapose the state violence and the state of his mind, in addition to his own interiority as a narrator. However, when we read the letter written by Dilawar to Swamy, his words plainly express their anguish about the failure of the nation-state. For Swamy, it was a moment to narrate his disillusionment not only with the Police Action but the very nature of the two governmental systems that destroyed the pluralist ethos of contemporary everyday life in Hyderabad.

Similar to "Yugantham," several stories in this collection describe diverse modes of everyday pluralism and Hindu–Muslim shared realms, specifically a cultural legacy produced as a result of popular Islam and Sufism in the city of Hyderabad. Swamy narrates how this secular space was forcibly erased from the public–private lives of Hyderabadis. Swamy's literary career and personal life were indeed defined by this everyday pluralist space, as he began his literary work with translations of Urdu writers and his exposure to local Sufi networks. The characterization of Dilawar in "Yugantham," too, portrays the dynamics of pluralist Hyderabadi life, but Swamy laments the way it came to an unfortunate end through the intervention of state violence. In the case of Dilawar, Swamy also mentions the migration of Muslims from Hyderabad to Pakistan. This is one of the few stories that depict the pain of migration and displacement of Hyderabadi Muslims. Few autobiographical accounts also describe this aspect of migration and displacement. For instance, General El-Edroos, the commander-in-chief of the Hyderabad state's forces, writes about these migrations:

> The Muslim problem in the Indian Union is a three-fold one. It concerns the government; it concerns the Hindus; and it concerns the Muslims themselves. With the partition of India, some Muslims who were residents of the territories which are now a part of the Indian Union migrated to Pakistan. In certain cases, this was the result of the communal riots in North India just preceding and during the Partition period, in which thousands of people of both the communities were slaughtered. Other Muslims went to Pakistan, because they were for the concept of Pakistan and could not adjust themselves to the new changes in India, as an Indian nation. A few others went because they thought they would have better prospects in Pakistan. Certain Muslims who moved from India to Pakistan moved away with their families, while in certain other instances, only a few members of the family migrated while the rest remained in India. This cause is creating a problem, as they are suspected of dual loyalties and are themselves at a loss about how to adapt themselves to their peculiar position.[45]

In "Yugantham," Dilawar represents this anxiety of divided loyalty when he speaks about his bleak future in Pakistan:

> Right now, I'm in Bombay. Of course, by the time this letter reaches you, I won't be here. If everything goes well, I will be somewhere in Karachi, getting ready for starting a new life in Pakistan. It's scary even

to think of! You know all the struggles of my life since I graduated from
the university. It took me so much time to settle in life and now I need
to start again. Now I don't even have those BA degree certificate papers
with me. I'm entering an abyss like nobody. I don't know how I would
survive! but, I got to go, no way but to go—to save my skin. If I stayed
there in Hyderabad state itself, they wouldn't rest until they see my
blood spilling. That fear made me leave even intimate friends like you.[46]

Although this story deals with several other themes which were key
events of his times, the fear and disillusionment about the failure of the
two nation-states remain central. The most intriguing aspect that many
works including this story reveal to us is the creation of a new religionized
identity. In this case, Swamy as "Hindu" and Dilawar as "Muslim" tell the
story of another disruption, one which is often considered to be an immediate
outcome of the Police Action: the end of the composite culture which was
the hallmark of Hyderabadi life.[47] Swamy's other stories, such as "Ruhi Apa,"
"Shareefa," "Bharosa," and "Vamsaankuram," likewise depict the ethics of the
coexistence of Hindus and Muslims.

Nevertheless, when it comes to "Yugantham," Swamy pushes this
narrativization further to show what the new avatar of the religion does
to individuals such as Dilawar and Swamy. As the story narrates, both
Dilawar and Swamy now acquire a new identity marked by state violence,
media strategies, and the divisive politics of Hindus and Muslims. Due to
these new developments, both Dilawar and Swamy, despite their longtime
friendship and interactions, suddenly become unknown entities to each
other. When Dilawar shared all the stories about his role as a Razakar with
Swamy, Dilawar appeared nothing but "a wild animal with a body drenched
in blood." This Dilawar is someone different from the man he had known as
an intimate friend during his college days. Similarly, Swamy, too, acquires a
new personality resulting from the hate politics of the 1940s.

SULTAN'S PREDICAMENT: TOWARDS A MODERN MUSLIM SELF

The epigraph of this chapter refers to the story "Vimukti" in which Sultan
writes a letter to his mother about his decision to marry the maidservant,
Shireen. Rejecting his noble heritage, Sultan openly embraces a newly
urbanized Hyderabadi identity with an emphasis on non-traditional modes

of social and religious life. Portrayed as an agent of the crucial historical shifts of his times, Sultan represents a life that pushes the boundaries of the personal. In the process, his story transforms into that of many Sultans in the city of Hyderabad—the Sultans who represent the new generation of religious freedom, pluralism, and gender equality. Though breaking away from the norms of *ashraf* Muslim practices, this young generation of Sultans strikes a balance halfway between the idea of Islamic modernity and the progressivist ideology of leftist politics. Whereas many historical and political archives fail to capture this key moment in the history of Muslims of Hyderabad,[48] the fictional world of Swamy holds up a realistic mirror to the making of a new Muslim and portrays diverse aspects of such new Muslimness of the late 1940s.[49] These new Muslims no longer desire to remain mere observers of yesteryear and the glorified past. Rather, like Sultan, they make a deliberate choice to pursue a dynamic life rooted in their individual comprehension of an emerging Islamic modernity, urbanization, and the hybridity of Hindu–Muslim everyday life.

In the aforementioned letter written to his mother or his entire family, Sultan describes their current social condition as "the contrived atmosphere of the *nawabi* families that are steadily in decline," filled with "loathsome customs and demeaning attitudes." Further, he also presumes that the shift in his life is "unacceptable" to her and considers his move as "good," a place from which he will, he says, "definitely not return." In fact, the language Sultan uses here provides clues for comprehending the contours of the puzzling world of Swamy's fictional realm too. Whereas the previous story, "Yugantham," demonstrates a political shift in Muslim life, "Vimukti" portrays an inner conflict about the remnants of the feudal life of *nawabi* Muslims in Hyderabad. Despite all his traditional schooling earlier on in his life, he tends to de-classify his identity and see himself as a product of modern education and reformist Islam—the key ideas prominent in 1940s Hyderabad. The recurring references to his Aligarh academic background mark Sultan's modernity and his engagements with the larger political and cultural developments in the city.

On learning about Siraj's abusive treatment of a maidservant (*dāsi*) and its tragic consequences, Sultan begins to hate the "wretched customs" in the family, specifically customs that treat maidservants as nothing but "sex workers." Sultan openly points out the unethical behavior of his brother Siraj who, after impregnating the *dāsi*, marries into a noble family. Sultan's rebellion against tradition redefines his relationship with Shireen. After an intense debate, he finally decides to leave home to marry Shireen and arrives in Aligarh to pursue higher education. While the storyline appears simple and straightforward, the ideas of resistance and progressivism have a devastating impact on Sultan's family. First, Sultan's contestation of *nawabi* customs is not considered to be merely a personal or family matter. From the perspective of his family, his actions would have serious implications for the immediate Muslim community in the city too.

> In a few days it became clear to him about Siraj's abusive behavior. And it was quite a surprise for him to discover that their liaison was being encouraged in the house. Would Siraj marry Jugnoo? Was it proper to go about like this without being married?[50]

For many family members, including his mother, this mode of questioning was indeed shocking. He could not digest the fact that his mother, for whom he also had great respect, approved of such behavior. Whereas the family dynamics are crucial, Sultan's discussions with Siraj and then with his mother speak more about the shift in his gender perceptions. Siraj openly points out Sultan's lack of knowledge about the family hierarchy and traditions by saying:

> Great! You are growing up so much faster than usual … but, then, my dear youngest brother, you can't as yet understand these matters. Still too young, aren't you? You'll understand everything in due course. In the meantime, don't wreck your head hard over such useless thoughts. Study hard like a good boy, go.[51]

In fact, Sultan's mother shares a similar worldview with Siraj, openly rejecting Sultan's ideas:

> "What? Siraj's marriage with Jugnoo…. Are you out of your mind? A servant-girl, a slave. Her place is just next to our shoes. Now you say, my son's marriage with such a woman?!"
>
> "But Ammi, Every day, bhai saaheb…."
>
> "Ooh, what's he doing?"
>
> "… Jugnoo … Bhai saaheb has Jugnoo in his room almost every single day."

"So what? That's what they're supposed to do. Don't they come to your room, tell me if not?"

"Not that Ammi ... Jugnoo is pregnant now...."

"Wretched whore! I'll set her right."[52]

Sultan fails to understand their responses as related to this entire episode, thus marking a disjuncture in the perceptions of the family—traditional and modern. Repeatedly, the entire family points out Sultan's failure to continue the legacy of the *nawabi* practices. One of his family members makes fun of him, saying "Sultan means what?! King, Emperor. But you hardly have any qualities of an emperor or a king!" These conversations in Sultan's family illustrate the tensions about the changing worldviews in the upper-class Muslim community of Hyderabad and the larger Islamic world of South Asia too. The title of this story—"Vimukti," meaning "deliverance" or "liberation"— compels the reader to consider two major aspects of the Hyderabadi Muslim identity: first, the critique of the noble legacy, and second, Sultan's emphasis on the reformism within the community. Sultan's major moment of resistance against the family traditions uncritically and unquestioningly resonates with the rise of a progressive, secular, and liberal Muslim's search for a repertoire of modern sensibilities and behavioral practices. As mentioned before, Swamy's literary mission in this context echoes that of the 1932 group of progressive writers who were also active around 1947 in the state of Hyderabad along with the Aligarh movement.

According to Jaini Mallaya Gupta, one of the participants of this conference, the giants of Urdu literature, such as Maqdoom Mohiuddin, Kaifi Azmi, Mazrooh Sultanpuri, and Ali Sardar Jafri made an impact on the political and literary activism in the city, which I will discuss more in Chapter 4. Kaifi Azmi's intimate knowledge of the city provided a new space for progressive writing too. In particular, the publication of the anthology of short stories titled *Angārē* offered a model for the new generation of short fiction writers in Hyderabad. Local writers and literary activists turned their attention to progressive icons such as Ahmed Ali and Rasheed Jahan, who focused on recasting the question of Muslim women in the light of modernity and social reformist movements in India.[53] Ahmed Ali's writings primarily focus on "the condition of women: poverty, domestic abuse, sexual desire, and longing experienced by widows, and the cruelties endured by women in everyday life." Makhdoom Mohiuddin, Rasheed Jahan, along with Zeenath

Sajida, were influential in the making of progressivism in the Hyderabad state.[54] Similarly, Muslim women take on a central role in Swamy's fictional world. Nonetheless, he was extremely selective when it came to portraying Muslim women from the noble Muslim community in Hyderabad. Most of his Muslim women characters struggle with the ideas of the new freedom, reformism, modern womanhood, and education as they tried to acclimate themselves to the local cultural idiom in 1930s–1950s Hyderabad. In addition, their journey with modernity is always tense and discomforting, though eventually they end up breaking their ties with traditional ways of being family and community, a move I discuss at greater length with regard to the next story, "Kevalam Manushulam" (We are just human beings).

In the story "Vimukti," Sultan's escape from his family and *nawabi* norms lands him in Aligarh—suggesting it also as an alternative destination for the new generation of Muslims. In Aligarh, Sultan envisions a new life with Shireen, a life shaped by the values of individualism, gender equality, and progressivism that counters the systems that he inherited from his family in Hyderabad. The story thus ends on a note of liberation of many kinds, from orthodoxy to political systems. This idea of deliverance from the chains of *nawabi* life finds much complicated and nuanced expression in the story "Kevalam Manushulam" (We are just human beings), this time with a focus on the life story of a young Muslim woman. Although the city of Hyderabad is known for its Shia Islamic practices including the public commemorations of Muharram, no literary work in Telugu has heretofore described the interior life of this community.[55] As is the case of many other stories by Swamy, this story also has multiple layers that unveil various public and domestic aspects of Shia Muslims in the city.

"WE ARE JUST HUMAN BEINGS": THE BEGINNINGS OF A CRITICAL MUSLIM

"Kevalam Manushulam" (We are just human beings) is a story about two families and their friendship that emerged in the wake of the new interactions between the Nizams and the Kayastha caste groups. Whereas both of these communities—Shi'i Muslims and Kayasthas—have certain shared features of urbanity and easy access to the authoritative structures of the Nizam state, the local history of the Kayasthas of Hyderabad was even more fascinating. Popularly known for their hybridity, fluidity, and an insatiable desire for upward mobility, Kayasthas played a key role in the making of modern Hyderabad, particularly in developing the bureaucratic structures of the Nizam's state.[56]

Kayastha families were also known for adopting elite Muslim cultures and even literary aspects of Urdu and Persian that allowed them to participate successfully in the Hyderabadi cultural and political milieu. Whereas many studies provide evidence for how their public selves were molded, the domestic aspects remain largely unstudied, particularly in Telugu literary writings. Once again Swamy takes on the task of dealing with such an uncharted realm of the modern history of Hyderabad, this time in the story "Kevalam Manushulam." The basic storyline is about the modern conceptualization of love and marriage between a Muslim and a Hindu—in this case, as mentioned before, a Shia Muslim and Kayastha Hindu. The story, however, creates tension between the two families who, despite their liberal and modern lifestyles, end up denying this love marriage and returning to their rigid religious boundaries.[57] This return to rigidity, in fact, mars our understanding of how communities, despite their fluid histories, respond to the changing religious circumstances.

Noticing the recent transformations in the religious behavior of these two distinctively authoritative communities in the city of Hyderabad, Swamy offers insights into their domestic spaces, but with a critical eye. While he was always hugely appreciative of the composite culture of Hyderabad, he had no qualms when it came to presenting the other side of this hybridity. Despite their liberal and secular public appearances, the domestic spaces of these two families still show an orthodoxy in the sense that they follow a strict religious code in the name of family honor (*izzat*). Being a pious Shi'i Muslim, Mirza performs the mandatory prayer five times a day and Swamy specifically mentions that he also made a hajj pilgrimage. He never displays any religious hatred either by his behavior or his words; yet, when it comes to Sunnis, he is never tongue-tied. His friend Saxena's father was a renowned scholar in the court of the sixth Nizam Mir Mahboob Ali Khan (1866–1911). As a mark of respect and devotion to the sixth Nizam, he named his son after the Nizam—Roy Mahboob Roy Saxena. Although he himself never participates in Hindu puja practices, he allows rituals and vows to Krishna out of respect for his wife's devotion. Nevertheless, the lifestyles of their children have all the features of an urbanized lifestyle, in that they celebrate the benefits of a new education and reformist cultural milieu. As such, Mirza's two sons settled in England and America, and the third child, Bilquis—the protagonist of the story—is a medical graduate. Similarly, Saxena's son Kamal too is a medical school graduate.

Like Sultan in the previous story, Mirza also graduated from Aligarh Muslim University and returned to Hyderabad. Conveniently using all the tools of urban life with a more utilitarian approach and not particularly obsessed with age-old sentiments, traditionalism, or feudalism, Mirza sells most of his ancestor's real estate and lives happily on the profits. To the surprise of Bilquis, he then begins to articulate a religious life singularly defined by Shi'i beliefs and practices, in which even Sunnis are nothing but *kāphir*s, non-believers! At one point, he even states that he is ready to marry his daughter into a Hindu family rather than into a Sunni family. Then, ironically, when it comes to accepting his daughter's love with a Hindu, he becomes utterly frustrated and rejects even the longtime friendship with the Saxenas. Mirza, thus, represents a category of Hyderabadi Muslims whose identity is being defined by new economic factors even though he continues his Shi'i identity. Bilquis and Kamal both realize that their parents represent a different urban modernity that fails to transcend their normative orthodoxy. In the end, before registering her marriage according to the civil marriage act at a government office, Bilquis states:

> In my view, religion is a personal matter and marriage is a social institution. They don't need to be contradictory to each other. We can be a husband and wife even without converting to the other's religion. Now and forever, we want to remain as Kamal Roy Saxena and Bilqis Mirza. After graduating, we're not even planning to live in this city, we will move out to a nearby village, and do service for the village, so that we will do justice to our medical profession. Humanism is our religion … so, we want to remain just human beings![58]

Swamy's focus here on the modernist conceptions of love and marriage is as crucial as the story of these two families and their shared histories. That way, the story is primarily about two family friends of two prominent religious communities who became great family friends; secondarily, it is a love story between Bilquis and Kamal who were exposed to new education systems similar to their parents, but the values of modernity, such as humanism, pluralism, and social justice, are more ingrained in their everyday lives. While acknowledging the entire shared history of Shia Muslims and Kayasthas in the city, Swamy's focus on these two different viewpoints of Hyderabadi urbanity allows him to show a larger picture of the city and its implications as related to the popularly known Hyderabadi *tehzeeb*. Despite their extremely close family ties, both parents decline the proposal and ask their respective child to convert to the other's religion. Bilquis and Kamal reject this idea and express their desire to stay just Bilquis and Kamal, not some Shia or Kayastha.

Swamy positions these four characters as two opposing arguments to launch a debate on the new Muslim self as it is reflected in the Hyderabadi *tehzeeb*. Benefiting from the tools of modernity, these four characters take diverse paths and represent a shift in the making of a Hyderabadi Muslim, one who is both progressive and critical. For Bilquis and Kamal, it is more about practicing the ethos of modernity and secularism in their everyday lives and their selfhood is central. For Mirza and Saxena, it was more of a socio-economic privilege, and they need this modernity to the extent that it contributes to their upward mobility. Swamy's description of how Hindu Kayasthas adapted Persian culture to their individual and social life offers fresh insights into the making of the city of Hyderabad, and this adaptation indeed works as a tool of modernization for Kayasthas. When Kamal and Bilquis challenge this convenient utilitarian adaptability of modernization, they also present a counterargument that puts them at odds with the worldview of the parents. In a way they are introducing their own mode of religious hybridity that unsettles the very structure of modern life fashioned by their parents. In the process, Swamy's Muslims emerge not as objects but as agents of modern Islam, and they reclaim their selfhood. In the next section, I will discuss how this agency and selfhood were gained in the social and religious milieu of the 1940s Hyderabad where Swamy's positionality in the Muslim discourse takes on a prominent role.

MODERN ISLAM AND MUSLIM AGENCY: SWAMY'S HYDERABAD AND ITS PEOPLE

When Swamy turned his attention to various Muslim characters, most of which were said to be from his real life, he specifically chose the era between the 1940s and 1956—the period marked by the Telangana rebellion and the formation of the linguistic state of Andhra Pradesh along with the new debates on Islam and Muslims. Like many writers and activists of this period, Swamy had also been intimately connected to various realms of personal and political life in the city since his childhood. Nevertheless, Swamy's focus on the agony of Hyderabadi Muslims, whose lives were impacted directly or indirectly by the Police Action, made his voice distinctive. Not limiting himself to portraits of these Muslim characters, Swamy was successful in creating a grammar of coexistence that counters the unprecedented antagonism and hate speech unleashed against the Muslims. By claiming their agency and selfhood, most of his characters are ready to embrace the fast-approaching shifts in religious, political, and socio-economic life. Their explicit contestation of the *nawabi*-centered practices functions as a first step towards deconstructing the prevalent political and religious systems.

A diverse set of characters, such as Sultan, Dilawar, and Bilquis, deny being defined by the stereotypical understanding of a Muslim or any rigid religious categorization. Arriving at this critical juncture, Swamy's characters (as discussed earlier) call for radical religious reforms and shifts in everyday life that echo the broader contextualization of progressivism and the idea of critical Islam in the state of Hyderabad. They found a way of life that transgressed the boundaries of the socio-political and religious systems of their times and refashioned a version of progressivism and critical approach. Whether writing about personal or political life, when it comes to Swamy's literary work, most such aspects begin with the story of Sultan. Before declaring his resentment openly, Sultan had already undergone turmoil and trouble by contesting many aspects of his family's *nawabi* practices. Questioning the already established notions of an *ashraf* and *nawabi* mode of life, Sultan was in favor of an alternative realm of "Islam" that he was trying to emulate in the continually shifting everyday life of Hyderabad. Similar to many literary narratives produced and circulated during this period in contemporary South Asia, Sultan also engages with a version of the postcolonial Muslim discourse including redefining religious identities, secularism, and the progressive politics of his contemporary life. Most importantly, like any of Swamy's characters, Sultan also participates in a new social imaginary that progresses towards modernity, and in so doing inaugurating an idea—what many of my interviewees described as "a new Hyderabad"—that was refashioned in the aftermath of the Police Action.[59]

For many of these shifts, the tensions between the *nawabi* traditionalism and the coming of modern consciousness (*ādhunika cētana*) remain a central theme. Clearly separating themselves from the *nawabi* practices, these young Muslims' desire for a reformist shift in the Hyderabadi Muslim community and this version of Islam as characterized by their desires to be inclusive of the new socio-political climate of the 1940s. However, very few fiction writers were as successful as Swamy in capturing the characteristics of such a new Muslim sense of being and belonging that continued further into the making of the public sphere of Hyderabad and Telangana of the late 1940s. By participating in a larger world of contemporary discourses on Muslim identity, these written narratives and oral accounts complement each other in comprehending the identity politics of the post–Police Action period of Hyderabad. In the process, Swamy's narrative elicits a debate on the intersections of tradition and modernity, inner conflicts within Islam in Hyderabad, the interfaces between Hindus and Muslims, but most importantly, the new Muslim identity, later termed *muslimīyata* (Muslimness) in Telugu.

Swamy returns to the art of storytelling to share not merely his passion for this specific genre; as we can observe from his body of short fiction, he was much more concerned about the loss of mutuality between Hindus and Muslims after the traumatic Police Action. The entire trauma of this military action and violence, however, always remains in the background of his writings and is barely described. In addition, he turns our attention to the rise of a dynamic middle-class and urbanized new generation of young Muslim men and women who had just started exploring an idea of modern Islam that resists the *nawabi* practices in the city.[60] Engaging with this new idea, Swamy's characters forcefully demonstrate their agency in the making of an alternative local modernity which was later characterized as "Telangana modernity" (*Telangāṇa ādhunikata*). As these two aspects determine the framework of each story, Swamy showcases the extremely strong, individualistic, urbanized, and dynamic minds of the new Muslim community in the city of Hyderabad, which were emerging in the aftermath of the Police Action.

These self-fashioning narratives of characters such as Sultan and Bilquis, as shown here, problematize the traditional Islamic definitions of many social institutions and everyday life in Hyderabad. On the other hand, like Sultan's letter to his mother, Swamy's fictional writing functions as a device of protest and resistance as the writer himself presents as a literary activist and positions most of his characters as activists. At another level, despite his identity as Hindu, Swamy's characters present a predominantly Muslim-centered lifeworld, which itself is a major cultural accomplishment in an era when Muslims were either being demonized or marginalized in the public sphere of the post–Police Action times. In a literary culture in which the Muslim lifestyle and Muslim portrayals were either extremely thin or totally underplayed or minoritized, Swamy ventures to create a repository of fictional testimony in which Muslims have a prominent voice.

As is the case with many writers and poets who wrote about the late 1940s transformations of Hyderabad, Swamy's literary personality has deep roots in the cultural legacy of Hyderabad. Swamy, nevertheless, travels further into the landscapes and the interiorities of Muslim consciousness. He indeed manages to capture that intriguing moment—what his many friends and writers fondly remember as the Hyderabadi *tehzeeb*. Similar to them and his various characters in his short fiction, in being a citizen of Hyderabad, he takes pride in his sense of belonging defined by this *tehzeeb*, which, in the case of Swamy's short fiction is symbolized by the iconic Char Minar, a huge memorial which towers in the heart of the old city of Hyderabad. Even a peripheral glance makes one feel the ethos of this historical site and the people inhabiting the surrounding neighborhoods. In Swamy's fiction, the entire landscape of the Char Minar and its inhabitants likewise come alive when he introduces us to various neighborhoods and people in these short stories. It is no surprise that Swamy's collection of short stories was given the title of *Char Minar* (1981), and the vivid descriptions of the surrounding places and people remain a recurring trope in his writing. In a preface to Swamy's *Char Minar*, the Telugu literary historian Ramalingam says:

> We learn about the distinctiveness of these stories just by its title Cār minār. Ever since Mohammad Quli Qutub Shah, as an emperor of the Golconda, built this structure, this remained a witness for the specific history, culture and civilization of Hyderabad. The Golconda that was known for its religious tolerance and culture later encountered many setbacks and then united with the Indian union. Blending all this history and its legacy, Hyderabad displays a specific culture, what we could call *Hyderabadu Samskruti* ("The culture of Hyderabad"). Swamy's work is the literary manifestation of this entire legacy and the title is a perfect fit.[61]

As mentioned before, Swamy's specific emphasis on Hyderabad's Muslim life made his voice distinctive in Telugu literary culture. His literary career and the focus on Muslim lives are paralleled with the focus on the public culture of Hyderabad. He was the secretary for the Sadhana Samiti, a literary and cultural organization, which was active between 1939 and 1950. The stalwarts of Telangana, such as Burgula Ranganatha Rao, Bhagi Narayana Murthy, Devulapalli Ramanuja Rao, Veldurti Manikya Rao, the Jammalamadaka brothers, Bhandaru Chandra Mouliswara Rao, and Pillalamarri Venkata Hanumanta Rao were all part of this organization. The activities of these writers were not limited to the genres of creative writing as they began to play a crucial role in the politics and social reformism in Hyderabad. In the words of his friend and short fiction writer Guduri Seetharam:

> Swamy was more than a storyteller. While writing extensively, he was also participating in the larger democratic movement initiated during his times. More concerned about the shifting dynamics between Muslims and Hindus in Hyderabad, he spent restless nights as he had intimate connections with the both groups. Amidst the terrible times of the political turbulence, he was lamenting the loss of longtime friends and their legacy of the Hyderabadi *tehzeeb*. His writing has a blend of literary and political activism.[62]

Throughout his life, Swamy had been proud of his Hyderabadi identity and never minced words when it came to speaking about his Muslim friends or Urdu legacy. Born and raised in the old city of Hyderabad, Swamy always defined himself as "half Muslim and half Hindu."[63] He read writers such as Prem Chand in Urdu, not in Hindi. During the early days of his writing career, he translated Prem Chand's stories from Urdu to Telugu.[64] He believed that Prem Chand's soul and heart were deeply embedded in Urdu and that he belonged to the same legacy. Later, Swamy read Sadat Hasan Manto's Partition stories, and these made an indelible mark on his style too. As I argued elsewhere, Swamy belongs to the story-telling tradition of Manto when it comes to his tone and style in the short story.[65]

Swamy deals with many aspects of the local Muslim neighborhoods of the old city of Hyderabad, almost like an ethnographer of the *qasbā*.[66] As he was thoroughly familiar with every neighborhood and alley of the old city, Swamy's fictional world accurately provides an accurate road map of various locations in the city. The idea of locality in his works begins with the geographical locations but extends to the interiorities of Muslim lives too. Specifically, his stories are set in the most "happening" neighborhoods, such as Dabir Pura, Meer Alam Mandi, and Chaar Kamaan. Swamy successfully captured the idiom of the men and women of the old city including the minutest details of Hyderabadi food and speech, but most importantly also the fading colors of the *nawabi* families, such as that of Sultan. As one reader told me, "When reading Swamy's stories, I instantly land into the lanes and alleys of the old city and feel like hanging out with many of my old friends there! Of course, it's all a memory now!"[67] He continued: "This entirely happy and friendly experience became a memory very soon as every aspect of the city life was deeply impacted by the wounds left by the traumatic Partition and the Police Action."[68]

Swamy's depiction of these places, however, does not end with a photographic memory. Swamy introduces us to his world of friends and their many dilemmas and ordeals related to religious identities and the sense of belongingness in the wake of the rise of the two nation-states. The tensions between personal and political, history and the present, and most importantly, the transformative consequences of the Police Action that changed the interactions between Hindus and Muslims, remain the central theme in many of his stories. During my field research in the city of Hyderabad among various literary circles and Muslim organizations, I was told that most of Swamy's writings are autobiographical and that several of his characters, both Muslim and Hindu, are in fact the accurate "representations" from the city of Hyderabad of the late 1940s, specifically, the early days of the post-Partition era and the Police Action of 1948 to 1950. In fact, the term "representation" (*prātinithyaṁ*) was used by Guduri Seetharam to emphasize the contemporary questions surrounding the idea of a new Muslim identity in relation to the political environment in Hyderabad. Nevertheless, his emphasis also resonated with the debates on Muslim representations and redefinitions of Muslim identity in the larger Islamic world.

Swamy grew up witnessing all these changes in the everyday life of Hyderabad and had close associations with various social and cultural organizations in the city. He was in his late twenties when the city was being reshaped by the post-1940s developments including the Police Action and the resultant religious shifts. Whereas many people even now recall Partition, Swamy's Muslim and Hindu characters speak more about the aftermath of the Police Action, and that in particular is what makes the literary work of Swamy so different from that of his contemporaries. During one of my conversations with the well-known Telugu–Urdu literary historian Sadasiva, he fondly remembered Swamy and said:

More than once, Swamy spoke extensively about the Police Action that he had witnessed. He was lamenting the disappearance of the

Hyderabadi Muslim legacy, particularly, the *tehzeeb* with which we all grew up and were proud of! Beyond this, being a writer, he always felt the loss of Urdu and its fabulous literary flavor. He was sad about the Police Action because he lost many Muslim friends as many of them migrated to Pakistan and never returned.[69]

Even now, Swamy's emphasis on narrating the transforming psyche of his Muslim and Hindu friends remains intriguing in light of the post-2014 Telangana separatist movement. His stories are more like overt lamentations for the loss of his Muslim friends in the old city of Hyderabad. Nevertheless, as mentioned before, they are not outbursts, but careful and genuine reflections pondering the implications of the shifting psyche of local Muslims and their movement towards modern sensibilities and urbanity.

Hyderabad has always been at the center of manifold arguments about developmental politics, from medievalism to modernism.[70] Many aspects of the late 1940s' manifestations of modernity were buried under the heavy arguments about the state of Hyderabad as a "feudal system." Whereas secular, nationalist, and even leftist historians marginalized such aspects, very few scholars have paid attention to Hyderabad as a fast-emerging modern state.[71] In a recent work, Bhangya Bhukya explained, "The British colonial state ensured that the princely states were picturized as backward enclaves that kept alive an older feudal polity characterized by autocracy and underdevelopment, while British India moved towards modernity and capitalist development." Nevertheless, when we take a closer look at various modern reforms that started during the era of Salar Jung (1853–1883), there was a strategic and consistent development plan that challenged both the British colonial and Indian nationalist states.[72] Even before these new observations, Karen Leonard said:

Hyderabad had in fact undergone many of the same 'modernizing' processes associated with British colonial rule, Western education had come to Hyderabad, through many channels including Osmania, and it produced in Hyderabad, the same kinds of voluntary associations, caste and linguistic mobilizations, Masonic orders, and sporting clubs as in British India. The Hyderabad government undertook significant modernizing projects, many of them initiated in the nineteenth century like the postal, railways, telegraph, public works, medical, and education departments.[73]

In addition to these material aspects, the state of Hyderabad had also produced elaborate networks of modernity, even at the intellectual and ideological levels, by providing space for new identity formations, gender discourses, and Islamic reformism. As mentioned before, within the Telangana literary culture, the idea of the "progressive" originates in the manifesto of the PWA, an offshoot of the leftist movement in India, particularly, the publication of the *Angāre*, an anthology of ten short stories published in 1932. Swamy's Telugu stories that focus on the Muslim culture in Hyderabad indeed resonate with the dominant themes in the *Angāre* to a significant extent. Describing the nature of narrative in the *Angāre*, Ali Hussain Mir and Raza Mir said:

> The stories dealt with prevailing familial and sexual mores, the decadence and hypocrisy of social and religious life in contemporary India, and took more than one potshot at religious orthodoxy....[74]

The 1936 manifesto further explains this new situation:

> Radical changes are taking place in Indian society. Fixed ideas and old beliefs, social and political institutions are being challenged. Out of the present turmoil and conflict a new society is emerging.... It is the duty of Indian writers to give expression to the changes taking place in Indian life and to assist in the spirit of progress in the country....

When the *Angāre* was released, the writers claimed that it was "intentionally penned as a provocation against religious and social orthodoxies among north Indian Muslims as well as literary conventions pervasive in Urdu letters."[75] However, when it comes to south India, we find these "provocations" working in a slightly different mode, as most of the writers were, in fact, writing in their local idiom in a language other than Urdu or Persian.

Despite the promulgation of Telugu as the state's official language, within the history of Telugu culture, various Islamic practices and Urdu linguistic and literary practices continue to be a significant influence. Despite all that, Muslim life and its transformations remain largely unexplored in modern Telugu short fiction. Not many writers have even attempted to broach this topic of social life in Telugu. Contrary to the dominant and hegemonic cultural domain, Swamy's Muslim characters speak the new idiom of Muslim selfhood, agency, and resistance by responding to contemporary social and political concerns rather than being trapped in the traditionalist debates on topics such as sectarian identity, normative and prescribed mode of womanhood, and conventional education and social institutions. Specifically, Swamy's portrayal of new Muslim women successfully captures the progressivists' vision of urban life. He also takes note of the various social aspects that pressurize these young, urban Muslims and illustrates the intense moments of multiple disconnects between them and the traditional communities.

While several studies focus on the violent side of the Hindu–Muslim interactions or gender issues during the post-Partition era, Swamy's hybrid literary narratives that blend Urdu and Telugu elements offer insights into the value of everyday life and help us understand the ethics of coexistence between local Muslims and Hindus, thus raising a pertinent question of what being Muslim means in a pluralist socio-religious and political context such as the city of Hyderabad. Although Swamy deals more with the concerns and worries of Muslims whose sense of belonging was both unsettling and intriguing at the same time, his fictional world produces a pluralist cultural model that forthrightly respects multiculturalism and values the idea of multiple identities—the hallmark of the Hyderabadi culture.

NOTES

1. Guduri Seetharam, ed., *Nelluri Kesava Swamy Kathalu* (New Delhi: National Book Trust, 2010), 83–96. The story "Vimukti" was first published in 1969 in the collection of Kesava Swamy's stories titled *Pasidi Bommalu* and later in various anthologies of Telugu short stories. An English translation of the story is now also available in the volume edited by Hasan and Asaduddin, *Image and Representation*, 271–281.
2. Interview with author (originally in Urdu), Hyderabad, India, January 29, 2019.
3. Mohiuddin, *Nizāṁlō Dōpiḍī Vidhānaṁ*.
4. Interview with author (originally in Urdu), Hyderabad, India, January 29, 2019.
5. Syed Jaleel Ahmed, "From the President's Desk," https://www.tameer-e-millat.org/index.php/about-us/.
6. For more on this organization, see M. A. Moid, "Muslim Perceptions and Responses in Post-Police Action Contexts in Hyderabad," *Deccan Studies* 6, no. 2 (2008): 65.

7. Interview with author (originally in Urdu), Hyderabad, India, January 23, 2019.

8. Interview with author (originally in Urdu), Hyderabad, India, January 28, 2020.

9. Interview with author (originally in Urdu), Hyderabad, India, January 27, 2020.

10. Interview with author (originally in Urdu and Telugu), Hyderabad, India, January 30, 2019.

11. The 1930s saw a proliferation of progressive nationalist literature. Newspapers like *Payam* and *Rayat* propagated ideals of freedom, democracy, and secularism. The monthly magazine under the editorship of Niaz Fatehpuri opposed superstition and religious fanaticism and was an anti-imperialist in its ideology. Several other progressive journals such as *Jamia, Parchum, Nayadab* inspired youth all over the country. Some of this progressive literature, along with the Communist Party literature, began to slowly finds its way into the Nizam's state. Young people, particularly the student community, were deeply influenced by this. See Lalita K., Vasantha Kannabiran, Rama Melkote, Uma Maheshwari, Susie Tharu, and Veena Shatrugna, *We Were Making History: Life Stories of Women in the Telangana People's Struggle* (New Delhi: Kali for Women, 1989), 9–10.

12. Interview with author (originally in Urdu), Hyderabad, India, January 25, 2019.

13. Zeenath Sajida (1924–2008) was an academician who published on the Deccan literary culture, but her Urdu book about the history of Telugu literature demonstrates an interest in the dialogue between Telugu and Urdu. When she died in 2008, both Urdu and Telugu newspapers published extensive tributes to her work. Zeenath Sajida, *Telugu Adab ki Taareef* [An appreciation of Telugu literature] (Hyderabad: Osmania University, 1960).

14. Interview with author (originally in Urdu), Hyderabad, India, January 29, 2019. Moid also mentioned many aspects of Hindu–Muslim exchanges during the Police Action. Summing up all his conversations, he said: "Hindus of Hyderabad too feared the new government because if they show sympathy for, or support Muslims they will also become its victims."

15. Moid, "Muslim Perceptions and Responses," 65; for more on this aspect, see K. L. Guaba, *Hyderabad or India* (Delhi: Rajkamal Publications, 1948).

16. Moid, "Muslim Perceptions and Responses," 65.

17. Adapa Satayanaraya's preface to the Telugu translation of Moulvi Chirag Ali's work describes how Salar Jung initiated the modern reforms in the Hyderabad state.

Salar Jung's reforms were aimed at transforming various systems in the Hyderabad state including traditions and ideology. He believed in a new educational system that would produce an educated and well-trained bureaucracy. Accordingly, he initiated several changes in the system. Along with Farsi and Arabic, he introduced the western educational system and promoted English. See Moulvi Chirag Ali, *Adhunika Haidarabād Caritra: Sālār Jang Saṁskaraṇalu*, trans. Gajula Dayakar (Hyderabad: Adugu Jaadalu Publications, 2015), 8–9.

18. The leftist definitions of the progressive writer and writings were limited to the contemporary political activism within the ideological base of the Communist Party. For more on leftist conceptualization of a progressivism, see *Abhyudaya*, the first issue of the Progressive Writers Association, October 1946: Chadalavada Picchayya, ed., *Abhyudaya Sacitra Māsa Patrika* (Bezawada: Progressive Writers Association, 1946). My conversations with Jaini Mallayya Gupta and Dasarathi Rangacharya too offer evidence for this multiplicity and pluralism in the Hyderabad state.

19. Muhammad Khalid Masud and Almando Salvatore, "Western Scholars of Islam on the Issue of Modernity," in *Islam and Modernity: Key Issues and Debates*, ed. Khalid Masud, Salvatore, and Bruinessen (Edinburgh: Edinburgh University Press, 2009), 45.

20. Adis Duderija and A. O. Zonneveld. "Transnational Progressive Islam: Theory, Networks, and Lived Experience," in *Handbook of Contemporary Islam and Muslim Lives*, ed. R. Lukens-Bull and M. Woodward (Cham: Springer, 2020); Omid Safi, ed., *Progressive Muslims: On Justice, Gender and Pluralism* (Oxford: Oneworld, 2003).

21. Adis Duderija, *The Imperatives of Progressive Islam* (New York: Routledge, 2017), xiii.

22. Around the 1940s, many short fiction writers in the south Indian languages seemingly followed certain paradigmatic and pragmatic features, as Preetha Mani observes, "considering the short story to be an exceptional medium for disclosing literary truth because of its narrowed thematic focus and compact portrayals of characters." See Preetha Mani, "An Aesthetics of Isolation: How Pudumaippittan Gave Pre-Eminence to

the Tamil Short Story," *South Asia: Journal of South Asian Studies* 43, no. 5 (2020): 926–942.

23. For a debate on Telangana modernity, see Srinivas, *Telangāṇa Sāhitya Vikāsaṁ*, 8–9.

24. Barbara Metcalf, *Islamic Contestations: Essays on Muslims in India and Pakistan* (New York: Oxford University Press, 2004), 186–187.

25. Heather Miller Rubens, Homayara Zaid, and Benjamin Sax, "Towards an Interreligious City: A Case Study," in *Interreligious/Interfaith Studies: Defining a New Field*, ed. Eboo Patel, Jennifer Howe Peace, and Noah J. Silverman (Boston: Beacon Press, 2018), 219.

26. Ibid.

27. Interview with author, Hyderabad, India, January 29, 2019.

28. For more on this history of the Comrades Association and progressive movement, see Rama Melkote, B. Pradeep, and B. Vijaya Kumar., *Living Those Times: Memoirs and Writings of Burgula Narsing Rao* (New Delhi: People's Publishing House, 2021).

29. Interview with author, Hyderabad, India, January 26, 2019.

30. Yasmin Saikia and M. Raisur Rahman, *The Cambridge Companion to Sayyid Ahmed Khan* (New Delhi: Cambridge University Press, 2019).

31. Ibid., 2.

32. Swamy as a writer was influenced by contemporary trends in Urdu and Hindi, particularly the new story movement such as *nayī kahānī*. In the 1950s and 1960s, most of these writers used a similar lens of an individual to portray the complexity of the post-Partition life. Stuti Khanna notes: "At a time when received norms and given 'truths' were so demonstrably at odds with the collapsing world order, the only means of authentic portrayal of life was through a focus on individual consciousness" (Ravikant and Saint, *Translating Partition*, 105).

33. Venkat, *Creating a New Medina*.

34. For an idea of feudal society of Hyderabad, see Sidq Jaisi, *The Nocturnal Court, Darbaare-e-Durbar: The Life of a Prince of Hyderabad* (New Delhi: Oxford University Press, 2004).

35. Karen Leonard, "Indo-Muslim Culture in Hyderabad: Old City Neighborhoods in the Nineteenth Century," in *Indo-Muslim Cultures in Transition*, ed. Alka Patel and Karen Leonard (Leiden: Brill, 2012), 165–188.

36. Noorani, *The Destruction of Hyderabad*.

37. Seetharam, *Nelluri Kesava Swamy Kathalu*, 141.

38. For the role of Deccan Radio during the Police Action, see Narendra Luther, *Hyderabad: A Biography* (New Delhi: Oxford University Press, 2006), 281.

39. Record of interview between Rear-admiral Viscount Mountbatten of Burma and Mr Jinnah, July 12, 1947, in Nicholas Mansergh, ed., *The Transfer of Power*, vol. 12 (London: Her Majesty's Stationary Office, 1983), 121.

40. Interview with Guduri Seetaram, September 20, 2010.

41. Rajeswara Rao Guthi's 1999 essay discusses various themes of Swamy's short fiction and highlights how his collection of short stories, *Char Minar*, portrays the diversity of the Muslims of Hyderabad. See "Nelluru Kesavasamy Kathalu," *Andhra Bhoomi*, March 22, 1999.

42. Seetharam, *Nelluri Kesava Swamy Kathalu*, 142.

43. Ibid., 141.

44. Ibid., 144.

45. Syed Ahmed El-Edroos and L. R. Naik, *Hyderabad of "Seven Loaves"* (Hyderabad: Laster Prints, 1994), 179.

46. Seetharam, *Nelluri Kesava Swamy Kathalu*, 80–81.

47. For more on the idea of the composite culture of Hyderabad, see Syed Akbar Hyder, *Reliving Karbala: Martyrdom in South Asian Memory* (New York: Oxford University Press, 2006).

48. A few exceptions: Khalidi, *Hyderabad*; Sherman, *Muslim Belonging in Secular India*.

49. Muslimness (*muslimīyata*) is now a specific concept being used in Telugu literary culture to mark the new Muslim identity that emphasizes progressive thinking and social consciousness. For more on this term, see Afsar Mohammad, "The Garden of Mirrors: Retelling the Sufi Past and Contemporary Muslim Discourse" in *Islam, Sufism and Everyday Politics of Belonging in South Asia*, ed. Deepra Dandekar and Torsen Tschacher (New York: Routledge, 2010), 247–261.

50. Seetharam, *Nelluri Kesava Swamy Kathalu*, 85.

51. Ibid., 86.

52. Ibid., 87.

53. For more on *Angārē*, see Ali Mir and Raza Mir, *The Anthems of Resistance: A Celebration of Progressive Urdu Poetry* (New Delhi: Roli Books, 2006), 2–8; Sarah Waheed Khan, *Hidden Histories of Pakistan: Censorship, Literature, and Secular Nationalism in Late Colonial India* (Cambridge: Cambridge University Press, 2021), 49.

54. For more on Zeenath Sajidaa, see Nazia Akhtar, *Bibi's Room: Hyderabadi Women and Twentieth-Century Urdu Prose* (Hyderabad: Orient BlackSwan, 2022).

55. For more on Shi'is of Hyderabad, see Hyder, *Reliving Karbala*.

56. Karen Leonard, *Social History of an Indian Caste: The Kayasths of Hyderabad* (Berkeley: University of California Press, 1978), 28–31.

57. According to Narendra Luther:

> Kayasths were the trusted and prominent civil servants of the Nizams. They had come with the first Nizam from the north and settled down in Hyderabad. They adopted the ways of the ruling elite and served as a bridge between the rulers and the subjects in all matters. They made good careers and some of them rose to high civil and military positions and even to the ranks of the nobility.

See Luther, *Hyderabad*, 132; for more on the changing notion of the idea of love and marriage in the background of urban modernity, see Dalmia, *Fiction as History*, 13.

58. Seetharam, *Nelluri Kesava Swamy Kathalu*, 190.

59. Interview with author, Hyderabad, India, September 14, 2014.

60. For more on various aspects of reformism, Islamic modernity and new discourses of public Islam, see Mehran Kamrava, ed., *The New Voices of Islam: Rethinking Politics and Modernity* (Berkeley: University of California Press, 2006).

61. Seetharam, *Nelluri Kesava Swamy Kathalu*, xi.

62. Interview with author, Karim Nagar, India, September 10, 2008.

63. Interview with author, Hyderabad, India, September 14, 2014.

64. Sangisetti Sreenivas, *Dastram: Telangāma Toli Taram Kathala Sūci* (Hyderabad: Kavile Prachurana, 2004), 77.

65. Afsar Mohammad, "Manto Beyond Urdu: Telugu Translations and Transcreations of Manto's World" (Talk at Hindi–Urdu Flagship seminar series, University of Texas at Austin, 2010).

66. Rahman, *Locale, Everyday Islam*.

67. Interview with author, Hyderabad, India, September 15, 2014.

68. Interview with author, Hyderabad, India, September 15, 2014.

69. Interview with author, Adilabad, India, September 12, 2014.

70. For more on these aspects, see Sheela Raj, *Medievalism to Modernism: Socio-economic Cultural History of Hyderabad 1869–1911* (Bombay: Popular Prakashan, 1987).

71. Bhukya, *History of Modern Telangana*, 2013.

72. Chirag Ali, *Adhunika Haidarabād Caritra*.

73. Karen Leonard, *Hyderabad and Hyderabadis* (New Delhi: Manohar, 2014), 97.

74. Mir and Mir, *Anthems of Resistance*, 3.

75. Snehal Singhavi, trans., *Angaray* (New Delhi: Penguin India, 2018), vii.

2

"ALL MUSLIMS ARE NOT THE RAZAKARS"

THE POLITICAL IDIOM OF AN INDEPENDENT HYDERABAD

It was a phase of unfortunate turns—everything so unexpected! Not about the Razakars or the Nizam, but most of the ordinary Muslims (*ām musalmān*) whom I know fully well since my childhood had a hard time. Particularly young Muslim men and women ... all suddenly became suspects and many of them from their homes leaving everything. They just wanted to live somewhere rather than dying in the bloody hands of the Razakars and Hindu fundamentalists.

—Razia Begum, a witness of the Police Action

When I met 75-year-old Razia Begum for the first time in 2007, she was reluctant to speak either about the Razakars, a paramilitary group between 1946 and 1948, or the Police Action. At first, I thought her memory was not serving her well. As we continued to speak, I realized that she was deliberately avoiding these topics. After a few years of extended conversations, she herself confessed that she had "an intense discomfort in speaking about the *action*, and was still struggling with anxiety and uncertainty ... related to that particular event." During our several conversations between 2007 and 2014, however, she spoke about many topics related to the Telangana peasants' rebellion of 1946 and 1949, famously known as the *Telaṅgāṇa sāyudha pōrāṭaṁ* in Telugu or *Telangana jung* in her colloquial Urdu. In every conversation, she tried to return to the idea of an ordinary Muslim—*ām musalmān* in Urdu and *māmūlu muslimlu* in Telugu. Her familiarity with leftist politics was sufficient to understand these class variations in her immediate community. At one point, she mumbled something about the Police Action and the Razakars, but quickly returned to her fond memories of the "party," which means the Communist Party. She was eager to describe how her young brothers became involved as couriers in the undercover activities of the party. She also narrated in detail the visits of several well-known party leaders who held secret party-related meetings at her home. Since her husband was also actively involved in the Telangana peasants' movement, their home was a secret den for at least a few years between 1946 and 1949, the period when the party had received exceptional praise for its radical historical event of the peasants' rebellion.[1] For her, this entire political story was intensely personal and strongly connected to her extended family of four brothers, along with their wives and children. Like many writers and activists of these times, this event was the mainstream narrative of their lives.

During this long journey of our conversations, when she finally became comfortable talking to me, at her own initiative she started talking about a few violent incidents between 1946 and 1948, mostly during the Police Action. Even then, it took a while for us to return to the question of the Razakars—the moment I had been eagerly awaiting. At the end of one such conversation, she said:

> It hurts me to hear that many keep saying the same thing repeatedly—that all Muslims were Razakars, despite all the sacrifices we made for the Telangana movement. Too bad that even now many people say that! You know, we lost everything in the movement. We lost our families, properties, and were even uprooted from our homes. Yet, it's hard to bear this blame! We never received so much as an ounce of sympathy either from the Nizam or the Razakars. It's time for all of us to remove this idea from our very heads and truly realize that not all Muslims are Razakars.[2]

I thought that marked the end of our conversation that day. She seemed to be tired of talking. Then she suddenly started speaking about her family. Razia Begum had an intriguing political life as her family was an extremely traditional Sunni Muslim one. She had finished her Quran when she was 11 years old, and by the time she was married into another traditional Sunni family of Mohammad Khasim, she was teaching Urdu and the first lessons of the Quran to the younger kids.

> Like many Muslims of those times, we had no conflict with practicing Islam in addition to our deep commitment to the Telangana movement now and then. Our immediate motivation was to fight against the Nizam and participate in the movement. My husband would go to the local mosque and perform prayers very religiously for five times a day and never missed a day of fasting in the holy month of Ramzan. And, of course, we never missed a single meeting or Party event either! In that way, we're real Muslims and really participating in every activity of the Party![3]

After this, as our conversation took off, I asked her again about the Razakars and their activities. Then I realized that for some reason she was not comfortable talking about the Razakars. Rather than narrating stories (which was her way of explaining things), now she was making more careful word choices and spoke in a measured manner.

> Interviewer [AM]: What do you think about the Razakars and their activities?
>
> Razia: First thing, I don't consider that any of those activities had anything to do with Muslims or Islam. Not at all! Me and my husband were very clear about it and also would share the same with our friends and family. Razakars were never real Muslims. Islam never teaches about such violence. Whatever the Razakars or the Nizam was doing, it had nothing to do with any form of Islam. Their acts made Muslims look like enemies of the Hindus with whom we always had cordial relations.[4]

In multiple ways, the conversations I had with Razia Begum resonate with some of the novelistic representations and written sources (such as autobiographies and memoirs) that I discuss in this chapter. With evidence from two autobiographical or semi-autobiographical novels, this chapter engages with various debates on the making of a Razakar and the afterlife of that idea in the wake of different waves of religious conflict and the separatist Telangana movement after 1984. Along with the family story of Razia

Begum, I include a few other eyewitness accounts of the Police Action and the Razakar movement as it is relevant to the larger argument.

THE NARRATIVIZATION OF A MUSLIM STATE AND RAZAKAR POLITICS

Most of the evidence presented here contests the homogeneous and linear narratives about the Razakar movement and the role of Muslims between 1946 and 1948. To comprehend this narrativization, it is imperative to take note of various political initiatives of the Hyderabad princely state after the Partition. Several political documents published by the Hyderabad princely state argue for its sovereign authority and special status as an independent state, which was gradually articulated as the Azad Hyderabad or independent Hyderabad. On June 11, 1947, the Nizam of Hyderabad, Mir Osman Ali Khan (1886–1967), issued a *firman* to declare the sovereignty of Hyderabad state. According to this *firman*: "The result in law of the departure of the Paramount Power in the near future, will be that I shall become entitled to resume the status of an independent sovereign."[5]

Following this *firman* and before the Police Action, on August 21, 1948, the Hyderabad state invoked Article 35 of the Security Council and made a complaint against the Indian government clearly stating "a grave dispute, one which was likely to endanger the maintenance of international peace and security."[6] In the appeal addressed to the secretary-general of the United Nations, the Nizam of Hyderabad said:

Hyderabad is an independent sovereign State within a territory of 82,692 square miles. Its population comprises seventeen million inhabitants. These figures do not include the territory and the population of Berar, which, although under the legal sovereignty of Hyderabad, is now under the control of India. The Administration of Hyderabad exercises normal governmental activities. Hyderabad possesses a legal system of its own administered by an independent judiciary. It possesses its own army, police, currency, post and telephones, State-owned railways, and its own State Bank. The Nizam is advised by a council of Ministers composed of fourteen members, eight of whom—four Muslims and four non-Muslims—are appointed from among elected members of the Legislature.[7]

Explaining the distinctive sovereignty of Hyderabad, this document discusses various dimensions of the Hyderabad state and Muslim matters including the post-Partition conditions. In the process, such efforts led to the articulation of an idea of a Muslim state.[8] As the Nizam sought the advice of Jinnah, in July 1947, he clearly warned that "if Congress attempted to exert any pressure on Hyderabad, every Muslim throughout the whole of India, yes, all the hundred million Muslims, would rise as one man to defend the oldest Muslim dynasty in India."[9] Nevertheless, as Sunil Purushotham analyzed in his recent work, "although press accounts in India raised a specter of a Hyderabad–Pakistan alliance, Jinnah would ultimately do very little to help the Nizam realize the project of Azad Hyderabad."[10] While trying to establish the legality of the Hyderabad state, these arguments produced by the Hyderabad state depend extensively on the role of the Majlis-e-Ittehad-ul-Muslimeen (MIM) and the Razakars.

> At this stage a note is necessary on the Ittehad-ul-Muslimeen and the Razakars, since they figure largely in the propaganda which has accompanied the violence and in the attitude of the Indian Government towards it. There has since the First World War been a growth in the strength and organization of political parties in Hyderabad. It is a sign of the Hyderabad Government's policy of steadily broadening the popular basis of government. The Ittehad was formed twenty years ago as a political party of Muslims in the State. It has steadily and quickly grown, and is now the only political party of the State Muslims.[11]

This document's heavy emphasis on the status of Hyderabadi Muslims after the Partition explains a shift in the very perspective of the Nizam and his government. In a similar mood, the Nizam's document also supported the Razakars, by specifically mentioning:

> The Razakars are a popular volunteer organization—"Razakars" meaning volunteers. It began in a small way as a body of volunteers to assist the Ittehad in electioneering campaigns, as is customary with most political parties. At the beginning of 1947 it had only a few thousand members, almost entirely in Hyderabad city. In 1947 and 1948, especially since 1947, it has grown very quickly, because of the feeling of insecurity engendered, first by the communal disturbances in India

and Pakistan, and later by the border incidents and the evident desire of India to take over Hyderabad.[12]

The appeal repeatedly stressed the importance of the Razakars in providing security to Hyderabadi Muslims by stating: "Hyderabad cannot stop its people defending themselves if nothing is done (by the Indian government) to stop attacks in them." In supporting the case, this document also provides evidence for "lawlessness," "inflammatory propaganda," and endless violence of the troops at the border districts.[13]

Recent debates about the question of Muslims in the wake of the Telangana movement after 2004 necessitated revisiting the accounts of the Nizam's rule, the state *firman*s, and a reappraisal of Razakar militarism too. Such revisiting of history allows us to question the constant conflation of the Razakars with the Muslims that still holds a privilege in the public memory.[14] Participating in a similar thread of debate, this chapter also analyzes the nationalist, leftist, and Hindutva narrativization of the Razakars with an emphasis on ordinary Muslims.[15] Two novels that I discuss show how different interpretations and readings help us rethink historical memory despite their limitations as related to the Razakars. Since most of these writers had a personal connection with such a history, I also draw on their life stories to corroborate my argument. Within the public sphere of Hyderabadi culture, however, this entire debate represents three major shifts through three different phases: first, the earliest phase of cultivating a sense of upward mobility among ordinary Muslims; second, the shift to Razakar militarism; and third and finally, the re-examination of the Razakar movement in the wake of recent Telangana and Muslim discourses after the Telangana separatist state between 2002 and 2010. This chapter discusses how these three phases are connected to the question of Muslim identity in the city of Hyderabad.

The conversation with Razia Begum and the reassessment of these novels and memoirs nonetheless took me back to the story "Yugantham" by Swamy that I have already discussed in the previous chapter. In "Yugantham," the protagonist Dilawar narrates what made him a Razakar despite his position as an employee of the Hyderabad state. After the Police Action, he returns to his previous self and faces an extremely hopeless situation. He considers himself to be a huge failure and decides to migrate to Pakistan, as did a few Razakars or *ashraf* Muslims of the city. Nevertheless, his conversation with his Hindu friend Swamy reveals many key dimensions of Razakar militarism. And, finally, he determines that Nizam's surrender was "a betrayal of the people of the entire state." What follows is an excerpt of the conversation between him and Swamy:

"Hey, Dilloo, why are you crying?!"

"Destroyed … everything utterly destroyed!"

"What?!"

"Our state has gone to dust now. Those Union people are already out there! By tomorrow, they will be in the city too! That brute Nizam has surrendered!"[16]

The Nizam did finally surrender—welcome news for Swamy. The same words that devastated Dilawar's heart make Swamy feel elated. As the conversation continues, Dilawar discloses more dimensions of the making of a Razakar, such as how Muslim employees were incorporated into the movement.

"So, the Union army is here. So, why are you afraid?"

"No … not about the army. But the Hindus here are going to cut me into bits and pieces!"

"Why? You didn't commit any crime, na!"

"Oh, then you don't know anything about me … I'm a Razakar!"

"You … you a Razakar! I don't believe it. Not at all! You're a state employee!"

"Hmm. What's the difference between state employees and the Razakars?! Haven't you heard about our dear friend, Iqbal?"[17]

Subsequently, Dilawar shares a story about Iqbal, one of the leaders of the Razakars. Like Dilawar, Iqbal was their childhood friend, and Swamy now realizes that most of such information about his Muslim friends were shocking surprises for him. Not only was he completely shaken and upset, but the things he heard now also made him afraid of Dilawar. Whereas only a moment ago he was a close friend, now Dilawar appears to him like "a wild animal." In his world, all these Razakars are nothing but wild animals. But if the conversation ends there, it is an incomplete story.

"We did everything for that crook—that crook!"

"Who's this crook?"

"The Nizam.... All of a sudden, he now surrendered, drowning the boat in the middle of the stream and then claims that he 'is totally innocent and Qasim Razvi did everything!'"

"Is it a lie?"

"Of course! When the Hyderabad state attains independence, would he leave the throne to Razvi?! Not at all! He would take all the benefits and claim his throne."[18]

Razia Begum's oral account and Swamy's fictional testimony disclose two separate viewpoints of the same Razakars. For Razia, any Razakar was a clearly defined enemy along the lines of the party.[19] In contrast, the narrator in Swamy's story encounters a dilemma in which he could not comprehend Dilawar's status, knowing fully well about his direct participation in many Razakar atrocities. In addition, Swamy's story also describes the way Muslim employees were forced into Razakar militarism, the role of Qasim Razvi (1902–1970) as the leader of the Razakars, the idea of a "Muslim State" as practically translated into the attainment of Azad Hyderabad (Independent Hyderabad), the idea of Pakistan, and most importantly, the terror created by the Razakars and then how all Muslims were misconstrued as Razakars. Throughout the history of Telangana beginning in 1946 and to this day, these aspects remain major constituents in the making of a Muslim identity discourse. Similar to the event of Partition, this too has become a means by which to appraise the Muslims in Telangana, and then to portray them as a demonized other. To a larger extent, even the nationalist, leftist, and revivalist narratives or the historical memory related to them project such biased viewpoints.[20]

Contrary to these hegemonic historical narratives, novelists such as Kavi Raja Murthy (1926–1985) and Bhaskarabhatla Krishna Rao (1918–1966) along with witnesses including Burgula Narasinga Rao, Vara Vara Rao, Ashfaq Hussain, Razia Begum, and several other interviewees, offer a contrasting view. Not that their testimonies totally support the Razakar movement, but they do decidedly contest the conflation of the Razakars with the entire Muslim community or the Nizam's rule. In a way, these novels and oral accounts evidence the first wave of an initial interpretation of Muslim identity and the Razakar from their close readings of various historical events. Their access and proximity to the events of the Police Action and its aftermath help us read that specific rupture of history through grounded reality. Not only what are considered to be Hindu nationalist texts such as *Razakar* by the Hindi novelist Neelkanth Vyas (2005), even various Telugu texts produced under the impact of the Telangana rebellion conflate the meanings of Muslim and Razakar.[21] In their eagerness to declare an immediate enemy, some of these ideological representations portray all Muslims as Razakars and the Nizam's entire rule as the Razakar's rule (*Rajākārla pālana* in Telugu often compared to Nazism by few Telangana poets).[22] Several of those who wrote about the Police Action have indeed touched upon these themes; however, the political and religious implications of the Razakar militarism in everyday life remain understudied.

I introduce the two novels in their chronological order: the first, Kavi Raja Murthy's 1949 novel *Mai Gharīb Hu* (I am the poor) describes the events before and after the Police Action from 1946 to 1948. The second, Bhaskarabhatla Krishna Rao's 1956 novel *Yuga Sandhi* (The transition) also depicts the developments around the formation of Andhra Pradesh. Written and circulated immediately after the turbulent period of the Police Action, these two novels present a close reading of Razakar militarism along with its different manifestations in the public and personal lives of the new generation Hyderabadis. Since the intellectual growth of these writers also plays a central role in the making of these times, I describe their life events as well.

THE EARLY PUBLIC LIFE OF THE RAZAKARS: MURTHY'S AUTOBIOGRAPHICAL NOVEL

The future is ours only if we live up to our faith. It does not lie in the lap of the gods, but it rests in our own hands. We can make or mar it.

—Choudhary Rahmat Ali, *Now or Never: Are We to Live or Perish Forever?*

In 1933, along with the "Pakistan Declaration," Choudhary Rahmat Ali, the earliest proponent of the state of Pakistan, created the map of the Continent of *Dinia* (Figure 2.1), which also included the imagined nation of

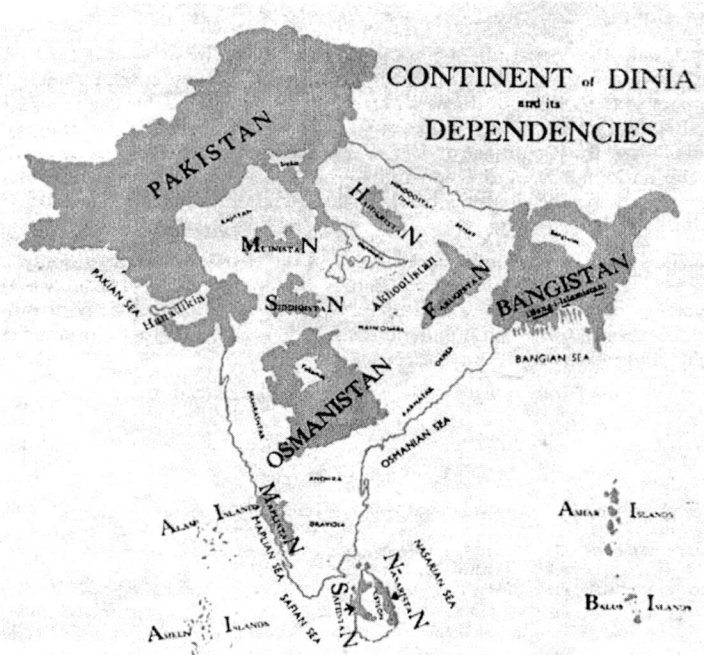

Figure 2.1   The map of the continent Dinia of Muslim states
Source: The Centre of South Asian Studies, University of Cambridge.

"Osmanistan" signifying the rule of the last Nizam, Mir Osman Ali Khan.[23] For Rahmat Ali and his followers, it was a dream to create a world of the *Din*—the faith, in this case clearly Islam. Although Rahmat Ali's idea, later renamed "Pakistan Declaration," was intended to create a separate Islamic nation limited to Punjab, the Northwestern Frontier Province, Kashmir, Sind, and Baluchistan, it had wider implications for politics and religious transformations in the Deccan too.[24] In fact, rather than "Osmanistan," it was popularly called Azad Hyderabad to suggest the idea of Pakistan becoming a goal or a single-minded dream for the Nizam and his private army of the Razakars, particularly when the Government of India started negotiations about incorporating the state of Hyderabad into the union. Rahmat Ali was in many ways popular among the educated young Muslims in the princely state of Hyderabad.[25] I was told that the above map was being circulated among some young Muslims of the late 1940s in Hyderabad to inspire the idea of Azad Hyderabad.[26]

Figure 2.2   Kavi Raja Murthy

Source: Courtesy of Kavi Raja Murthy's family.

I had an opportunity to see the printed copy of this map in the hands of Kavi Raja Murthy (henceforth Murthy) in my hometown of Khammam, a few hundred miles from the city of Hyderabad (Figure 2.2). One evening at his home, introducing the map to me as one of his precious treasures, Murthy told me:

> This was the map that created a sensation when I was very young…. We always had a fascination for the maps and we collected so many maps. We were curiously discussing how borders were made in these newly imagined maps! Particularly, this one! We would put this on a table and then start discussing each *stan* that Rahmat Ali was dreaming about! Of course, *Osmanistan* then also became a dream for Qasim Razvi and his army of the Razakars too. That made our life a hell!

Being a victim of the brutality of the Razakars and the Nizam's authority, Murthy's experiences through the turbulent 1940–1948 period offer insights into the early phase of the Police Action, the Razakar militarism, and the idea of a Muslim state. Whereas his other writings including translations from Urdu to Telugu, personal essays, and memoirs describe this early phase, most importantly, his novel *Mai Gharīb Hu* (I am the poor) (1949), functions as a political testimony of these tense times. Although written in an experimental style that blends his favorite authors such as the Russian fiction writer Fyodor Dostoevsky (1821–1881) and the Urdu short fiction writer Sadat Hassan Manto, Murthy's novel is one of the earliest fictional testimonies that depicts the immediate political complexity in Hyderabad state. Whereas the situation of the Nizam further aggravated by the Police Action led to unprecedented violence, this young 22-year-old communist, like many, had to run from one place to another to save his skin. Being very much at the center of many debates and political movements of his times, Murthy provides a portrait of the life of a young man who was disenchanted with the entire political system. Since most of these aspects from the fictional account have an autobiographical element at its base, various political and historical events in the life story of Murthy help us see multiple layers of this narrative.

Born into an extremely traditional Shaiva Brahmin family, Murthy grew up in a milieu that embraced diverse strands of political and religious thoughts of nationalism, modernity, and Marxism. His elder brother Sarva Devabhatla Ramanatham, who was considered to be the first communist in Telangana, known for his deep commitment, was a huge influence on Murthy.[27] Unlike Ramanatham, Murthy developed an interest in literature and early on fell deeply in love with Urdu poetry and short fiction. It was said that during a *mushaira* in Hyderabad, the Nizam so appreciated his Urdu poetry that they conferred on him the title of "Kavi Raj." Yet things quickly took a drastic turn: Murthy became a political activist and then the same Nizam's authority and his private army of the Razakars began to chase him. The Razakars even put a bounty on his head. To escape the Razakars, Murthy, along with his newlywed wife, Varalakshmi, became a fugitive and was forced to spend no more than a day or night in any one place. As things settled down following the Police Action, Murthy finished writing this novel along with several translations of Urdu ghazals into Telugu. According to Varalakshmi, "Those days, a lot of his friends and leftist activists would make copies of his writings by writing down every page in a long hand to share with each other."[28] Later, when things were still tense in the city of Hyderabad, he had another idea, which was, according to Varalakshmi, "even more dangerous"—to establish a Marxist publication center called Prajā Sāhitya Pariṣat along similar lines to the People's Publishing House of the Communist Party. Murthy and his friends started translating and publishing Marxian literature for the newly created local reading clubs even in the remote villages of Telangana and the

Hyderabad state. Then, Giduturi Suryam, Murthy's friend and a well-known translator of Russian fiction, translated Murthy's novel into Telugu with the same Urdu title.

Between 1940 and 1950, during the prime of Murthy's life, the state of Hyderabad witnessed the rise of a new political vocabulary along with various strands of Islam. Murthy's novel incorporates this entirely new political language including several extensively debated terms, such as Muslim state (Murthy used a Telugu equivalent, *Mahammadīya rājyaṁ*), *jihad* for "righteous war," *an'l malik* for "the declaration of divine sovereignty," *majlis* meaning "the council," *ittehad* for "unification," *razakar* for a "volunteer," *mulki* for "natives," and finally, the most important concept of Azad Hyderabad.[29] Murthy's long-time friend and Telangana activist, Mallayya Gupta, said:

> Some of these words that had religious meanings acquired a political interpretation with an emphasis on the idea of Muslim state and the Razakar militarism. These Urdu and Persian terms now have become very local Telugu terms as we were all trying to understand their shades of meanings in our everyday conversations and writings too.[30]

Throughout their activism and cultural work, both Murthy and Gupta were exploring such possibilities to offer political interpretations for this entirely new discourse. For depicting such an intense environment, Murthy's novel *Mai Gharīb Hu* remains one of the earliest documents in Hyderabad state that fictionalized the story of the beginnings of the idea of a Muslim state and the making of the Razakars. Although Murthy tried to follow an impressionistic and abstract style of the narration, his political references are extremely local and completely situated in the post-1940s politics of the Hyderabad state. In 2007, during the early phase of my field research for this work, I had an elaborate conversation with his wife Varalakshmi, who told me:

> He drafted the entire novel in just one month after the Police Action. He would write late into the night and read it to me in the morning after a cup of chai. He would read it as if he had a high fever and speak out of the fever. Although he also read the novel to me in Telugu, his Urdu reading was more emotional and passionate. After reading the Telugu versions of the novel, he would say "no, this is not my voice and it reads like some stranger's story. This language doesn't speak my life. I don't feel like I'm telling my story." In fact, what I get from my

limited knowledge of literature and politics, I think he was not writing some fiction; he was more into writing about himself and his deeper associations with the politics of our turbulent times.[31]

According to Varalakshmi and Murthy's younger brother, Viswanatham, Murthy had a fascination not only for the maps but also for how modern politics were, to use their word, "created and how they impacted the ordinary people." Murthy's other writings, too, focus on similar aspects and demonstrate his continuous engagement with contemporary political and religious discourses (Figure 2.3). Being an active member of the Progressive Writers Association and newly formed Telangana Writers Association, Murthy's intellectual life took a radical turn, and she said:

> He was always meeting leftists from other states including north India. He had lengthy correspondences and almost every day he would get one book of leftist writing either Urdu or English. He would invite leftists for talks and gatherings. When police and the Razakars started hunting him, all this came to an end.[32]

Figure 2.3 A group of young communists who attended the 1937 political training camp in Kotta Peta in the Madras Presidency (the Murthy brothers were key figures in this camp)

Source: Courtesy of K. Mutyam (Hyderabad).

Viswanatham held similar viewpoints and agreed with these comments about the political situation. Between 1940 and 1950, the Hyderabad state had witnessed the rise of several political, social, and cultural organizations including the Andhra Maha Sabha, which was a deep influence on Murthy's entire family, as it was on many young activists in Telangana in the 1940s. Viswanatham said:

> The entire climate was so intense and fluid that we had hard time digesting what exactly was happening. I was a Gandhian and very active in the local Congress party, while Murthy was still a Communist. We were sincerely working for our parties and we would meet only to fight with each other.[33]

He continued, laughing:

> So, not only new politics were being created. Along with the new politics, there were new tensions in the family, too. There was some new fight almost every day among us, the three brothers and our wives too! I remember the day—February 5th, 1946—when Gandhi visited our hometown of Khammam. That day, too, we were in a pretty heated debate. Of course, Murthy was there just to see Gandhi! The political concepts were being created and even remote villages were undergoing a revolutionary transformation. In many ways, we were forced to discuss how all these things would end up.[34]

Whereas Viswanatham was a Gandhian in every way, for Murthy and his progressive friends the new political climate of the late 1940s was more about class conflict as explained by Marxian theory. Like many Marxian writers of his day, Murthy's early writings, too, focus heavily on economic determinism. Yet, I suggest that Murthy's novel takes a detour from such economic determinism to engage with the shifts in the religious environment that were affecting everyday life between 1946 and 1948. Whereas Murthy's activism still forced him to use the progressivist framework of the class conflict, his characters push him the other way, specifically motivating him to talk about the Muslim question and the aftermath of the Independence and the communal pre–Police Action setting in general. Whereas the making of such intellectual life remains largely buried or at least barely discussed in the Telugu literary sphere, during our conversations, Murthy and his contemporaries elaborated on how the new trends in the short fiction of Urdu—as represented by Manto, Ismat Chughtai, and the entire group of the pioneering anthology of the *Angāre*—made a huge impact in Telugu. Growing up in this composite cultural milieu of Urdu and Telugu literary exchange, Murthy developed his distinctive style of prose by blending Urdu and Russian narrative modes. His friends, including his wife and brother, however, always mention that he would indeed write everything in Urdu and then translate it for the Telugu audience. Explaining the writing process of Murthy, Varalakshmi said:

> He would read me Manto, Chughtai, and Qurratulain Hyder. Of course, those days we read more Urdu writings than Telugu. He actually read Prem Chand in Urdu, not Hindi. But the specific chapters he would read they all speak about contemporary politics, Hindu–Muslim conflicts. He cared less about other things of life in the story. I would ask him: why do you censor non-political aspects of a writing? Then he would laugh and respond: if you're not speaking about contemporary politics, you're revealing the real secret of present life.[35]

Now the question is: what makes this novel a political testimony? Despite an emphasis on Murthy's uncompromising self and extremely leftist stance, this novel unravels a subtle lifeworld of Muslim politics and Hindu–Muslim encounters in Hyderabad state that resonate with the larger Islamic world. Even a cursory reading of the novel tells us that Murthy was dealing with the immediate political reality of his times. Interestingly, this is a novel in which the author gives the characters no names. Thus, the protagonist himself goes by *aparicituḍu*, meaning "the stranger." The very first layer of the novel speaks about the migrations from a village to Hyderabad, the industrialization of the city, and then the political climate of the city. Since Murthy was a communist activist during this time, he speaks more about the rise of the working class and the making of an industrial city as the major themes of his narrative.

In four brief and compact chapters, Murthy opens a narrative space for multiple aspects of this new political climate. The very first chapter begins on the very first morning after Indian Independence on August 15, 1947. The description of that day, once again, reminds us of a commonplace trope in the Partition narratives widely discussed in Urdu literary culture. I heard Murthy himself reciting the couplet of the Urdu progressive poet Faiz Ahmed Faiz's phenomenal poem in Urdu, and again in Telugu:

> *these tarnished rays, this night-smudged light,*
> *this is not that dawn for which, ravished with freedom,*
> *we had set out in sheer longing,*
> *so sure that somewhere in its desert the sky harbored,*
> *a final haven for the stars, and we would find it.*[36]

In an essay on Partition literature, Ravikant notices how "the occasion for celebration is also one for mourning."[37] Extending the same metaphor, Murthy translates the entirety of the agony into his fictional narration along with a critique of the pressures of nationalism and developmental politics in post-Independence India. Indeed, these two aspects run deep throughout the narration, as the author continually engages with local politics and their immediate transformations between Indian Independence and the situation before the Police Action. Similar to Swamy's story, this novel also deals with the making of a Razakar in the city of Hyderabad against the background of three major themes: (*a*) various modes of the public appearances of the Razakars; (*b*) the rise of fundamentalism that worsened the economic and social status of poor people; and finally, (*c*) the metaphorization of the idea of a stranger. When it comes to the fictional representations in this novel, these three major themes overlap and mutually depend on each other, thus producing a trajectory of the tragedy of Hyderabad.

THE PUBLIC FACE OF THE RAZAKARS

Murthy describes the activities of the Razakars at three levels: first, he portrays the actual political figures of the day, such as Qasim Razvi and other Majlis leaders whom he witnessed during his youth, however, as other characters in the story, he barely mentions any of their names; second, he provides an in-depth description of the interior and exterior mindscapes that were affected by the Razakars along with the fear psychosis their politics produced. Finally, he uses many Razakar idioms of the day, thus documenting the political language of the Razakars. In "Yugantham," Swamy shows how Razakar activity partitioned the community into two diagonally opposing groups. In addition, he shows how conflicting news reports broadcast by

Deccan Radio and also by All-India Radio (AIR), inflamed this polarization. Narrowing down this effect further, Murthy also focuses on the public appearances—and thus both the verbal and non-verbal violence—instigated by the Razakars and the religious fanatics. The stranger in the novel, while searching for a piece of bread for that day, approaches a public meeting where the president of a Razakar group was addressing a gathering. In this context, Murthy does not disclose the details of this organization or the person.

> We're the Muslims. It's the time now to fight against the attacks of the non-Muslims and kafirs. We should be prepared even to sacrifice our lives for the cause. This is our jihad and each Muslim [is] a soldier in this war. The flag of our nation should touch the skies. Indeed, each of you should rise like a flag. If not, that would be the final day for Islam ... and Satan is already there to take us over. Now it's the time for all of you to don your colorful wings and ascend to the heaven of the Muslim state.[38]

Such mentions of the different versions of the public speeches were not uncommon in various fictional accounts published after the Police Action either in Telugu or other languages.[39]

Initially, the entire goal of the Razakars under the leadership of Qasim Razvi was to provide military support to the Nizam, and then the Razakars became indispensable for the Nizam to enforce the idea of a Muslim state. The Razakars, too, took advantage of the entire political situation with the growing popularity of the Majlis among the Muslims. The historian Taylor Sherman notes:

> The bluster of the chauvinist forces of the Majlis-e-Ittehadul Muslimin, who declared that the Asaf Jahi flag would fly over the Red Fort in Delhi, and the thuggish behavior of the Razakars easily created the impression that all Muslims had acted as oppressors against the state's Hindu Population.[40]

During my college days, Murthy himself narrated a few stories about the stalwarts of the Hyderabadi Muslims including Bahadur Yar Jung, Qasim Razvi, and Ibraheem Jalees, mostly about their public speeches, acts, and their impact on the Hyderabad state. Murthy and his brothers explain how a leadership that started with a charismatic personality such as Bahadur Yar Jung (1905–1944) finally ended in the "terrible hands" of Razvi:

If you had an opportunity to listen to Bahadur Yar Jung, it is not that easy not to be trapped into all that idiom. Then came Razvi, not even comparable to Bahadur, but [he] knows how to use ordinary language that could appeal to the lower strata of society. Despite these differences in personalities and the leadership skills, both of them were extremely influential and captivating in their own way. And, now there was one more person—Ibrahim Jalees of Deccan Radio! That's how they could attract hundreds of young Muslims, not only men, but also women, into their private army.[41]

Although during those college days, I was familiar with the names of Nawab Bahadur Yar Jung and Qasim Razvi, I knew very little about their histories and barely heard about Ibrahim Jalees or Deccan Radio. Later I learned that Ibrahim Jalees was one of the popular Urdu orators during the days of the Police Action.[42] According to Murthy and his brother Viswanatham, "Bahadur Yar Jung in the early 1940s, was successful in sowing the seeds for the Muslim state too."[43] Many oral testimonies and written sources explain how he circulated the concept of *an'l malik*, meaning "I am the Ruler!" As the Hyderabad-based biographer Narendra Luther observes in his memoir:

According to this theory, sovereignty did not vest in the ruler, but in the Muslim community. The Nizam was merely a symbol of that sovereignty. Every Muslim in the state thus became a participant and stakeholder in sovereignty. It was in the vested interest of every Muslim to protect his sovereignty and its symbol, the Nizam.[44]

Murthy's fictional testimony likewise describes how religious and political vocabularies were blended to create the idea of a Muslim state—he uses the Telugu term—*Mahammadīya rājyaṁ* in the early phase of the Razakar militarism in Hyderabad. Nevertheless, Murthy's novel also depicts the other side of this situation—the protest against the Razakars. Viswanatham, who was also a witness to many such incidents, said:

Since me and my brothers were highly critical about the Nizam, and added to this, our own party affiliations, we were strong enough to question them! Moreover, we had vigorous training from our political classes to deal with this situation and intense debates, too, prepared us for staying strong through and through. Bahadur was so expressive and persuasive that despite our dislike for the content, we were totally in awe listening to him. Each sentence is like a powerful slogan, *buland nara*! Now you can imagine a Muslim's situation in such an overwhelming flow of the greatest words and concepts![45]

In a similar way, the protagonist in the novel questions the leaders of the Majlis and Razakar militarism.

"Is this all about Muslim state? Or also about the food and clothing for the poor?"

The leader responds: "Under the high flag of a Muslim state, there would be no poor and impoverished!"

"How?! Are you going to poison them all at once?"

"I repeat there'll be no poverty in a Muslim state!"

"Don't believe him! It's a big lie. These words are like cheap liquor! Don't forget that even the Prophet lived in utter poverty. It's the rhetorical trap of the State. Don't fall into the trap!"[46]

Although several Telugu writers of the late 1940s had similar experiences of observing or witnessing these speeches either directly or through Deccan Radio of Hyderabad, not many literary narratives describe such a direct engagement with the leaders of the Razakars. However, Murthy's narration extends further, telling of more implications of this activity that lead to the polarization of religious identities, thus establishing fixed categories for "Hindus" and "Muslims."

THE MAKING OF RELIGIONIZED IDENTITIES

In local poetry gatherings, Murthy was a regular, and he would often begin his own poem with a couplet in Urdu. Poets such as Josh Malihabadi (1894–1982) and Faiz Ahmed Faiz's couplets were always on his lips, ready to be recited for any context. While I heard Murthy reciting many such couplets by Malihabadi and Faiz at different private and public gatherings, I noticed that a similar questioning mode and emotionality runs through most of his writings, and the conversations about his life and work, too, provide testimony of the dilemma of Hindu–Muslim interactions.[47] During the literary discussions, Murthy would emphasize the end of what he called the idea of cultural openness or inclusivity which was a strong constituent in the making of his intellectual and everyday milieu. Such an emphasis was always appreciated and typically included several references to Partition writings. He would share his reflections on Manto (1912–1955), Rajinder Singh Bedi (1915–1984), and Krishna Sobti (1925–2019). However, Manto was always his favorite. Murthy's other writings, including the short pieces of prose, too, demonstrate Manto's influence in the making of his prose. Heeralal Moriya, a long-time friend of Murthy and a well-known Urdu writer, said:

> Among us, Murthy was the one who was deeply influenced by Manto's style of writing. But, I don't want to see this as a literary matter. For all of us, Manto remains a powerful expression of the Hindu–Muslim conflict and the devastating experiences of the Partition. In the case of Murthy, that theme of Partition was replaced by the Police Action.[48]

Moriya also mentioned that Murthy's perspective had undergone an explicit shift after the Police Action, noting that "he could not forgive the authoritative structures and political forces that pushed the community to that cliff of hatred and killings." Here I see a continuity between Swamy and Murthy's lifeworlds that hinge on the consequences of the Police Action. Most writings of Swamy and Murthy share the concerns of the progressivist Urdu poets and writers, yet seek to articulate in their local idiom, like several writers who began their literary careers after 1940 in Telugu. Such an aspect of plurality has attracted larger debates within many languages including Urdu and Telugu in the Indian literature of the 1940s, and it was also revisited during the rise of the new Muslim writing after the Babri mosque demolition in 1992 and during the recent religious conflicts. The idea of diversity and commonality is prominent in such writings, as Mushirul Hasan observed:

> The voices are not in unison; there is no reason why they should be, because the country's vivisection signified different things to different people. Neither do they sharply focus on or consciously underline a particular theme. Yet there is an unmistakable commonality of concerns, an underlying coherence and unity of thought. They distinctly share and convey to us the agony, pain, sorrow, and indignation of a generation

that was unwittingly caught up in the internecine "communal" conflicts of the forties.[49]

Hasan's observations citing the example of the Urdu fiction writer Intizar Hussain's work against the background of the Partition help us see a connection with the writings on the Police Action too. Not limiting themselves to sharing the emotionality of these developments, both Swamy and Murthy also were motivated to envision the consequences of the Action. Along with the political effects, they were also aware of the ongoing cultural consequences that affected the composite culture or the Hyderabadi *tehzeeb*. Discussing such cultural aspects, Hasan noted:

> Some of his other works reflect on how an ongoing cultural process was stalled in a "very unnatural way" by a few Muslims and Hindus who, with their puritan frame of mind, contributed to the tragic events afflicting the subcontinent. The cultural process, according to him, was not denominational. Nor the "Indian–Muslim" culture, which had its own individuality and was discernibly different from the culture of other Muslim countries, of any less significance.[50]

Comparable to the progressivist generation of Urdu poets and writers, the question of Muslim identity and its immediate creative expressions along with the new ongoing processes also had a deep impact on Murthy. Like the Partition, the aftermath of the Police Action had forced writers to ask a new set of questions related to the Hindu–Muslim dilemma. While reflecting on the consequences of the communal conflict (in the case of Hyderabad), writers such as Murthy also lament the failure of the Independence. Murthy describes the newly gained independence in an extremely disillusioned tone. By representing the angst of the younger generation growing up in the 1940s, Murthy's novel presents a local lifeworld extremely disappointed by the Indian Independence and disenchanted with the nationalistic project. Despite his strong sense of political activism, Murthy extended this dialogue further to cultural and literary matters that pushed him to embrace the Urdu and Muslim writings of the Partition.

In the novel, this intriguing moment arrives when the protagonist engages with the physical spaces of a temple and a mosque, which, in his ideal world, should be an embodiment of humanity and compassion. Murthy's narrations capture the early phase of the hatred and hate speech by documenting how even the utterance of Urdu words such as *gharīb* was a target of anti-Muslim sentiment. In this context, even the title of the novel *Mai Gharīb Hu* functions as a tool of resistance against hate politics. At the temple, the priest who was about to give the sacred food (*prasādam*) to him, asks him about his religious affiliation.

Priest: Who are you?

Me: I am a *gharīb*.

Priest: What is your caste?

Me: I am a *gharīb*—the poor! Poverty is my religion too. Poverty is my dharma. Poverty is my karma.

Scared of a Muslim presence, the priest started shivering, then, screamed: "Oh, my god! He is Turk!"

The bhaktas then started chasing me. Then, I had no idea what happened when I woke up in some alleyway after a long while. The nerves that kept swallowing me, now woke up, opening my eyes to face sheer darkness. My blood smeared lips were still tightly shut. Then I slowly recognized myself and the surroundings. On the street, there were two khaddar-clad persons, they were trying to walk away from me, saying "oh, some Turk … some Muslim!" They stared at me, as if I were a wild animal. Since I saw a human being after a long while, I gathered all my energies and tried to move. Then I heard them saying "let him die … die!"[51]

Recollecting the earliest experiences of such hate speech as articulated in the novel, Dasarathi Rangacharya, an intimate friend of Murthy, explained:

At that point, we all thought that even the title of the book, *Mai Gharib Hu*, was a statement of resistance. Me and my brother Dasarathi asked Murthy repeatedly about this title. Although such Urdu words were very common in everyday speech, when they appeared in any Telugu writing in the '40s, there were some concerns. There were questions around: Why Urdu words? Why Muslim language?! Why not translate that into Telugu? Of course, there was also resistance even to the very idea of translating Ghalib, Josh or Makhdoom into Telugu![52]

Rangacharya then recounted several experiences of these earliest forms of hatred and hate speech. He also explained various ways that the Telangana writers discovered to counter such "conspiracy of language politics" after the Police Action. According to him:

> The hate speech particularly after the Partition and the Police Action was doing nothing but imposing thick dividing lines. Yet, most progressivist writers in the Hyderabad state were cautious about such transformations, as Urdu gradually became relegated ... to a Muslim language, popularly called *turakala bhāṣa*—the language of the Turks. Dasarathi's insistence on not only translating Urdu poetry, but also his stress on introducing and circulating the poetic forms such as *ghazal*, *rubaai*, and the very idea of autobiographical elements used in his prose were actually ... tools of resistance too.[53]

Whereas poets and writers from Telangana tended to follow Urdu literary paradigms in their Telugu writings, Murthy's emphasis on the value of Urdu emerges in its fullest form in the translations as well. While this novel provides fictional testimonies from everyday life, according to his wife Varalakshmi, throughout his life, Murthy continued to call Urdu "one of his mother tongues." After the formation of the Telugu linguistic state in 1956, Murthy returned to Urdu poetry and translated extensively from Urdu to Telugu. Murthy's novel and other writings emphasize several strategies of countering hate speech that was primarily centered on Urdu and then extended to the question of religious identities such as "Hindu" and "Muslim." Participating in these larger debates on identities, Murthy's novel openly challenges the practice of labeling individuals as either Hindu or Muslim by naming his protagonist "the stranger," thus motivating the readers to think in terms of fluid identities and the liminality between Muslims and Hindus.

OPENING THE TEXT AND THE DEBATE

According to Viswanatham, with whom Murthy would usually share the earliest rough drafts of his writings:

> I was one of the few people who read this novel's earliest and tentative drafts. I asked Murthy several times why there was no name for the protagonist. We kept suggesting that he make their religious identity

clear by identifying them as either Hindu or Muslim. We thought that would make the novel more understandable. But Murthy, who would usually take our suggestions seriously, never cared for this one. He had a clear strategy for not giving a name to his characters and he said that he would leave it to his reader to give them the names![54]

In the novel, both the narrator and the protagonist remain strangers until the end, leaving space for a reader to interpret the story in multiple ways. In the era in which historical fiction in Telugu was filled with closed texts that privileged the glory of historical figures including Krishna Deva Rayalu of the Vijayanagara Empire (1336–1565), Murthy's open text was a challenge and departure from this norm both in content and structure. Deeply inspired by the models provided by the recent Urdu literary culture after the Partition, this novel remains an innovative narrative. Nevertheless, Murthy's protagonist narrates an experience of the migrant within the home being a victim of what the historian Sunil Purushotham calls "internal violence."[55] Whereas Manto's characters depict the distress of the borderlines between India and Pakistan, Murthy's stranger shows another dimension of such irony, madness, and dark reality of everyday life after the Police Action. At first, the characterization of the stranger challenges the idea of a hero and the making of their histories, as characterized by the privileged texts of the Telugu linguistic nationalism.[56]

Oh, this is my India. We tirelessly praise the greatness of our Hindu land in tens and thousands of words. Nothing goes into the minds of the rich people who're busy sucking the blood of the poor. You know, my country is so rich in agriculture, industries and then in its spirituality. Any civilization including Chinese and Egyptian are tinier against us. My country takes pride in its Taj Mahal, Amaravati, Ajantha, Ellora and what not! Beginning with the great Ashoka and then the great Mahatma, we taught the virtue of non-violence to this world! … You know, thousands of people die here out of hunger! Why?! Only the patriots should respond to my question: what made my country a golden sparrow, bhaktas!?[57]

Building on this, Murthy used three narrative strategies to dehegemonize the "authority" of the privileged textual culture in contemporary Telugu literature. First, an anti-hero "stranger" shatters the dominant image of a valorized hero constructed from the Hindu-centric historical figures; second, he interrupts the stereotype of a Muslim, being portrayed as a "Razakar" or "anti-social" as popularized in the leftist writings between 1940 and 1956.[58] And third and finally, by making such a choice he raises concerns about displacement and homelessness experienced by both Muslims and Hindus that signify the erasure of a discrete religious identity.

The stranger here imagines a place which is quiet and beautiful, one far removed from the everyday violence of his hometown. Rather than indulging in romanticized nostalgia, he is forced to respond to multiple queries from another stranger. This questioning invariably pushes him to return to his normal social life. Unable to escape the persistent questions, the stranger begins to share his story which indeed represents the anxiety and victimization of an ordinary citizen in the post-Independence Hyderabad state. Murthy's stranger narrates that being ordinary was the ultimate heroism and that a common man/woman were the real heroes in times of extreme state violence and the added entanglement of polarized religious groups. Murthy notes how an ordinary citizen was forced to become an insane and anti-social being. In addition, Murthy tried to connect multiple threads that complicate the social and religious life of his times. Deeply conscious about the fast-changing religious conditions and also about his mental state, he introduces himself as follows:

> I am the poor, the *gharīb*. Not just once, I would say it hundred times, I am utterly poor. After introducing myself as an utterly poor person. Now you don't need to know about my caste or religion. Once you know I am poor, you don't even need to know my name! If I weren't a poor being, that name might carry some special meaning, there must have been some caste or religion. There must have been a church, temple or mosque for my prayers or worship. Since now I am just a poor being, I am deprived of all of them. Did I say that clear enough? I have lost my mind too. If my terrible karma still haunts me here and if you're a patriot, then I am doomed! Now I will also lose this small space I have![59]

Disenchanted by the self-serving politics, repressive government, the booming industrial economy, and most importantly, the overwhelming communal violence, Murthy's stranger wanders the in-between spaces of life. By imagining a quiet narrative space for himself, the stranger—and of course, the narrator, too—were trying to escape into some deep solitude, some place of safety in a no man's land. At this point, particularly after Independence and the Police Action, Murthy was still a strong believer in the Marxian approach, and his characters—here and in various other short stories too—articulate similar class conflict and the tensions between politics and everyday life.

Furthering this debate, Bhaskarabhatla's novel entitled *Yuga Sandhi* (The transition) reveals more layers to life in this era, as I discuss in the next section. Though it depicts a similar everyday life and intellectual milieu as Murthy's novel, Bhaskarabhatla's novel attends more closely to the Razakars and the Police Action by situating the characters more concretely in the reality of Hyderabad. Whereas Murthy's descriptions and locations are more abstract, Bhaskarabhatla provides what almost amounts to an ethnography of the city of Hyderabad and its surroundings, and also locates his characters right in the eye of the storm.

YUGA SANDHI: THE POLITICS OF THE MAJLIS AND RAZAKARS

To have been born in the city of Hyderabad and grown up with its cultural and religious ethos—famously known as the Hyderabadi *tehzeeb*—has always been a source of pride for many Muslim and non-Muslim writers, cultural activists, as well as for its ordinary citizens. Most of them take pride in using the phrase *paidāyiṣī Haidarābād*, meaning "born in Hyderabad." This phrase encapsulates certain features that signify the Hyderabadi culture: multilingualism, cosmopolitanism, and also the "Ganga–Jamuna *tehzeeb*"— the composite culture metaphorized as the meeting of the two rivers, the Ganga and the Yamuna.[60] As his friends and literary critics describe, Bhaskarabhata was an embodiment of such a Hyderabadi *tehzeeb*. Like Murthy, Bhaskarabhatla Krishna Rao was likewise born into an extremely traditional Brahmin family (Figure 2.4). However, like Swamy, he was born in Hyderabad and grew up there and was exposed to its more cosmopolitan elements. Bhaskarabhatla likewise studied Urdu and Persian at school, and was surrounded by Muslim friends and their specific religious and cultural manners. Unlike Murthy and Swamy, he traveled far and wide. Graduating from Calcutta University meant he was exposed to Bengali languages and cultures too. As Calcutta was another colonial city at that time, he read and discussed new ideas in British and American literature. Being a voracious reader of English fiction, his innovative narrative style also reflected that heritage and sensibility.

Figure 2.4 Bhaskarabhatla Krishna Rao
Source: Courtesy of Bhaskarabhatla's family.

Bhaskarabhatla's intellectual and personal life took on another key dimension when his scholarship in Urdu, prompted by a deep passion of his, led him to join Deccan Radio in Hyderabad. Even before that, he was on the editorial staff of the *Golconda*, the Telangana newspaper that became one of the tools of resistance in Telangana. After the Police Action, many local governmental institutions were nationalized, and Deccan Radio was converted into AIR. Bhaskarabhatla stayed with this radio station until his retirement. Unlike Murthy, Swamy, and several other contemporaries, Bhaskarabhatla's intellectual journey largely reflects European modernity and places him among the modernist prose writers of the erstwhile Madras state. As the literary critic Mudiganti Sujatha Reddy notes:

> His college life in Calcutta had exposed him to various modern movements including social and cultural reformism such as women's education and colonial changes. As a writer, Tagore and Sarath Chandra Chatterjee remain extremely strong in the making of his literary personality. Similarly, he followed the innovative writers and thinkers such as Chalam, Bucchi Babu and Gopi Chand in his prose style.[61]

Following Chalam (1894–1979) and other writers mentioned above, Bhaskarabhatla focused more on narrating various social and cultural issues encountered by the new middle-class produced by the educational and socio-political consequences of the late 1930s. Known for his proto-feminist ideas, Chalam inspired many fiction writers of his time. Buchi Babu (1916–1967) is even now known for his innovative prose including the stream of consciousness (*caitanya sravanti* in Telugu) and high emphasis on gender dimensions. Blending these two stylistic strategies, Bhaskarabhatla's prose provided a new direction to the Telangana short fiction. His emphasis, however, on the city of Hyderabad and its new middle class of the 1930s and 1940s made his voice distinctive even among the other coastal and Telangana writers. Like Murthy, Bhaskarabhatla too described the new political environment effected by the Muslim politics in Hyderabad. His trenchant observations about the politics of Majlis and the Razakars warrant a reassessment in the wake of the recent Telangana activism and Muslim discourse, which I discuss in the third section of this chapter.

C. V. Krishna Rao, another prominent writer from the same period, said:

Bhaskarabhatla was twelve-years old when the politics of Majlis were unfolding and impacting the composite culture of the city. It was also the time when the Telangana was undergoing a religious transformation as both Hindu and Muslim communities were equally responding to various fundamentalist or reformist activities. He was deeply concerned about these changes that would forever transform the city's cultural and religious life.[62]

Extremely fond of the Hyderabadi Irani chai and the city's Islamic milieu, Bhaskarabhatla represented the multiplicity of the Hyderabadi *tehzeeb*. Malathi Chandur, a well-known literary columnist, said:

Bhaskarabhatla was a person of few words and extremely shy. But his love for Hyderabad was so unbounded that he could not stay in Madras that long and immediately sought a transfer to Hyderabad. Passionately attached to the Hyderabadi chai and its night-long mushaira culture and everything about Hyderabad's life made him impossible to integrate into the life in Madras. We were familiar with him and his writings, but nothing more than that. However, since he wrote the novel in Madras, we always enjoyed reading it when published in the popular magazine, *Telugu Svatantra*. For us, it was another classic comparable only to Bucchibabu's *civariki migilēdi*.[63]

During one of our conversations, Chandur likewise mentioned how Bhaskarabhatla's quiet personality and love for Hyderabad were evident in his fictional work. She said: "Very particularly, at some point, some of the chapters read like historical documents. His portrayals of the Razakars and the Muslim question reveal many dimensions of those critical times." Being a voracious reader of Western literature, particularly fiction, Bhaskarabhatla tried adapting certain modernist techniques in his prose too. Writing from the perspective of an angry, urban, educated, middle-class young man, this novel was considered to be one of the milestones in the early prose of Telangana literary history. Chandur describes this novel as the earliest of the modernist tradition novels (*ādhunika navala*) from Telangana. However, Bhaskarabhatla's emphasis on city life and the narrations of Hindu–Muslim communities as related to its growing urbanity read more like an ethnography. Unlike Murthy, who imagines a place to escape and then describes the city as a part of his memory, Bhaskarabhatla's entire novel is set in the actual physical environment of Hyderabad. When reading the novel, one gets a clear sense of the neighborhoods, roads, and modes of transportation as well.

YUGA SANDHI: NEW CONVERSATIONS IN A NEW CITY

By the time *Yuga Sandhi* was serialized in the *Telugu Svatantra* magazine in 1956, the city of Hyderabad had undergone significant modernization. Many aspects of the new forms of education, reformism, political shifts, gender dynamics, religious identities, and most importantly, several manifestations of urbanity, permeate deep into the everyday life of the city. Along with several political developments of his day, Bhaskarabhatla also focused more extensively on how a new generation—in a way, the products of Osmania University—were crucial in the making of the new Hyderabad. Nevertheless, unlike Swamy and Murthy, this new Hyderabad, as described by Bhaskarabhatla, narrates the life stories of an urbanized middle-class educated youth, particularly those aged between 16 and 25. Offering evidence for a new set of ideas, ideologies, and conversations, this novel also functions more like an intellectual biography of the post-1930s new generation in Hyderabad state.

Presented as the coming-of-age story of Raghu who, like Bhaskarabhatla, was born and grew up in the village of Premavati Peta and then migrated to the city of Hyderabad, this novel depicts major themes including Telangana local modernity, which is called *Telangāna ādhunikata* in Telugu. Characteristics such as the engagement with the new educational system, shift in gender discourse, transformation of a new self, and most importantly, growth of new sensibilities in the cultural and literary sphere remain central in this version of the *ādhunikata* (modernity). As mentioned in the introduction of this book, the specific emphasis on local modernity pays attention to the factors that led to the emergence of Telangana activism since the beginning of the twentieth century. This novel, however, specifically depicts how the trajectory of the new education, social reformism, and gendered sensibilities evolved together. Many events, particularly the political and cultural ones, represent the making of a new generation in the city after the Telangana activism of the 1940s.

Explaining the larger canvas of Bhaskarabhatla's fictional world, the literary historian Sangisetti Srinivas said:

> Bhaskarabhatla captured the life stories of the newly emerging middle-class in Telangana. This middle-class consists of the young lawyers [who] just started practising law at the courts of Secunderabad and Hyderabad, the lecturers working in various colleges in the city and the government employees. This middle-class was very different from the British Andhra and Yuga Sandhi shows those differences too. The middle-class in Telangana emerged from the bureaucracy created by the Nizam's offices and also the new working class from various cigarette and textile factories.[64]

Since Bhaskarabhatla likewise belongs to the same middle class of the late 1940s, his novelistic representations reflect several autobiographical elements. Many social, cultural, and political aspects as perceived and interpreted by the protagonist offer insights into the making of a milieu that the author inhabits. Like Murthy and Swamy, Bhaskarabhatla also represents the new Hyderabad (*nayaa* Hyderabad) that emerged in the wake of the post-1940s political environment. In the preface to the first edition of the novel, the literary critic Srivastava mentions how the author engages with the new changes in the city along with the paradigmatic shifts in family life.[65] The life stories of Raghu, Rukmini, and Ramana represent three distinctive angles of such a shift, as they move from one system to another. All three characters originate from typically conservative families and gradually embrace a modern life, one of the most significant aspects being shifting from a joint to a nuclear family and then being forced to take up middle-class jobs in an agriculture-based economy. Reflecting deeply on this new "transition," or *yuga sandhi*, Raghu speaks to himself as an existentialist who was struggling to find meaning in his life and work.

> In this new context, he began to reflect on the differences in the ways he and his father understood life. He could see a vast difference between his father, who strongly believed in the traditions, and himself as the one who [had] lost all the beliefs. Relatively, his father sometimes feels a little sad or perplexed, but himself—always confused and lingering in between many things. Maybe, that's where both of them differ. He is like this modern being who lost everything but could not regain anything. With no base, he's flying endlessly in the emptiness. Certainly, he lost all the old value systems, but could not reach out for the new values. He's that modern being living constantly in a period of transition (*yuga sandhi*). Everything is in the state of confusion and uncertainty.[66]

Similar monologues throughout the novel represent the anxieties of his times, thus offering insights into the interiorities of the self. Living under this constant anxiety, not only Raghu but also the other characters, undergo some kind of psychological trauma and continuously search for a resolution.

In the process, he portrays multiple manifestations of modern selfhood that contest the boundaries of the existing family system while debating a new set of values grounded in the new Hyderabadi context, one such aspect being the arrival of a modernity that fits into the recent educational reforms and urbanization of the city. Still in college, Ramana speaks emphatically about her sense of individuality when it comes to love, marriage, and her social life.

> "You believe that anything related to your marriage is in your control? You're now speaking as if you're the maker of your own life and future?"

> "Of course, not until now! But today onwards I'm taking that responsibility fully," she said as a modern young woman who realized her own rights and responsibilities.

She continues:

> "One thing that you should learn is that I'm not living in the times of my grandmothers. Those were old days when parents made matches and we just have to say yes for anything. Since they had no education, they

had no discretion about which was a good match and which wasn't.…
Now living in the twentieth century, I don't want to remain in that utter
darkness. I have decided to take responsibility for myself and my rights
and then my future too. If I keep saying this, people have already started
branding me a revolutionary."

Continuing the similar mood, Ramana said:

"I know I don't have enough worldly knowledge. But how would it be
if I'm left to my own freedom not trying to chain me in their decisions
about me and my future!"[67]

Through this long and intense conversation, Ramana touches on a few
aspects of her sense of being and belonging with respect to her everyday life
and its complications. She also endeavors to create her own meaning and
interpretation of universal concepts such as love, marriage, and freedom in
the light of reformism, urbanity, and gender dynamics. Along similar lines,
the male protagonist of the novel also articulates parallel ideas, sharing
evolving discourses about social and cultural matters. In the case of the
male protagonist, this is further complicated by the advent of new political
momentum and its public sphere. Nevertheless, both Ramana and Raghu
along with many young men and women in this novel experience a similar
break from the past as the family system undergoes a rapid change in 1940s
Hyderabad.

Bhaskarabhatla's other writings likewise engage with similar shifts in
the family system, representing a new wave of generational transformation
in the city. Even extremely traditional characters such as Rukmini were also
forced to undergo similar changes and participate in the redefined realms of
love, marriage, and family interactions. Bhaskarabhatla introduces us to a
new reading culture that allowed these innovative dialogues. For instance,
he offers a close description of the specific reading experience of an English
newspaper:

To understand things better, it's always said that we must read the
newspapers. But, Raghu never read what's called like a newspaper
before. How about buying a newspaper and start reading it on a daily
basis? How is it possible to go to the city every day for the newspaper?
In Premavati Peta, there's no post office. If you subscribe, it takes
four days to be delivered to this village. What's the use of reading the

news four days delayed? But, he wouldn't miss reading the newspaper when he's in the city. That day he bought *The Hindu*. He couldn't even understand where to start reading the contents in the newspaper. He was familiar with reading the Telugu newspapers, but not these English ones. Wherever he starts, he thought it would be better to read the entire newspaper … for a long two hours, he read it until he gets tired of reading![68]

Such specific observations about newspapers are only examples of broader changes in the culture, such as the growing culture of new reading practices and exposure to western literature. The latter we find in this novel:

When he joined the college, he started reading more books outside the class including classical texts and modern classics. He read the volumes of Keats, Shelley, Wordsworth and Byron enthusiastically. Scott and Dickens became his regular reads. Then, he paid attention to the Russian writings. Dostoevsky, Tolstoy, and Gorky were his passion. Later, he turned towards the modernist writings of James Joyce and Virginia Woolf. He realized how literary culture was impacted by World War II and the "New Writing" movement led to an entire group of new writers. He read Eliot, Auden, Spender, Dylan Thomas, Ezra Pound and most of the novelists such as Maugham, Isherwood, Hemingway, Huxley, Sartre, Andre Ziede, Saroyan, Faulkner, Forster, Zola and Balzac. He enjoyed reading the plays of Shaw, Eugene O'Neill Tennessee Williams. These readings have introduced him to a new brilliance. He made it a habit to spend hours and hours reading these authors.[69]

Yet, these humble beginnings of the new reading culture affected the younger generation's lifestyle and outlook. Indeed, Bhaskarabhatla's descriptions provide evidence of the rise of a new reading public that gradually created a refreshing public political conversation as in the case of various characters in this novel.

The reading culture was not confined to literature. It led to a serious view of contemporary politics including national and local. Most importantly, the local politics of the Itteḥād. In the Nizam's state, everything is now under the control of the Itteḥād. The very idea of the two nations is totally unacceptable to him and also, he doesn't believe in the separation of Muslims and Hindus as two entirely opposing groups. All these tensions and conflicts are merely the creation of the Itteḥād.[70]

For the urbanized and educated new middle class in the city, such reading habits became an inseparable part of their identity formation and the new self. According to the cultural activist Jaini Mallayya:

> Most of our generation's young men and women just started reading almost everything that appeared in the print which was like a magical world for us. We were introduced to every type of modern writing in prose and poetry. Even the remote urban town in Telangana now started either a printing press or a magazine. More than that, numerous translations from English, Hindi and Urdu along with other languages such as Marathi as well appeared in Telugu. Not only many writers such as Bhaskarabhatla in prose, Dasarathi in poetry, but also ordinary people, too, became new readers.[71]

Within these new conversations around various aspects of modernity, the public sphere, and the rise of alternative political organizations, discourses about Muslim politics and Hindu–Muslim hybridity evolved into a larger theme in the city. Depicting this political environment, this novel explores different layers of the Ittehad and new Muslim politics.

THE METAMORPHOSIS OF MUSLIM POLITICS: FROM ITTEḤĀD TO RAZAKARS

Narrating the brutality of the Razakars, *Yuga Sandhi*, like the previous novel, turns our attention to how the idea of the Muslim state, which Murthy translates as *Maḥammadīya rājyaṁ* into Telugu, was circulated. In doing so, however, he clearly emphasizes the perils of conflating the Razakars with the local Muslim community. Established in 1927, the Majlis-e-Ittehad-ul-Muslimeen (initially known as the Itteḥād and later popularly known as the Majlis) very soon emerged as a pressure group in Hyderabad state. Through its different phases during the political manifestations between 1927 and 1948, the Majlis played a crucial role during the Police Action. In the novel, Bhaskarabhatla depicts how these different phases of the Majlis made interventions into everyday life in the city. According to him, during the first phase, the Majlis had no political agenda and had the simple goal of uplifting the lower strata of the Muslim community. In a conversation,

Ramanatham, one of the witnesses of the Police Action and the Razakar activities, explained:

> When the Majlis started working in the 1930s, even non-Muslims were appreciating all its efforts to bring ordinary Muslims into a social dialogue. Until then, none was really concerned about these lower sections—the *ajlaf*—of the community. It started almost like the Andhra Mahasabha with an emphasis on improving ... literacy and cultivating a new reading culture among the Muslims. And, later history of the Razakars had reversed all these efforts. It was such a painful turn of the events not only for the Muslims, but also for the entire community of the city. That's how the actual purpose of the Majlis was defeated![72]

Along similar lines, the memoirs published by various Muslim families who migrated to Pakistan also narrate the early history of the Majlis. Most importantly, a former diplomat Qutubuddin Aziz (1929–2015) in his memoir narrates the earliest phase of the activities as a "reaction to the subversive activities fomented against the Nizam's government by hawkish and chauvinistic Hindu political and religious parties based in India."[73]

Along with this, the portrayal of the Hyderabadi community in this novel takes on further heights by presenting a few characters such as Rasheed, Ayesha, and Rehana. Like Swamy, Bhaskarabhatla's Muslim characters represent a dynamic and progressive Muslim community which participates in the new public sphere. Rasheed, who works as a supervisor in a cigarette company in the city, helps Rukmini by offering her a job. Later, they enter into a relationship too. On learning about this, the Razakars start pressuring Rasheed to leave Rukmini because she is a Hindu woman. The heated conversations between Rasheed and the Razakars explain more about the two different viewpoints within the local Muslim community as related to the Razakars and show how Muslims like Rasheed were against the extremist activity of the Razakars. Here, Bhaskarabhatla takes an opportunity to narrate the early phase of the Razakar movement when the Ittehad Muslimeen (later known as the Majlis) was gradually shifting towards extremist politics.

The narrativization of the Razakar activities in the novel indeed documents various phases beginning with the early 1940s. According to

Bhaskarabhatla, the very definition of the term Razakar had undergone several interpretations:

> The term now that has become popular or in wide circulation in various levels of discourses was a late phenomenon. In those days, Razakars were confined to the Ittehad as volunteers and there was no militaristic turn. The entire movement was limited to the spread of the idea of the two-nation theory and the Ittehad's activity was confined to create hatred among various religions. During this phase, the members of the Ittehad put enormous pressure on Rasheed to make Rukmini convert to Islam and they also demanded him to join the Ittehad. Rejecting both the proposals, Rasheed openly disagreed with the two-nation theory too.[74]

This resonates with what Omar Khalidi said:

> The very word disappeared from the vocabulary of Urdu journalism for volunteer, as the dictionary's innocuous meaning—volunteer—sank under the weight of its association with an armed militia resisting the Indian army. Despite the passing of more than half a century since the events of the 1940s, Urdu newspapers in Hyderabad still laboriously avoid the word Rizakar when referring to volunteers of any kind.[75]

Nevertheless, the debate between Rasheed and Rukmini is crucial in portraying their religious identities that, according to the filmmaker and one of the witnesses of the Police Action, B. Narasinga Rao, actually represent the larger portion of the Muslim community.

> Not only literature and autobiographical writings, even the popular imagination in the movies, folk cultures too inform us about the value of co-existence even in the wake of the Police Action. Literary portraits might be partially successful in capturing those moments, but the Razakar group was absolutely smaller and their brutality had nothing to do with either Islam or Muslims.[76]

The debate between Rukmini and Rasheed about these aspects also reveals more layers of this everyday grammar of co-existence in times of extreme violence. While Rukmini is totally supportive of the idea of religious conversion to save Rasheed's life, he simply laughs this off and says:

> "If you say so, I don't even consider myself a Muslim in that way. Then, what's the real purpose of converting yourself into Islam now?"

> "Then who are you?"

> "I'm an Indian!"

> She had no idea what does "Indian" mean and asks him back:

> "Just stop making fun and now do all that needed to convert me to Islam."

> "Not at all! I simply hate those who convert from one religion to another!"

> "Even if you hate it, I need to do it to save our family!"

> "I've respect for you only as long as you don't fall into this trap of conversion!"

> Then too, she is adamant and repeats the same, and he says:

> "Then you just go ahead with it!" as if he has nothing to do with it. She knows he is not going to budge even an inch when it comes to such ideas.[77]

Even before this conversation, Rasheed tries to explain what Muslim means in an Indian context. As his nationalist outlook defines his identity, he openly condemns whatever the Razakars or other fundamentalist groups were doing in the period of late 1940s. Bhaskarabhatla describes this situation:

> The politics of the Ittehād were against the nationalist spirit too. They were inspired by the communal violence instigated by the Muslim League in the British India. They all strongly believed that Hyderabad would be an independent country by all means. The leaders of the Ittehād were in communication with Jinnah who also supported the independence status for the Hyderabad state. Now, Ittehād almost started functioning like a military under the new leadership of Qasim

Razvi. Rasheed is against all these acts of violence and militarization of the Muslim politics. Moreover, he is living together with a Hindu woman. Some of his childhood friends, too, joined the Razakars and they all started pressurizing him.[78]

While representing the tensions of distinctive new ideologies and their conversations, this novel discusses at some length how the Ittehād transformed into the Razakar militia and how some groups of Muslims subscribed to its militaristic program. With an emphasis on the life story of both male and female protagonists, the author describes the polarization of the student body into two groups—the nationalists and the followers of the Ittehād. Narrating how the situation led to the United Nations, this novel portrays the entire political and religious complexity that culminated in the Police Action. In this case, the novel almost provides a testimony for various incidents and political debates that led to an extreme military action. What follows is an example:

On September 11th, 1948 Jinnah died. Two days later, on 13th was the doomsday for the Razakars. Under the supervision of Lt. General Rajendra Singh, the union army invaded the Hyderabad state from three directions. Major General J. N. Chodhary led this team and gradually the army progressed towards the city. Except in Naldurg, no resistance anywhere in the city. As soon as the Police Action started, all the streets in the city were desolate. The parades of the Razakars stopped almost suddenly. There was an artificial quietness throughout the city. As there was also a fear of communal riots, there was no motion. All the doors of the houses were shut and people didn't even dare to walk an inch outside. The army was so surprised to see that there was no resistance from anywhere. The Indian army was quite astonished about all those highly brave speeches of the Razakars. On the day of the Action itself, there was a huge migration of Muslims into the city.[79]

Although Murthy and Swamy also describe such intense moments of the Action, Bhaskarabhatla's descriptions portray the order of the events as a direct witness, as he was on the staff of the Deccan Radio. Beginning with the first day of the Police Action and until the arrest of Qasim Razvi, he portrays almost every event closely. In addition, he also documents the role of Jinnah throughout this period.

> Moin Nawaz Jung led the team that made a trip to Paris via Karachi to convince the United Nations. Meanwhile, Mir Layaq Ali, too, met Jinnah who was already on the deathbed. Then, the rumours about the invasion already swept through the state. It was also told that Jinnah promised Layaq Ali that if the Indian army invades the Hyderabad state, Pakistan would provide all the help whether this invasion takes fifteen days or three months. Assured by Jinnah, the Nizam was ready for the battle. He gathered Arabs and Rohillas extensively.[80]

Within this political environment, the everyday life of Rasheed and Rukmini, as representatives of a pluralist religious culture, demonstrates a dilemma that has both Muslim and Hindu elements. Both Rasheed and Rukmini, despite their religious associations in their everyday lives, fail to meet the expectations of their conservative religious groups. The sudden shifts in their everyday life in the late 1940s were defined by the Razakars and the Hindu groups that made a shift to violent politics. Whereas the life stories of Raghu, Ramana, and Padma struggle with the advent of modernity and its multiple transformations, Rasheed and Rukmini are forever stuck in the politics of the Razakar.

According to the political activist Burgula Narasinga Rao, who witnessed such violent incidents, particularly in 1948:

> This specific killing reminds the murder of Shoebullah Khan, the young journalist who was murdered by the Razakars in the city on 22nd August of 1948. Shoebullah was a liberal nationalist with progressive ideology and his writings against the Razakars attracted unfathomable hatred among the Razakars and the pro-Nizam forces. Finally, they killed him brutally by chopping off his right hand as a revenge for his writings.[81]

Although whether the Razakars killed Shoebullah or not remains a contentious issue, Khalidi argues, like many incidents, this too was reconstructed to place blanket blame on the Razakar militarism.[82] Nevertheless, Bhaskarabhatla narrates such incidents to articulate multiple layers of the politics of the nationalists, the local activists of Azad Hyderabad, and the extremism of the Razakars. According to Heeralal Moriya, a contemporary of Bhaskarabhatla and a well-known Urdu–Telugu bilingual writer:

> Bhaskarabhatla indeed took many such events of the everyday life of the 1940s and documented them carefully. Whenever I read this novel and read specific chapters related to Rasheed, specifically, about his killing, that entire incident reminds me not only of Shoebullah but many young Muslims who were the victims of the violence unleashed by the Razakars and also the union army around 1948. For me, this novelistic representation of Rasheed portrays such brutality that has no religious intentions.[83]

Moriya's comments resonate with several oral testimonies that I documented during my field research between 2007 and 2014. Abdul Quddus was 75 years old when I met him in 2007, and he used to sing *marsiyas*—the elegies for the martyrs of Karbala—during his teens and early twenties. In fact, when I met him I was intending to document his experiences of the *marsiya* songs in the late 1940s and 1950s. Then, he suddenly started talking about the Police Action.

> You know, what happened because of the Police Action … of course, we all know how brutal those Razakars were! Not just Hindus, even a big number of Muslims too were the victims of this entire brutality. Maybe, some ashrafi or the Nizam-related upper class Muslims were in line with the Razakars. But how about thousands and thousands of Muslims who were poor or lower middle-class! They were never part of this Razakar movement. Because of this entire violence, even the public appearance of Muslims was complicated and Razakars had become the only one *pehchaan* identity for all of us. Muslims were scared of even walking in the streets those days![84]

Quddus's emphasis on the local term of *pahecān* for identity depicts not only his pain but also of the entire neighborhood of his small town hundreds of miles away from the city of Hyderabad. During this trip, I heard from many Muslims and Hindus about such false assumptions that conflate the identities of Muslims with the Razakars. Srinivas, a local poet and folk performer, said:

> In the name of these Razakars and the stories we heard about them, we lost many Muslim friends and even now that image still lingers heavily in the back of our minds. We never know what actually happened, but the hurt remains deeper.[85]

Bhaskarabhatla, too, portrays such an intensely violent situation of the late 1940s. Most of his characters such as Rukmini, despite their extremely traditional Hindu upbringing, publicly articulate their positive interactions with the Muslim community even in times of communal violence. Nonetheless, despite her traditional Hindu family background, Rukmini eventually develops an empathy for Rasheed and tries to revise her many prejudices about Muslims. Whereas Swamy's Dilawar, being an employee of the state, joins the Razakars, despite many pressures Rasheed sticks to his liberal nationalist viewpoint. For him, Razakars represent the "worst form" of state violence, and their activities elicit barely any sympathy from the local Muslim community. In addition, several literary writings and oral history narratives, including these two novels, speak about how upper-caste Hindu landlords became Razakars in service of their authority.

CONCLUSION

Since 1948, Razakars have always been there in everyday conversations and media in the Telugu and Urdu bilingual realm of Telangana. Recent debates about Muslim identity in Telangana, specifically in the city of Hyderabad, return to the violent incidents caused by the Razakars. On the other hand, literary writings such as Neelkanth Vyas's Razakar, as analyzed by the literary critic Nazia Akhtar, are infused "with divisive and patriarchal present-day Hindutva understanding of nationhood, citizenship, and belonging."[86] With evidence from oral histories of various groups of Muslim women, the sociologist Suneetha Achyuta discussed the part played by the Razakars in the Police Action, and the subsequent dimensions in the postcolonial politics of Hyderabad.

Conflating the Razakars with Muslims has always been a dominant strategy in the post–Police Action socio-political narrativization in the Telugu-speaking states of Andhra Pradesh and Telangana. Even during my recent field research between 2007 and 2014, I heard several historians and public intellectuals expressing antagonism about the role of the "entire" Muslim community in the 1940s Hyderabad state. In 2011, Moriya said:

> Most historians and writers fail to understand the reality of the times of the late '40s in the Hyderabad state as they're blinded by an emotion filled with the anti-Nizam's rule. Not many people were conscious about the general Muslim community, however, most people were using every tool to criticize the Nizam and ordinary Muslims were the victims of this kind of imbalanced and emotional state.[87]

As witnesses to all this violence and the rise of a new Muslim discourse in the Hyderabad state, several bilingual writers such as Moriya, Murthy, Bhaskarabhatla, and Swamy continued their efforts to present an empathetic portrayal of the then Muslim community. Nevertheless, the debates after September 17, 1998, when the Government of Andhra Pradesh celebrated fifty years of liberation of Hyderabad, popularly called Hyderabad *vimochana*, raised concern about the very term "liberation." Such concerns also have implications for the recent Muslim discourses that found expression in the Muslim debates on identity formations known as *Muslim vādaṁ* (Muslim-ism) or *maināriṭī vādaṁ* (minority discourse) in Telugu.

> For long, the majority of Muslims kept themselves away from anti-feudal struggle because of the influence of the Muslim communal organizations. The nationalist Muslims hesitated to join the State Congress because of its links with some Arya Samaj leaders. However, as the crisis deepened, a section of democratic and nationalist-minded Muslims started opposing Nizam's rule. Many radical Muslims like Maqdoom Moinuddin, Rafi Ahmed, Mirza Haider Hussain etc., joined the communists. Shoyab-ulla-Khan, the editor of the Imroze, at the cost of his life, criticized the atrocities of the Razakars and the Nizam's police in Bibi Nagar and Nizamabad. Many Muslim leaders also appealed to the Nizam to disband the razakars, dissolve the government and accede to the Indian Union.[88]

These two novelists and many of the interviewees I met to document their personal experiences of the 1940s Muslim debates, including Jaini Mallayya, Burgula Narasinga Rao, Heeralal Moriya, and many others, were intimate friends with this section of radical Muslims too. In addition, Muslims who were not part of the Nizam's administrative structures also shared their experiences about being Muslim in the times of the Razakar violence. Abdul Quddus Zaimi, who was a homeopathic doctor in the city of Hyderabad, said:

> While some administrators such as Tahsildars and other employees were forced to participate in the Razakar activities, the violence was not exclusive for Hindus. Even ordinary Muslims, too, were the victims of this violence. In fact, Muslims were the victims of several forms of violence. My own family is evidence for this. We were national-minded Muslims and totally supported the freedom struggle and in the emotional upsurge of anti-Muslimness such aspects had no impact. All Muslims were labelled as Razakars! Even after the Police Action, too, those feelings had continued and ordinary Muslims suffered heavily under this burden of hatred.[89]

In the wake of the Telangana separate state movement after 1994 and the rise of new Muslim discourse, a group of scholars and writers from Hyderabad have continued to explore the multi-layered realm of the Razakars and the Muslims of Hyderabad state.

NOTES

1. Raj Bahadur Gour, *Glorious Telangana Armed Struggle* (New Delhi: Communist Party of India, 1973).
2. Interview with the author, September 20, 2013.
3. Interview with the author, September 20, 2013.
4. Interview with the author, September 20, 2013.
5. Nizam's *firman*, June 11, 1947, file no. 68, pt II, AISPC Papers, NMML. For a discussion about this *firman* in a Telugu political context, see Kandimalla Pratap Reddy, *Haidarābād Rāṣṭraṃ Bhāratadēśamlō Vilīnaṃ: Cāritraka Nēpathyaṃ* (Hyderabad: Nava Chetana Publishing House, 2017).
6. *The Hyderabad Question before the United Nations* (Documents and other materials prepared by the Hyderabad Delegation to the United Nations, Karachi, 1951).
7. *Hyderabad Question*, 38.
8. Purushotham, *From Raj to Republic*, 69.

9. Mansergh, *The Transfer of Power*.

10. Purushotham, *From Raj to Republic*, 71.

11. *Hyderabad Question*, 38.

12. Ibid.

13. Ibid., 38–42.

14. About the Hindutva stance on the Razakars, Tanika Sarkar said:

> … revenge must be taken on present-day Muslims both for historical wrongs and for the future danger they embody … for the Muslim of today embodies all past offences and future threats that have been allegedly committed and could be committed. Therefore, revenge may be taken on any Muslim anywhere for anything that any Muslim do or had done.

Tanika Sarkar, "Semiotics of Terror: Muslim Children and Women in Hindu Rashtra," *Economic and Political Weekly* 47, no. 44 (2002): 2874, https://www.epw.in/journal/2002/28/commentary/semiotics-terror.html (accessed November 20, 2021).

15. K. M. Munshi, *Report on the Razakars of Hyderabad* (Bombay: Bharatiya Vidya Bhavan, 1948).

16. Seetharam, *Nelluri Kesava Swamy Kathalu*, 145.

17. Ibid., 146.

18. Ibid., 147.

19. For the perspective of the Communist Party, see P. Sundarayya, *Telangana People's Struggle and Its Lessons* (Calcutta: Communist Party of India [Marxist], 1972).

20. For such a biased viewpoint of the Razakars and Muslims, see Kishorilal Vyas Neelkanth, *Razakar* (New Delhi: National Publishing House, 2005).

21. "Neelkanth holds all Muslims guilty for Razakar violence, thereby effecting a smooth narrative fusion between the term 'Razakar' and 'Muslim' so that both become synonymous in his writing, every Muslim becomes a justified target for surveillance and persecution." See Nazia Akhtar, "Hyderabad, Partition, and Hindutva," in *Revisiting India's Partition*, ed. Singh, Iyer, and Gairola, 305.

22. For more on these silences and gaps in the historiography, see Suneetha Achyuta, M. A. Moid, and R. Srivatsan, eds., *Broadsheet on Contemporary Politics: Nizam's Rule and Muslims* (Hyderabad: Anveshi, 2010), 2–5.

23. Tahir Kamran, "Choudhary Rahmat Ali and His Political Imagination: Pak Plan and the Continent of Dinia," in *Muslims against the Muslim League*,

ed. Ali Usman Qasmi and Megan Eaton Robb (Cambridge: Cambridge University Press, 2017), 82–108.

24. Ayesha Jalal, *Self and Sovereignty: Individual and Community in South Asian Islam since 1850* (London: Routledge, 2000), 392–393.

25. For an understanding of Rahmat Ali's worldview, see Choudhry Rahmat Ali, *The Millat and the Mission* (Cambridge: National Movement, 1944); Choudhry Rahmat Ali, *Osmanistan: The Fatherland of the Osman Nation* (Cambridge: Osmanistan National Movement, 1946).

26. The Telugu novelist Dasarathi Rangacharya (1928–2015), too, explained about this map and its reuse in the years between 1946 and 1948. His autobiographical work *Jeevana Yaanam* (The journey of life) explores many aspects of the Police Action and the dividing lines between Muslims and Hindus. Dasarathi Rangacharya, *Jīvana Yānaṁ* [The journey of life] (Hyderabad: Nava Chetana Publishing House, 2015).

27. For a recent study of the life story of Sarvadevabhatla Ramanatham, see Mutyam and Sivalingam, *Kaṣṭāla Kolimi*.

28. Interview with the author, September 20, 2012.

29. Some of these terms, specifically *jihad*, are now most debated concepts. For more on this, see David Cook, *Understanding Jihad* (Oakland, CA: University of California Press, 2015).

30. Interview with the author, December 25, 2019.

31. Interview with the author, Khammam, India, September 1, 2007.

32. Interview with the author, Khammam, India, September 2, 2007.

33. Interview with the author, Khammam, India, September 2, 2007.

34. Interview with the author, Khammam, India, September 2, 2007.

35. Interview with the author, Khammam, India, September 1, 2007.

36. Faiz Ahmad Faiz, "The Dawn of Freedom," trans. Agha Shahid Ali, *Annual of Urdu Studies* 11 (1996). Following Murthy and his brother's suggestion, this author also translated the poem into Telugu. Afsar, *Rakta Sparsa* [A touch of blood] (Khammam: Ravali Prachuranalu, 1985), 63–64.

37. Ravikant and Saint, *Translating Partition*, 160.

38. Murthy, *Mai Gharīb Hu* (Hyderabad: Praja Sahitya Parishat, 1949), 61.

39. Ashoka Mitran in his 1981 Tamil novel *Padunettuvadu Lakshatagalu*, later translated into English as *The Eighteenth Parallel* (1993) and Telugu as *Janta Nagarālu* (1985), describes the situation that led to violence. Ashokamitran, *Janta Nagarālu* (New Delhi: National Book Trust, 1985), 117–125.

40. Sherman, *Muslim Belonging in Secular India*, 8.

41. Interview with the author, Khammam, India, September 1, 2007.

42. A Telugu translation of a chapter from Ibrahim Jalees's *Dō Mulk Ēk Kahānī* was published in *Andhra Jyothi*. "Nalimela Bhaskar, Reṇḍu Dēśālu – Katha Okkaṭē!" (Two countries and one story), *Andhra Jyothi*, September 19, 2015.

43. For more on Bahadur Yar Jung and Ibraheem Jalees, see Shefali Jha, "Democracy on a Minor Note: The All-India Majlies-E-Ittehadul Muslimeen and Its Hyderabadi Muslim Publics" (Unpublished manuscript, University of Chicago, Chicago, 2017), 177.

44. Luther, *Hyderabad*, 222.

45. Interview with the author, Khammam, India, September 1, 2007.

46. Murthy, *Mai Gharīb Hu*, 63.

47. For more on Josh Malihabadi and Faiz Ahmed Faiz's influence on the Telugu literary sphere, see Dasarathi Krishnamacharya, *Yātrā Smṛti* (Hyderabad: Literacy House, 2006); Sadasiva, *Urdū Bhāṣā Kavitva Saundaryaṁ* (Hyderabad: Telugu University, 2004).

48. Interview with the author, Khammam, India, August 20, 2006.

49. Hasan and Asaduddin, *Image and Representation*, 9.

50. Ibid.

51. Murthy, *Mai Gharīb Hu*, 70.

52. Interview with the author, Hyderabad, India, September 20, 2008.

53. Interview with the author, Hyderabad, India, September 20, 2008.

54. Interview with the author, Khammam, India, September 3, 2007.

55. Sunil Purushotham, "Internal Violence: The 'Police Action' in Hyderabad," *Comparative Studies in Society and History* 57, no. 2 (April 2015): 435–466.

56. For more on Telugu linguistic nationalism, see Mitchell, *Language, Emotion, and Politics: The Making of a Mother Tongue* (Bloomington: Indiana University Press, 2009); Peter L. Schmitthener, *Telugu Resurgence: C. P. Brown and Cultural Consolidation in Nineteenth-Century South India* (New Delhi: Manohar, 2001).

57. Murthy, *Mai Gharīb Hu*, 18.

58. For a detailed discussion of this specific period's writers and their emphasis on Telangana movement, see Vara Vara Rao, *Telaṅgāṇa Vimōcanōdyamaṁ* (Hyderabad: Sweccha Prachuranalu, 1983).

59. Murthy, *Mai Gharīb Hu*, 11.

60. For a recent portrayal of this idea of the Ganga–Jamuna *tehzeeb* in the movies, see C. Yamini Krishna, "Language and Cinema: Schisms in the Representation of Hyderabad," *South Asia: Journal of South Asian Studies* 44, no. 6 (2021): 1027–1040.

61. Mudiganti Sujatha Reddy, *Bhāskarabhaṭla Kṣṇārāvu Racanalu – Kathalu, Navalalu* (Hyderabad: Visalandhra Publishing House, 2013), iv.
62. Interview with the author, Hyderabad, India, September 3, 2006.
63. Malathi Chandur, "Pāta Keraṭālu," *Swathi* (May 1986).
64. Sangisetti Sreenivas in Mudiganti, *Bhāskarabhaṭla Kṣṇārāvu Racanalu*, xiii.
65. Mudiganti, *Bhāskarabhaṭla Kṣṇārāvu Racanalu*, 4
66. Bhaskarabhatla, *Yuga Sandhi*, 84.
67. Mudiganti, *Bhāskarabhaṭla Kṣṇārāvu Racanalu*, 50–51.
68. Ibid., 94.
69. Ibid., 135.
70. Bhaskarabhatla, *Yuga Sandhi*, 136.
71. Interview with the author, Hyderabad, India, January 29, 2019.
72. Interview with the author, Khammam, India, September 11, 2008.
73. Qutubuddin Aziz, *The Murder of a State* (Karachi: Islamic Media publication, 1993), 37.
74. Mudiganti, *Bhāskarabhaṭla Kṣṇārāvu Racanalu*, 192.
75. Omar Khalidi, *Muslims in the Deccan: A Historical Survey* (New Delhi: Global Media Publications, 2006), 156.
76. Interview with the author, Hyderabad, India, August 30, 2020.
77. Mudiganti, *Bhāskarabhaṭla Kṣṇārāvu Racanalu*, 192.
78. Ibid., 192–193.
79. Ibid., 200.
80. Ibid., 199–200.
81. Interview with the author, Hyderabad, India, January 26–29, 2019.
82. Khalidi, *Muslims in the Deccan*, 147.
83. Interview with the author, Khammam, India, January 20, 2012.
84. Interview with the author, Karim Nagar, India, September 20, 2006.
85. Interview with the author, Karim Nagar, India, September 20, 2006.
86. Akhtar, *Revisiting India's Partition*, 320.
87. Interview with the author, Khammam, India, May 20, 2011.
88. H. Srikanth, "Liberation of Hyderabad State," in *Making of the Indian Union: Merger of Princely States and Excluded Areas*, ed. Sajal Nag, Tejimala Gurung, and Abhijit Choudhury (New Delhi: Akansha Publishing House, 2007), 141–142.
89. Zaimi's interview published in Paravastu Lokeswar, *Nizāṁ Pai Nippulu Kuripiṁcina Vīrulu* [The warriors who fought against the Nizam] (Hyderabad: Gandhi Prachuranalu, 2011), 53.

3

"I AM GOING TO FIGHT ..."

MUSLIM WOMEN'S POLITICS AND GENDER ACTIVISM

I am a woman and I can sense and feel the sound of an impending danger sooner than anyone. Now writers have to pay more attention to this world than ever before. The new knowledge, the dangers of the new politics have flared up this world. The darkness of hostility, destruction, and disenchantment are everywhere and constantly increasing!

—Jeelani Bano

In Jeelani Bano's 1963 novel *Aiwan-e-Ghazal* (The palace of the ghazals), two *ashraf* Muslim women, Qaiser and her daughter Kranthi, join the radical squads of the Telangana armed rebellion led by the communists that fought valiantly between 1946 and 1951.[1] Members of an extremely conservative family known for its absolute loyalty to the Nizam and its conservative Islamic practices, Qaiser and Kranthi take a path that unsettles the entire family and the local community. In fact, Qaiser's cousins Chaand and Ghazal had been predecessor rebels in the family; however, Qaiser's leftist politics—according to one of her elderly family members—"create nothing less than extreme chaos in the family." The entire confrontation begins with what historian Mahua Sarkar terms an "invisible everyday agency."[2] However, in the case of these four Hyderabadi Muslim women characters whom I will introduce in this, this everyday agency gradually becomes strikingly visible in their interactions with the family, thanks to their explicit interventions in the political sphere of Hyderabad. Along with Qaiser and

Kranthi, Chaand and Ghazal demonstrate two modes of gender activism with their participation in the Hyderabadi public sphere. In what follows, I discuss the magnitude of such gender activism and of the political dimension of Muslim women's selfhood as manifested in this novel. This chapter explains how amidst the intersections of the rise of new politics in the city, the system of modern education, the Telangana activism of the 1940s, and the progressivist ideology—all four of these women forcefully demonstrate their agency as resistance against traditionalism, and specifically against the normative definitions of Muslim womanhood and the hegemonic patriarchy. During my interviews and field research, I came to realize that the life story of the author also plays a crucial role in the making of this compelling political agency of Muslim women and their participation in the public sphere. For that reason, I will connect Jeelani Bano's biography—which functions as what Dale Eickelman calls "social biography"[3]—along with the oral histories of a few living witnesses of the Police Action that further contributes to our understanding of the possible topography of this discourse. Despite its limitations as a fictional work, I suggest that this novel functions as a testimony that unveils key historical aspects of Muslim gender discourse and its foundational tensions, possibilities, and political subjectivities that shaped Hyderabadi Muslim women's lives after the Police Action. I discuss how Qaiser and Kranthi on the one hand, and Chaand and Ghazal on the other, approach this gendered self—or, to use Banu's term *nayī aurat*, meaning "the new woman"—with an emphasis on how differently they understand gender discourse. Rather than submitting to the reigning hegemonic social and gender inequality, and rather than remaining victims, all four of these women forcefully claim their agency and individual voices. This novel testifies to the rise of a political dimension of this resistance almost around the time of the end of British colonial rule and the beginning of postcolonial politics. Major themes that I delineate in this chapter are part of the debate on the shaping of Muslim women's agency that disrupted the nationalist narrative of home and feminine characteristics as what Partha Chatterjee calls "essential spiritual virtues."[4] Departing from such a broader gender base, however, recent scholarship advances this debate specifically through its much nuanced understanding of the category of "Muslim woman."[5] In her 2018 work, the historian Siobhan Lambert-Hurley stresses the importance of using the category of South Asian Muslim women "considering them as a distinct group," which she characterizes as a "fairly fluid cultural category."[6] Furthering this debate, various Muslim

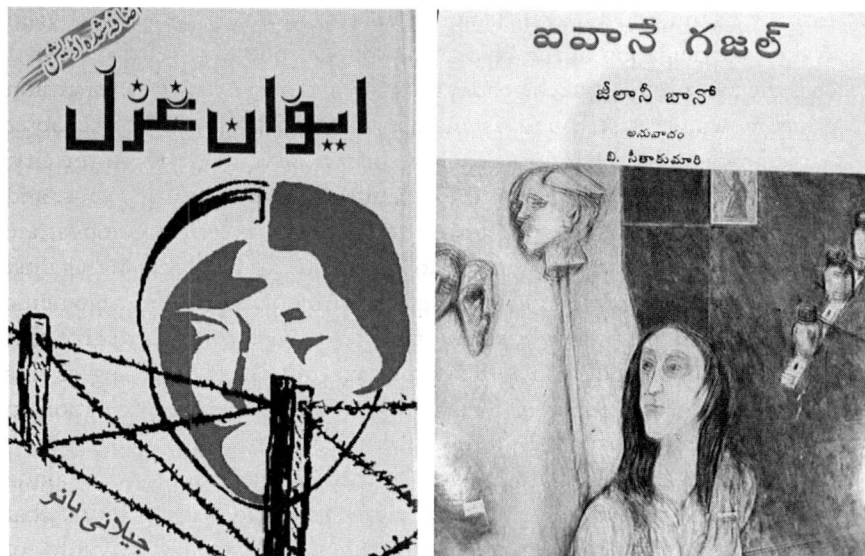

Figure 3.1 *Aiwan-e-Ghazal*: Urdu and Telugu versions
Source: National Book Trust of India.

women characters in Banu's novel demonstrate this fluidity along with their emergent political persona that allows us to use the alternate term of the "new Muslim woman" to describe themselves.

Focusing on how the spaces of the *zenana* evolve into a theater of multiple political discourses and alternative gender debates, this chapter demonstrates the newly available sources of power and resistance that shaped the lives of these Muslim women in diverse ways. Although *Aiwan-e-Ghazal* (Figure 3.1) indeed deserves a more nuanced study as regards several aspects of Muslims and then the interactions between Hindus and Muslims in Hyderabad as a larger community, this chapter focuses on how this novelistic representation of gender activism disrupts the boundaries of domesticity of the *zenana* and *purdah* systems. Set amidst various happenings in the public sphere of the city, the novel portrays the recasting of a modern Muslim woman in the wake of colonialism, Partition, and most importantly, the 1948 Police Action. These fictional representations provide evidence of a process that prompted Muslim women to define a modernity that embraces political discourse of the late 1940s in Hyderabad, including the leftist movement. In connecting both personal and political realms, this novel raises several questions related to the making of Muslim women and their engagements with a new set of ideas, including modern Islam, nationalism, progressivism, linguistic and cultural partition, and the recasting of the role of Muslim women in postcolonial India. Through these dialogical movements between multiple themes that made the city of Hyderabad a site of tensions among various discourses, this novel morphs into a historical and political testimony that crosses the boundaries of the fictional domain.

As the pioneers of a proto-feminist wave in this upper-class Muslim family, all four of these women encounter several challenges, ranging from the personal to the public. Chaand and Ghazal lose their lives, while Qaiser and Kranthi join the Communist squads.[7] Living almost in the same period around the 1940s, they effectively transgress many boundaries of domesticity epitomized as *zenana*, the interior space traditionally and patriarchally specified for women. Using the recently available tools of western education, performance arts, reformist Islam, and the tools of the modern public sphere of the city, all of them embrace a public persona. Engaging with this trajectory, Bano's novel projects a history of various groups of Muslim women fighters that the normative and mainstream historiography of Hyderabad state has not acknowledged (Figure 3.2). Even leftist historians have failed to recognize this dimension of the historical Telangana armed rebellion.[8]

In their pioneering work, *Women's Writing in India*, Susie Tharu and Lalitha emphasize how fictional works function more like documents rather than as "monuments to existing institutions of cultures (classics are, by definition, monuments) but as documents that display what is at stake in the embattled practices of self and agency."[9] Within the dynamics of Urdu and Telugu hybridity of the Hyderabadi literary culture, Bano's novel has narrative elements that characterize it as a document. As the novel encompasses most possible groups of women, including various shades of traditionalism, reformism, and modernity, it acquaints us with more Muslim women from the *zenana* to various public spaces. As the political climate changed after the Police Action, many women underwent a multifarious attitudinal transformation, which was not comprehensible to men in the family. Such failures in understanding, and the increasingly nuanced and new multi-layered idioms, further complicated the interactions between men and women, which I argue, are primarily premised on the constantly shifting gender discourse.

Within the novelistic representation of this history of Hyderabad in the post-Police Action era, this chapter aims to discuss: What were the implications of such a crossing of the *zenana*, and how did they fashion the rise of a new kind of Muslim woman subject in the public sphere of Hyderabad? How might we understand this new Muslim woman, who conducts her life through the trajectory of reformist Islam, progressivism, and gender discourse as manifested in a vernacular milieu, specifically in the wake of a violent historical event such as the Police Action? What were the responses of the new generation of Muslim women who were simultaneously experiencing the aftermath of this political violence and the rise of Muslim identity politics?

The story indeed begins with Chaand, the eldest and favorite granddaughter of Wahed Hussain—an epitome of the *ashraf* and feudal way of life.[10] His son-in-law Haider Ali Khan represents the early phase of leftist politics in the city by becoming an active member of the Progressive Writers Association (PWA). Being his daughter, Chaand continues the legacy of a progressive individual. Rejecting the legacy of both male heads of the family, Chaand adopts a version of modern life that asserts her individual freedom. Taking advantage of the benefits of new education and the resultant opportunities, she engages with contemporary social and political organizations in the city, including local clubs and performing arts groups.[11] Following her lead, Ghazal subscribes to similar ideas, with some ambiguous commitment to the family. By contrast, Qaiser and Kranthi take a leftist approach that revolutionizes almost every aspect of their personal life, disrupting the established *ashrafi* life of the Hyderabad state. Continually demonstrating their political agency and gender activism through everyday life, all four of these women cross the domestic boundaries of a typical *zenana*. Not surprisingly, their entire family was devastated by their revolutionary actions. More than their personal life or the consequences of their radical choice, the entire family, particularly Wahed Hussain, was quite concerned about how the Nizam would respond to these "dangerous" acts.

Qaiser's revolt arrived at the point when the history of this long decade reached its peak around 1946 as the battle between the Nizam and the leftist radical squads entered an extremely violent phase. With a nod to the paramilitary of the Razakars and the violent activities, along with the agenda of the Azad Hyderabad, the Nizam was tightening the grip of the forces of law and order to suppress the leftist activities and the nationalist organizations in Hyderabad state. The Nizam was also successful in "banning" the entry of Mahatma Gandhi into the state. On August 27, 1948, in a place called Bairan Palli, the Communist party squads had fought with the Razakars, and eighty-seven leftists were killed brutally. Fictionalizing almost every historical event in detail, Bano's novel corroborates how these developments impacted local Muslims, and particularly the Muslim women in the city. Bano's focus on Wahed Hussain's family, in fact, provides a theatrical setting for the entire drama that blends the personal and the political. Most zamindars like Hussain were following the Nizam's instructions to the letter in hopes of attaining Azad Hyderabad. Amidst these developments that encompassed both personal and public life, Qaiser's move to go into exile in the forest to intensify her revolutionary activities was like a bombshell dropped on the family. Qaiser's revolutionary politics were an alternative strategy that unsettled many aspects of the male monopoly that defined the very legacy of this zamindari family and its *zenana*. In addition, she also contested the gender inequality practiced within the leftist movement by being prepared to participate even in deadly and extremely risky activities. Through this process, we also encounter additional questions, such as how Muslim women like Chaand, Ghazal, Qaiser, and Kranthi engage with the new debate about gender reforms, leftist movements, and the rise of the Telangana movement against the background of the Police Action. To connect these ideas with the current scholarship on gender studies, Qaiser's perspective fits perfectly in what Margot Badran characterizes as "a kind of feminism and a public activist mode without a name."[12]

Rejecting the prescribed *zenana* way of life, Qaiser and Kranthi make their own choices of personal and public activism by defining their roles in the community and public life. While participating in this resistance, they also contest derivative modernities, including a version of Western modernity that shaped the gender identity of Chaand and Ghazal. Despite her recent theoretical engagements with the feminist movement and the larger Telugu and Urdu hybrid literary sphere, Bano in our several conversations also described Qaiser as a Communist. "Qaiser and Kranthi both were the products of the long history of leftist politics and social ideology. I just wanted to show that there were Muslim women who were active in the leftist resistance struggles and that we need to recognize their work and [the] several ways they sacrificed their families and personal lives." Likewise, we see Chaand for the first time in the history of the family embracing the idea of individual choice and modernity by taking advantage of new education benefits. Ghazal contests the boundaries of domestic and public life by raising concerns about the marriage system and then participating in the performative arts in the city. Then, we meet Kranthi who, like Qaiser, again

Figure 3.2 Women in the historical Telangana armed rebellion
Source: People's Democracy.

declares openly that she will join the political movement to revolt against the "entirely rotten systems of the family" that aim "at killing the individuality" of a woman. Whereas Chaand and Ghazal continue to believe in the securities offered by the family system, Qaiser and Kranthi clearly abhor those aspects, thus representing another mode of Muslim self that involves the political life as well. What makes Qaiser and Kranthi arrive at this point of a political revolt? And what are the implications of such a role in a conservative Muslim *zamindari* family in the city of Hyderabad? How do we understand such a shift in the life stories of Chaand and Ghazal on the one hand, and then Qaiser and Kranthi on the other? We can clearly draw a line connecting the two different paths they took in the public sphere of the city of Hyderabad.

FROM *ZENANA* TO *DAḶAM*

By writing about the intriguing journey of Qaiser and Kranthi from being in *zenana*s to being in *daḷam*s of the communist squad in a forest, Bano was indeed tapping into one of the rarely studied political dimensions of the history of Hyderabad and Telangana. While such stories are not unique or isolated, most of them remain unknown and undocumented in the official histories and mainstream literary narratives either in Urdu or Telugu. Despite the recent upsurge in feminist historiography, these stories about Muslim women have remained largely undiscovered. Along with the novel, Bano's own experiences with leftist organizations and gender activism tell the story of Muslim women's politics in the late 1940s. To that extent, although this novel is not autobiographical in its strict sense, Bano's experiences as a witness and participant play a prominent role in this testimony. Structuring the novel in a distinctive mode of blending as an autobiography, a historical narrative, and fiction, Bano persuasively negotiates a path between history and literature, thus finding her own way to blend facts and fiction.

Unlike her two cousins Chaand and Ghazal, whom I will introduce later in this chapter, Qaiser questions every aspect of patriarchy, including the legacy of the local-specific religious and political hegemony defined by the Nizam state and the male authority in the zamindari families. By juxtaposing these two modes of interventions into the public sphere of the Hyderabadi culture, Bano also gives us a lens through which to capture the shaping of an *ashrafi* Muslim women's discourse of the late 1940s. Experiencing adventurous undercover forest life as a member of the Communist Party squad, she meets Sanjeeva, a lower-caste Hindu, and marries him. Sanjeeva and Qaiser give birth to a baby whom they name Kranthi, meaning "revolution," symbolizing their extreme leftist ideology. Following the model provided by her mother, Kranthi likewise joins the revolutionary group towards the end of this novel. Bano describes this intense moment as follows:

On one side it was the Communist ideology which was gaining momentum even in the interior districts; on the other, the Indian government was emphasizing the merger of the states. Going beyond the stage of negotiations, the matter threatened to become violent. Qasim Rizvi was whipping up passions by giving inflammatory speeches. Parade was made mandatory for every youth.[13]

Qaiser's choice was utterly shocking and groundbreaking for the family considering the ongoing battle between the Nizam and the communists about the liberation of Hyderabad state. As one might expect, that moment creates a massive uproar among the male and female members of the family, men withdraw into an undefinable silence and remain helpless. Unable even to imagine such persistent action, the women of the *zenana* in the family "were agape in wonderment." On the other hand, this entire family drama reaches a crescendo when Qaiser's daughter, Kranthi, openly announces her decision likewise to join the radical political squads in Telangana. Unable to understand the choices Kranthi is making, her godmother Ghazal asks her:

"Would you mind telling where you are going and what for?"

"I am going to fight," she said and then brought out a white sheet to cover boxes that lay on the floor. "Did you see the newspaper today? In Warangal seven people were hanged to death. Is human blood so cheap? Tell me?" Pacing up and down the room, she picked up a few things from different nooks and corners and stuffed them into her pocket. "Is it wrong to ask for succor and justice? Will it always incur punishment? Death?" she hurled another question at Ghazal.[14]

This conversation raises a key question: What inspires Kranthi to make this particular political choice as the history of Hyderabad unfolds during these troubled times? Kranthi's intervention towards the end of the novel offers a possible resolution to many conflicts that these women, beginning with Chaand and ending with Kranthi herself, experienced during this period. Against the background of the hegemonic nationalist narrative and the Nehruvian idea of socialism, and the Nizam's oppressive rule, Bano's novel seemingly suggests a political alternative. To comprehend this entire journey as told in the novel, we must look at the beginnings of Muslim women's activism within the Hyderabadi public sphere.

As the waves of new educational opportunities and reformist Islam stimulated fresh discourses in the city, the *zenana* of the *ashraf* families was also deeply impacted. Fused with the emerging new politics, economic shifts and the rise of an urban economy, these two aspects stimulated a debate about the limits of domesticity, thus questioning many aspects of *zamindari* life in Hyderabad. While the very act of interrupting the patriarchal discourse has its own implications, these life stories of Muslim women reveal a historical process that evolved into constructing a political agency, selfhood, and gender activism within the limits of Hyderabadi culture. In addition, the mutuality of the Urdu/Telugu public sphere and new literary discourses remain key in the making of gender activism—and it is this rationale that makes Bano's Urdu writings and activism relevant for my work and the larger arguments in this book.

When I started reflecting on this novel, my initial thoughts were confined to Muslim women characters as described, narrated, and evolved through the story. At that point, I had planned to analyze various aspects of this fictional work against the backdrop of the Police Action in Hyderabad. Although she wrote primarily in Urdu, Bano's role was not confined to the Urdu language or the Muslim community. Being an active participant in the cultural politics of Hyderabad ever since she started publishing in the 1950s, Bano has crossed many boundaries of local religious and political systems. In one of her interviews, she explained how the impact of the shifting political and literary climate made her renounce the *purdah* that signifies a turn in her personal life too.[15] Similar to this, her characters, too, demonstrate such a shift and, via this entire narrative process, Bano likewise emerges as one of the "characters" within the novel with her deeper engagements with various socio-political and cultural movements in Hyderabad. Within the sphere of the post-Partition era—or, as more relevant in the case of Hyderabad the period before, during, and after the Police Action—this historical narrative captures a moment that foregrounds the key feminist idea that the personal is political.[16] More precisely, these personal life stories evolve into a multi-layered political and social history of Muslim women in Hyderabad. In the next section, I introduce Bano's novel with a focus on its major themes.

AIWAN-E-GHAZAL: THE TRAJECTORIES OF GENDERED MUSLIM HISTORY

During those days the upper rung of the social ladder in Hyderabad had two types of women; the representatives of one were in Wahid Hussain's family who still travelled in curtained cars, could not pronounce English words correctly (even if they signified the designations of their husbands who held government jobs) and fulfilled all the norms of piety and nobility.

The representative of the other type was the one that was being fashioned at Haider Ali Khan's. These women studied at Punchgani, Delhi, Dehradun and so on, and danced at clubs meant for the British officers. They wore sleeveless blouses, cut their hair short and applied make-up. They addressed their parents with the English words of endearment like 'dear' and 'darling.' They married out of their own choice but sought divorce because of the compulsions clamped on them by others.[17]

Describing the status of Muslim women in the *ashraf* families of the city of Hyderabad, Bano observes the above two categories that portray the adoption of a version of western modernity in everyday life in Hyderabad. As the story unfolds, however, we begin to realize that this categorization is insufficient, and more nuanced gender identities were at work during the historical events between 1940 and 1960. Throughout the novel, we encounter multiple layers of Muslim politics and the key personalities that contest the normative understanding of a *zenana*. Such portraits, nevertheless, undergo huge shifts as they engage deeply with the contemporary socio-political setting of the late 1940s.[18] In this section, I discuss how these dynamics of gender representation and histories mutually construct a new Muslim gender discourse or *nayī aurat* as they play a significant role in the public sphere of the post-Police Action in Hyderabad. Such an engagement also increased the visibility of various sections of Muslim women in multiple fields, such as social reformism, politics, and the performing arts.

Recollecting the experience of actually writing the novel, Bano said, "The title also had some political history, the initial title given to the novel—*ahad-e-sitam* ('The Age of Tyranny') was in fact more suitable for all that history that I tried to capture in the novel. Unfortunately, the title was 'censored' by the Government of India." Although the story begins with the life events of Wahed Hussain, who was an administrator in the Hyderabad state, the focus shifts to four female characters—Chaand, Ghazal, Qaiser, and Kranthi—and their battles with various institutions of public life in the city, including nationalist politics, the Police Action, the Telangana peasant rebellion, and finally, the rupture caused by the progressivist politics. In addition, the Partition and the idea of Pakistan from the lens of a political viewpoint also impact the life world of these women.[19]

The novel begins with the interventions made by the Hyderabadi Muslims into nationalist politics that likewise remain undocumented even now after an enormous effort to retrieve the history of Telangana in the post-Telangana separatist movement around the 2000s. Whereas my larger argument in this book raises the question about why mainstream historians fail to document such Muslim participation, this novel offers few responses that cross the fiction/literary boundary. This novel, nevertheless, had a precursor for such narrativization: the 1951 novel *Zohra* by Zeenuth Futehally which, as the literary critic Ambreen Hai observed, unfortunately "remains unheard of even among scholars of English literature."[20] Taking note of the failures in the reception of this novel, Hai points out:

> Nor did they note the novel's political effort to represent (some) Indian Muslims not as separatists demanding a breakaway country (Pakistan), but as loyal nationalists and active participants in the anticolonial struggle for a free, unified India.[21]

Since this novel was set in the 1920s and 1930s, Futehally documents the emerging ideology of nationalism, noting that "the questions of loyal citizens and [the] Muslim sense of belonging were also dealt [with] as the novel was written after the Partition." This political aspect becomes more complicated, the literary critic Suvir Kaul notes, when two Muslims—Hamid and Bashir—debate the idea of the "independent" state being circulated in the Hyderabad state.[22] Whereas such debates go nowhere, Futehally in many ways was successful in capturing that intense moment of Muslim participation in nationalist politics. These two essays offer fresh insights into how Futehally was "deeply concerned with appropriate forms of national belonging and citizenship," and "the emancipation of women as a foundational necessity for both political and personal demands for freedom."[23]

Furthering this discussion, Bano's novel likewise introduces a new dimension—a radical leftist version of the political activism as explicitly articulated in the characterization of Haider, Qaiser, and Kranthi that indeed provides a counter-narrative to the stories of Chaand and Ghazal. Inspired by the activities of the Progressive Writers Association in the city of Hyderabad under the leadership of the first-generation Anglophone poet and nationalist Sarojini Naidu, Haider becomes the chief organizer of a conference. This historical moment as narrated in the novel resonates with the oral testimony of Razia and Baji in *We Were Making History*:

> Right from the beginning we were close to the left front. There was this Progressive Writers' Association started in 1941. Makhdoom and Nazar Hyderabadi used to come regularly. We four sisters attended these meetings openly. Even my mother came. Some used to sit behind the chilmans. Even Tasadduq Panjethan who had returned from England

did not attend the meetings openly. Many like Sajjad Zaheer and Omkar used to stay in our house for months when they were underground. After Independence, we attended the Hindi Conference (Maulana's Asiatic Conference) in Lucknow. We hoisted red flags. Many were arrested. I became a member of the party in 1946.[24]

During my conversations, Bano shared several such stories about the Muslim women who were active both in the political and literary spheres— the histories which were never documented even at the height of the cultural activism of the 1940s or 1980s in Telangana. Qaiser and Kranthi in Bano's novel represent a similar political consciousness, akin to Razia and Baji, thus pushing the boundaries of the Muslim gender discourse further. However, in between, we also meet several women who are battling with an emerging social, political, and cultural climate following the Police Action. Growing up against this background, Chaand, Ghazal, Qaiser, and Kranthi define the terms of their own lives, explicitly announcing their agency and representation.

First is a story about a family led by Wahed Hussain, who passionately desires to live in the past era of glory, signified by a romanticized version of the ghazal.[25] The novel begins with a conversation that marks the tension between the two diametrically opposing viewpoints that were defining the history of Hyderabad in the 1940s. Hussain, to use his own words, "was least bothered with what was happening in the world. There should be peace in my own land. That's all that matters, at least to me." In this context, "my own land" means his "Palace of Ghazal," the location that gradually becomes the stage for many historical and political developments. In a way, the palace turns into a microcosm of an *ashraf* Muslim life of the entire Hyderabad state, now being exposed to leftist politics, a radical dimension that was represented by his son-in-law Haider Ali Khan. Whereas the narrative continues to portray how this tension turns the family upside down, the lives of women within the palace experience a different set of problems.

Nonetheless, Wahed Hussain was always troubled by the progressivist politics while still celebrating the established authority of the *ashraf* symbolized in his philosophy of the "ghazal." Throughout the novel, Bano delves deeply into the tensions between several binaries—the traditional and the modern, the feudal and the progressive—which continue to define or recast the domestic and public lives of the women in the family.

Despite the invention of all kind of watches and the progress made in science and technology, Wahid Hussain still used the sun and its shadows to know the time which, according to him, was the best means to serve this purpose.[26]

Although this novel unravels many untold stories and multiple dimensions of Hyderabadi life, the central idea is how peace in "The Palace of Ghazal" was disrupted as several political and religious developments evolved before, during, and after the Police Action. Hussain's romanticized notion of the peace and beauty of life undergoes a setback when young women such as Chaand, Ghazal, Qaiser, and Kranthi almost declare battle. Whereas the grandfather was still struggling to restore at least the remnants of feudal life and the *zamindari* legacy, these four women of the family turn towards new ways of womanhood, now defined by modern education, cultural life, and the shifting social climate. Indeed, the entire novel portrays the historical moments both from the perspective of the family and through political events in the city; while Wahed Hussain was busy weaving beautiful ghazals, his son-in-law Haider Ali Khan, with his leftist ideology, offers a counter-narrative to whatever Hussain represents. With Haider, the abode of the beautiful ghazals until now turns into a stage for the political debates too, as his resolute perspective through the narrative marks many dimensions of nationalist politics and the disruption of the *ashraf* Muslim life of Hyderabad. Bano uses this opportunity to connect various national and local political developments, which also impacted the literary world of Urdu. In a way, they stand as an example of a counter-narrative to the romanticized ghazal worshipped by Wahed Hussain:

From Bhagmati to Bibi the story of the Deccan was splashed with myriad colours of love. Of course, the times were different now. The most outstanding sign of this change was Basheer Begum's husband, Haider Ali Khan, who was also her distant cousin. He had been to London to do a course of law and was a great nationalist, though Hyderabad was yet to be familiar with nationalism. Ittehadul Muslimeen was not known yet, but Bahadur Yar Jung, who was dead against the merger of Hyderabad, and wanted to see it as an independent state, was gaining political importance. Opposed to him were some people with great insight, like Haider Ali Khan, who had studied the political movements of Europe and liked Pandit Jawaharlal Nehru's policies for the Congress Party. These people also realized the impending danger of fascism. Though most of the Indians were united against Hitler and Mussolini, the people of Hyderabad knew very little of the political scenario of the world. When Haider Ali Khan married Basheer Begum, Hyderabad had just started showing signs of awakening. The poetry of Josh Malihabadi and the efforts of Qazi Abdul Gaffar had succeeded in sowing the seeds of new trends. Sarojini Naidu had joined the Congress. Her leadership gave rise to a whole group of people who were receptive to new ideas. The most active member of this group was Haider Ali Khan. This was also the time when Iqbal wrote *Bal-e-Jibreel* in an effort to awaken Indian youth.[27]

These two personalities represent two different worldviews, which correspond to contemporary times. The political events and the public intellectuals mentioned above invariably reshaped the personal and public lives of women in the family too. These consequences also demonstrate how the Hyderabadi public sphere was refashioned in the aftermath of nationalist politics, the idea of the Azad Hyderabad (independent state), the role of the Congress party, various global political movements along with the resistance groups that motivated civil society in the city, along with the frequent interventions made by nationalist and progressivist personalities such as Josh Malihabadi, Khan Abdul Gaffar Khan, Sarojini Naidu, and Muhammad Iqbal.

The life stories of these four women begin as they embrace a modern lifestyle initiated by Chaand. Of course, Chaand inherits some of these ideas from her father, Haider Ali Khan:

Haider Ali Khan had decided to make his daughter Chaand Sultana a doctor and also an independent, liberal woman of today's new world. So she went to a convent school, joined dance classes, and wore skirts. Like English ladies, she wore her hair short and conversed with her father in English.[28]

In the extremely restricted and restrained domain of the *zenana*, how does this idea of "independent, liberal women of today's new world" work? The successes and failures of Chaand and Ghazal, as narrated in the novel, portray all possible dimensions of such a shift. In her father's family, Chaand was exposed to multiple aspects of a new culture that in fact landed her in trouble when she had to live with her traditional grandfather's family. The novel provides extremely detailed descriptions of these political changes and tensions too. Early on, Chaand developed an interest in the performing arts by watching movies, thus displaying another tool of modernity entering this noble family. She was a "mere seven-year old at that time but remembered the story of every film she saw. She was especially fond of Leela Chitnis." Leela Chitnis (1909–2003) was one of the prominent actresses who represented modernity on the screen.[29] She was one of the earliest female romantic leads who wore what was then considered male apparel. Described as "the first society lady graduate on the screen from Maharashtra," several of her films were characterized as "mighty drama of a modern maiden of India." Despite being a popular young woman, Chaand undergoes a major transformation throughout her life as she embraces almost every device of popular culture from movies to local performative arts. Being a strongly individualistic person, Chaand faces antagonism very early on among the local conservative Muslim community for her new ideas and behavioral practices. Her friendships with lower-caste Hindu friends such as Narayana and Sanjeeva become a community talking point:

"What am I to say sir? I hear that Nawab Wahed Hussain's granddaughter is having an affair with a Hindu boy."

"Yes, I have heard the same. They also say she wears lipstick and goes to a boy's college to study."

"I am speechless. Moral values are going to the dogs."[30]

Many things, even extremely personal ones, related to Chaand now become a huge concern for the entire local Muslim community: first her education, her attire, and then her love interest. In addition, Chaand attracts the Hyderabadi leftist political groups:

This was the period when the progressive writers held their first conference in Hyderabad. Haider Ali Khan took his daughter along to show off his progressive thinking which had allowed her to be so modern. Muslim women of Hyderabad had not yet started attending public meetings. And for a girl like Chaand, it was a bigger taboo. The inevitable happened; they forgot all of their progressive slogans. There was hardly any poet who did not compose poetry on Chaand.[31]

Nevertheless, this remains an episode which is followed by an absolute reversal of the life events in the story of Chaand. Although there were always concerns and disappointments about the "waywardness" of Chaand, the entire family turns against her when she makes her own choices in the matter of love and marriage. Even her leftist father Haider Ali Khan is unhappy when Chaand falls in love with her friend Narayana, a lower-caste Hindu.

> Although Haider Ali Khan himself remarried soon after his wife's death and also considered himself the torchbearer of truth, reality, and liberalism, he too was unhappy with the course of his daughter's friendship with Naraina. Chaand now realized that her father, who was so gentle otherwise, could sulk like this....[32]

On the other hand, her grandfather was already critical of her ways. The very presence of Chaand made him nervous and prompted him to complain about her manners and demeanor. Bano explains that "in Wahid Hussain's family, Chaand was the only woman who represented the new trends," and notes that

> for a person like Wahid Hussain, a granddaughter who studied medicine with boys, roamed around without a veil and played the violin, was quite a bitter pill to swallow.... In a very short span of life, Chaand experiments with many aspects of life and challenges several social and religious institutions.[33]

As a pioneer of new ideas and modes of life, Chaand is an inspiration to the new generation of women in her family. Ghazal is one of those who was immediately influenced by Chaand. Since her childhood, Ghazal indeed worshipped Chaand:

> Chaand was Ghazal's ideal; her role model, though she did not meet her often or for long durations ... but whenever she had the chance of meeting Chaand she touched her again and again as if to make sure she was real. She looked like one of the pictures in a movie, singing and dancing. Her appearance made her decide [that] if she ever married, she would marry Chaand aapa![34]

Ghazal's life story leads to much deeper social complications as she associates herself with more social and cultural institutions and challenges their biased treatment of women. Whereas Chaand's life is centered more on the domestic aspects of a Muslim woman, Ghazal walks straight into the center of various social circles of the late 1940s. In her admiration for a modern lifestyle, Ghazal once declares that "Chaand *aapa* is mine!" to articulate her possessiveness for her intimacy and declare Chaand as a role model. Eventually, she contests many family and community norms that surprise even Chaand. Ghazal's interactions with various social and cultural institutions in the city of Hyderabad also draw attention to the gendered bias of those organizations, and Ghazal vigorously challenges those male prejudices, demanding gender equality and justice. Her approach unsettles the dominance of the male-centric social norms, and her admiration for modernity speaks more about how Chaand's life and career demonstrate a major shift in the domestic space of the palace:

> Ghazal thought ruefully that her Chaand *apa* was always short of time. Whenever you went there you found her drawing room full of all kinds of people. Some of them rehearsed a play while Chaand sang over the violin or put up her paintings for display. Smoke coming out from their cigarettes merged with laughter.
>
> Everything that related to Chaand testified to her refined taste and education. There was no fashion which did not suit her. Though Razia had done her Junior Cambridge and Rashid had been abroad for his higher degree, their social circle was next to inconsequential. It was because of Chaand that they had become really sociable. Razia started going out in her car without curtains; she shed most of her inhibitions. She talked and laughed with men freely, went out to parties all decked up. When she did her hair in the latest style and deftly made-up her face, Rashid fell in love with her all over again.
>
> Chaand was not an artist in name; she was quite versatile. After attending her classes in the medical college, she went to a famous artist of Hyderabad in the evening to learn to paint. She was a rare combination of medical science, music and painting. People waited impatiently for her to finish her education so that they could benefit from her healing touch.[35]

While this description provides a picture of a multi-faceted modernity adapted by Chaand and Ghazal, we also note that the very space of the drawing room becomes a playground of shifting identities and the anxieties triggered by Chaand and other young women in the family. In such a challenging environment, Chaand acquires the status of a central public figure, in so doing unsettling both the patriarchy of her grandfather and the leftist aspirations of her father. By embracing multiple forms of modernity, the drawing room now also attracts a counter-narrative to whatever Hussain taught or practiced until now, and Chaand and Ghazal both symbolize this turn. In contrast to this, the world of men within the palace begins to shrink as their status declines, with a resulting decline in their political and economic power and engagement. At one point, Hussain laments: "Nobody had ever worked in our family, though. Not even in the hundred generations that passed before us. But we, the feudal landlords of today, have to see such bad times as these when we had to run after jobs, much below our status."[36] Wahid Hussain's world was caught up in "the whirlwind of a massive debt and Rashid was desperately looking for new ways of earning some extra bucks."

Haider Khan on the other hand formally joins the Communist Party. "Although he worked as the secretary of the Progressive Writers Association and attended its office regularly, it was only for the public eye. In reality, he was an active member of the raiding squads of the Telangana movement."[37] By narrating the story of Haider, Bano introduces the reader to another major event in the history of the Hyderabad state—the Telangana armed rebellion between 1946 and 1951. Whereas numerous fictional and autobiographical writings memorialize this guerilla struggle, Bano's focus on the Muslim participation and the connections between the Progressive Writers movement and the Telangana armed rebellion portray a Muslim-centered domain of political activism of the late 1940s.[38] The events as narrated in the life story of Haider represent this dimension through his engagements with the Hyderabadi public sphere and the leftist activism, which purposefully deepen and impact the *zenana* too.

When this moment of resistance arrives during the Police Action, the tensions between personal and political spheres build up dramatically in the family. Each character in the novel acquires a political dimension by responding to the polemics of the day as the daily newspapers and radio special bulletins circulate extensively among the family members. The women of the *zenana* now also read the newspapers and debated with each other, particularly regarding the tensions between the union army and the Nizam along with the updates on Pakistan. These women are quite taken aback by the political developments, as the newspapers "spoke of riots all around, filling hearts with terror."[39] Politics quickly became a key aspect of their daily conversations.

> "Where have all the peacemakers gone? Are they dead already?" Langdi Phuphu would ask with trepidation.
>
> "I hear Gandhi is trying his level best. He goes to riot-hit areas in person and stops people from killing the Muslims." Razia repeated what she had heard from her husband.
>
> Bibi was visibly upset. "It is all quiet here. Hope and pray that the riot mongers do not turn to us."[40]

While these conversations continued, it also became routine for Hussain to listen to the radio and then read the newspapers, rather than merely enjoying the ghazals. At this point, the author herself intervenes to describe what prompted them to care for the external political happenings, particularly after the Police Action.

> On one side it was the Communist ideology which was gaining momentum in the interior districts; on the other, the Indian government was emphasizing the merger of the states. Going beyond the stage of negotiations, the matter threatened to become violence [sic]. Qasim Rizvi was whipping up passions by giving inflammatory speeches. Parade was made mandatory for every youth.[41]

At this point, Hussain's routine also undergoes a major shift:

> He had stopped going out completely. Army vehicles, trucks, and the environment that prevailed outside made him feel highly disconcerted. People were living in a state of terror. Nobody could think of organizing a mushaira or any other cultural function for that matter.[42]

The politics of the Ittehād'ul Muslimīn also now affect life in the palace. Shaheen and Ayaz, the grandsons of Hussain, now join this group of volunteers, who were popularly known as Razakars. We read that "particularly, Ayaz knew all of Qasim Razvi's fiery speeches by heart. In fact, he had become the leader of all those young boys of the locality who had pledged their last drop of blood to defend the Asifid Sultanate."[43]

Almost every aspect of the family evolves into something that Hussain cannot digest, and most importantly the changes within the domestic space appear more than disgraceful to him. In a family that was strictly defined by Hussain's authority and his allegiance to the Nizam, "Now, following Chaand, believing everything she said, was mandatory for everyone in the family."[44] That was also the moment when Chaand left home to marry a lower-caste Hindu, Sanjeeva, a big shock that disrupts the well-kept world of Hussain for two specific reasons: first, because Sanjeeva was a lower-caste Hindu, and second, because he was a political activist working for a communist squad, namely *dalam*.

Following the model offered by Chaand, Qaiser and her daughter Kranthi make this circle of change complete through their further interventions into the more radical political spaces. Indeed, the most intriguing moment arrives in the life of the palace when Qaiser joins the Red squads of the communists *dalam*. With their new politics, both Qaiser and Kranthi targeted the very center of the palace: its false privileges and feudal lifestyle. Qaiser even gives up living in the palace and ends up in a forest with the communist activists, while Kranthi, still a student, openly declares she will join the extreme leftist political party of the Naxals. As one of the conservative female characters in the novel comments: Great are the ways of God; people are imitating Chaand. I have heard that Fatima's daughter, Qaiser, is studying in college. All these are tell-tale signs. The end of the world is coming closer.[45]

Qaiser and Kranthi further complicate the family setting at the palace. In a family that was eagerly waiting for the moment of independence for Hyderabad, Qaiser introduces the idea of extreme leftist politics by openly participating in an armed struggle that was responsible for the killings of feudal landlords. Whereas Qaiser lives underground as police and military search for her, though living in the palace, Kranthi likewise actively participates in the extreme leftist politics of the Red squads. Then, the novel begins with the modern lifestyle introduced by Chaand and it ends with Kranthi's direct initiation into extreme leftist politics. Since this imaginary is closely connected to the biography of the writer as well, we need to understand the crucial historical events that shaped Bano as a writer and cultural activist in the Hyderabadi public sphere.

AN ALTERNATIVE VOICE IN TIMES OF VIOLENCE

In the last week of January 2019, I was just about to wrap up a whirlwind tour of Hyderabad. Then I thought of meeting Jeelani Bano (Figure 3.3) for a casual chat and to check in with her about her health. We had met several times previously as a part of this project and also on many public occasions, such as literary gatherings and Muslim activist events. Her lively engagement with the Telugu public sphere always fascinated me, though such a mutuality between Telugu and Urdu is not surprising throughout various phases of the history of the Deccan and Telangana.[46] In our conversation, Bano touched upon several personal memoirs and the events of the modern history of Hyderabad and Telangana since the 1940s. Specifically, my last few conversations with her usually came to an end with a segment that summed up her entire story in just three or four sentences, when she said:

> The story is more complicated when we turn our attention to Muslim women which we often never dare to touch for the fear of the depths of that suffering. That's one reason why not many women writers either in Urdu or Telugu wrote about Muslim women during the police action.[47]

Figure 3.3   Jeelani Bano
Source: Photo by Nagara Gopal.

Almost eighty-three years old at that time, she was having a really hard time recollecting the past, yet she was intent not to mix up the chronology of the overlapping and intersecting historical and political events of the Partition, the Telangana Armed struggle, Police Action, the fall of the Hyderabad state, the beginnings of the new Telugu state of Andhra Pradesh, the radical left politics of the Naxalite movement, and the early phase activity of the Telangana separatist movement. She said:

> My journey both as a person and writer would not make any sense if I skip any of these political events in the Hyderabad state, specifically, the city. They are all part of my life as much as they are related to the city and the rise of new Muslim community of the '40s. In fact, I deliberately made them part of my life with my long-time association with the political and social activism of the city. My interactions with the Progressive Writer's Movement made it an obligation too.[48]

She uses the term "political" not merely in the sense of power politics, but truly as defined by the hybridity of both leftist and gender activism of the late 1940s. According to her, "both leftism and gender identity movements taught us all the political idiom that we needed to comprehend the new contexts in the city and Telangana." Simultaneously, she was not only thoroughly particular about the events of her personal life but also about providing the minute details of various historical events. Over the course of several conversations, she explained how the processes of these historical and political turns molded her personality as a writer, and at the same time, the ways in which these events were key in the making of her characters:

> During the police action, the Muslims of Hyderabad were in utter despair and frustration as they grappled with the aftermath of this unexpected turn of violence in their life. As some of the upper class and rich Muslims migrated to Pakistan, many left their home and underwent a deep agony of displacement. On the other hand, the new generation of Muslims had an extremely hard time finding employment or any economic support. All this resulted in intense psychological trauma that impacted gender relations too. Disenchanted with the changing scenario, not many writers were in a situation to capture the shifting emotionality embedded in the gender dynamics.[49]

Her writings prove how fictional narrative merges into testimony form for many marginalized historical events in Hyderabad state. Three prominently recurring tropes define her entire corpus of literary writing—the redefined Muslim women politics of the 1940s, the religious dynamics of the Hyderabadi *tehzeeb* including the mutuality between Muslims and Hindus, and the rise of a new Hyderabad as the post-feudal systems of politics, social identities, economic dimensions and, most importantly, the fluctuating religious politics, came into effect. These three aspects logically culminate in the emphasis on a new Muslim women's identity in the works of Bano. Her other writings, including short stories, novels, and essays, likewise offer an insider's perspective of the heretofore untold story of Muslim women in the wake of the shifting religious and political identities that followed the Police Action.[50] This newly defined realm of Muslim women's politics produces a richly diverse discourse that marks a concrete departure from the previous lives of *purdah* and polygamy.

According to Bano, most of her women characters were either "real or close to reality." To use her own words, they are "almost like biographical sketches with some amount of fictionalization, but I would say they are mostly real." Although the distinction between the real and imaginary as represented in this novel is not that simple, the multi-layered narrative provides a graphic description of various political happenings and the many ways that prompted the lives of Muslim women through three key decades between 1940 and 1970 in the history of Hyderabad. Bano and her many contemporaries also witnessed the phase when an expansive body of advice literature from men fueled a passionate reading culture among Muslim women.[51] While the *purdah* and other restrictions were either still being debated or had been only partially implemented, Muslim women from the noble and elite sections of society began to publish and participate in other ways in the public debates. As the story unfolds through different phases of the history of Hyderabad between the 1940s and the late 1960s, the novel explores a gradual unlocking of the private spaces of women in the city of Hyderabad. Through the socio-political and cultural engagements outlined in the above section, there emerges a new portrait of a Muslim subjectivity breaking through the extremely restricted barriers of the *zenana*.

In addition, reading Bano's fictional writing is an emotion-packed double movement between the past and the present, global and local ideas of Islam, the private and public, and the bilingualism of Urdu and Telugu. Whereas she takes the utmost care with the aesthetics of the genre that borrows elaborately from the history of modern Urdu fiction and the emerging Marxian aesthetics as defined by the Progressive Writers' Association, her way of dealing with the politics of Hyderabad remains distinctive as it delves deeper into the locally produced idiom of these historical events than do other writers. Despite her sincere commitment to the model of socialist realism, which was gaining momentum in the post-Telangana armed rebellion, Bano pushes those boundaries further to focus more on gender inequality along with new questions of religion and gender. As a result, we find robust evidence in her novel of the shifting paradigms of gender politics when the city of Hyderabad embraces the modern tools of education, urbanity, and a redefined Muslim self that was liberating itself forcefully from the remnants of feudalism.

During and after the Police Action, the entire discourse took off as more Muslim women made what Bano calls "decisive interferences" into the public spaces. Whatever long strides they took at a personal level to position themselves at a distance from the *zenana*, they all signify their key role in the making of postcolonial progressivist Muslim women. In fact, Bano strongly believes that these interventions made her rethink the boundaries of her creative writings too. She said: "It was the time to contemplate how history, particularly Muslim women's history, should be rewritten." In this way, whereas the novel itself documents this turn effectively, her own life story also functions as a testimony to the various transformations that occurred after the Police Action. In many ways, her authorial voice that runs through this narrative acquires central prominence in the unfolding of the historical process that motivated the reconstruction of the Muslim community of Hyderabad. The category of the new womanhood (*nayī aurat*), as used prominently in this context, privileges the female agency in these debates by locating Muslim women within a larger network of gender discourse. In addition, Bano's fiction also discusses other issues such as the migrations and life of Hyderabadis in Pakistan.

> The idea of Pakistan and the aftermath of Partition were crucial in the then everyday life in the city of Hyderabad too. Then, the Police Action added to this and made our lives hell. Any writer or even an ordinary person who was growing up with these two modes of violence had to deal with all that trauma. It's not true that Partition was confined to north India, as we were constantly haunted by its specter.[52]

Along with these larger ideas about the city of Hyderabad, Bano also portrayed the more rural areas of Hyderabad state in her writings. Her engagements with rural life and its dialects are clear in the novel *Barish-e-Sang* (*A Hail of Stones*), where she provides a thick description of a village named Cheekat Palli.[53] To gather data for this novel, like an ethnographer, she traveled widely in the urban and rural areas in the Telangana region and interviewed different sections of villagers. Experiencing these diverse worlds made her participate actively in the debates on Muslims, women, and various social and political discourses in Hyderabad ever since the formation of the Telugu linguistic state in the 1950s. Though she has many accomplishments, thanks to her long literary and public life since then, her direct interventions into the public sphere made her voice even more distinctive, specifically by allowing a debate on aspects of gender in Hindu and Muslim shared public life in Telangana. In Urdu literary circles, she is well known for her progressive and leftist ideology, particularly her longstanding affiliation with the Progressive Writers' Association. A close reading of her activities both as a writer and activist, however, informs us that this affiliation does not define her entire role as a public intellectual. During our several conversations between 2010 and 2019, more than once, she certainly emphasized the influence of the Progressive Writers' Association and her contemporary mentors, including Makhdoom Mohiuddin, Faiz Ahmed Faiz, and Ismat Chughtai, but she also spoke highly about the recent feminist discourses as represented in the Telugu public sphere. This emphasis makes complete sense when we understand her role within the vernacular public sphere that necessitates the amalgamation of Hindu and Muslim solidarity in gender activism. She said:

> One of the tools that I found extremely useful is: the emphasis on politics. A few writers of my generation might have felt that this emphasis was overly stressed. But I should say it was not. I have no words to describe how much I have learned about politics and being politically conscious. Most of my writings particularly that speak about the Partition, Police Action, and the Telangana peasant's movement led by the leftists, undoubtedly have this unavoidable political base. I was too young to understand the implications of these historical moments when I was growing up. But the lenses provided by the leftist ideology made me think through these aspects deeply and enriched my perspective. In fact, this ideology also helped me in developing my own

stance on gender issues, specifically as they are relevant to the Muslim women of Hyderabad and Telangana.[54]

Being an active member of the Progressive Writers Association, she sincerely believed that politics and economic disparities are at the center of all contemporary social and cultural developments, and she understood that the recent politics defined the shifting worldviews in Hyderabad. In many of her stories and novels, she used the Telangana dialect, thus producing a new idiom of Telugu and Urdu hybridity in a literary text. She learned the Telangana dialect of Telugu to conduct conversations with the women of rural Telangana that resulted in a novel *Barish-e-Sang* (*A Hail of Stones*) known as "the first novel in Indian languages in respect of its theme, regional location, and its historical setting."[55] Her ability to navigate the Telangana region at various linguistic, cultural, and political levels enriched her corpus of prolific writing in Urdu—writing that ranged from personal essays to fiction. This Telangana aspect also made her work stand out among the core progressive writers of the 1950s.

In many interviews, Bano fondly remembered the well-known Urdu writer Ismath Chughtai (1915–1991) whom she calls "Ismath Aapa" (*aapa* meaning "elder sister"). Like Ismath Chughtai, she was also born into a north Indian Muslim family in Badayun in Uttar Pradesh. Nevertheless, Bano clearly makes a distinction between their literary expressions and their different priorities in creative writing:

> Ismath *aapa* was one of the best friends of my mother, and they were always in touch with each other. That way, Ismath *aapa* also used to visit us in Hyderabad. We had great times together. Her take on literature is completely different from me. As she wrote more about life in Uttar Pradesh, I have focused entirely on Hyderabad and Telangana. Also, rather than telling the story of a limited section, I tried to bring extremely ordinary Telangana women into the fictional world. I think that's what made my Urdu fictional work different from other Urdu writers including Ismath *aapa* and Qurratulain Hyder. I would say I am closer to the narrative style of Kishen Chandar, who represents a realist turn.[56]

That her father Hyrat Badayuni was a well-known poet and their house was a meeting place for poets and writers of those days, all helped her to develop a passion for creative writing very early on. One of seven children in the family, she has survived several long periods of illness. She learned to fight the chronic illness and the consequent loneliness with the help of books and music. As a child, she grew up watching and listening to the literary stalwarts of Hyderabad, such as Makhdoom Mohiuddin, Alam Khundmiri, Raj Bahadur Gaur, Akhtar Hasan, and Zeenat Sajeeda, in short, the group that became a "vanguard of young Hyderabad artists and intellectuals" in the 1940s and 1950s. In her early days as a writer, Bano was influenced by Ismat Chugtai and Rasheed Jahan, the new generation of short story writers of the *Angare* team who stirred controversy about gendered narratives first in Urdu and then in Indian literature. When Bano first published her short story around the 1950s, it was immediately recognized by writers such as Kishan Chander, Faiz Ahmed Faiz, K. A. Abbas, and Ahmad Nadeem Qasimi, who also subsequently became her close friends. Published extensively in India and Pakistan, Bano's writings have also been translated into many Indian languages. In addition to two novels, she has more than twenty books of different genres, including short stories, stories for children, and radio and television plays. Her writings reflect, as she herself described, "a rebel girl." She said:

> I am always fascinated by that rebel-girl hiding in a cave of a high mountain, waging a lone battle for her rights. Whenever a father commits suicide for failing to arrange a dowry for his daughter, or a mother cannot control tears on the birth of a daughter, or a husband destroys the life of his wife by simply pronouncing the words *Talaq, Talaq, Talaq* … that girl emerges in front of me—the courageous girl who is struggling against tradition, customs, and against the soldiers of social and religious persecution, simultaneously. That ideal girl has come to stay within me. I do not remember how many times I have presented myself to her, seeking hope and courage, and each time she has lit yet another lamp before my eyes.[57]

Growing up in an intensely paradoxical world of tradition and modernity, communal and communist ideologies, and the diverse realm of Hindu–Muslim/Urdu–Telugu hybridity, Bano truly represents the spirit of her times and the ethos of the city of Hyderabad. Indeed, her life story as an individual and a Muslim progressive writer reads like an adventurous and meaningful story filled with many memorable events and accomplishments.

As described by Mehak Hyderabadi, who translated her Urdu writings into Telugu, "she is just another immortal character that grew out of a world extremely tense with communal conflicts, but undergoing a social and religious transformation."[58] During the early days of her writing career, Bano faced similar issues to any young Muslim woman. In a recent interview, she said:

> Even in an ambience of art and culture, there were restrictions and the strict diktats of the purdah system. My mother was very particular and never allowed me to read Ismat Chughtai's novels, which I used to hide and read. We were not allowed in the room where poetry recitations and concerts used to go on. Instead, we used to sit in the courtyard of our house and listen to it from a distance. Later, my brothers used to mimic the writers and poets and entertain us.[59]

Whereas Bano remembers several historical events during her lifetime, the memories of the Police Action and the Telangana peasant's rebellion remain fresh as if "they happened just yesterday." She recollected various incidents from the Police Action that caused both the Hindu and Muslim community's trauma "that was in fact worse than the Partition as we were directly facing the military action in our very neighborhood." While the novel *Aiwan-e-Ghazal* focuses more on the post-Police Action gender aspects, her other novel, *Barish-e-Sang* (*A Hail of Stones*) describes various historical moments of the turbulent times of the late 1940s with a focus on the Telangana peasants' rebellion. She portrays how both everyday Muslims and Hindus were entangled in the political turmoil of this period:

> Times were not peaceful, though. There was commotion all around. The air was thick with the rumours that the state would be merged with the Indian Union. Everybody was at a loss to know the future course of events. Guerilla squads of Telangana had spread terror in the villages. Ranga's life had become most insecure because his district guerillas had captured a few villages. Consequently, His majesty had come down on [the] tehsildars, patels and patwaris of the village. Every event was being reported to His majesty. Also, a department called "Redress of Atrocities on Man" was set up, which made sudden raids on bungalows and farmhouses and interrogated servants and maid servants employed in them.[60]

Although this novel's focus is primarily on the bonded labor system (*veṭṭi cākiri*) in Hyderabad state, aspects of communal conflict and Hindu–Muslim identities were also described in detail. Bano captures a political and social condition which was completely controlled by violence, and in so doing, she tries to show different forms of violence that were prevalent in Telangana. She said:

> Here in the city even ordinary people—irrespective of their religion— were extremely frustrated and helpless too. Every person and every incident of those days was still fresh in my memory. Particularly, I remember the women of those days just like yesterday. Undoubtedly, they had undergone more trauma than men.[61]

Her women characters, both Hindu and Muslim, represent a new political and social reality that portrays various key moments from the everyday life of an emerging modern urban center, always with an emphasis on the making of a new Muslim woman. Bano has always been a self-conscious writer, ever since the early days of her writing. Many times, she refers to her gender identity as being deeply affected by the times and spaces of the city of Hyderabad, and particularly the life of Hyderabad during the Police Action. In the next section, I will discuss how we could locate her novel within the local gender discourses of the Hyderabadi public sphere.

TOWARDS A NEW GRAMMAR OF MUSLIM GENDER POLITICS

When it comes to the depiction of the *zenana* or domestic spaces in the *ashraf* and *zamindari* families of Hyderabad, *Aiwan-e-Ghazal* is not an exceptional and singular example. In the 1944 novel *Purdah and Polygamy*, Iqbalunnissa Hussain (b. 1897) likewise describes life inside a *zenana*, namely Dilkusha. Like Bano's *Aiwan-e-Ghazal*, the palace of Dilkusha was a building whose "high blind walls made a stranger take it for an unguarded jail."[62] In another novel entitled *Zohra* (1952), Zeenuth Futehally (1904–1992) also uses a similar setting but adds another key dimension—the migrant Muslim families from north India. Belonging to the *ashraf* family of Hyderabad, Zuhra and Zohra—interestingly basically the same names—undergo similar struggles in the *zenana*. Whereas Hussain's Zuhra remains in the *zenana*, Futehally's Zohra moves out of the *zenana* to face the world outside the palace, where her life takes on shades of the life stories of Chaand and her cousins in *Aiwan-e-Ghazal*. Like Bano, Hussain and Futehally were also witnessing political turmoil during their lifetimes between the 1940 and 1950s, but their writings portray that turmoil only in limited ways.[63]

Departing from the narrative frameworks of these two novels, *Aiwan-e-Ghazal* describes how the city of Hyderabad transforms into a site for the interplay of various global and local Muslim politics, that description also being through a gendered lens. Throughout the narrative, women both traditional and modern, including Chaand, present an entirely distinctive facet of this political life, as mentioned before, namely a steady and explicit political agency and self-representation. Bano introduces several traditional and semi-traditional Muslim women, who speak about contemporary politics from their own lifeworld and female viewpoint. This aspect of the political consciousness comes full circle when Kranthi unambiguously announces her desire to fight, not within the *zenana*, but in the forest—the then center of the Telangana armed rebellion.

Before arriving at this point of revolutionary politics, however, Bano observes four different phases of Muslim women's agency: (*a*) nationalism, (*b*) progressive politics, (*c*) Telangana armed rebellion, and finally (*d*) the Police Action. Whereas portraying the history of nationalism from a vernacular lens is itself a major shift, the other aspects further enrich the ways vernacular histories are reconstructed. In addition to these, reformist Islam also participates in this making of a politically active Muslim gender identity. As shown in the previous sections, any discussion about such a public face of Muslim women in Hyderabad clearly begins with the emphasis on girls' education since 1907 when the first *zenana* school was established.[64]

Moving beyond this phase of primary educational efforts, Bano's novel shows the impact of the next phase of women's education in the city by taking note of how higher education disrupted the authority of *ashraf* and purdah-centered practices. In 1940, Iqbalunnisa Hussain published a collection of essays entitled *Changing India: A Muslim Woman Speaks*, followed in 1944 by her novel *Purdah and Polygamy: Life in an Indian Muslim Household*. The retrieval of these two works in contemporary scholarship emphasizes the return to a debate on women's education and purdah practices in the 1930s and 1940s, Asiya Alam explains that they "involve[ed] Islam and revelations between the 'East' and the 'West,' childhood and early education, gender inequality, domesticity, and sexual politics in the family."[65] Reminding us of the importance of these "mutual encounters" between the East and

West, Margrit Pernau likewise discusses how this advanced the "formation of an identity and an internal cohesion of this group of ascending families, demarcating them sharply both from the traditional nobility and from the lower strata of the society."[66] In many ways, Chaand's life explains a process that shows how one could, in Hussain's words, challenge "an authoritative attitude of commanding influence at home."[67] By contrast, Chaand herself takes on such a commanding position for a while, ascending almost to the level of her grandfather's authority. Most importantly, she provides a model that characterizes modernity and gender equality, in so doing reversing the traditional female roles in the *zenana*. Her idea of freedom and self-representation deconstructs and dehegemonizes the structures of authorities and hierarchies, and of course, as mentioned before, this also attracted considerable criticism from the elders of the family.

As the life stories of Chaand, Ghazal, Qaiser, and Kranthi unfold in the novel, the consequences of the Police Action remain central in the evolving process. While the entire community was traumatized and struggling hard to remake its everyday life, women's education became a significant force by which to redress the larger concerns. It was also the time when Chaand begins to use a different idiom of emancipation that she drew from the new cultural milieu of education reforms and reformist Islam. That moment peaks when Chaand openly says to an elderly person in the family, "Oh come off it, *Khaloo pasha.* You and your lopsided, old fashioned ideas! You are no less than grandpa in hanging on to them."[68] While engaging with the complexities of the *zenana* and the public sphere, Chaand here introduces a new language that transforms into a favorite model for the new generation of women in the family. This new idiom of liberation fashioned by Chaand demonstrates to Kranthi a particular kind of significance when the patriarchy modeled by the palace still believed in the feudal system, specifically, the times when Hussain still holds a strong desire that the Nizam "could invade Delhi to take over the entire Hindustan, making the Asifid dynasty reign supreme."[69]

In many ways, while the men in the palace remain less concerned or even passive about the happenings outside its boundaries, the new generation of women in the palace push their way through those boundaries to embrace the tools of modernity, and most importantly matters related to politics in Hyderabad state and Pakistan. Whereas, as the head of the family Hussain desires to command every aspect of the fast-approaching changes just to save his romanticized version of the ghazal-like poetic beauty of the palace, Khan and his son Rashid turn towards a more urbanized lifestyle by inviting into their lives various modes of new commercialization and shifting politics. In the characterization of Rashid, Bano documents a newly forming nexus between urban economics and city politics. Being an engineer, Rashid was exposed to new business ventures in the city of Hyderabad while his father Haider Khan was deeply involved in the leftist politics of Hyderabad. The tensions between the rise of an urban market and leftist politics reached a climax when both intensified their activities on daily basis. For Hussain, who always desired to celebrate life as a "pure" ghazal, these intense moments become unbearable and destroyed his vision of the palace. After morning prayer, his routine typically began with writing a couplet. The morning news about "Europe in flames," "Nazi intrigues," or "Gandhiji's non-cooperation movement" bother him little. In an environment where the lack of such ghazal-like conversations has lost its significance, he starts speaking instead to a little bird with beautiful feathers and begins to compose a ghazal about flowers and birds. Into such a highly romanticized and quiet world, Haider Khan brings the message of the Progressive Writers, who by then had started experimenting with the very form of the ghazal by replacing that old, romanticized world with freshly minted leftist ideals.[70] Their way of writing ghazal was different too, quite far from the imagination of Hussain. Moreover, the names of the progressive poets that Khan mentions were utterly shocking for Hussain. Given these two diverse political viewpoints, which also encompass two diametrically opposed gender perceptions, plus the materialistic market-centered vision of Rashid, Hussain's authority was in shambles. Now, amidst the tensions between three diverse worlds, ideologies, and modes of power, the new generation women of the palace begin defining their own terms of life by exercising their own long-dormant agency. When the union military enters the state of Hyderabad, for the first time in their lives, the people in the palace begin to care about listening to the news on the radio to learn about the political developments in the city.

In such a politically charged milieu, Bano presents portraits of three generations of Muslim women, from Bibi to Kranthi, and positions their life experiences within the trajectory of the Police Action, leftist politics, and the reformist Islam of the 1940s. Since most of these events overlap and are mutually influential, it is imperative to read them in their chronological order as represented in the novel. Unlike many of its contemporaries both in Telugu and Urdu, this novel focuses extensively on the idea of Pakistan and the Azad Hyderabad (Independent Hyderabad). The very portrayal of Wahid Hussain as a patriarchal head of the family in many ways symbolizes this intensely conservative moment of the "Azad Hyderabad."[71] This entire movement shaped by the Majlis and the newly formed "Nizam's Subject League," (1933) further complicated the larger question of Muslim representation and citizenship. Hussain and Haider Khan represent two opposing dimensions of Muslim citizenship. The *ashraf* Muslims (such as Hussain in the novel) represent this dimension of loyalty to the Nizam and the establishment of Azad Hyderabad following the model of Pakistan. Khan represents a counter-narrative to this idea of Pakistan and a separatist agenda. They took a path of progressivism led by the Comrades' Association that further precipitated the prominent Telangana peasants' rebellion that both Qaiser and Kranthi embraced.[72]

Even within the fictional realm, this novel remains exemplary for its engagement with political resistance among *ashraf* Muslims. Such class distinction Hussain mentioned repeatedly to discourage his granddaughters from armed rebellion or any leftist politics or even from participating in public life at all. That all begins with his hatred for Chaand when she develops an interest in the theater, yet he remains helpless and fails to discipline her. He was partly successful in the case of Ghazal, but Qaiser and Kranthi were totally out of his control as their entire philosophy is grounded in contesting the normative patriarchy of *ashrafi* families. Nevertheless, the novel portrays how different modes of agency work in their everyday lives, as they try to emulate a new model of Muslim womanhood (what Bano calls *nayi aurat*) that contests the normative pattern of the *zenana*. Despite her higher education and the broader engagements with the public cultures in the city, Chaand, too, never dares to cross the physical boundaries of the *zenana*. Living within those high walls, she tries to break certain chains and remain a model for Ghazal, who passionately admires Chaand's modernist ways as well as her love of theater. However, their continuing ties with the *zenana* and its wide variety of people still show the centrality of its location in their lives. Despite all their digressions to different places, personalities, and philosophies, their life stories still revolve around the *zenana* to a certain extent.

Not Bano herself, but several writers both in Urdu and Telugu consider this location of the *zenana* to be a crucial site in the making of upper-class Muslim gender identity. The novels and short fictional narratives written between the 1940s and the 1960s consequently prioritize this location, not merely as a physical location, but also as a metaphorical site that represents the tensions between traditionalism and modern definitions of Muslim womanhood. Set in Lucknow, Attia Hosain's *Sunlight on a Broken Column*, deals with similar tensions, as Tarun Saint explains: "Hosain sensitively depicts antagonism and self-destructive domestic feuds that enfeeble women within the cloistered *zenana*."[73] In contrast to this, Bano's novel takes note of the changing perceptions within the *zenana*—from women's education to social reforms. Within the context of Hyderabad, Sheela Raj notes how women's education further strengthened the cause of modernity:

> From the small number of schools and of girls in them, it can be seen that female education made slow progress in Hyderabad. There is no doubt that insuperable obstacles retarded such progress. Compared to the Hindus of Hyderabad, however, Muslims were better in taking advantage of the benefits of education. Hindus had not shown any enthusiasm to educate their girls till the end of the nineteenth century.[74]

The evidence from fictional writings and memoirs demonstrates this power of modern education, such as through medicine, the theater arts, and literature. In their 2006 essay, Asha Islam Nayeem and Avril Powell discuss how the colonial efforts resulted in "redesigning the zenana," by cultivating a passion for learning both local and global subjects.[75] In the case of Hyderabad, however, there was an endeavor that successfully created an alternative realm for women to study beyond the interventions of any governments, including the colonial officers and also the Nizam's rule. In his essay, Moid discusses how a local Muslim organization named Tāmīr-ē-Millat extended this idea of education further to vocational training.[76] Not limiting itself to education, this organization, launched in 1951, gradually focused on other social problems of Muslim women.

> The issue of women's income and especially that of widows was another urgent problem. After the police action they became the most vulnerable group and their security was under threat. It resulted in their voluntary and forced confinement. The loss of family members and income sources compounded their problems.[77]

These efforts, however, were not confined to the formal school system; religious organizations too changed their course and took up literacy and literary activism. During a conversation, the present head of this organization, Zia Uddin Nayyar, further explained that the Tāmīr-ē-Millat has been a constant presence in the lives of Muslim women in Hyderabad ever since the

Police Action. First, they encouraged them to learn Urdu script and reading so that they could speak for themselves and share their pain related to the Police Action; next, they encouraged Muslim women to participate in the newly forming public sphere with a focus on literary campaigns, lectures on political and social issues, and reinterpretations of the prophetic teaching as relevant to the current situation.[78] Departing from the colonialist and nationalist project, the educational activities promoted by the Tāmīr-ē-Millat indeed changed the direction of the entire gender discourse by finding a middle ground between religious teachings and modern tools and ideas of education.

During my field research, several political and cultural activists acknowledged this extensive literacy activity combined with various welfare programs. Along with Bano, freedom fighters like Jaini Mallayya explained to me how such educational missions refashioned a new Muslim womanhood without class distinctions.[79] Indeed, their activities motivated more non-*ashraf* Muslim women to participate in the Hyderabadi public sphere. However, such efforts beyond the *zenana* seem to be undocumented. On the other hand, this aspect of literacy intensified, as Mallayya explained, thanks to the activities of the Comrades' Association founded by leftist Muslim intellectuals and political activists.

CONCLUSION

In her 1940s work *Changing India*, Iqbalunissa Hussain observed:

> Regeneration of the Muslim nation is only possible when its women are educated and are efficient and independent. The goal of the young girl's life should not just be marriage, but also efficiency and culture. The contemptuous attitude of the superiority of man and the inferiority of woman should be replaced with equality. Real and good education, based on certain fundamental principles, should be given to women to enable them to realize self-worth and their duty to home and society. Any woman educated on such lines will not stoop to silly and useless social customs. Any effective change in the conditions of women is bound to affect those of men. The regeneration of our nation is possible only when our women become efficient, intelligent, and brave.[80]

Recall that Hussain published *Purdah and Polygamy*, a novel in which she debates similar issues in a fictional mode.[81]

By reading the life stories of all the women in *Aiwan-e-Ghazal*, from Chaand to Kranthi closely, we also notice that, as shown in this chapter, these four women barely fit into those two categories. From a close reading of this novel, we learn that these four women were deeply affected by the new political and social developments that followed Partition and the Police Action. In his pioneering work, Mushirul Hasan shows how Muslims of the late 1940s faced various degrees of uncertainty, including economic, political, and social vulnerabilities. Muslims "felt overwhelmed by the climate of hostility, suspicion and distrust."[82]

Along similar lines, Bano's novel also tells the story of Muslim political life before and after India's Independence from the British. Before Independence, Muslims had no option between the 'nationalist' Congress and the 'separatist' Muslim League. In her essay on Muslim Women in Indian Politics, Karen Karlekar observes that "those who remained in India included long-standing Congress supporters as well as a number of prominent members of the Muslim League." Eventually, after Partition, the community 'lost credibility' and its efforts to reorganize itself politically were regarded with suspicion and hostility." [83] Most of these studies fail to notice the impact of leftist politics on Muslims and their role in the locally produced political discourse of the Communist Party, let alone on Muslim women. In many ways, the leftist politics certainly provided a new space for progressive Muslims such as Waheed Khan and his other grandson Shaheen, the two characters in Bano's novel.

Whereas both Chaand and Ghazal reject the legacy of her grandfather's politics, Qaiser and Kranthi proudly own the Telangana armed rebellion and openly participate in the underground battles of the Communist Party. At this point in history, Bano's novel reads more like a political story of these two leftist women, who grew up in the city of Hyderabad and then eventually denied all the luxuries of metropolitan life. The traditional historiography of Hyderabad, with its nationalist, communist, Arya Samaj, and even minority politics, fails to capture this intense moment, while Bano offers a vivid description of the entire dilemma and political activism of Qaiser and Kranthi. The novel concludes by suggesting that the new history of urban women in Hyderabad is incomplete without studying their role in modernist or leftist discourses.

NOTES

1. Several works of Jeelani Bano have been translated into Telugu since her early days. *Aiwan-e-Ghazal* was translated into Telugu with the same title in 1998 by the National Book Trust, New Delhi. Later, it was also translated into English by Zakia Mashhadi and published by the National Book Trust in 2016. I have used these three texts as my primary sources in this chapter: Jeelani Bano, *Aiwane Ghazal*, trans. B. Seetha Kumari (New Delhi: National Book Trust, 1998); Jeelani Bano, *Aiwan-e-Ghazal*, trans. Zakia Mashahhadi (New Delhi: National Book Trust, 2016); Jeelani Bano, *Aiwan-e-Ghazal*, trans. B. Seetha Kumari (New Delhi: National Book Trust of India, 1998).

2. Mahua Sarkar, *Visible Histories, Disappearing Women: Producing Womanhood in Late Colonial Bengal* (Durham, NC: Duke University Press, 2008).

3. Dale Eickelman, *Knowledge and Power in Morocco: The Education of a Twentieth-Century Notable* (Princeton, NJ: Princeton University Press, 1985), 15.

4. Partha Chatterjee, *The Nation and Its Fragments: Colonial and Postcolonial Histories* (Princeton, NJ: Princeton University Press, 1993), 9.

5. The idea of the "New Woman" has generated significant debate in the western literary and public spheres, including the question about "who or what was the New Woman." For more on this, see Clare Francisca Mendes, "Representations of the New Woman in the 1890s Woman's Press" (PhD diss., University of Leicester, 2013). However, my idea of the New Woman is strictly confined to various vernacular sources in Telugu and Urdu in the context of the modern Telugu public sphere that emerged around 1910. For more on this discourse in Telugu and a few life stories from the city of Hyderabad, see Kannabiran, Vasantha and Olga, *Mahilāvaraṇaṁ* [Womanscape] (Secunderabad: Asmita Resource Centre for Women, 2001).

6. Siobhan Lambert-Hurley, *Elusive Lives: Gender, Autobiography, and the Self in Muslim South Asia* (Stanford, CA: Stanford University Press, 2018), 8.

7. Within the Hyderabadi public sphere as regards Telugu literature, the post-1940s writings advance this version of proto-feminism and identity-based literary works. Gogu Syamala, in her anthology of Dalit women's writings, discusses how Dalit women writers were engaging with these gender issues. See Gogu Syamala, *Nalla Poddu: Daḷita Strīla Sāhityaṁ 1921–2003* (Hyderabad: Hyderabad Book Trust, 2003), xv. Another Telugu feminist writer and theorist, Olga likewise observes such an early wave of feminism

in various literary writings. See Olga, *Sahita: Sāhitya Vyāsālu* (Hyderabad: Sweccha Prachurnalu, 2010).

In addition, during our conversations, Jeelani Bano likewise referred to the impact of the women writers who were affiliated with the Progressive Writers Association. Interview with author, Hyderabad, India, January 2019.

8. Although historians and literary critics from various sections of the organizations in the current Telangana state have published prolifically on the armed rebellion, very few of their writings focus on women's participation. However, the Telangana women activist and revolutionary writer, Ratna Mala, published a detailed essay on the Telangana armed rebellion entitled "Telangana Sayudha Poraatam – Streelu" [Telangana Armed Rebellion and Women], in *Sṛjana ādhunika Sāhitya Vēdika* [Modern Literary Forum] (Warangal: Sahitee Mitrulu, October 1982), 83–92, a monthly literary magazine.

9. Susie Tharu and Lalitha, *Women Writing in India: 600 BC to the Present* (New York: Feminist Press at the City University of New York, 1990), 39.

10. For an insider story of the feudal way of life, see Bilquis Jahan Khan, *A Song of Hyderabad: Memories of a World Gone By* (New York: Oxford University Press, 2010).

11. For an idea of how clubs and specifically the associational life of the "inner workings" of club life related to women, see Benjamin Cohen, *In the Club: Associational Life in Colonial South Asia* (UK: Manchester University Press, 2015), 147–64.

12. M. Badran, "Gender Activism: Feminists and Islamists in Egypt," in *Identity Politics and Women: Cultural Reassertions and Feminisms in International Perspective*, ed. V. M. Moghadam (Boulder, CO: Westview Press, 1994), 202–227. For more on this perspective, see Margot Badran, *Feminism in Islam: Religious and Secular Convergences* (Oxford: OneWorld, 2009).

13. Bano, *Aiwan-e-Ghazal*, 190.

14. Ibid., 346–347.

15. Interview with author, Hyderabad, India, January 25, 2019.

16. Lalitha in her pioneering work returns to this historical moment using the lens of feminism. K. Lalita, *Manaku Teliyani Mana Caritra: Telaṅgāṇā Raitāṅga Pōrāṭaṃlō Strīlu, Oka Sajīva Caritra* [The history we don't know: Women in Telangana armed rebellion, a live document] (Haidrābād: Strī Śakti Saṅghaṭana, 1986).

17. Bano, *Aiwan-e-Ghazal*, 102–103.

18. Puccalapalli Sundarayya, *Telaṅgāṇā Pōrāṭamlō Strīlu* (Haidarābād: Prajāśakti Bukhaus, 1999).

19. For a study on Pakistan as a political idea, see Faisal Devji, *Muslim Zion: Pakistan as a Political Idea* (Cambridge: Harvard University Press, 2013); David Gilmartin, "Partition, Pakistan and South Asian History: In Search of a Narrative," *Journal of Asian Studies* 57, no. 4 (November 1998): 1068–1095; Ayesha Jalal, *The Sole Spokesman: Jinnah, The Muslim League, and the Demand for Pakistan* (New York: Cambridge University Press, 1985).

20. Ambreen Hai, "Adultery behind Purdah and the Politics of Indian Muslim Nationalism in Zeenuth Futehally's Zohra," *Modern Fiction Studies* 59, no. 2 (2013): 317–345.

21. Ibid.

22. Suvir Kaul, "Women, Reform, and Nationalism in Three Novels of Muslim Life," in *A History of the Indian Novel in English*, ed. Ulka Anjaria (Cambridge: Cambridge University Press, 2015), 141.

23. Ibid., 145.

24. For a detailed story of Razia and Baji, see Lalitha et al., *We Were Making History*, 172–179.

25. Carla Petievich discusses the gender politics of ghazal in an essay entitled "Gender Politics and the Urdu Ghazal: Exploratory Observations on Rekhta versus Rekhti," *Indian Economic and Social History Review* 38, no. 3 (2001): 223–248.

26. Bano, *Aiwan-e-Ghazal*, 25.

27. Ibid.

28. Ibid.

29. Meera Kosambi, *Gender, Culture and Performance: Marathi Theatre and Cinema before Independence* (London: Routledge, 2015), 366.

30. Bano, *Aiwan-e-Ghazal*, 104.

31. Ibid., 105.

32. Ibid.

33. Ibid., 102–103.

34. Ibid., 118.

35. Ibid., 119.

36. Ibid., 127.

37. Ibid., 151.

38. Jawad Razvi's documentation of the leftist history in the princely state of Hyderabad, too, shows this dimension as it impacted the new generation

throughout Telangana. Jawad Razvi, *Haidarābād Samsthānamlō Rājakīya Caitanyaṁ: Vidyārthi-Yuvajanula Pātra* (Vijayawada: Visalandhra Publishing House, 1985).

39. Bano, *Aiwan-e-Ghazal*, 189.
40. Ibid.
41. Ibid., 190.
42. Ibid., 192.
43. Ibid., 193.
44. Ibid., 121.
45. Ibid., 117.
46. The interconnected histories of Telugu and Urdu have now also become key in the contemporary debate. For more discussion on this, see Chapter 4.
47. Interview with the author, Hyderabad, India, January 29, 2019.
48. Interview with the author, Hyderabad, India, January 30, 2019.
49. Bano, *Aiwan-e-Ghazal*, 102–103.
50. Bano's works are widely translated into the Telugu language, and her recent collection of short stories *Antā Nijamē Ceptā* [I will tell the truth], published in 2018, is the latest. In the preface to the 2018 collection, Bano briefly mentions the role of Hyderabad city and Telangana in the making of her personality. Jīlāni Bānō, *Antā Nijamē Ceptā: Jīlāni Bānō Kathalu*, trans. Mehak Hyderabadi (Hyderabad: Nava Chetana Publishing House, 2018).
51. Margrit Pernau, "Schools for Muslim Girls: A Colonial or An Indigenous Project? A Case Study of Hyderabad," *Oriente Moderno* 84, no. 1 (2004): 263–276.
52. Interview with the author, Hyderabad, India, January 29, 2020.
53. Jīlāni Bānō, *Bārish-e-Sang* (Dihlī: Ejūkeshnal Pablishing Hā'ūs, Aḥmadābād, 2018).
54. Interview with author, Hyderabad, India, January 25, 2014.
55. Jīlāni Bānō, *A Hail of Stones*, trans. Rajinder Singh Verma (New Delhi: Sterling Publishers, 1996).
56. Interview with the author, Hyderabad, India, January 29, 2019.
57. Sahitya Academy, November 11, 1999.
58. Conversation with Mehak Hyderabadi, January 26, 2019.
59. *The Hindu*, January 19, 2012.
60. Bānō, *Hail of Stones*, 21.
61. Interview with the author, January 26, 2014.
62. Zeenuth Futehally, *Zohra* (Delhi: Oxford University Press, 2008).

63. Pointing out such limitations in the novelistic representations of Hussain, Suvir Kaul noted:

> [However] the problem is that Purdah and Polygamy suggests none of the highly visible contemporary currents of "emerging modernity" (Gandhian and progressive politics, westernized education, movements for social reform) then changing the Hyderabadi and Indian public and domestic spheres, and therefore reads as a *cri de coeur* about the forms of women's oppression rather than as a novel that locates possibilities of change in an India mobilizing against colonialism, or indeed in parallel energies and relations within the household.

See Suvir Kaul, "Women, Reform, and Nationalism in Three Novels of Muslim Life," in *A History of the Indian Novel in English*, ed. Ulka Anjaria (New York: Cambridge University Press, 2015). Ambreen Hai has made similar observations about the novel *Zohra*:

> Given that *Zohra* was completed in the turmoil of these years, yet makes no mention of them, and ends in 1935 before the violent agitations and communal polarization began, several questions emerge. Once we understand the extreme exigency for the Indian Muslims in the time of *Zohra*'s completion and publication, what are we to make of its silence regarding those difficult years? If that silence could be understood as reluctance to address trauma, loss, and political controversy, how are we to read the shaping effect of the events of 1938-48 on the retrospective slant cast on the earlier period that the novel does address? How indeed does Zohra desire to remember and memorialize Hyderabadi culture and history prior to those years, to offer a different (forgotten) narrative of the 1920s and 1930s and suggest an alternative, more complex reading of at least some of its intellectuals and their families? (Hai, "Adultery behind Purdah," 317–345)

64. For a brief take on women's educational activities in Hyderabad, see Bhangya Bhukya, *History of Modern Telangana* (Hyderabad: Orient Blackswan, 2017), 87–88; Roosa, *The Quandary of the Qaum*, 1998.

65. Iqbalunissa Hussain, *Changing India: A Muslim Woman Speaks* (Karachi: Oxford University Press, 2015 [1940]), xiv.

66. Margarit Pernau, "Schools for Muslim Girls: A Colonial or An Indigenous Project? A Case Study of Hyderabad," in *Perspectives of Mutual Encounters in South Asian History, 1760–*1860, ed. Jamal Malik, *Social, Economic, and Political Studies of the Middle East and Asia*, vol. 73 (Leiden: Brill, 2000).

67. Margrit Pernau, "Schools for Muslim Girls."

68. Bano, *Aiwan-e-Ghazal*, 173.

69. Ibid., 183.

70. For more on this progressive resistance moment, see Mir and Mir, *Anthems of Resistance*, 26–49.

71. Narendra Luther explains, "Outside the fold of the Ittehad, there were three—or rather four—broad categories of Muslims who favored an independent, sovereign Hyderabad like Abid Hussain, Mohammad Siddiqui, Syed Hasan and others. The 'Nizam's Subjects League' was their forum." Narender Luther, *Hyderabad: A Biography* (New Delhi: Oxford University Press, 2006), 311.

72. Luther notes:

> A younger lot was being nurtured by the secular and letist writings of Jawaharlal Nehru, Jaya Prakash Narayanan, and the teachings of newspapers like the payam, the Nigar, and the Imroz. It also drew inspiration from international events and progressive thought reflected in socialism and anti-Fascism. The Russian Revolution and its achievements had fired their young minds. Some of them, like Alam Khundmiri, Syed Ibrahim, Ahsan Ali Mirza, Gulam Hyder, Raj Bahadur Gour, Onkar Prasad, Srinivas Lahoti, Jawad Razvi, and Mirza Hyder Hussain, set up the "Comrades' Association" in 1939. Makhdoom Mohiuddin, a lecturer in the City College, and a poet was their leader. (Luther, *Hyderabad*, 312)

73. Tarun Saint, *Witnessing Partition: Memory, History and Fiction* (London: Routledge, 2010), 131.

74. Sheela Raj, *Medievalism to Modernism: Socio-economic and Cultural History of Hyderabad 1869–1911* (Bombay: Popular Prakashan, 1987), 247.

75. Asha Islam Nayeem and Avril A. Powell, "Redesigning the Zenana: Domestic Education in Eastern Bengal in the Early Twentieth Century," in *Rhetoric and Reality: Gender and the Colonial Experience in South Asia*, ed. Avril Powell and Siobhan Lambert-Hurley (New Delhi: Oxford University Press, 2006), 50–81.

76. M. A. Moid, "Muslim Perceptions and Responses in Post-Police Action Contexts in Hyderabad," *Journal of Deccan Studies* 6, no. 2 (2008): 52–74.

77. Moid, "Muslim Perceptions and Responses," 63.

78. Interview with author, Hyderabad, India, January 21, 2019.

79. Jaini Mallayya is another prominent Urdu activist in the then public sphere who promoted literacy among Muslim and non-Muslim women between 1948 and 1955. I will discuss his interventions at more length in Chapter 4 where I address Urdu–Telugu discourses related to the rise of a post-Police Action Muslim public sphere.

80. Hussain, *Changing India*, 23.

81. As mentioned earlier, Suvir Kaul critiques, that this novel

> suggests none of the highly visible contemporary currents of 'emerging modernity' (Gandhian and progressive politics, westernized education, movements for social reform) then changing the Hyderabadi and Indian public and domestic spheres and thereby reads as a *cri de coeur* about the forms of women's oppression rather than a novel that locates possibilities of change in an India mobilizing against colonialism, or indeed in parallel energies and relations within the household. It may well be that Hussain's observational realism was so scrupulous that she could not, in 1944, see progressive change in the public sphere altering the traditionalism of a rentier family, whose properties, the diminishing remnants of a feudal inheritance, insulated them from contact with modernizing political or professional energies in Hyderabad or in India. (Kaul, "Women, Reform, and Nationalism," 137)

82. Mushirul Hassan, *Legacy of a Divided Nation: India's Muslims Since Independence* (Boulder, CO: Westview Press, 1997), 178.

83. Karen Deutch Karlekar, *In a Minority: Essays on Muslim Women in India*, ed. Zoya Hasan and Ritu Menon (New Delhi: Oxford University Press, 2005), 232.

4

FOR THE LOVE OF URDU

RELOCATING URDU IN POSTCOLONIAL HYDERABAD

When I met 90-year-old Jaini Mallaya Gupta on January 23, 2019, at his Hyderabad apartment, he had just finished reading the Urdu daily newspaper, *Siāsat*—his morning ritual of almost seventy years. Not surprisingly, our conversations found a relevant beginning with his long journey with the *Siāsat*, a paper launched in the aftermath of the Police Action.[1] For Mallayya Gupta, reading *Siāsat* was a major source of his passionate engagements with the progressive literature in Urdu and the rise of Muslim discourse against the background of the Police Action. He said:

> At that moment of excessive violence, Urdu was more than a language for us. In an endless tirade of hate speech and religious hatred, the very utterance of any Urdu word was indeed a political statement. On the one hand, it had the seal of authoritarianism as the Nizam's administrative language of the Hyderabad state and then it also became the language of progressivism and resistance.

"Look," he insisted, "we used the same weapon to fight against the Nizam and all that gruesome violence of the Police Action." Elaborating further, he continued:

> Despite all the violence, we had two great sources of inspiration. First, contemporary Urdu writings including the short fiction from Urdu and their translations into Telugu, and secondly, the *Siāsat* daily

Urdu newspaper. Both have taught me religious tolerance and love for humanity. They both played a great role in the times of extreme violence and, no doubt, my entire understanding about Marxism and progressivism comes from reading those Urdu writings and the *Siāsat*.[2]

For many young political activists of 1940s Telangana, the progressive literature (Gupta used the Urdu equivalent throughout our conversations, *taraqqī-pasand*), particularly in Urdu, was a major source of inspiration and political resistance. Gupta was barely eighteen when he started a reading group in his hometown of Nalgonda in the late 1940s (Figure 4.1). It was a humble beginning that attracted a significant number of the new-generation writers and readers who had just started engaging with a vibrant political and cultural climate in the princely state of Hyderabad. Major trends and writing modes in contemporary Urdu literature provided a paradigm for most of these writers and readers who grew up in the late 1940s and played crucial roles in the early phase of various publications and reading groups in Telangana.

Figure 4.1   Jaini Mallayya Gupta
Source: Photo by Vommy Ramesh Babu.

As the reading group became more recognized, the Razakars and the state police began to harass him, and he was forced to migrate to the city of Hyderabad.[3] Detailing his underground activities in the late 1940s, he said:

> Like me, many leftist writers and activists had migrated to the city at that point and they became popular by using pseudonyms. Hyderabad was like a sanctuary as it could hide us in its remote neighborhoods where we were supported by local Muslim community too. But we all became really closer to each other and more connected to the Urdu literary culture that indeed provided a model for our activities.[4]

Even now, Gupta's love and passion for Urdu language and literature is boundless, and he continues to read Urdu writings every day, along with the *Siāsat*. According to him:

> *Siāsat* and the other local Urdu newspapers were more than any newspaper, and Urdu was more than a language. During the military invasion, it was almost like a resistance movement that focused more on rebuilding the Muslim community using education, creative writing, and engaging with the newly available print sources along with other welfare activities. More than anything, they used Urdu as a weapon of Progressivism and a language of secularism.[5]

Then he explained in detail how the teams of the readers' clubs used Urdu literature as a device to rebuild the Hindu–Muslim community during and after the Police Action of late 1940s Hyderabad.

Within the cultural and religious milieu of Hyderabad state, Gupta's work remains crucial even now.[6] His life story resonates with many activists and writers who still resist the language politics that disrupt the much-admired *tehzeeb* (composite culture) of the Telangana state. As contemporary Telugu literary activists continue to return to the Muslim question in the aftermath of post-2014 Telangana politics, this moment of the Police Action—which was a major event in Gupta's life—is being replayed and revisited. Gupta's words resonate with the larger discussions about three key developments: language politics in South Asia, the arrival of modernity, and discourses around the Hindu–Muslim divide.[7] Although the debates between Hindi and Urdu are still relevant in this case, several other studies in the context of Hyderabad state likewise discuss this communal divide at length.[8]

More relevant for our purposes is the study by Kavita Datla who specifically analyzed how Urdu language had developed a secular idiom in the context of Hyderabad, particularly around the 1930s as a result of the establishment of Osmania University and other educational initiatives.[9]

In her argument about the idea of Urdu literary modernity, Jennifer Dubrow describes a variety of developments in the Urdu culture that led to the rise of modern prose.[10] A similar paradigm could be extended to the history of exchanges between Telugu and Urdu beginning with everyday life and extending to a broader composite culture that is considered to be one of the hallmarks of Hyderabadi cosmopolitanism and pluralism.[11] Whereas several studies describe such a collaborative literary and cultural dialogue between Telugu and Urdu, the other side of the production of this pluralist culture—the reception and its effects—remains understudied. Gupta's interconnected journey with Urdu and Telugu gives us valuable information about this other side of literary production, and about the exchanges between the two languages specifically in the cities of Hyderabad and Telangana.

Many oral accounts, including the above one, made me ask myself numerous questions related to linguistic histories, literary politics, and the Muslim networks of Hyderabad state, thus compelling me to revisit the earliest memories of reading publications such as Biruduraju Ramaraju's *Qutub Sultānulu – Ṣāhī Andhra Sanskṛti* (The Qutub Shahi sultans and Andhra culture);[12] *Makhdūm Kavita*, a Telugu translation of the Urdu poems of Makhdoom Mohiuddin;[13] the Telugu poet Dasarathi's *Yātrā Smṛti* (The memories of a journey); and, finally, Adluri Ayodhya Rama Kavi's long folk-narrative *Haidarābādupai Pōlīsu Carya: Burra Katha* (Police Action of Hyderabad: Burra katha folk narrative).[14]

Thinking through these multiple dimensions, I also realized that these texts demonstrate four totally diverse viewpoints as related to the linguistic history of Hyderabad—not only cultural viewpoints but also political ones. The long journey of Hyderabad-Deccan from 1518 to 1948 is one of enormous diversity and various political shifts. The first text, *Qutub Ṣāhī Sultānulu – Andhra Sanskṛti*, is a collection of literary essays about the literary contributions of the Golconda sultanate (1518–1687).[15] The Deccan historian H. K. Sherwani describes the nature of the cultural uplift inspired by the Golconda and specifically mentions how the Sultanate promoted "a complete understanding between the Hindus and the Muslims in spite of constant conflicts with Vijayanagar."[16] Such understanding also had an influential bearing on their linguistic perceptions. According to the historian

Richard Eaton, the Golconda sultans were also famous as "Telugu Sultans," as Telugu was the language most widely spoken in the region, and because the Qutub Shahi rulers made it a mission to promote the Telugu language and literature.[17] As Biruduraju Ramaraju explains in his book, the Qutub Shahi Telugu literature, known as *acca telugu* (pure Telugu), and its politics of de-Sanskritization produced a new repertoire of narrative and stylistic tropes. Rather than depending more on Sanskrit, these poets were successful in mixing words taken from other languages including Persian and Urdu. Later, this phase of the de-Sanskritization of Telangana literature after the 1900s opened up a creative space for the blend of Telugu and Urdu literary paradigms. For me, who grew up witnessing various forms of hate speech between Telugu and Urdu, Hindus and Muslims, it was fascinating to read something that speaks about the blend of Muslim and Hindu religions and languages. Also interesting to me was that this Telugu book was published by an Urdu organization called Idar-e-Adabiyat-e-Urdu (Urdu Literary Publishing House, founded in 1931).

In light of the divide created between these two languages after the Police Action and the formation of the Telugu linguistic state of Andhra Pradesh, these exchanges demonstrate a different history. In contemporary politics of fundamentalism and religious conflict, these dynamics present a case of what the historian Margrit Pernau calls "a cosmopolitan and tolerant Islam."[18] Along a similar line of argument, historian Seema Alavi, too, articulates Muslim cosmopolitanism as a consensus in rituals and devotion and one inspired by liberal reforms.[19] Various examples from the Hyderabad state and Telangana build up on such possibilities of convergence and consensus around a historical moment in order to comprehend and deal with a crisis that is now laden with a greater amount of hatred and misinformation.

Re-reading Biruduraju's text in the wake of the contemporary language politics of Urdu and Telugu raises an important question about how, after the Police Action, the Hyderabad state was portrayed as the "enemy" of the Telugu language and how gradually Urdu became an alien or "foreign" language.[20] Dasarathi's aforementioned autobiography *Yātrā Smṛti* narrates some of these language politics between Urdu and Telugu.[21] Even in the scholarly debates on the composite culture of Hyderabad state, the mutuality of Urdu and Telugu remains undermined. Poets such as Dasarathi return to this dimension not theoretically but through the lens of everyday life and Hyderabadi culture. The segments from his autobiography compel us to think about how the community of Hyderabad state was adapting and appropriating the literary paradigms of modern Urdu in many ways including prose, poetry, and literary criticism. Despite his emphasis on the Telangana rebellion and anti-Nizam perspective, Dasarathi's life story offers testimony about multiple dimensions of the Urdu literary sphere that emerged in the wake of the Progressivist movement in the city and then gradually spread to the remotest parts of the region. Rather than as a literary piece, I read this more as a historical document that explains the archaeology of emerging knowledge systems in Hyderabad state, particularly after the 1940s—the long decade that witnessed the metamorphosis of the Deccan and Telangana.

Simultaneously, I was also captivated by the Telugu translations of the Urdu poems of Makhdoom Mohiuddin (Figure 4.2) which I consider a key aspect in the making of my own self as a poet. The collection of his poems, *Makhdūm Kavita* (The poems of Makhdoom), was published in Telugu and ran into several editions.[22] Early in my life, it was one of my favorite

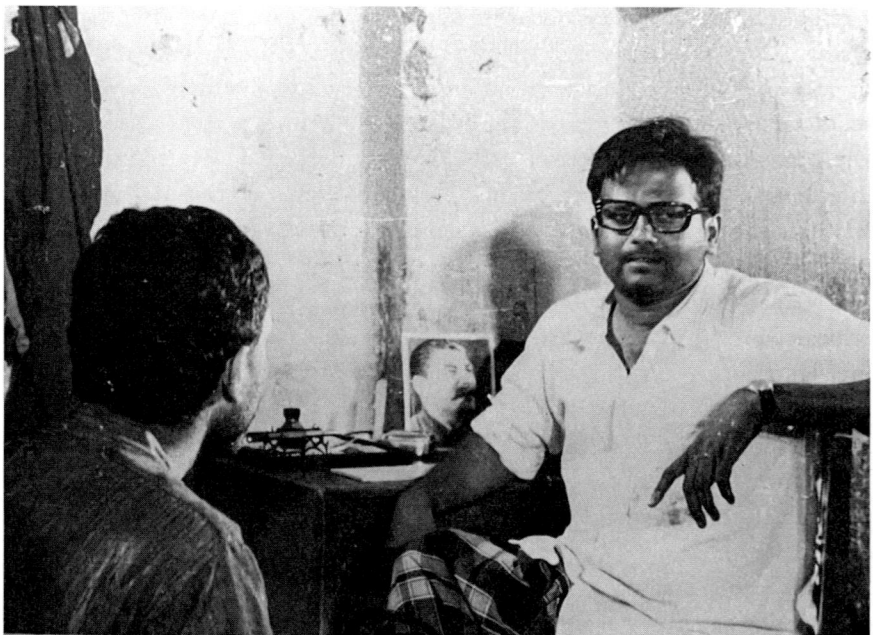

Figure 4.2 Makhdoom Mohiuddin remains a symbol of a progressive Muslim even in contemporary imaginary. Ram Gopal as Makhdoom in a Telangana landmark movie, *Maa Bhoomi*, 1979.

Source: Photo by Kamal Naik.

collections of poetry to read. While reading repeatedly, I recognized many continuities between Dasarathi and Makhdoom's literary and political careers. Makhdoom's short poems, beautifully translated into Telugu (my father and Progressivist writer Kaumudi was one of the four translators of this volume) made me realize the potential of a literary piece that centers on the local history, particularly, Hyderabad and Telangana. Makhdoom's life story and his engagements with the Telugu public sphere speak more about the Telugu and Urdu interactions too.

Within the scholarly debate about Urdu and its role in Hyderabad, this dimension is still a major lacuna. In 2013, Kavita Datla analyses how Urdu was successful in promoting a language of secular Islam in Hyderabad.[23] From the textual choices and literary practices that I will discuss in this book, I argue that this creation of a secular language and intellectual sphere is incomplete if we do not consider the role of Urdu and Telugu interactions. Discussing this specific dimension of mutuality between Urdu and Telugu, this chapter shows that in the case of Hyderabad and Telangana, such a refashioning of the modern self and its being and belonging was never a singular or homogeneous process. For many of these post-1930s literary figures, the question of identity and belonging was not about a prescriptive religion, but "an ethical inheritance," and the proper understanding of the key concept of ethical conduct, or *adab*, that has both ethical and literary interpretations.[24] Historian Sarah Waheed's 2021 work on Urduphone writings discusses how progressivist writings were deeply rooted in the long tradition of *adab*.[25]

Many of my interlocutors speak passionately both about the literary and ethical value of *adab* within the Telangana literary culture and also everyday life. Jaini Mallayya's life story and cultural activism demonstrate the moral efficacy of this term. While Gupta is one of the few living witnesses of the Police Action, this chapter is not entirely about him. Most of his ideas about Urdu and Muslim discourse during the Police Action can be corroborated through the writings of two of his contemporaries, both celebrated writers and cultural historians: Dasarathi Krishnamacharya (1925–1987) and Samala Sadasiva (1928–2012), whom Gupta fondly remembers. These three personalities, I argue, represent three dimensions of this broad discourse centered on Urdu modernity as it affected the Telugu literary sphere: production, transmission, and reception. Influenced by the Urdu language and cultural practices, this triangle of literary sphere was in dialogue with the rise of the modern public culture in Hyderabad and Telangana.

Gupta's story, along with those of Dasarathi and Sadasiva, further enriches the understanding of the Police Action, Muslim politics, and the cultural dynamics of Urdu at a time when the idea of Telugu linguistic nationalism engulfed this region in the 1950s. Given the recent debates on the politicization of Urdu and its forced separation from its history of diversity and pluralism, this story of Urdu from Hyderabad offers particular insights into two aspects of this dynamic: first, how Urdu works even in a situation of overwhelming politicization by forces of Hindu nationalism; and second, the extended realm of Urdu beyond the linguistic limits of Urdu, meaning in a non-Urdu setting such as Telugu. Whereas most studies and debates about Urdu and Muslimness are limited to north India, this chapter turns our attention to locating Urdu within the South Indian public sphere with an emphasis on Hyderabadi Muslim discourses. The two autobiographies and the life story of Gupta, as I discuss in this chapter, describe a process that made Urdu an influential language and cultural system, as it played a crucial role in the new selfhood and community formation in the local history of Hyderabad and the Telangana state. Like many writers and activists that we met in this book, the life and work of these three prominent figures underwent deep transformations through their engagement with Urdu and the rise of new Muslim discourses in the turbulent 1940s and the era of the Police Action. In fact, Dasarathi, Sadasiva, and Gupta signify multiple manifestations of the same story: being a poet, Dasarathi's life tells the story of the production of a literary culture that has deep roots in the Urdu culture, and we learn about how Telugu writers repositioned their writings on the Urdu models. Being a critic and cultural historian, Sadasiva devoted his entire life to documenting the other side of this story—the dynamics of the literary transmission with detailed descriptions of the reading public as related to the Urdu writings in Telangana. By contrast, being a political activist Gupta offers insights into the history of reception, stressing how these two languages and their literatures journeyed together in times of political violence and religious conflict.

In what follows, I first introduce the two autobiographies of Dasarathi and Sadasiva. I then connect their life stories with the cultural activism as documented in my elaborate interviews with Gupta along with other witnesses of the Police Action. Whereas the autobiographies of Dasarathi and Sadasiva were both well circulated and debated in the Telugu literary sphere, Gupta's story is, in a way, a heretofore unwritten autobiography that I documented through my extensive interviews in 2019.

Throughout their lives, Dasarathi and Sadasiva have documented or reconstructed the key dimensions of the history of the Police Action and the Muslim question with an emphasis on the language politics of Urdu and Telugu. Based on their autobiographical writings and personal memories, I shape my argument around three central ideas: first, the cultural memory of the Urdu legacy in the times of the 1948 Police Action; second, the alternative discourses initiated by the mutuality of Urdu and Telugu; and finally, the production and transmission of a new genre of autobiography as a marker of new consciousness generated by these exchanges. These three personalities grew up not only witnessing the religious conflict and hate speech as an immediate consequence of the Police Action; they also unveil the history of local resistance as demonstrated in the literary domain and the arena of cultural activism, thus disrupting the mainstream historiography. They were in dialogue with the new tools of modernity, such as the multi-lingual educational system, religious reformism, and political resistance, which were deeply grounded in the cultural specifics of Hyderabad state and the early Telangana activism initiated by various political and literary organizations.[26] Before I elaborate on the alternative discourses engendered by the autobiographical narratives of Dasarathi, Sadasiva, and Gupta, I begin by introducing these three personalities within the Hyderabadi context.

THE SMALL BEGINNINGS OF A LONG CONVERSATION

In the first week of September 2006, it was drizzling in Adilabad, a town bordering the present states of Telangana and Maharashtra. During field research in this region for my previous book, *The Festival of Pīrs*, I ran into Samala Sadasiva, whom I know for more than two decades as a writer and friend. Our easy banter that day surprisingly turned into a larger and more serious conversation. Having met him several times before, I was aware that conversations with him tend to be protracted, as he fills every *chai* hour with numerous anecdotes about Urdu poets and couplets. This time, however, Sadasiva took me to a different time period—the Police Action which he called *miliṭarī durākramaṇa* in Telugu, meaning "military invasion." Recollecting the trauma and its shocking consequences, Sadasiva said:

> There was some undeclared censorship or a selective silence about the police action and usually nobody would dare to touch that particular

moment of the history of the Hyderabad state. We started pretending silence about the entire event and its consequences, as it hurts to remember certain things. We just learned to forget it quickly![27]

Of many pieces of that conversation, one stayed with me for a long time, when Sadasiva recalled:

When we were growing up, we were in an exciting *caurasta* (intersection) of languages and literatures. Between 1948 and 1956, that intersection came to an end, and each one of us funneled into a narrow lane of one language and one literature—Telugu for Hindus, and Urdu for Muslims! Similarly, the Hindu–Muslim dialogue too! We ended up in a lane where we could not even imagine that once upon a time we all shared the same histories and cultural moments. Most importantly, the *adab* of shared values between Hindus and Muslims. Whatever the delightful essence of our shared culture, that has gone forever now! We lost that compassionate love and started living with an unforgiving hate![28]

Dasarathi shared similar concerns about the loss of the same intersection of the shared literary and religious life, particularly, the exchange that was shared mostly through Urdu language and Muslim traditions in Hyderabad. Recounting the stories about the mutuality between Telugu and Urdu, Dasarathi's autobiography, *Yātrā Smṛti*, documents this separation repeatedly as he speaks about everyday life and the literary cultures of Hyderabad state. Several autobiographical writings published in Hyderabad and Telangana state endeavor to convey that intense angst of linguistic and cultural partition as experienced by many personalities such as Dasarathi, Sadasiva, and Gupta. Narrating the Telangana cultural and political awakening of the 1940s, most of these writings detail various historical moments related to the Police Action. In their writings that span from the 1940s until their deaths, these autobiographers offer testimonials for how the Police Action had forcefully erased the practices of the shared literary and religious culture in Hyderabad state specifically in the 1940s and later solidified with the formation of Telugu as the official language (*adhikāra bhāṣa*) of the state. In the process, they also narrate the life stories of various Telangana-based personalities that relate to the diverse manifestations of multilingualism that adapted Urdu paradigms in the making of their new identities.

Undoubtedly, Dasarathi and Sadasiva too found distinctive ways to cherish the memories of those days throughout their literary careers, though they never failed to remind us of the growing chasm between Telugu and Urdu cultures, in other words, between Hindus and Muslims.[29] For me, their story is not merely about the waning beauty of Urdu in Deccan but also about the fluctuating interactions between Muslims and Hindus. Throughout their narratives, they were both trying to delve deeper into the interactions between Hindus and Muslims symbolized in their love for Urdu. Nevertheless, with an unwavering determination and profound devotion to Urdu, they made this story an extremely captivating and memorable journey that reflected the traumatic times of post-1948 communal conflicts and violence. In the process, they indeed set an example for an ideal cultural dynamic and shared the remedies for sustaining the love for a shared community life.

Born into an extremely traditional *śrī vaiṣṇava* Brahmin family in a remote village in the Warangal district in 1925, Dasarathi began writing poetry when he was in high school in the town of Khammam. This medium-sized town has been the scene of many historical moments since the late 1920s. Dasarathi was in his prime during the times of the Police Action and the Telangana armed rebellion led by the Communist Party. He was one of the earliest generations of writers who were imprisoned for their political views, and his autobiography narrates those prison experiences in detail. Later, Dasarathi published extensively about Urdu literature, and most importantly, his translation of the great Urdu poet Ghalib became popular and ran into several editions. Dasarathi's translation activity also tells us about the importance of Urdu literature in the Telangana literary sphere, and it celebrates the times when Dasarathi was considered to be one of the cultural bridges between the two languages, cultures, and religions in Hyderabad. Dasarathi was a prolific writer until his death in 1987 and published numerous collections of poetry along with a few short stories, plays, and translations from Urdu.

Whereas Dasarathi focused on creative writing including poetry and poetry translations, Sadasiva intentionally blazed a new path by turning his attention to personal essays, a genre that emerged as an immediate outcome of the new journalism and print media in Telangana in the late 1940s. Sadasiva also started writing sketches about Urdu poets and various Telangana personalities who specifically contributed to the bilingual cultural history of Telangana. Like Dasarathi, Sadasiva first published his personal narratives in a newspaper and only later in books. Sadasiva also began his literary career around the time of the Police Action and published extensively, beginning with poetry and then moving to various genres of prose including the autobiography *Yādi* (remembrance). Although he began his career with creative writing such as classical metrical poetry, very soon, he realized the importance of writing more about Urdu–Telugu interactions. Having settled as an employee in the department of education, Sadasiva travelled widely in the districts of Telangana and had close connections with local literary figures who helped him document various marginalized life stories. Born in 1928 in the village of Tenugu Palle in Adilabad district, he was actively writing and lecturing until his death in 2012.

Despite different personal backgrounds and regional and family histories, both autobiographies portray the turbulent period of the Police Action. Both tried to capture those moments of the rise of a new Muslim discourse defined by the shifting Hindu–Muslim encounters, and Telugu and Urdu identities. Providing a testimony to the making of the distinctive Hyderabadi literary culture, the autobiographical genre as developed by these two writers has also introduced a new mode of prose writing, which in turn opened a space for the Telangana identity that evolved in the 1940s. In times when most prose writings in Telugu were endeavoring to create a new or alternative idiom for the Telangana historiography, this space initiated more experimentation. During this period when printing presses, small magazines, and readers clubs were also spreading to the remote villages of Telangana, several writers turned to personal essays and other autobiographical modes of writing.[30]

Within this new realm, Dasarathi and Sadasiva were equally successful in creating a cultural discourse with a double movement between the personal and political by engaging the concepts of nationalism, post-colonialism, and Telangana cultural activism. While both of them spend a good amount of time describing personal matters including family relations and inner circles, many political topics such as governmental changes, public administrative affairs, caste, and religious issues unavoidably become a major part of their autobiographical writing. In the process, they also pushed themselves into a center of the growing movement of identitarian writing that provided tools of cultural resistance during this period. In multiple ways, the personal stories of Dasarathi and Sadasiva are firmly rooted in the history of Hyderabad state, and they have parallels with the timelines of the local and global histories, beginning with the Persian links of the Qutub Shahis, the 1884 declaration of Urdu as an administrative language, and the formation of Osmania

University—all in some way related to contemporary Muslim history of Hyderabad.[31] In addition, they also provided detailed descriptions of the early Telangana public sphere, including the establishment of the Telugu libraries, writers' associations, readers' clubs, the beginnings of Telugu and Urdu journalism, the printing presses, the early publications of various Telangana-based publishers, and the establishment of several literary and cultural organizations. Since 2000, most of these aspects are now again part of the discourse as a result of the political movement advocating for a separate Telangana state. Nevertheless, one of the prominent features that made the life stories of Dasarathi and Sadasiva intensely effective was their involvement with locally produced Persian and Urdu cultures in Telangana.

The first time I met Dasarathi, he was a guest speaker at our middle school anniversary. Despite my inability to grasp what he was talking about, I remember him sprinkling Urdu couplets into his conversations with my father and his colleague in the activities of the Progressive Writer's Association between 1950 and 1987. In my child's world of Deccani Urdu and Telugu oral poems and folk tales, he was a delightful presence with refreshing ghazal recitals and fascinating stories about his Urdu literary friends. When he passed away in 1987, my father said: "You know, he was like an innocent kid throughout his life—never influenced by any impurities of politics!" Yet, when I began to reflect on his various works in Telugu, mainly his autobiography, I started realizing that, contrary to my father's evaluation, Dasarathi was in fact not that "innocent kid": he had become stuck in the turbulent times of his twenties for his entire life, tied totally to the political environment before the Police Action. Several events narrated by Dasarathi describe the beginnings of the Razakar militarism that also affected the local literary culture. For the first time, we find evidence of the Razakars' interventions in the Telugu literary realm—he explains how the Razakars interrupted the historical event of 1944 when the Andhra Saraswata Parishat (Andhra Literary Council) held its first Telangana literary conference in Warangal. The Razakars set fire to the venue to scare off the writers. Yet even such violence failed to stop Suravaram Pratapa Reddy, the president of the Parishath, from conducting the event. According to Dasarathi, Suravaram openly challenged the Razakars by holding the conference successfully—an incredible political statement at that time.[32]

The Razakar militarism was one of the major factors in creating an anti-Muslim discourse even within Telugu literary circles. Like many poets and writers of the 1940s in Telangana, Dasarathi's early literary life was hugely influenced by the Urdu and Persian cultures. This crucial part of literary history was either silenced or marginalized by the hegemonic narrativization of Telugu nationalism and the formation of the Telugu linguistic state of Andhra Pradesh. In addition, both Urdu and Persian were now marked as "Islamic," and their influence was defined as a dark moment that disrupted the continuity of the history of Telugu literature and culture.[33] In times when British colonialism and its forms of knowledge defined the entire reach of modernity, these two autobiographies opened a window onto a parallel world of Telangana modernity that contested the English-centered colonial modernity—which I will discuss in the last section of this chapter. In the next section, I introduce Dasarathi's text and its role in the contextualization of the Hyderabadi Muslim discourse.

FACING THE TRAUMA: DASARATHI'S JOURNEY
THROUGH VIOLENCE AND RESISTANCE

"Why does Dasarathi speak so much about the Police Action and Urdu poetry? Don't you think he is unclear about his perception of the Nizam and Urdu?" It was an immediate response when Dasarathi first started publishing his autobiography in *Andhra Jyothi*, one of the largest circulated weeklies in Telugu in the late 1980s (Figure 4.3). Since it was a weekly feature, as I continued to read, at least a few contemporary writers continued to ask the same question. At this point, many had started to believe that the Police Action was a "reasonable and much-needed political decision in the wake of the Nizam's authoritarian rule." As they explained: "The entire Muslim community in Hyderabad state was heading towards absolute anarchy and unprecedented communal violence." They also subscribed to the idea of Urdu as a "language of Muslims" (*turakala bhāṣa*).[34]

These three misconceptions, which were also depicted in some literary narratives, in many ways led to a bias against local Muslims irrespective of their nationalist, secularist, or leftist ideologies. In my conversations with several Muslim writers and poets who have been now writing in Telugu since the 1980s, there was a consensus about how "Urdu" and "Muslim" were collapsed or conflated into one idea of an anti-Hindu debate after the Police Action. Divi Kumar, an activist and the editor of the *Prajā Sāhiti* literary magazine said:

Figure 4.3 Dasarathi Krishnamacharya, Nerella Venu Madhav, and C. Narayana Reddy

Source: Courtesy of Dasarathi's family.

The Police Action has become a measure for the patriotism of a Muslim. If you condemn the brutality of the Union army that represented the Indian government, you're traitor or pro-Pakistan. If you're supporting the Nizam, you are an anti-communist. By all means, Muslims were considered evil, it does not matter if they are lower class or upper class, meaning *azlaf* or *ashraf*. Even secular progressive Muslims were labelled *jihadi*s. Many aspects of Muslim cultures, such as Urdu, the public religious festivals including Muharram, and even talking about Muslim writings in Telugu have become "anti-national" or Jihadist.

It's not surprising now that even the so-called progressive Hindus view the Police Action as a legitimate act and the only solution for the second wave of the Partition in Hyderabad.[35]

At least for some of them, the Police Action was brutal, and memories of it should be erased to avoid inciting communal tensions. However, this mode of approach was nothing new and Dasarathi himself during the time of the publication of his autobiography experienced similar encounters. In one of our conversations, he shared such concerns with me and said: "How many of those memories could you erase? And why should you erase a memory at all?" And, in his quite natural poetic way, he said, "*smṛtiki lēdu mṛti, vismṛti*" (Memory has no death and no erasure). Dasarathi's autobiography, I argue, is a deliberate effort to retrieve and reconstruct the memory of the Police Action—yet with an emphasis on the legacy of Urdu in Hyderabad state. Nevertheless, Dasarathi's life story is not merely confined to the narration of the Urdu cultural practices; he also details multiple experiences of violence, Hindu–Muslim interactions, the beginnings of the new print culture, and most importantly, his schooling and the migration from a mufassil area to Hyderabad. Despite his exceptional accomplishments, Dasarathi's experiences reflect many contemporaries' lives of his generation who were fighting against the conservative social and political order of their day. With a deeper empathy toward these developments, his insights problematize some of the normative narrativizations of the Police Action that were grounded in an anti-Muslim discourse.

Despite his family background of a middle-class Vaishnava, Dasarathi was one of the beneficiaries of a multilingual and multicultural environment of the princely state of Hyderabad that defined his everyday life and work until his death in 1987. Throughout his autobiography, Dasarathi narrates how this pluralist milieu made his personality similar to that of most of his contemporaries in the late 1940s. He belongs to the generation that the literary scholar A. K. Ramanujan describes as follows:

> After the nineteenth century, no significant Indian writer lacks any of the three traditions: the regional mother-tongue, the pan-Indian (Sanskritic, and in the case of Urdu and Kashmiri, the Perseo-Arabic as well), and the western (mostly English). Thus, Indian modernity is a response not only to contemporary events but to at least three pasts. Poetic, not necessarily scholarly, assimilation of all these three resources in various individual ways seems indispensable.[36]

Dasarathi's engagements with Urdu, Farsi, and English literature, and their assimilation into his personality, both personally and scholarly, demonstrate the pluralist culture that he inherited from his contemporaries including Suravaram Pratapa Reddy (1896–1953), Burgula Ramakrishna Rao (1899–1967), and Makhdoom Mohiuddin (1908–1969). Dasarathi's school days in the town of Khammam likewise embody a shared space where multiple languages and ideological worldviews intersected—a cultural ethos which Sadasiva describes as a "friendly intersection." During his school days, he was active in left-leaning political groups, and this motivated him to join the freedom movement as well. As the state-sponsored oppression and violence were extremely unbearable in mufassil places such as Khammam, he moved to the city of Hyderabad. In 1947, while the entire nation was joyously celebrating the newly gained independence from the British, the Nizam government of Hyderabad jailed Dasarathi for his ferocious speeches and poetry recitals. The state police seized all his books, manuscripts, and he was forbidden to use either pen or pencil during his prison time. Consequently, following ghazal tradition, he started reciting couplets and scribbling them on the prison walls with a piece of charcoal. When he was released from prison, he and his friends wrote down all these couplets from memory. Indeed, Dasarathi's prison narratives, some of them as told in this autobiographical text, deserve careful study too. As he describes in one chapter, "The oppression was so intense that it's comparable only to a Nazi concentration camp. Actually the entire Telangana was a concentration camp."[37]

How then did Dasarathi's autobiographical narrative depict different manifestations of Urdu connected to the Hyderabad-based Muslim discourse, public aspects that illustrate the impact of the Police Action and the rise of Hyderabad as a cultural center in the late 1940s? This autobiographical text deals with three major features: first, early schooling that draws on the tensions between traditionalism and modernity; second, the Urdu-centered literary and cultural personalities; and third, the common ground of Urdu and the Telugu literary sphere. Throughout these shifts in his literary career, Dasarathi unreservedly embraces the idea of Urdu as a tool of progressivism, as reflected in leftist Urdu poets such as Kaifi Azmi, Faiz Ahmed Faiz, Kaifi Azmi, and Makhdoom Mohiuddin.[38] Many examples and experiences about which he writes demonstrate his intellectual progression, and the diverse influences on him, whether Urdu practices initiated by the Progressive Writers movement in Hyderabad or national events. The entire autobiography exemplifies the making of the rebellious worldview of his generation, a generation that was struggling between traditionalism and resistance in the wake of the Telangana uprising.

Via the sixty chapters of this autobiographical work, Dasarathi documents sixty different memories of the Telangana uprising. All in one way or another refer to the violent Police Action or the historical events of Hyderabad. Unlike Sadasiva, who narrated his story in fragments that lacked any chronological order, Dasarathi's chapters follow a clear chronology. Nonetheless, Dasarathi describes various key historical moments that in some way locate Urdu within Hyderabad state and the Telugu cultural sphere. His narration of the Police Action and Hindu–Muslim interactions strengthens the entire discourse as he leads us to the final point of the rise of the modern Telangana (*ādhunika Telangāṇa*) in the late 1940s.

EARLY SCHOOLING AND THE POLITICS OF LANGUAGE

Dasarathi's *Yātrā Smṛti* (Figure 4.4) begins by recounting that the linguistic tension of his early days of schooling was a combination of Sanskrit, Persianized Urdu, and Sanskritized Telugu, while his everyday language was

Figure 4.4 Title image of the *Yātrā Smṛti*

Source: Courtesy of Dasarathi's family.

a hybrid of the spoken Urdu and Telugu that he tried to emulate in his later writings. He recounts:

> At home my father forced Sanskrit upon us, even in everyday conversations! He would never use Telugu even to ask questions such as "where are you going?" He would always say "*twam kuthra gacchasi.*" I literally hated that linguistic fundamentalism! And, at the school my classes would begin with the excessively Persianized Urdu praise song for the Nizam. There was no day that went happily, I was always in tears and never uttered any of those syllables accurately. And, the teacher was so tough that I had to suffer cane-beating almost every day! I just wanted to speak ordinary Telugu, nothing but my ordinary Telugu! Then I realized that you've got to fight for everything, and that's how I started being a rebel![39]

For Dasarathi, this was a life-changing moment. He began to explore diverse possibilities of these three languages and their place in his personal and literary life. His linguistic dilemma reached its apogee when he migrated to the city of Hyderabad and became fully engaged in the literary sphere of the city. He began attending Urdu *mushairas* besides various Telugu gatherings.[40] He started reading local Urdu magazines and made friends with the poets who had migrated from north India to Hyderabad. Indeed, the location of Hyderabad provided an ideal space for his growth, and he then expanded his realm from print magazines to oral cultures of *mushaira* along with broader exposure to global cultural and literary movements, reading extensively about world literature and also Sufism. For him, it was truly an intersection—or to use Sadasiva's Urdu term *milan sār caurasta* (an intersection of many interminglings)—that blended the local, national, and transnational. Nevertheless, it was obvious that his favorites were Urdu poetry and literary groups that were affiliated with the Progressive Writers' movement.

Dasarathi's literary career and the history of the Urdu language and literature in the city of Hyderabad run parallel at various key moments, such as the establishment of the Osmania University, the first university created for a regional language, Urdu.[41] Dasarathi narrates this phase of Urdu's progress and then turns his attention to explain several processes that made Urdu a link language in the public sphere, including how Urdu became a model for the new journalism and print culture in Telangana. Dasarathi's younger brother Rangacharya shared several cultural interests in common with his brother, such as the politics of language, the Hyderabadi public sphere, and the Urdu–Telugu conversations. He said:

> Strangely enough, Telugu had no respect in our own family. My father always believed that Sanskrit and Dravidam were the better languages, and in his worldview, Telugu was not even a language. In school, if we even mentioned the letters of Telugu, it was considered a demerit. In such a situation, we two brothers developed a love for Telugu.[42]

Rangacharya thus details how Urdu became an influential tool in their early schooling. Though both of them were also concerned about the limited usage of Telugu in everyday life and administrative institutions, their love for Urdu as a literary and cultural link was particularly pronounced. During one of our informal conversations, Rangacharya said:

> My early education in Urdu started when I was in the first grade. If I have any knowledge about cultural history, geography, or poetry, that was because of my Urdu teachers, who were actually not Muslims. Some of my best Urdu teachers were Hindus. In addition, our Urdu class was not about the language, but about different forms of new knowledge. I am even now totally indebted to my foundational courses in Urdu. I also mentioned this in my autobiography, of course![43]

Throughout their long literary careers spanning between 1945 and their deaths, the two brothers tirelessly wrote with appreciation of how Urdu had shaped their social and cultural identities by allowing them to participate in the larger discourses, both local and global. Several autobiographical works (including these two) that narrate the tense times between the late 1940s and the early 1950s unavoidably describe how Urdu became a "Muslim's language," thus alienating the entire language from its cultural history and everyday life before the 1950s. Both Dasarathi and Rangacharya describe the way Urdu was "politically manipulated" by the Nizams and the fundamentalist elements of their day. Indeed, Rangacharya said: "Tying Urdu to Islam is just a political conspiracy."[44]

The historian Taylor Sherman discusses how before and after the Police Action there were competing viewpoints about the position of Urdu in society, and this led to a debate on the question of mother tongues such as Telugu, Marathi, Kannada, and the official language of Urdu. Rangacharya remarks:

"All of a sudden Urdu now becomes a religious language—*mata bhāṣa*—something that was not even imaginable in our school days." Despite the fact that Urdu was a medium of instruction in their schools, these autobiographers never perceived it as a "religious or Muslim's language." For them, Urdu was simply another language of power similar to English in British India. However, they took considerable pride in owning the foundations provided by the Urdu literary culture and the contributions made by several Urdu newspapers and literary organizations in refashioning their everyday life and literary careers.

The history of the Urdu language in Hyderabad state has three clear phases: first, before 1884 when it was given official language status, Urdu was a vernacular language like any local language in the Deccan, and it became totally marginalized as Persian took center stage under the Nizams. Narendra Luther recalls:

> Soon after the death of Salar Jung I, two important events took place, which helped the transition to a new order. One was the replacement of Persian by Urdu as the language of administration in 1884. The medium of administration thus came to be intelligible to the people. It also encouraged the growth of higher education in the State. The second was the extension of the railway line to the mining area of the state, and to Vijayawada. Hyderabad was thus connected to the three principal presidency towns of the British—to Calcutta and Madras through Vijayawada, and to Bombay through Wadi. During the second phase after 1884, Urdu was declared as the official language and gained a certain authority as a language of power.[45]

Most Deccani scholars acknowledge the enhanced status of a vernacular such as Urdu. Telugu scholars including Dasarathi and Sadasiva have always appreciated the way it promoted new connections with other places and the larger cultural discourses. The vernacular languages and places thus connected began to disseminate cosmopolitan worldviews that redefined the ethos of the Hyderabad-based scholars and writers. When this process was underway, there began a new phase, one that Rangacharya describes as "religious" language, meaning "Muslim language." The Telugu poet Kaloji Narayana Rao (1914–2002) likewise refers to the early debates between the Persian and Urdu experts, charting the journey of Urdu through diverse periods. While Dasarathi refers to various literary moments that privilege "excessively Persianized Urdu," Kaloji goes another step and describes how a vernacular language such as Urdu de-hegemonized the Persian-centered literary cultures, particularly in the Deccan. According to Dasarathi and Kaloji, the act of writing in vernacular languages such as Urdu and Telugu was a radical cultural statement during the 1940s.[46]

But perhaps most important about Dasarathi's story is his assessment that the younger generation of writers who wrote in both languages struggled to prioritize their "home language" (*inti bhāṣa*) as a literary language, meaning the Telangana hybrid usages of Telugu and Urdu. Several examples from his life story explain the strategies that he discovered to use this hybridity of Urdu and Telugu into a literary text. Nevertheless, many writers including Dasarathi, Kaloji, and Rangacharya were also aware of the "political conspiracy" of the Nizam in using Urdu as an "Islamic language." Their autobiographies show the progression of this crucial shift of the Urdu language and they deliberately de-construct the politics of the "official" language, which was pitted against vernaculars such as Telugu. Recognizing this shift also made them conscious about locating Urdu in the social space of Hyderabad state.

LOCATING URDU

Many fictional and non-fictional works in the post-Partition literary sphere discuss the process of locating Urdu within the new discourses that evolved in the late 1940s. For instance, Ahmed Ali's novel *Twilight in Delhi* describes how Urdu became an "alien language" as the Hindu extremists pushed the agenda of nationalism and majoritarianism.[47] During post-Partition, this tension led to limiting the choices, even though interest in reading and writing Urdu poetry continued.[48] Many Telugu writers from Hyderabad state appear like the characters from Ahmed Ali's novel and walk straight into the reality of the social and political drama of the times of the Police Action. Most of these Telugu writers, including Dasarathi, C. Narayana Reddy, Kavi Raja Murthy, and many others identified more with Urdu writers who represented socialist liberal positions. In the case of the Telugu and Urdu literary cultures in Hyderabad, such a process of mending the rift between the vernacular languages started much earlier in the 1930s. Describing such efforts, Mohammed Ayub Ali Khan said:

> The 1930s were eventful years in the history of Hyderabad with a relative increase, as compared to the rest of the subcontinent, in communal

mobilisation and intense debates about the princely state's future. This marked the early beginnings of polarisation of the population on communal and ideological lines. Fissures in the Muslim community between nationalists and those who wanted to maintain the status quo also began to appear. However, contentious politics was not the only thing on the minds of Hyderabadis. There was a thriving cultural scene in the state where Hyderabadis of all persuasions came together. Their love for poetry and Mushairas led them to admire and celebrate poets and persons across religious and linguistic divides.[49]

Furthering this conversation, the activities of Osmania University and various local literary associations were instrumental in creating a dialogue among these languages, including Telugu and Urdu. The early chapters in Dasarathi's story provide a detailed description of the Urdu literary practices in the city of Hyderabad that have made him a poet. He narrates the story

Figure 4.5 The Telugu translation of Ghalib's ghazals

Source: Courtesy of Visalandhra Book House.

of Urdu in Hyderabad in multiple modes, including through references to the memories of various Urdu poets and scholars connected to Hyderabad, translation activity between Urdu and Telugu, stylistic experiments in Telugu based on Urdu poetic forms such as ghazal and *rubaayi,* and the role of the Urdu press in Hyderabad (Figure 4.5). Many such references help us to locate the place of Urdu within the Hyderabadi public sphere. However, as most discussions related to Urdu in the late 1940s turn also to the question of Muslim identity, Dasarathi's narration also provides a framework by which to comprehend these dynamics, including Hindu–Muslim exchanges, Razakar activity, and the Telangana peasant struggle led by the leftists.

Dasarathi's passion for Urdu began with stressing the pluralistic values supported by the Urdu literary tradition, which Jaini Mallayya Gupta and Burgula Narsinga Rao describe as a "major contribution to the development of a global educational system that opened a dialogue between liberal arts and sciences."[50] Many of these Telugu–Urdu bilingual scholars including Dasarathi and Sadasiva specifically appreciate the efforts by Osmania University that, as Kavita Datla explained, provided "instruction in all subjects through an Indian vernacular," adding proudly that this "happened first in a territory not directly ruled by the British, but in the princely state of Hyderabad."[51] Telugu writers, such as Bhaskarabhatla Krishna Rao, whom we met in Chapter 2 of this book, likewise discuss how this mode of higher education contributed to cultivating a modern self in the Hyderabad state. But above all others, it is Dasarathi's autobiography that privileges the role of Urdu in the making of a literary modernity specific to the Telangana cultural sphere, which has become a source of pride in the post-2004 separate Telangana movement.

Towards the specific goal of reconstructing the memory of the Urdu-centered cultural sphere, Dasarathi provides multiple examples from his own story: first, at a personal level, and then from the lens of a literary historian. To discover himself as a poet and distinguish himself from the other mainstream Telugu poets of his day, Dasarathi remade his entire literary career after the models provided by Urdu poetry. He described himself as blending both the revolutionary (*angāraṁ*) and the erotic (*śṛmgāraṁ*) to offer a new type of poetry in Telugu. In fact, Dasarathi was experimenting with the well-known poetic grammar of the Urdu progressive poets including Josh Malihabadi, Faiz Ahmed Faiz, and Makhdoom Mohiuddin, and he was successful in introducing and translating such grammar into Telugu.

In addition, during the peak of his poetic career, he translated Ghalib (1797–1869) into Telugu in *Gālib Gītālu* (poems of Ghalib, 1961) a book that ran into several editions.[52] Fascinated by Ghalib's life story, very early on Dasarathi fell in love with his poetry too. He recalled:

> It was my childhood practice of reading and reciting Ghalib that led to [my] ultimate desire of translating him into Telugu. As my life was completely tense and restless, I never thought that that desire would be fulfilled. My experiences with Ghalib's poetry reading and translating made me realize that his expressions of love were just a mask for his endless search for freedom that was suppressed by colonial rule, both personally and politically.[53]

When the Telugu translation of Ghalib was published in 1961, it was no surprise that critics such as Burgula Rama Krishna Rao, Bejawada Gopala Reddy, and Devulapalli Ramanuja Rao identified many common traits and tropes between the two poets despite their diverse cultural and historical backgrounds. Ghalib's idea of love has provided an alternative to the classical *kavya* tradition such as *prabandha śṛngāra*—a mode of eroticism modeled by the medieval *kavya*s in Telugu. As many critics have noted, this mode of *prabandha śṛngāra* had become an artificial device by then. Among them, the Telugu–Urdu bilingual scholar Gopala Krishna Rao said:

> Ghalib's descriptions have a refreshing feel as many Telugu poets were really confused by the structural confinements of the *prabandha śṛngāra*. At this point, Ghalib was not merely another translated Urdu poet, but a pioneer in fulfilling the long-time desire of the Telugu poets to experiment with the ideas of love and freedom.[54]

Many critics including Gopalakrishna Rao were successful in figuring out the affinities between Ghalib and Dasarathi. However, Dasarathi's search for an idea of an alternative love and freedom did not end with Ghalib, and he continued further into the translations of Ghalib's contemporaries including Mir Taqi Mir and Bahadur Shah Zafar, the last king of the Delhi Empire. The refined sensibilities of both these poets, according to his younger brother and writer Rangacharya, have truly impacted the literary personality of Dasarathi.[55]

REFASHIONING THE SELF

Clearly, Dasarathi's life story offers fresh evidence for the making of Telangana modernity in the late 1940s. Yet, he was not an exception. Several dimensions—such as the exchanges between Urdu and Telugu, the dialogue between political matters and personal journeys, the reading public that evolved as a result of the mutuality of Telugu and Urdu, the public sphere of new intellectuals, new journalism and cultural associations, and their activities—also resonate with the life stories of many of his contemporaries who grew up witnessing the key historical moments in Hyderabad and engaging with multiple cultures that pervaded the city. To find parallels, Dasarathi used a new prose style that agrees with the rise of modern journalism in Telangana analogous to what his contemporaries such as Nelluri Kesava Swamy and Kavi Raja Murthy also accomplished in their writings, as discussed in Chapters 1 and 2 of this book. Similar to his contemporaries who were assiduously producing various types of prose works, Dasarathi's journey begins with the early phase of the print media and the new prose genre of the personal essay in Telangana, but with Hyderabad at the center. Whereas several chapters from his autobiography narrate the violent manifestations of the idea of Azad Hyderabad—a new idea promoted by the Nizam to empower his political hegemony—he also provides a detailed description of how a new Telangana discourse was emerging in the public sphere with its distinctive vernacular features.

Dasarathi describes literary publishers such as the Aṇā Grantha Māla that started in 1938.[56] Selling each book for a one-sixteenth subunit of a rupee, which is an *aṇā*, this experiment became extremely successful in creating a reading public for the new writings in Telangana. Explaining how this publication emerged as a major source in the transmission of the new prose from Telangana, Dasarathi connects it to the current political situation too. The Aṇā Grantha Māla was successful not only in producing new prose works from Telangana but also generated a political discourse of resistance and created its own avenues by which to market the books. In his memoir, Veldurti Manikya Rao said:

> This publication was initially a protest to the new political situation emerging in the Hyderabad state. We accomplished two tasks, first, we created a public opinion against the Nizam and secondly, we in fact electrified the print culture by selling books more cheaply and also

making them easy to access. The books published by Anaa Grantha Maala were available even at the small tea stalls.[57]

Most publications from the Aṇā Grantha Māla were about political matters in the state, and only a few were devoted to literature and culture. Dasarathi said:

> At the local tea stall, the vendor would serve one dosa and one coffee along with some publication of the Anaa Grantha Maala. Those books all had 80 pages, and were easily accessible. In those days I used to finish one book a night.[58]

Soon the Nizam's government recognized these "dangerous ways"—to use Dasarathi's phrase—of this press and banned its various publications. Dasarathi explained how new prose writers developed a lucid and direct style that actually paved the way for creating public opinion and led to the public's direct engagement with political matters. Along with several magazines, such as *Golconda, Telangana*, and *Sujata* in Hyderabad, many activists started printing presses even in the remote Telangana which were instrumental in creating a new generation of prose writers between the 1940s and the 1950s.[59] Dasarathi said:

> It's not an exaggeration to call it a revolution in the print culture. Along with the Telugu books, Aṇā Grantha Māla had an impressive Urdu unit too. In fact, it's Anaa Grantha Mala that published the poetry of Makhdoom Mohiuddin for the first time.[60]

Dasarathi's autobiography provides evidence for the new literary activism of the post-Police Action times along with the creation of the new journalism and alternative literary culture. Dasarathi's documentation of these literary and print activities helps us to picture how they shaped various literary and cultural institutions, such as Andhra Saraswat Parishat, Sadhana Samiti, Sahiti Mekhala, Telangana Rachayitala Sangham, and several locally organized writers' centers that were a significant part of the political and cultural discourse of the times.[61] These organizations were extremely active gathering even the writers from the remote regions of Telangana, and they were instrumental in creating a new curiosity in the language and literature. They started organizing the *mushaira*-type poetry gatherings in the remote villages too, which Sadasiva described in detail in *Yaadi* which I will discuss in the next section.[62]

The publication of Urdu materials by various Telugu presses and the Telugu poetry gatherings modeled on the Urdu paradigm reflect a continuum of the Urdu literary culture in Telangana, thus providing us with a transition to the discussion of the role of Urdu and the Muslim question in 1940s Telangana.[63] In Dasarathi's writing, we find several instances of these deeper interactions, such as the ongoing dialog between Hindus and Muslims and Telugu and Urdu cultures. At the very beginning of his autobiography, Dasarathi's memoirs foreshadow his argument by citing extensively Urdu legends such as Ghalib, Muhammad Iqbal (1877–1938), and Josh Malihabadi (1894–1982). Indeed, his own work was deeply indebted to Josh Malihabadi's autobiography *Yādō Ki Bārāt* (The procession of memories). During our conversations, Dasarathi quoted extensively from this autobiography, and when it came time to write his own story, he followed Malihabadi's textual model.[64]

While Urdu as a language and literary culture is a constant topic in his progression as a writer and literary activist, Dasarathi's narrations in *Yātrā Smṛti* represent a tension between the history and memory of Urdu and Urdu literary centers of the 1940s. In the process, Dasarathi was also successful in relocating Telugu literature to Telangana with his descriptions of various emerging literary centers there. Whereas several historical writings of Telugu literature restrict themselves to the British Andhra, Dasarathi took a different challenge, centering history on the city of Hyderabad. Unlike Dasarathi, who focused more on the public culture of various Telangana literary organizations and print sources, Sadasiva has tried to broaden the search for the Urdu culture in Deccan. Although Sadasiva also mentioned the role of various literary organizations, he focused more on the value of cultivating a taste for Urdu poetry and aesthetics. In the next section, I will describe how Sadasiva furthered this mission of Telugu and Urdu mutuality by providing elaborate descriptions of Urdu literary practices as related to Telangana, and again also by engaging with the Muslim discourse.

RESISTING TELUGU NATIONALISM: SADASIVA'S SEARCH FOR URDU

"November 1, 1956 will remain a black day in the history of Telangana." More than once I heard this comment from Samala Sadasiva (1928–2012), both in his interviews and writings (Figure 4.6). When I asked him about this provocative statement, he said:

> We lost that real essence of the Hyderabadi *tehzeeb* and Telangana's sense of belongingness when the linguistic state of Andhra Pradesh was formed. Most aspects related to language, literature and culture were solidified in the name of Andhra and the culture of the two coastal districts of Krishna and Gunturu became the standardized Telugu, thus erasing all the nuances of what we can say about Telugu. Specifically, Telangana Telugu lost its place and it took lots of struggle to retrieve it.[55]

Figure 4.6 Sadas va in 1948
Source: Courtesy of Samala Rajavardhan.

Sadasiva certainly believed that the standardization of coastal Telugu as an act of dominance; more importantly, the declaration of coastal Telugu as an "official language." He explicitly said:

> The linguistic purification of Telugu after the formation of Andhra Pradesh as a linguistic state was one of the worst things that happened to Telangana, as many Urdu words from the local Telangana language were considered to be impure and then we were all forced to use the standardized language of the coastal area Telugu—that resulted in ignoring the idiom of Telangana.[66]

Soon after this realization, Sadasiva made it his mission to return to the pre-Police Action days when the Telugu and Urdu cultures represented a shared history, and the linguistic boundaries were not so thick. Sadasiva's autobiography *Yādi* (*yād* from Urdu, then Telugized as a vowel-ending term *yādi*, meaning memory) touches on all these aspects of Telangana, with an emphasis on Urdu–Telugu interactions. Published in *Vārta*, one of the largest circulated Telugu daily newspapers between 2002 and 2003 for fifty-five weeks, this autobiographical column was well received for its retrieval of the cultural history of the Hyderabad state and Telangana.

Born into a middle-class lower-caste family, Sadasiva grew up in a multilingual and multicultural environment. In 1949, when he was still in his twenties, he was busy writing metrical poetry when he met the historian and Telangana activist Suravaram Pratapa Reddy, who suggested that Sadasiva write a few prose pieces about how Urdu literary traditions influenced Telangana writings.[67] For Sadasiva, that was a life-changing event. He left poetry once and for all to devote himself to the new task of writing about Urdu poetics. Prior to this, Sadasiva had published four volumes of poetry and one novel between 1949 to 1952. Until his death in 2012, Sadasiva never talked about or mentioned these early creative works again, as he was fully engaged with these new writings on Urdu poetry and literary practices. With gratitude to Pratapa Reddy, Sadasiva started his Urdu journey with a few translations and then dedicated himself to the Sufi poetry of Urdu and Persian literature. His first-ever translation of the Hyderabad-based Sufi poet Amzad Hyderabadi (1888–1961) was published in 1963, along with the translation from Urdu of the history of Urdu literature by a prominent literary historian and the progressivist, Ehtesham Hussain (1912–1972).[68] These translations he followed with ones of Rumi's long narratives such as *masnavi*, Ghalib's biography, and then several other works.[69]

Like Dasarathi's *Yātrā Smṛti*, the *Yādi* is more than a personal memory, although he emphasizes his subjective perceptions of various Urdu and Telugu literary-historical moments and movements in Telugu. *Yādi* could be described as a mnemonical text of a cultural activist that blended the personal and the political and was based on the vernacular cultural history. More than an autobiography, this work is a collage of several personal and collective cultural memories that document the vernacular history of Urdu and Hindustani music in Telangana. I use the term "collage" to denote that Sadasiva indeed paints a verbal picture of diverse scattered memories of these two traditions. Unlike Dasarathi, he barely follows any chronological order and frequently digresses from one topic to another. *Yādi* is a nostalgic return to 1940s Hyderabad and Telangana cultural spaces. However, an analysis of this text remains incomplete if we fail to recognize the connections he makes with contemporary cultural politics and social activism in Telangana after 2004. While narrating the past and recounting aspects of Urdu culture, Sadasiva relates them to the new questions of the Hindu–Muslim dilemma, language politics, and the value of shared/multiple cultures as a direct response to the politics of Hindu nationalism of the post–Babri mosque era. Sadasiva's narrative strategies are comparable to Partition writings that tried to connect the past and present as an emotional chronicle. Sadasiva's mode of narration calls to mind what the literary critics Ravikant and Tarun Saint noted about Partition writing: "a contrast is sought to be established, nevertheless, between the composite culture of yore and the breakdown of the trust in the present."[70]

Sadasiva's autobiography portrays almost every historical event between 1940 and the recent Telangana separate state movement. He was not merely compiling facts and figures but showing his emotional engagement with those specific moments and movements, juxtaposing the past with the present. After the Police Action and in the times of both political and cultural violence solidified with the formation of the separate Telugu state, Sadasiva continually laments the loss of Urdu culture that shaped his literary personality. In Sadasiva's writings, the recurring references to Urdu writings and the non-Muslim appreciation of Urdu literary culture function as a device for the recovery of these larger aspects, reminding us of the cultural partition that affected more than two generations. Indeed, these writings demonstrate how Sadasiva remains a successful emblem for having cultivated a taste for Urdu literary practices among the Telugu literary community since the late 1940s. To accomplish this mission, Sadasiva used three modes of autobiographical narrative strategies: First, re-writing the stories from the Police Action related to the history of Urdu and Telugu cultural spheres; second, presenting the stories and anecdotes of various personalities that were marginalized in the mainstream historiography in Telugu; and third, making elaborate references to Sufism and Sufi poets in the context of Hyderabad.[71]

RE-WRITING THE PAST: URDU AND PROGRESSIVE MUSLIMS

Like Dasarathi, Sadasiva frequently returns to his childhood and his early formative years which coincided with the times of the Police Action. Most important were his memories of the Police Action itself in Hyderabad and the events associated with it. From 1947 to 1948, during times of intense violence in Hyderabad, Sadasiva was a student at the Intermediate Teachers Training College in Hyderabad. At a time in which most Muslims of the city were simply portrayed as either supporters of the Razakars or sympathizers of the Nizam, Sadasiva narrates the stories from a diagonally opposing viewpoint that document the role of the progressive Muslims in Hyderabad. During a time at which even a simple utterance of Urdu words was considered to be pro-Nizam or anti-Indian government, Sadasiva plainly took the side of progressive Muslims. Specifically, he mentions a new group of Muslim educators who were active in circulating ideas about modern Islam and its engagement with the discourses of modernity, secularism, and socialism. He tells appreciatively of his experiences at the Teacher's Training College, noting the efforts of this new generation of Muslim educators in promoting new ideas such as modern education, technology, and progressivism.[72] During my conversations with Sadasiva in 2011, I asked him about this explicit usage of the categories of "Hindu" and "Muslims." He said:

> We were not that comfortable using those labels at all. But, the politics of those days forced us to see segregation. Within our circles, we never identified each other with similar religious markers, however, the outside world was something else by that time. Even at my institute, there was a fear and as I wrote in my memoir, we were in separate "Hindu" "Muslim" groups which I hate even now. Literally, even my friends were using different linguistic styles that mark these labels. Earlier we had never experienced such segregation.[73]

Sadasiva elaborates on many such experiences of religious segregation including the very context of the Police Action or the post-Police Action politics of religious hatred that remains a trope at the crux of his narrative. As for Dasarathi, so too for Sadasiva, those were intense moments in his life that shaped his worldview. These stories about the progressive Muslim groups resonate with the worldview that he shared throughout his autobiography. One such element had to do with contextualizing the mutuality of Urdu and Telugu within the pluralist setting of his early years. Whereas Dasarathi pays more attention to the linguistic tensions, Sadasiva emphasizes the value of the multiple literary cultures that defined the beginnings of the Hyderabad-based Telangana renaissance launched by stalwarts such as Suravaram Pratapa Reddy (1896–1953). Undoubtedly, most of his early schooling experiences were deeply influenced by both academic and informal engagements with Urdu. Throughout his autobiography, he fondly remembers the beginnings of his Urdu learning process, recollecting the experiences with teachers who were exceptionally familiar with multiple languages and their literary cultures.

> Of course, Urdu was the official language, yet there were no restrictions about learning Telugu or any other language. However, it was not because Urdu was an official language that me and most of my friends fell in love with urdu, I would even now say, it is the passionate teaching of our Urdu teachers. If I had no such teachers, it would have been impossible for me to gain interest in Urdu, Telugu and Farsi. They were not merely language teachers explaining the grammar, their passion for literature and aesthetics made me develop a curiosity not only in Urdu, but also in Telugu. My initial writings about either Urdu and Farsi poetry were just to share my love for those languages with my friends.[74]

During one of our conversations, he explained how various Urdu-centered cultural and literary patterns helped to counter Western thought and in particular the colonial policies promoted by the British. He said:

> Definitely, the advent of Urdu was a progressive turn in the cultural life of Telangana. The very idea of modern education was indeed a major contribution of the Osmania University that had invited world level intellectuals to Hyderabad and opened a conversation between local and global. But I would say the princely state of Hyderabad was

already a fertile land of creative and intellectual engagements by that time. Thanks to Urdu progressive writings and their constant visits to Hyderabad, we were all well-informed about various global and Indian trends in arts and literatures.[75]

Through his writings, Sadasiva contributed to the cultural history of Urdu and Muslim writings. He (*a*) introduced the Urdu poets whom he admired and celebrated by reading and reciting their work repeatedly; (*b*) translated the Urdu verses and focused specifically on their beauty; (*c*) introduced others to the cultural milieu and lives of these poets; (*d*) compared Urdu and Persian poetic devices; (*e*) located such poets within the literary history of Urdu; and, finally (*f*) elaborated the specific cultural aspects that define these poets.[76] Most of these literary accomplishments from the late 1940s onward were indeed well received and appreciated by Telugu readers.

Sadasiva published more than twenty books, and most of these writings focus on Urdu, Farsi, and their interactions with the diverse literary traditions of Hyderabad. Their genres were numerous, from the personal essay to the historiography of these particular literary fields. Nor did he merely introduce or appreciate the poetic elements of Urdu or Farsi literary traditions. Instead, he also retrieved the past that celebrates the hybridity of the connected Urdu and Telugu histories and the cultural landscape of Hyderabad state. In the process, Sadasiva also retrieves the memory of everyday life during the times of the Police Action.

LIFE STORIES FROM THE MARGINS

Knowingly or unknowingly, Sadasiva has drifted away from the normative autobiographical styles that were popular during his time. Most of the autobiographers had, like Rangacharya and Kaloji, followed a coherent, retrospective, and linear narrative style, very often loyal to the chronological order of the events. To a certain extent, Dasarathi too followed the chronology of the events that read like a diary. Unlike them, Sadasiva chose a fragmented style of narrative which allowed him to blend the historical account with a personal essay or letter. Each piece in Sadasiva's *Yādi* reads more like a personal letter with several digressions from the original topic. While narrating a past event, Sadasiva very often returns to the present and connects two different time periods that in fact helped him make thematic connections, specifically the issues related to the Police Action, the role of

Urdu, the hybridized intellectual landscape of the late 1940s, and the Muslim question. That way, Sadasiva could accommodate many stories from the margins that failed to capture the attention of normative historiographers and autobiographers. Furthering the mode of narrating about the Urdu-centric cultural systems, he writes extensively about themes such as *mushaira*s and intellectual exchanges between north Indian and Hyderabadi scholars, Urdu and Telugu cultural activists, and most importantly, the devices of modernity that defined the Telangana activism. He recalls:

> I have noticed very distinctive aspects in this local culture when people attend any Hindustani musical concert or Urdu poetry gatherings. Not merely the dignitaries of the town, even the ordinary people who lived on daily wages would listen with a rapt attention. And, it was difficult to find a place to stand on your feet, and none could turn back until the *mushaira* came to an end. Throughout the mushaira, there was a quiet and pleasant ambience. That means, people observe a self-imposed discipline while paying full attention to the entire event.[77]

In Sadasiva's lifeworld, *mushaira*s and musical concerts were almost everyday events although most events that he described were from Hyderabad since Sadasiva's father was a teacher, and due to frequent transfers from one place to another, he also had the opportunity to experience the happenings outside the city of Hyderabad, even in remote parts of Telangana. The value of telling the story from the margins has its own significance in terms of the literary history of Telangana or Hyderabad state. Sadasiva also refers to various non-Muslim Urdu poets, such as Kaloji Rameswara Rao, who participated actively in this composite public culture.[78] Indeed, he mentions that his non-Muslim teachers such as Ramanatha Rao were a major influence in cultivating a taste for Urdu poetry.[79] In one example, Sadasiva begins by describing the intellectual landscape of Asifabad which, according to him, was one of the unknown cultural centers of his day:

> In fact, there were many such centers in Telangana outside the city of Hyderabad that were popular for the language arts, literature and music. But most of this history remains unnoticed as we are still under the heavy influence of the history constructed by the Coastal Andhras. It's not surprising that even the historians such as Suravaram Pratapa Reddy were ignored. Unlike the people from Coastal Andhra, the

scholars from this region had no desire for fame and money. They just live for their art and never use it as a ladder to reach somewhere in a materialist sense.[80]

Both Dasarathi and Sadasiva repeatedly share the experiences of the various *mushaira*s in the city of Hyderabad. Nevertheless, their stories differ, as Dasarathi speaks more as a poet and Sadasiva from the lens of the reception. Sadasiva's experiences and anecdotes about these *mushaira*s characterize the making of a new audience of the late 1940s that was represented by both Muslims and Hindus, demonstrating the captivating hybridity of the *mushaira*s. Dasarathi too described various events of *mushaira*s and their role in the making of a public culture in Telangana. But his focus was more on the events in Hyderabad, whereas Sadasiva also described events from remote Telangana.

BACK TO SUFISM AND HYDERABADI POETS

The passion for Urdu poetry opened up possibilities for Sadasiva to explore further the Deccani roots of Sufism too. He specifically refers to the interconnected histories of Urdu literature and Sufism. He said:

> In the 14th century, despite the dominance of Farsi, Urdu was in wide circulation during the Bahmani empire. Mostly, Sufi saints contributed to the spread of Urdu to circulate their Sufi message. Most of the writings from this period were hybrid narratives of both poetry and prose.[81]

Most poets who were born and grew up in Hyderabad were equally well-versed in both languages. However, very few poets wrote in their native Deccani Urdu. Sadasiva's essay traces this shift from Farsi to Urdu to stress the power of the ordinary or vernacular language. Sadasiva's exploration into the connected histories of Sufism and Urdu begins with the translation of the work of the Hyderabadi poet, Ahmed Hussain Amzad (d. 1961). Considering the limited scholarship available about modern Sufis in South India, Amzad's story has its own importance as his life also epitomizes the connected histories of Sufism and Urdu poetry.

Amzad was one of the influential personalities in Sadasiva's life. Known for his simple and humble lifestyle, Amzad was, as described by Sadasiva, a "modern Sufi, who really was devoted to the ideals of true Sufism." In

1911 during the floods on the Musi river in Hyderabad, Amzad lost all his family—mother, wife, and daughter. He also lost his small house and whatever he had from his meager earnings. Sadasiva describes how "for many years he remained utterly silent just staring into the emptiness and enjoying the solitariness like some classical Sufi."[82] After a while, his friends and relatives came to his rescue, and then he married Jamalunnisa who was also equally spiritual in thinking and everyday life practices. Following the debates between the two of them, he published a spiritual text, "Jamal-e-Amzad." Influenced by her ideals, Amzad returned to poetry and studied the poetic genre of *rubaiyat* which eventually made him popular in the city of Hyderabad.

When Sadasiva was in college in the late 1940s, Amzad was a delightful center of many *mushaira*s in Hyderabad. Sadasiva narrates a story of one such *mushaira*, at which the Nizam was present too. When Amzad started reciting, the Nizam who was sitting in the front row began chatting with the person next to him. Instantly, Amzad was mad, stopped his recitation, and said: "Why should people who are busy with their royal matters come to a mushaira?!" At that point, Amzad was a minor employee in the accountant general's office. So impressed was he by the integrity of his personality and poetry that the very next day, the Nizam sent a letter to Amzad saying that he would be sending payment every month to his home, and he need not come all the way to work but should instead devote the rest of the years to poetry. Rejecting this proposal, Amzad replied that he would not accept any *khairat* (charity) and that his conscience would not allow him to accept money if he were not working. Nonetheless, the Nizam was so appreciative of his poetry that very soon Amzad received a significant salary increase.

Although Sadasiva translated several *rubaiyat* composed by Amzad, the real learning experience for him was when he set out to translate his Sufi verses. Since Sadasiva was not familiar with the precepts of Sufism at that point, he had to begin by studying closely various Sufi textual materials and meet the masters from different schools of Sufism (*silsila*s). Being an atheist, it was an extremely difficult exercise for Sadasiva. In the process, he discovered a few Sufi masters from the Deccan. Among them, his meetings with the saint Yaseen Shah were particularly influential. It was told that Yaseen Shah was also one of the scholars with whom Maulana Abul Kalam Azad (1888–1958) consulted during the translation and *tafsir* (interpretation) of the Quran. After several meetings with Yasheen Shah, Sadasiva translated nearly twenty-five *rubaiyat*s of Amzad. For the first time, these translations introduced Amzad to the Telugu literary audience and also launched a new career for Sadasiva. This work made Sadasiva realize the importance of connecting the realms of Sufism and the Deccani literary sphere with an emphasis on Hyderabad. In addition, Sadasiva also records how Telugu readers received Amzad and other Sufi poets.

Whereas this autobiography includes many such examples, his other works on Urdu and Farsi poetry delve further into their interconnected local histories. Following the translation of Amzad, he published extensively about the poets who balanced both Sufism and poetry; among them were his translations of Maulana Rumi in 1967 and Ghalib in 1969. While translating these poems, he also published monographs, first on Urdu poetic traditions with the title *Urdū Kavula Kavitā Sāmagri* (The poetic devices of Urdu poets) in 1970 and the second on Farsi poetic practices entitled *Phārasī Kavula Prasakti* (Speaking of Farsi poets) in 1975. In 2014, he published another monograph on the aesthetics of the Urdu language entitled *Urdū Bhāṣā Kavitva Saundaryaṁ* (The beauty of Urdu language).

In a sense, Sadasiva devoted his entire life to spreading the message of Urdu and Sufi writings. However, his particular success lies in the way he connected both Urdu and Telugu literary cultures between 1948 and until he died in 2012. Throughout the *Yādi* and also in his other works, Sadasiva narrates in detail these interactions between Urdu and a non-Muslim audience with an emphasis on various intersections of Telangana and Urdu networks. Despite their diverse perspectives, these two autobiographies by Dasarathi and Sadasiva have a few powerful commonalities that address the concerns of the post-Police Action consequences in Hyderabad state. At first, both of them were narrating the same era from different localities. However, their roads merged in the city of Hyderabad—the city they were trying to reimagine through the lens of Urdu language and literary cultures. Both works include elaborate descriptions of the larger Urdu literary networks, but they make explicit connections with their immediate social and political reality of violent Police Action. In the next section, I explain how these three personalities and their intellectual journeys were in dialogue with the broader aspects of contemporary Muslim discourse.

THE VERNACULARIZATION OF COSMOPOLITAN HYDERABAD

Popular for its multi-lingual and pluralist ethos, Hyderabad was known to be one of the cosmopolitan centers since early modern times. In his 2015 study,

Eric Beverley analyzed the global networks developed and promoted by the Nizams by using two concepts "Islamicate cosmopolitanism" and "Asaf Jahi cosmopolitanism" to define the political idiom of the Hyderabad state. Eric Beverly observes:

> The Nizam's capital served as a key concourse for transnational connections between global networks linking South Asia not only to Britain and other parts of their empire but to fellow Muslim-ruled states, other European polities, and other locations seen as exemplary models for institutional modernization projects in the state.[83]

In the process, he notices how two key ideas—Muslim internationalism and institutional and political modernity—"supplied the logic and content of intellectual and human connections."[84]

Although Beverley elaborates more on the political aspects, his emphasis on a specific modernity—an "acolonial" one—that was evolving in Hyderabad state around this period is relevant here. Within this worldview, Hyderabad was a melting pot of several cosmopolitan and vernacular languages and cultures too. Along with Persian, Sanskrit, and English, the wide circulation of the vernaculars such as Telugu, Urdu, Kannada, and Marathi represent the linguistic diversity of the Hyderabad state. As a marker of the Mughal empire, Persian remained an administrative language until 1884, and the debate about the use of Persian and Urdu until then tells us more about the language politics of Hyderabad state as well. Muzaffar Alam's pioneering work *Languages of Political Islam* documents the heated debates about the Persian-Urdu dynamics during the prime ministership of Salar Jung, who openly declared till his last breath that Persian would be the language of the empire. Instead, the political and cultural environment at this point metamorphosed so radically that Salar Jung himself had to yield to the proposal of Urdu as an "official" language.[85] The radical decision to switch to Urdu also had a political purpose that was necessitated by the reformist program initiated by Salar Jung himself.[86] Within the Telugu print media and polemical discourses, the rise of the vernacular—in this case, Urdu—was a huge event that spread the seeds of resistance, resulting in an upsurge of progressive writers and leftist political activists, along with yielding space for a widely debated reformist Islam.[87] In turn, these language politics also redefined the social status of the Telugu as an idiom of local modernity, which later became known specifically as a version of Telangana

Figure 4.7 Urdu literary activities in the public sphere of Hyderabad with the presence of Telugu personalities

Source: Courtesy of Samala Rajavardhan.

modernity (*Telaṅgāṇa ādhunikata*) within which the rise of a progressive Muslim community plays a pivotal role.[88]

Within the Telangana public sphere, many cultural and political activists at a broader level have embraced the idea of Urdu as an official language (Figure 4.7). The discourses developed around a vernacular acquiring the status of a new official language, and as Sadasiva said, "opened a real democratic space in the Hyderabad state and in fact made a huge impact as related to various cultural aspects." In his autobiography, Kaloji too has perceived this shift as paradigmatic both culturally and politically. He said:

> Urdu was the language of the ordinary people (*prajala bhāṣa*) Until now we heard all the greatly praised classics and puranas in the *dēva bhāṣa* ("the language of the gods") and we with no hesitations accepted the privilege of the *dēva bhāṣas*. Despite the fact that, Urdu benefitted a specific class, the rise of a vernacular itself should be considered a major development.[89]

For several scholars, such as Narendra Luther and cultural activists such as Gupta, Urdu was a "platform" for Hindu–Muslim unity.[90] In general, most of these scholars and activists consistently acknowledged that Urdu provided a model for the Telugu print culture including for a new wave of journalistic writings and modern prose in the late 1940s. This moment also led to the rise of a new genre of autobiography that marks the beginnings of a locally produced self or subjectivity deeply rooted in the Telangana identity, hybridizing Telugu and Urdu along with Hindu–Muslim practices.

By locating Urdu within the public sphere of Hyderabad, we can comprehend the contours of an anti-colonial discourse for which Urdu became a focal point at this time. Privileging Urdu undoubtedly unsettled the hegemonic role of Hindi as a tool of nationalism, particularly in the Hyderabad state. Those who argued in favor of the idea of Telangana modernity now discuss the paradigms produced by the Urdu legacy, including the ideas related to modern education and cultural forms that created an alternative public opinion grounded in the Hyderabadi composite culture. While several studies debate the interactions between Urdu and Hindi, the relationships between Urdu and other vernaculars remain understudied. Along with dealing with the larger question of a Muslim sense of belonging, these debates inspire us even now to focus on the dialogical elements between Urdu and Telugu.

With a focus on the Hindi public sphere, the literary historian Francesca Orsini discusses how Hindi was influential in constructing a singular and normative public that promoted nationalism, described as a "culturally homogeneous harmony."[91] Similar to what happened in north India under the leadership of Mahatma Gandhi from 1918 to 1919, the British-ruled Madras state likewise responded by promoting Hindi as a singular national language and it was hoped a more united public opinion that was institutionalized as the *Dakshina Bharata Hindi Prachar Sabha* ("the South Indian Association for the Hindi Promotion"). Learning Hindi was considered to be a privilege, and many middle-class and upper-class political and cultural leaders were connected to the Hindi Prachar Sabha, thus declaring their allegiance to the nationalist mission. By contrast, Hyderabad state promoted a vernacular language such as Urdu as its official language (*raja bhāṣa*). For many Telugu writers, Urdu, at this point, is a source of idiom for a secularism and progressivism that was defined by the ideals of the Progressive Writers' Association and the composite culture, otherwise known as the Hyderabadi *tehzeeb*. Growing up in such a milieu,

Dasarathi and Sadasiva were dealing with Urdu in the times of what Ali Hussain Mir and Raza Mir noted:

> The Progressives also had to come to terms with the growing communalization of the polity, an issue that became increasingly after the Partition of the country along religious lines. An unfortunate corollary was the communalization of Urdu itself in India. Urdu suffered a debilitating blow when it became identified as the language of Pakistan, and by specious extension, the language of Muslims, resulting in, among other things, a loss of state patronage.[92]

Along with several historical and cultural moments including the Partition, Urdu has always been a contentious issue since the beginnings of the debates on nationalism, progressivism, and secularism in late twentieth-century Hyderabad. In the case of Hyderabad, the Police Action too became a major historical event that defined many issues around the question of Muslims and the mutuality of Urdu and Telugu. Despite numerous manifestations of the aforementioned key ideas, as demonstrated in the life stories of our three cultural activists, Urdu plays into this discourse as more than some linguistic identity. For the late 1940s generation, as Gupta noticed, Urdu was more than a language; even a peripheral survey of the contemporary developments informs us that Urdu continues to be a similarly contentious topic as more debates gather around it during the Police Action and the formation of the Telugu linguistic state until 1956.

In analyzing how British rule was instrumental in constructing "Hindi/Hindu" "Urdu/Muslim" categories, Shamsur Rahman Faruqui observes that, "At the time that modern Hindi was being groomed to occupy center stage on the Indian literary and linguistic scene, Urdu was being denigrated on moral and religious grounds." He points out how anti-Urdu voices developed an anti-Muslim discourse.[93] David Lunn's 2018 essay provides another framework with which to understand the gray areas between Hindi and Urdu, and suggests that we pay attention to the spaces created across the divide of the discrete religious communities.[94] Moving beyond this framework, this chapter has tried to push the debate further to include a south Indian language, Telugu. The above evidence from Hyderabad-based narratives about the Urdu language politics with the testimonials from the non-Muslim community's passion for Urdu problematizes the colonial categories of Hindu/Muslim and also Urdu/Muslim. While figuring out how these two languages functioned in the local history of Hyderabad and Telangana, this discussion advances the reconstruction of the history of Muslim and Hindu conflicts in the post–Police Action Hyderabad. The new genre of autobiography has opened up larger questions with a focus on discrete religious identities that were being reshaped by the Police Action in politics and everyday life. These debates also contributed to expanding the discourse on linguistic diversity and the arrival of a vernacular shift in the public sphere of Hyderabad state.[95]

RETHINKING THE URDU–TELUGU DEBATE

After more than three hours of conversation, Jaini Mallayya Gupta returned to my earlier question about the violence of the Police Action and Partition in Hyderabad. Picking up one of his old paper clippings of *Siasat*, he started reciting a couplet from the Urdu poet Bashir Badr (1935–):

> *Log tuut jaate haiñ ek ghar banāne meñ*
> *tum taras nahīñ khāte bastiyāñ jalāne meñ*
> People are dying to make one house thrive,
> Mercilessly, you burn neighborhoods alive.

He continued by insisting, "Any private or public issue perfectly fits in that genre of ghazal, just in a couplet. Of course, Urdu is always something larger than the genre of that kind of couplet." Like Gupta, Dasarathi, Sadasiva, and many Telugu writers have explicitly declared their return to Urdu in the times when, as the literary historian Jennifer Dubrow noted, "Urdu is seen as a language of loss, death, mourning and nostalgia."[96] Gupta's instant referencing of Urdu couplets exemplifies that Urdu is still a language of life and everyday emotions. As Gupta insisted, "It is not *turakala bhāṣa* (Muslim's language)." Similarly, the autobiographical texts and a few personal narratives that I have discussed in this chapter demonstrate various ways in which Telugu writers in the post-Police Action times have found to resist the idea of the "death" of Urdu. Considering Urdu as an alternative paradigm, these personalities and their contexts participate in a larger milieu that connects the local and the global, and different faces of modernity including highlighting the Telangana-specific local modernity known as *Telaṅgāṇa ādhunikata* and the popular theme such as the Hyderabadi *tehzeeb*, the inter-community life in the city. Their emphasis on the mutuality of Urdu and Telugu specifically begins by narrating the inter-community and interlingual life in Hyderabad. In 2008, analyzing the shifts in the inter-community life of the city, Javeed Alam noted:

> Coming back to the present, there is a huge change in inter-community relations, a clear-cut discontinuity, even though some of the earlier structural features continue and the social forces they gave rise to remain intact. The Majlis continues to be a major force among the Muslims. There has not been any diminution of its influence in the politics of the city. The VHP together with the rest of the Sangh Parivar is there with the same social and political positions, perhaps a little less shrill.[97]

In such a climate, literary and cultural activists such as Gupta, Dasarathi, and Sadasiva, have definitely contributed to the dialog of inter-community life by reminding people of the value of pluralism, multilingualism, and the need for the mutuality of the everyday practices of Hindus and Muslims. Their specific emphasis on Urdu as a dialogical tool shows the continuing legacy of the *Hyderabadi tehzeeb* in which they took considerable pride too.

Although it is not documented systematically, we see several phases of the cultural and political returns of Urdu in Hyderabad and Telangana state at different points in history. Drawing on sources from the early history of the Telugu textual traditions, the bilingual scholar K. V. Gopala Krishna Rao analyzes the beginnings of the dialog between Urdu-Farsi and Telugu literary cultures in his pioneering work in Telugu, *Telugupai Udū Phārasīka Prabhāvaṁ* (The influence of Urdu and Farsi on Telugu) published in 1968.[98] Although it was not the first of its kind of work in Telugu, Gopala Krishna Rao's observations about the dialogical relationships among these three languages remain foundational as related to the comparative linguistics and literary cultures. With numerous textual examples, Rao primarily shows that the inseparability of these three languages is a built-in feature of the local histories of Hyderabad and has been so since medieval times.

In modern times, such a moment arrives when, with the rise of new printing presses, newspapers, and literary magazines after the 1930s, most writers understood the role of a personal narrative in articulating the new consciousness that does not fit in any religious and literary categories.[99] In newspapers such as *Golkonda* and *Telugu Swatantra*, the letters-to-the-editor columns which had typically been brief, single paragraph responses to the contents of the newspaper or magazine now turned into more extended conversations and features. For instance, bilingual writers such as Kavi Raja Murthy's column written as a letter with the title *Palle Nunchi Uttaram* (Letter from my village) was a significant turn towards this consciousness.[100] Murthy explains the personality transformations as he migrated from a small town to the city, while Dasarathi and Sadasiva dwell more on various cultural locations in the city itself. The latter two writers extended this mode to an elaborate autobiographical narrative, which they improvised into a fully developed genre in the modern history of Telangana writing.

In *Literary Cultures in History*, Sheldon Pollock notes that

> the literary needs to be understood as a historically situated practice: how people have done things with texts. This approach suggests that the problem of history may also be addressed, at least in part, by exploring how people have done things with the past and by taking seriously how different modes of temporality may have worked to structure South Asian literary cultures for the participants themselves.[101]

Discussing this "historically situated practice," Pollock remarks on the value of the *tazkirah* in Persian and Urdu literature. In the making of this specific genre, memory plays a pivotal role. In various conversations, both Dasarathi and Sadasiva express high regard for this particular genre that privileges personal and collective memory at the same time. Despite the fact that Dasarathi and Sadasiva were writing to a modern reading public, their recurring references to Urdu and Persian literary genres clearly speak extensively about what inspired them to write these autobiographical narratives. Both begin their autobiographies with two Urdu couplets that invoke the past with a passion, yet do so to connect with the present.[102]

These writings, however, raise a question about what kind of past was their point of reference, and how to locate this "past" within the "present" times, thus redefining their notion of historiography. Like many who were writing about the Police Action and its consequences in Hyderabad, Dasarathi and Sadasiva were also disenchanted with the mainstream historiography that was stuck describing Telugu nationalism. Due to this emphasis on the formation of the Telugu linguistic state, many historians and writers were busy glorifying the Telugu past. As a counterpoint to that mainstream Telugu-centric historiography, Dasarathi and Sadasiva returned to the bilingual cultural sources of Hyderabadi *tehzeeb*, specifically in the cities of Hyderabad and Telangana. Whereas Dasarathi limits his observations to

Hyderabad, Sadasiva narrates the story of Urdu even beyond Hyderabad, this being demonstrated in the recurring references to popular Urdu events and literary figures from outside the city.

In writing these pieces, both autobiographers have a clear sense of their temporality and the aspects that define this temporality, particularly the bilingual literary culture produced and circulated in Hyderabad that developed into a cultural center in the late 1940s. Due to emotional entanglements created by the Telugu separate state during this period, the earlier bilingualism was clearly and visibly marginalized, and the aftermath of the Partition and Police Action too led to marking Urdu as a "Muslim's language" (*turakala bhāṣa*). In this case, the observations made by the historian Sudipta Kaviraj, particularly in the context of the Bangla literary sphere, are relevant to Hyderabad as well. He said:

> Writing the history of Bangla literature was part of the project of the literary modernity, and since this was entirely dominated by a Hindu upper stratum of society, the initial historical accounts tended to ignore Islamic elements by suggesting either that they belonged to a separate cultural strand (Mussalmani Bangla), or that these texts were not of sufficient literary quality to find a place in the exalted history of literary art.[103]

For Dasarathi, Sadasiva, and Gupta, this element of Islam and Urdu were crucial in the making of their new identities. The Urdu scholar Syed Akbar Hyder presents a similar case in his essay about two Hyderabadi Urdu poets Sarwar Danda and Suleiman Khatib who used the Telugu idiom in their Deccani Urdu verses.[104] Akbar Hyder notes: "It is not just one linguistic entity that wonders about the postcolonial direction that the state has taken, but two languages speak in unison."

Either explicitly or implicitly, these two texts participate in the debate on the idea of the nation-making, postcolonial, and post-Partition Hindu–Muslim divide in South Asia. This question of a postcolonial Hindu–Muslim divide has its roots in the rise of a new Muslim discourse and the remaking of an Urdu–Telugu cultural dialog in post-90s Telangana. While Dasarathi presents his immediate responses as a witness to the Police Action, Sadasiva adopts a different viewpoint extending further into the post–Babri mosque demolition politics. Dasarathi's way of dealing with histories and culture was more from his creative side as he perceives the changes from the viewpoint of a poet, a true insider in cultural production. A careful and sensible reader, the success of Sadasiva's literary career hinges on the singular axis of his reception of Urdu aesthetics. In many ways, their autobiographies could be defined (to use Pollock's words from a different context) as "a form of ethnohistory." [105] Reading the autobiographies of Dasarathi and Sadasiva as historians will certainly benefit our interpretive exercise in understanding the understudied period of the post-Police Action in Telangana. In fact, both Dasarathi and Sadasiva entered the Telugu literary domain from a geographically and culturally marginal site, two remote places far from the cultural center of Hyderabad. However, their connection to Hyderabad (Dasarathi migrated to the city and Sadasiva was always traveling back and forth) made them explore a new identity formation, filled with urban sensibilities and religious transformations. Their autobiographies describe the intense struggle to participate in the mainstream literary public sphere of their times and remain an effective testimony of their celebration of the shared/multiple cultures of Hyderabadi *tehzeeb*.

NOTES

1. Many writers and cultural activists, during my conversations, have expressed similar sentiments about the Siasat. Some of them even mentioned how *Siyāsat* pages were pasted on the front walls of their office which, in fact, resulted in increasing the reading public. According to the journalist J. S. Ifthekhar, "The wall newspaper is a trademark of Hyderabad. The *Siasat* is pasting its paper on the wall from day one – August 15, 1949 to be precise. Other dailies like *Payam*, *Nizam Gazette* and *Rahnuma-e-Deccan* also followed this practice for sometime." J. S. Ifthekhar, "Wall Newspaper Has Come to Stay," *The Hindu*, December 6, 2011, Hyderabad. For more about the work of these newspapers as related to the Telugu public sphere, see Mandumula, *Yābhayi Samvatsarāla Haidarābādu*, 41.
2. Interview with the author, Hyderabad, India, January 27, 2019.
3. Telangana villages, particularly those in the Nalgonda district were under heavy oppression, for details see Panneeru Ramesh, *Telangana Armed Struggle in Nalgonda District: A Case Study of Kadavendi Village, 1930–51 A.D.* (Hyderabad: Prajasakti Book House, 2010); for a general understanding of the Telangana rebellion, see Barry Pavier, *The Telangana Movement, 1944–51* (Delhi: Vikas, 1981).

4. Interview with the author, Hyderabad, India, January 27, 2019.

5. Interview with the author, Hyderabad, India, January 27, 2019.

6. For an idea of the language politics of Telugu and Urdu, see Lisa Mitchell, *Language, Emotion, and Politics in South India: The Making of a Mother Tongue* (Bloomington: Indiana University Press, 2009); Kavita Datla, *The Language of Secular Islam: Urdu Nationalism and Colonial India* (Hyderabad: Orient Blackswan, 2013); Karen Leonard, "Hyderabad: Mulki–Non-Mulki Conflict," in *People, Princes, and Paramount Power: Society and Politics in the Indian Princely States*, ed. Robin Jeffrey (New Delhi: Oxford University Press, 1978), 65–106; Raju, "Library Movement in Telangana," in *Comprehensive History and Culture of Andhra Pradesh*, ed. B. Kesava Narayana, *Modern Andhra and Hyderabad, AD 1858–1956*, vol. 7 (Hyderabad: EMESCO Books, 2016), 919–935; K. V. Narayana Rao, *The Emergence of Andhra Pradesh* (Bombay: Popular Prakashan, 1973).

7. For such debates on Hindi–Urdu, see Christopher King, *One Language, Two Scripts: The Hindi Movement in Nineteenth Century India* (Bombay: Oxford University Press, 1994).

8. I am particularly indebted to the work of Francesca Orsini in broadening my understanding of the "multilingual local." See Francesca Orsini, "The Multilingual Local in World Literature," *Comparative Literature* 67, no. 4 (December 1, 2015): 345–374.

9. Datla, *The Language of Secular Islam*, 8–10.

10. Jennifer Dubrow, *Cosmopolitan Dreams: The Making of Modern Urdu Literary Culture in Colonial South Asia* (Honolulu: University of Hawaii Press, 2018), 3.

11. For a fictional account of the role of Urdu, see Huma R. Kidwai, *The Hussaini Alam House* (New Delhi: Zuban, 2012).

12. Biruduraju Ramaraju, ed., *Qutub Ṣāhī Sultānulu – Āṁdhra Saṁskṛti* [The Qutub Shahi sultans and Andhra culture] (Hyderabad: Idaar-e-adbiyate, 1962).

13. Makhdoom Mohiuddin, *Makhdūm Kavita*, trans. Gajjela Mallāreḍḍi, Dāśarathi, Sī Nārāyaṇa Reḍḍī, Rāmbhaṭla Kṛṣṇamūrti, and Kaumudi (Vijayawada: Visalandhra Publishing House, 1970).

14. Adluri Ayodhya Rama Kavi, *Haidarābādupai Pōlīsu Carya: Burra Katha* [Police Action of Hyderabad: Burra katha folk narrative] (Secunderabad: Konda Veerayya, 1948).

15. Biruduraju Ramaraju (1925–2010) was also known for his book *Muharram Songs in Telugu*, the first-ever documentation of the songs of the public ritual of Muharram.

16. H. K. Sherwani, *History of Medieval Deccan (1298–1724)* (Hyderabad: Government of Andhra Pradesh, 1973), 444.

17. Richard Eaton, *A Social History of the Deccan 1300–1761: Eight Indian Lives*, vol. 1 (New York: Cambridge University Press), 142–143.

18. Margrit Pernau, *Emotions and Temporalities* (Cambridge: Cambridge University Press, 2021), 2.

19. Seema Alavi, *Muslim Cosmopolitanism in the Age of Empire* (Cambridge, MA: Harvard University Press, 2015).

20. For more on this aspect, see Lisa Mitchell, "Making the Local Foreign: Shared Language and History in Southern India," *Journal of Linguistic Anthropology* 16, no. 2 (December 2006): 229–248.

21. Dasarathi's *Yātrā Smṛti* first appeared in the *Andhra Jyothi*, a weekly magazine between 1997 and 1998, when the question of Hindu nationalism and Muslim discourse was in the debate.

22. Makhdoom Mohiuddin, *Makhdūṃ Kavita*, trans. Gajjela Mallāreḍḍi, Dāśarathi, Sī Nārāyaṇa Reḍḍī, Rāmbhaṭla Kṛṣṇamūrti, and Kaumudi (Vijayawada: Visalandhra Publishing House, 1970).

23. Datla, *The Language of Secular Islam*.

24. Anand Vivek Taneja, *Jinnealogy: Time, Islam and, Ecological Thought in the Medieval Ruins of Delhi* (Stanford, CA: Stanford University Press, 2017), 10; for more on the concept of *adab* in South Asian Islam, see Barbara Metcalf, *Moral Conduct and Authority: The Place of Adab in South Asian Islam* (Berkeley: University of California Press, 1984).

25. Sarah Fatima Waheed, *Hidden Histories of Pakistan: Censorship, Literature, and Secular Nationalism in Late Colonial India* (Cambridge: Cambridge University Press, 2021), 31.

26. For a brief history of various literary and cultural organizations in Hyderabad, see C. Mrunalini "The Role of Literary Associations in the Promotion of Telugu Language in Hyderabad," in *Languages and Literary Cultures in Hyderabad*, ed. Kousar J. Azam (London; New York: Routledge, 2018), 227–231.

27. Interview with the author, Adilabad, India, September 12, 2006.

28. Interview with the author, Adilabad, India, September 12, 2006.

29. For more on the role of Urdu in the Nizam's era, see Datla, *The Language of Secular Islam*; for a larger discussion on Urdu as a "Muslim" language and religions politics in South Asia, see Tariq Rahman, *From Hindi to Urdu: A Social and Political History* (New Delhi: Orient BlackSwan Private Limited, 2011). Anita Desai's novel, *In Custody*, portrays the tensions between Hindi

and Urdu in north India: Anita Desai, *In Custody* (New York: Harper and Row Publishers, 1984).

30. Anjali Nerlekar's observations about the role of little magazines and new spaces of literary writing in the Marathi literature of the 1960s are relevant to understand these broader implications. Nerlekar said:

> The little magazines of Bombay could be seen similarly as the De Certeau-like "tactics" of the marginal writers who undermined the cartographic reach of the institutionalized gaze and created underground or guerilla tactics in order to be heard. (Anjali Nerlekar, *Bombay Modern: Arun Kolatkar and Bilingual Literary Culture* [Illinois: Northwestern University Press, 2016], 42)

31. For a detailed analysis of the role of Persian in medieval times, see Muzaffar Alam, *The Languages of Political Islam: India 1200–1800* (Chicago: Chicago University Press, 2004).

32. Dasarathi, *Yātrā Smr̥ti*, 21.

33. For more details of these new prose genres from Telangana, see Mudiganti Sujatha Reddy, ed., *Telangana Toli Tharam Kathalu* (Hyderabad: Rohanam Publications, 2002); Sangisetti Sreenivas, *Dastraṁ: Telangāṇa Toli Taraṁ Kathala Sūci* (Hyderabad: Kavile Prachuranalu, 2004; Mudiganti Sujatha Reddy and Sangisetti Sreenivas, eds., *Telangāṇa Tolitaraṁ Kathalu Bhaagam* [Stories from Telangana, 1910–1956] (Hyderabad: Navodaya, 2005).

34. Interviews with the author, Khammam, India, September 20, 2016, and Hyderabad, India, January 10, 2020.

35. Interview with the author, April 20, 2019.

36. Dharwadker and Blackburn, *Collected Essays of A. K. Ramanujan*, 333.

37. Dasarathi, *Yātrā Smr̥ti*, 76.

38. Dasarathi's autobiography has several references to these personalities and their work. The recently published translation of Shaukat Kaifi's Urdu memoirs *Yaad Ki Rehguzar* into Telugu describe the 1947 events in Hyderabad along with the interactions with local poets. N. Venugopal, trans., *Talapula Tōva: Kaiphī Ajmītō Artha Śatābdi* [The path of many memories: Half a century with Kaifi Azmi] (Hyderabad: Veekshanam Publications, 2016), 8–9, and 11–26; for a recent analysis, see Farha Noor, "Negotiating Nostalgia: Progressive Women's Memoirs in Urdu," *South Asian History and Culture* 12, no. 4 (2021): 371–384.

39. Dasarathi, *Yātrā Smr̥ti*, 16.

40. For a detailed narration about the importance of *mushaira*s in Hyderabad city, see R. S. Sharma, "A Tentative Paradigm for the Study of Languages and Literary Cultures in Hyderabad City," in *Languages and Literary Cultures*, ed. Azam, 1–34.

41. Tariq Sheikh argued that this idea of a modern university in a regional language was inspired by "Tokyo's success at creating a system of education that taught modern science and humanities in Japanese"; for more, see Tariq Sheikh, "When Princely Hyderabad Looked to Imperial Tokyo," https://maidaanam.com/when-princely-hyderabad-looked-to-imperial-tokyo/?fbclid=IwAR2Whj2PIwnzXBW290WuDS6Z4RTMG7u1ZYMXWN2_DEXlcPxF8STDgCSvV30 (accessed November 20, 2022).

42. Dasarathi Rangacharya, *Jīvana Yānaṁ: Gaḍicina Gurtulu* (Hyderabad: Nava Chetana Publishing House, 2016), 75.

43. Interview with the author, Hyderabad, India, September 20, 2013.

44. Rangacharya, *Jīvana Yānaṁ*, 84.

45. Luther, *Hyderabad*, 180.

46. Interviews with the author, Hyderabad and Vijayawada, India.

47. Ahmed Ali, *Twilight in Delhi* (New York: New Directions, 1994 [1940]).

48. Saint, *Witnessing Partition*, 197.

49. Mohammed Ayub Khan, "Rabindranath Tagore's Visit to Hyderabad: When Poetry Triumphed over Politics," https://www.thenewsminute.com/article/rabindranath-tagore-s-visit-hyderabad-when-poetry-triumphed-over-politics-155721?fs=e&s=cl (accessed October 22, 2021).

50. Interview with the author, Hyderabad, India, January 26, 2019.

51. Datla, *The Languages of Secular Islam*, 7.

52. This translation of Ghalib's poetry into Telugu has a fascinating history in Telugu literary culture. First published in 1961, the collection became a device that cultivated a taste for Urdu poetry, particularly, Ghalib's tradition. Dasarathi, *Gālib Gītālu* (Vijayawada: Visalandhra Publishing House, 1961).

53. Dasarathi, *Yātrā Smṛti*, 35.

54. K. V. Gopala Krishna Rao, *Telugupai Urdū Phārasīka Prabhāvaṁ* [The influence of Urdu and Persian on Telugu] (Hyderabad: Andhra Pradesh Sahitya Academy, 1969), 134.

55. Interview with the author, Hyderabad, India, August 20, 2008.

56. Anaa Grantha Maala—one of the popular publishers in the early phase of Telangana print culture. Established by Gupta in 1939 from Hyderabad. Well-known Telangana historian Veldurthi Manikyala Rao was the editor

of this publication. Most of the publications between 1945 and 1948 were banned by the Nizam. For more, see Dasarathi, *Yātrā Smṛti*, 66–75.

57. Veldurti, *Haidarābād Svātantryōdyama Caritra*, 85.
58. Dasarathi, *Yātrā Smṛti*, 66.
59. K. V. Ranga Reddy, *The Struggle and the Betrayal: The Telangana Story* (Hyderabad: Vignana Sarovara Prachuranalu, 2010).
60. Dasarathi, *Yātrā Smṛti*, 73.
61. Ranga Reddy, *The Struggle and the Betrayal*, 53–56.
62. Dasarathi, *Yātrā Smṛti*, 196.
63. For more details about the Urdu press, see Kaloji, *Idī Nā Goḍava* [Here's my story] (Hyderabad: Kaloji Foundation, 2015), 128–129; for a contemporary understanding of the Mushaira, see Ali Khan Mahmudabad, *Poetry of Belonging: Muslim Imaginings of India, 1850–1950* (New Delhi: Oxford University Press, 2020).
64. Dasarathi, *Yātrā Smṛti*, 196; for more on Josh Malihabadi, see Josh Mahilabadi, *Yādoṉ kī Bārāt* [The procession of memories] (Lāhaur: Maktabah-yi Sh'air o Adab, 1975); Saleem Kidwai, "Josh Malihabadi: There Will Never Be Another Like You," in *Same-Sex Love in India*, ed. R. Vanita and S. Kidwai (New York: Palgrave Macmillan, 2000).
65. Interview with the author, Adilabad, India, September 26, 2007.
66. Interview with the author, Adilabad, India, September 26, 2007.
67. Interview with the author, Adilabad, India, September 26, 2007.
68. Sayyid Iḥtishām Ḥusain, *Urdū Adab kī Tanqīdī Tārīkh* (Na'ī Dihlī: Taraqqī-yi Urdū Biyūro, 1988).
69. Sadasiva's translation of Iḥtishām Ḥusain, *Urdū Adab kī Tanqīdī Tārīkh*, was published in 1963. See Sadasiva, trans., *Urdū Sāhitya Caritra* (Hyderabad: Andhra Pradesh Sahitya Academy, 1963).
70. Ravikant and Saint, *Translating Partition*, xviii.
71. Sadasiva, *Urdū Bhāṣā Kavitva Saundaryaṁ* (Hyderabad: Telugu University, 2004); Sadasiva, *Urdū Kavula Kavitā Sāmagri* [The poetic devices of Urdu poets] (Hyderabad: Andhra Pradesh Sahitya Academy, 1970); Sadasiva, *Phārasī Kavula Prasakti* [Speaking of Farsi poets] (Hyderabad: Andhra Pradesh Sahitya Academy, 1975).
72. Sadasiva, *Yādi*, 46–47.

> At the teacher's institute, we Hindus were thirty and [there were] nearly a hundred Muslims. We were all like siblings and then suddenly things changed. As the Police Action was approaching, Laiq Ali's

government arrested Ramanand Teertha, then the tensions increased. Every day, Deccan Radio would broadcast the emotion-packed hate speeches by Qasim Rizvi. There were loudspeakers throughout the city and the speeches were audible everywhere. Listening to these speeches, we would walk in the city with fear. In the evenings, both Muslim and Hindu teachers gathered in two opposing sides and there was an intense fear among us all. That fear was totally new; it was something that we had never experienced before. However, the Muslim educators in the institute were totally supportive of their students and always would say: "Qasim Razvi is just a day dreamer. Nothing of what he says would be possible in Hyderabad state, which will certainly be aligned finally into the Union government of India." Most of these Muslim educators were progressive in their thinking and forward looking. Their words gave us lots of relief and they were totally critical about the new developments in Hyderabad. Now in the so-called democracy, we have been watching the people who could not even utter a single word against their governments. But, during our college times, and particularly at that unusual moment of tension and conflict, our Muslim teachers were completely vocal about the atrocities of the Razakars and the dictatorial policies of the Nizam. My Muslim teachers were never scared of any consequences, either for the security of their employment or their lives. They taught us the lessons of ethical righteousness and now I remember all those Muslim teachers from whom we learned being ethically bold and speaking out.

73. Interview with the author, Hyderabad, India, July 10, 2011.
74. K. Jithendra Babu, ed., *Jayanthi* (special issue for Samala Sadasiva, Visalandhra Publishing House, Hyderabad, 2012), 434.
75. Interview with the author, Adilabad, India, October 2012.
76. Jithendra Babu, *Jayanthi*, 217.
77. Sadasiva, *Yādi*, 2.
78. Ibid., 82–91.
79. Ibid., 107.
80. Although, Sadasiva stressed these specific politics of discrimination against the Telangana and Hyderabad states in his autobiography, he continued to emphasize the same during several interviews published at various sources including the special issue edited by Jithendra babu, *Jayanthi*; Sadasiva, *Yādi*,

14; Sadasiva, *Dakṣiṇa Bhārata Dēśamlō Urdū Sāhityaṁ* [Urdu Literature in South India].

81. Jithendra Babu, *Jayanti*, 4.

82. Interview with the author, Adilabad, India, October 2012.

83. Eric Beverley, *Hyderabad, British India, and the World, Muslim Networks and Minor Sovereignty c. 1850–1950* (Cambridge: Cambridge University Press, 2015), 100–101.

84. Ibid., 101.

85. For more on the politics of Persian and Urdu language, see Muzaffar Alam, *Languages of Political Islam: India, 1200–1800* (Chicago: University of Chicago Press, 2004).

86. For more on the modern reforms initiated and promoted by Salar Jung, see Ali, *Adhunika Haidarabad Charitra*.

87. For the role of reformist Islam, see Roosa, *The Quandary of the Qaum*, 180.

88. See Srinivas, *Telangana Sahitya Vikaasam*.

89. Kaloji, *Nā Goḍava*, 36.

90. Luther, *Hyderabad*, 185.

91. Francesca Orsini, *The Hindi Public Sphere (1920–1940): Language and Literature in the Age of Nationalism* (New Delhi: Oxford University Press, 2009).

92. Mir and Mir, *The Anthems of Resistance*, 12.

93. Shamsur Rahman Faruqi, "A Long History of Urdu Literary Culture," in *Literary Cultures in History*, ed. Pollock, 814.

94. David Lunn, "Across the Divide: Looking for the Common Ground of Hindustani," *Modern Asian Studies* 52, no. 6 (2018): 2056–2079.

95. In a 2019 article published in the *Diplomat*, Shahzaman Haque discussed recent issues related to Urdu:

> The strength of Urdu lies in its diversity and broad appeal. It has united people in the past and it still has the potential to reunite and shrink the distances between different communities in today's turbulent times. It is a pity that powerful Hindu nationalists take such an exclusivist and hostile attitude toward Urdu, as such an attitude is hardly representative of India's deeper identity and long coexistence of multiple regions, peoples, faiths, and languages. To purge Urdu is to purge a part of India, and one can only hope that the contributions of Urdu to Indian history and culture today as well as in the past will be celebrated, not suppressed to the satisfied whims of the narrow-minded and intolerant. (*The Diplomat*, July 15, 2019)

96. Dubrow, *Cosmopolitan Dreams*, 5.

97. Javeed Alam, "Inter-Community Life in Hyderabad: Reconfigurations," *Deccan Studies* 6, no. 2 (2008): 23–24.

98. Rao, *Telugupai Uaū Phārasīka Prabhāvaṁ*.

99. For a detailed study of Telangana journalism between 1886 and 1956, see Sangisetti Srinivas, *Shabnavis: Telangana Patrikaa Ranga Charitra* (Hyderabad: Kavile Telangana Research and Referral Center, 2003).

100. Deviprasad, ed., *Palleturu: Samskrutika Masa Patrika* [A village: Cultural monthly magazine] (Sanga Reddy, 1952).

101. Sheldon Pollock, ed., "Introduction," in *Literary Cultures in History: Reconstructions from South Asia* (Berkeley: University of California Press, 2003), 1–36.

102. Dasarathi, *Yātrā Smṛti*, 15; Sadasiva, *Yaadi*, 1.

103. Sudipta Kaviraj, *The Invention of Private Life: Literature and Ideas* (New York: Columbia University Press, 2015), 41.

104. Syed Akbar Hyder, "Up, Urdu's Progressive Wit: Sulaiman Khatib, Sarvar Danda, and the Subaltern Satirists Who Spoke," *Annual of Urdu Studies*, no. 20 (2005): 99–126.

105. Pollock, *Literary Cultures in History*, 19.

CONCLUSION

THE AFTERLIFE OF THE POLICE ACTION
AND CONTEMPORARY MUSLIM DEBATE

How could we forget a violent massacre of such a massive magnitude that occurred at the very heart of the country? How do we read such a historical event in the wake of an authoritarian Hindu Raj and the making of contemporary Muslim discourses?

Although these are the same questions that I have been attempting to explore at a conceptual level throughout, the origins of such questions lie in the everyday lives of my interlocutors of the Police Action. My documentation of oral histories about the Police Action started in 2006 and came to an end in the first week of January 2020 when I witnessed a huge "million people march" in Hyderabad (Figure C.1) against the National Register of Citizenship (NRC) and Citizenship Amendment Act (CAA). Mass protests during this period have registered a "high visibility" of common Muslims in the public sphere of South Asia. As Akeel Bilgrami suggested, "The common Muslim has done what even Gandhi, Nehru, Ambedkar, or Azad couldn't."[1] Some of my interlocutors, since they were also active in the political sphere during their twenties, tried to make connections between 1948 and 2020 when the citizenship of Muslims metamorphosed into a "national problem."[2] As a result of Hindu nationalism or ethnonationalism, the being and belonging of Muslims in India have become a major "problem," both empirically and theoretically. As Manan Ahmed noted: "To be a Muslim in India today is to be a problem. The Muslim is a theological problem, a social problem, a cultural problem, and critically, a geopolitical problem."[3]

Figure C.1 Million March 2020 by various sections of Hyderabadis against the Citizenship Amendment Act

Source: *Sakshi* newspaper, Hyderabad.

While working on this book between 2012 and 2021, I also witnessed the Black Lives Matter movement (BLM) in the USA. The question of why some lives do not matter became a major debate, as the minoritized voices of African Americans, Muslims, and women marched along the main streets throughout the nation. As a student who has an interest in the making of everyday religious lives of marginalized communities, particularly Muslims, I began to make a few connections of questions such as Muslim being and belonging, the idea of citizenship, and the hegemony of a nationalist narrative that became prominent in everyday debates in the USA and India too.[4] For a broader understanding of the Muslim community of 1948 Hyderabad, at first, I wanted to document the stories of the victims and survivors of the Police Action of 1948. As expected, it took me enormous time, effort, and patience to find people who had actually witnessed or survived any or all of the Police Action. Even once I had located some, few victims were ready to share about this dark episode of their lives, as the memory itself was utterly sad and frustrating. Several of these interlocutors openly refused to respond to my question, saying that they "don't want to return to that most bitter part of their life." Then came the new phase of Hindu nationalism in 2006 which, according to the political scientist Christophe Jaffrelot, demonstrated the rise of the authoritarian Hindutva state. According to him, this majoritarian state "targeted minorities in a more official and direct way than the vigilante groups, making Muslims second-class citizens."[5]

It was during this period after the Hindu nationalism that I met most of my interlocutors, those from the city of Hyderabad to the remotest corners of Telangana state. My fieldwork was further complicated by these political developments. During this period, I witnessed many forms of fear and psychosis that the Muslim community in the city and Telangana state had suffered. First, there was a subjective "fear" that did not allow them to retrieve the dark memory, and now, the fear of the authorities made them remain silent forever. Hence, each life story in this book uncovers unending pain and invisible injury. As I traveled from place to place and as more interlocutors began to share their long-suppressed stories, they helped me understand the forgotten history that was marked by silences.

Soon I realized that rather than covering them in abstract theorization, I should try to learn from the concrete reality of their testimonials. At the heart of this book is the desire to uncover this reality of an event that had been pushed to the margins of history. My search began with a question of why this violent event remains invisible in mainstream historiography and public discourses, despite an assertive identitarian movement of Muslims, Dalits, and feminism in the late 1980s.[6] During our many conversations, my interlocutors too asked the same question and tried to offer many interpretations in their own ways. Many of these interlocutors called the Police Action the "Hyderabad Massacre"—*ūcakōta* in Telugu, or *qatal-e-aam* or *khoonrezi* in local Urdu. Since most of them were politically conscious, despite their reluctance to speak of long-ago events they nonetheless tried to voice their story that was about to become drowned under what they called "the heavy flood of Hindu nationalism."

The five-day-long "battle" of the Police Action was certainly still fresh in their memory. But they also stressed that the "main history" or "official history" (*pradhāna caritra* or *adhikāra caritra* in Telugu) was centered on the celebration of the formation of the Telugu linguistic state of Andhra Pradesh and the leftist-centered Telangana armed struggle. The celebrations of the formation of a new state of Andhra Pradesh became a form of nationalist rhetoric, while the Telangana armed rebellion turned into a leftist campaign for the general elections of 1952. According to the Deccani Urdu literary historian Samala Sadasiva:

> The very usage of the term Andhra was meant to relegate the history of Hyderabad and Telangana into some immemorial past. While growing up in the late 1930s or '40s we all identified ourselves with the term

Telangana as it represents the mixed history of Urdu and Telugu. Along with the new usage of Andhra, the state-sponsored histories gradually erased the centrality of Hyderabad and its Muslims. The *khoonrezi* ("massacre") of the Police Action was totally removed from the recorded histories.[7]

Sadasiva's comments took me back to what the folk singer Abdul Quddus Saheb said in the introduction of this book. In 2006, when I was about to wrap up our conversation, he mentioned the statements made by the Bharatiya Janata Party (BJP) in 1998.[8] Specifically, Quddus Saheb spoke of the Home Minister L. K. Advani's speech in Hyderabad—a mammoth public meeting and, in fact, one I attended. Referring to the Police Action, Advani made a call to "celebrate" September 17 as a "day of the liberation," later translated as *vimōcana dinaṁ* in the Telugu public sphere. Advani's usage of the term "liberation" triggered a new debate about the Police Action in the local print and electronic media, as well as in various political writings after 1998. Responding to Advani's statement, several historians and social activists also began to revisit the history of the Police Action.[9] Along with the events that led to the Police Action, what to do with Muslims of Hyderabad was again a question, while Muslims were also in dilemma about their future. The chronology of this history was repeatedly considered in the public discourse as activists from different social and political groups continued to debate.

Quddus Saheb said:

Advani and BJP had actually stirred the hornet's nest for their own political benefits! Not that we have all forgotten about it, but the way Advani fueled this issue was quite disturbing! We should talk about the Police Action, but the way Advani and his followers entered into this debate was all hate speech that caused a new antagonism between Muslims and Hindus. He and his party were just using this entire history—*tārīkhu*—of the Police Action to take advantage of Hindu vote.[10]

Either Islamic or Hyderabad-related, the events from history—*tārīkh*—had always been a source of passion for Quddus Saheb. Growing up in the critical era of the late 1930s and 1940s, he had developed a keen interest in reading history materials both in Urdu and Telugu. Being a well-known folk performer and a public figure during the late 1940s, Quddus Saheb had also witnessed many historical events during his lifetime—from the powerful public speeches of Nawab Bahadur Yar Jung (1905–1944) to the beginnings of the Telangana separatist movement in 2004.[11] Quddus Saheb recalled for me that

> Bahadur Yar Jung's party Ittehād, later known as Majlis-e-Ittehād'ul Muslimīn (MIM) became extremely powerful and led many political and social movements. He was such an inspiration—*josh*—to the young Muslims of Hyderabad that we [knew] all his words by heart. He actually provided a language for our emotions and thoughts. Most importantly, he made us realize that young Muslims need to speak out about the contemporary politics and understand how Islam could contribute to improve them.[12]

Many times, during our conversations, Quddus Saheb tried to compare the late 1990s to the late 1940s. Of particular and significant concern for him was the lack of "proper" leadership—in his eyes—in the Muslim community. Even now I remember how Quddus Saheb's eyes glowed when he spoke about Bahadur Yar Jung's accomplishments (Figure C.2). In the midst of his enthusiastic recollections of the speeches of Bahadur Yar Jung, he concluded, "These days we need such an orator and activist who can inspire with words and actions. More than that we need a force that unifies the entire Muslim community from the city to the remotest village in Telangana." When Quddus Saheb said these words, he was not so much being nostalgic, but he was speaking from a pragmatic viewpoint. Bahadur Yar Jung, according to Quddus Saheb, was a combination of many dimensions—including leadership qualities, oratory, and political awareness—that the Muslim community should emulate in any period, and he emphasized, "particularly after the saffron wave of Hindutva."

In speaking about the Police Action, Quddus Saheb repeatedly referred to the Battle of Karbala (680 CE), which he described as "the historical event that demanded many sacrifices from the Muslim community." It took me a while to understand that he was making an important connection between the life story of Bahadur Yar Jung and the martyrdom of Imam Hussein in Karbala. "Just like the Imam Hussain, Bahadur Saheb was also a martyr in the battlefield."[13] While Quddus Saheb's own life was filled with many tragic events, such as the loss of family members and close friends in the violence of 1948, he had also witnessed many persons who had gone incognito, been

Figure C.2 Bahadur Yar Jung with young Hyderabadi Muslims
Source: Mohammed Ayub Ali Khan.

displaced, or had had their lives uprooted, and had seen a new generation of Muslims face the stigma of "being Muslim." Explaining further about this stigmatization, he said:

> You know how hard it was when you were being labelled as a criminal and anti-social in the name of the Razakars. All Muslims, particularly, the younger generation between the age group 18 and 30 were stigmatized as the Razakars and hunted down. They had a hard time finding work, food, and shelter in their own hometown.[14]

I included several such testimonies from my field research in Chapter 2; some of those testimonies also stressed that "not all Muslims are extremists or Razakars." Conflating the identity of ordinary Muslims with the Razakars was one of the narrative strategies in many nationalist writings too. According to Quddus Saheb, such demonization was due to a lack of "proper" leadership. He said:

> As the times had changed, Muslims had also lost that support and empathy. Now the very word Muslim arouses some fear for many

people. Things have gotten even worse now and I feel so bad about the current generation of Muslims. Where have we come?![15]

Quddus Saheb stressed the Urdu term *hamdardi* (empathy) and noted a lack of empathy towards Muslims and Muslim issues. Despite all the hardships and tragedies in his personal life, Quddus Saheb had also contributed much to the making of this new generation of Muslims. A devoted performer, he successfully inspired at least a few young men, both Muslims and Hindus, and trained them in the folk performances of Muharram (known as *pirla pandaga* or "the festival of *pirs*") that memorializes the martyrdom of Imam Hussain and the Prophet's family in the Battle of Karbala. As a performer of Muharram songs, Quddus Saheb had travelled extensively in various regions of the Hyderabad state and the current state of Telangana. Since he feared having to abandon such public performance, he was also passionate about training at least ten or twelve young men to continue the tradition. That way, he was always in communication with the new generation Muslims and Hindus wherever he traveled. He said:

> Of course, I can say I was really successful in training more than twenty young men and then it arrived—the saffron wave of the Bharatiya Janata Party. At this moment, even young Muslims were not ready even to participate in any public rituals related to Muslims. I then started witnessing another phase of hatred. For Muslims now in India, it is like every day is a Karbala. Muslims are being killed for no reason and just for few political motives.[16]

Quddus Saheb was not alone in comparing the fate of Muslims under Hindutva to Karbala. Many interlocutors and contemporary political activists use similar metaphoric language, particularly to speak about their condition in the times of what the political scientists like Angana Chatterji call "a normalized majoritarianism and hostility to Muslims."[17] During our many conversations, Quddus Saheb often referred to the Babri mosque demolition on December 6, 1992. According to him:

> It was nothing but another mode of Police Action, as both religion and governmental politics had joined hands once again to destroy the entire Muslim community in India. In fact, this demolition was more than destroying a mosque and a direct attack on the Muslims. As a person

who witnessed the Police Action, I felt like this one is another testing moment, not only for Muslims, but also for Hindus. Here we are at the end of the twentieth century, and I just also heard about what is happening in Gujarat—the killings of Muslims.

As a response to Advani, several Muslim activists returned to the Muslim question discussed during the Police Action. They were concerned about how the "hasty" decision of the "military invasion" by the union government of India had led to its tragedies. Some now describe those five days between September 13 and 17 as a "battle" and as the earliest phase of Hindutva.[18] These discourses remind us of how the Indian government under the leadership of Nehru and Sardar Patel initiated the "military invasion" as the Security Council of the United Nations was about to convene on September 16, 1948, in Paris. The documents related to this delegation to the United Nations were published in 1951 with the title *The Hyderabad Question before the United Nations (Documents and Other Materials)* (Figure C.3). The document reported:

The Nizam, who has been a prisoner and compelled to sign whatever decrees were wished by the Indian Military Governor, in November, 1949 issued a *firman* accepting the Instrument of Accession by which Hyderabad would be incorporated into the Union of India, subject to approval by a Constituent Assembly to be elected by the people of Hyderabad.[19]

During the post-1998 debates about the Police Action, several activists referred to the entire process of accession or integration *vilīnam* in Telugu, meaning "unlawful" and "undemocratic." As documented in the oral histories of this book, the Police Action remains an influential trope in the narratives of public culture.[20] After the declaration made by Advani in 1998, one such folk song from the public imagination was circulated widely:

How many colors you don,
Nehru, oh, Nehru!
How many colors you take on,
Nehru, oh, Nehru!

Now the real color of yours is out,
Nehru, oh, Nehru!

Figure C.3   The Government of India declared the Nizam as Raj Pramukh

Source: Mohammed Ayub Ali Khan.

Tatas on the right
Birlas on the left
Truman on the head
you call yourself a socialist
Now we know your real face,
Nehru, oh, Nehru!

Published in a document titled *1948 Septembar 17 Vidrōhaṁ* (1948 September 17, betrayal) by the Communist Party of India (Marxist-Leninist) of Andhra Pradesh, this folk song had returned to the public discourse with all its leftist connotations, however, with a pungent critique on Nehru. Similar viewpoints were also expressed in a 1966 novel by M. A. Seljouk *Corpses*:

On Nehru's death nearly everybody wrote what a saint he was. The corpses I saw, and some of hundred corpses I buried with my own hands in each one of those years 1949 to 1957 when I fled from the country, were some of the achievements of this saint. The corpses of Moslems and Christians who lay rotting in the fields of Hyderabad were the achievements of this saint and his silent admirers abroad.[21]

Capturing the core of the argument made by leftist groups and political activists, the song explicitly critiques the idea of "liberation" as a "betrayal."[22] Drawing a comparison between the 1948 public speeches by Sardar Patel and then the 1998 speech by Advani, this publication was also instrumental in debating multiple dimensions of the Police Action. For leftists, the Police Action was one of the tools to suppress the popularity of the Communist Party's armed struggle known as *Telangana sāyudha pōrāṭaṁ*, in Telugu, which was famously described by the leftists as the replica of the Yan'an, the wartime stronghold of the Chinese Communist Party in the mid-1930s to 1949.[23] However, Muslim activists of the late 1990s contested what they felt was leftists' overemphasis on the Telangana armed struggle in explaining the Police Action.

Between 1998 and 2010, a few writings in the Telugu public sphere have returned to various dimensions of the Police Action, and of these the newfound Telangana Historical Society's *17 Septembar 1948: Bhinna Dṛkkōṇālu* (17 September 1948: Different perspectives) declaration stands out.[24] Focusing on all possible dimensions of a marginalized history in Telangana, this society successfully gathered a public discourse against the nationalist "celebration" of the Police Action. The debate around the Police Action centered around three topics: first, the realities about the nature of the Nizam's rule; second, the status of Muslims in Hyderabad state and then in the newly formed Telangana state; and, finally, questions related to historiography. To discuss these issues, most historians and activists realized the importance of using sources contemporary to the Nizam's rule. Whereas many of these historical and political writings have generated a significant debate about various aspects, the discussion of an ordinary Muslim has so far been elusive. Emphasizing the need to locate ordinary Muslims, this book has tried to define a Muslim turn in the historiography of Hyderabad state and Telangana.

In a 2010 essay published in the Urdu daily newspaper *Etemaad*, a senior journalist of the city, M. A. Majid, uncovered multiple layers of the Police Action and contested the idea of "liberation." The title of this essay "Mere Taboot Par Jashan" (A celebration on my coffin) generated a heated debate.[25] Majid began by questioning the very intention of the Hindutva and its mission after almost sixty-two years of the Police Action. Describing the "celebration" as an "evil suggestion," he said:

"Independence day," "liberation day," "victory day,": these are the different names of the demand to celebrate the 17th September. Why?

Is the accession of Hyderabad freedom from colonialism? Why, after 62 years, is there a demand to celebrate this day officially? Was Hyderabad state, the only Princely state that acceded to India?[26]

Towards the end of this essay, Majid also said:

How can the brokers of power and their sycophants know the meaning of love for the land? Whenever this land called for it, its real lovers spilled their blood. Commander Abdul Razzak Laary knew that he was fighting a mighty emperor who was pious and diligently copied out the Quran. Rather than religion or military might, it was a question of Deccan culture and self-respect that drove Laary. Today this question exists in every Hyderabadi's mind. How can they accept the celebration on the coffins their dear ones whose blood was spilled in the aftermath of 1948? While their celebration will result in mockery and humiliation, the ultimate aim for which these power brokers are harping on 'celebration' will not be achieved. The celebration of the Accession of Hyderabad is a wound on 'Hyderabadiness.' Saffron and Red flags may become one, but we must remember that Aurangazeb put the Mughal empire in a coffin after defeating Golconda! History will repeat itself on those who want to celebrate Hyderabad's liberation.[27]

Considered to be one of the most poignant and emotional responses to Advani's speech, this piece refers to concepts such as the identity of Hyderabadiness, Deccan Islam, and the historical memory of Abdul Razzak Lari, who fought against the Mughal Empire, and various political dimensions of the Muslim dilemma, which together present a strong case for the Hyderabadi Muslim discourse.[28]

Majid's writing demonstrates the importance of Muslims speaking out about not only the Police Action but also on behalf of the larger task of retrieving Deccani culture. Whereas this process of retrieval still needs more work, several writings in the Telugu public sphere show a certain level of Muslim agency by having produced translations of personal memoirs, biographical sketches, and autobiographical writings about the Police Action. Between 1998 and 2020, there has been a continuous effort to publish or reprint memoirs, autobiographies, and personal essays that demonstrate the pluralist essence of the Hyderabadi *tehzeeb*. Published both in English and then Telugu, these works have endeavored to present a multi-layered texture of Hyderabadi identity. I have discussed various narrative strategies that questioned the hegemonic and canonical writings about the Police Action and Hyderabadi Muslims. Any story that digresses from the mainstream historiography (if only briefly) offers insights into how historical events shaped the histories of their own group and the community as a whole. In this book, I tried to gather many such personal stories of ordinary people and literary figures, whose lives were deeply connected to the history of the Police Action.

BETWEEN THE PERSONAL AND THE POLITICAL: THE MAKING OF A COUNTER-NARRATIVE

Each chapter in this book has been a blend of personal and political dimensions, given that many oral accounts and written sources blur the lines between these two aspects. For many of these accounts, the long 1940s, when most personal lives were defined by their immediate political sphere, were critical. By connecting these two aspects—the personal and the political—we can visualize the larger implications of the Police Action. Hence, when discussing the making of literary personalities in the wake of the Police Action, this book has shown how their everyday lives were intricately connected to various political events, figures, and discourses between the 1930s and 1950s. However, I also noted particular aspects of marginalization that these interlocutors and political activists explained. During my field research and archival work, I heard repeatedly that political writings and activities were confined to certain elite classes and categories. Most of them had complained that such political writings and activities were meant and designed for the upper class and caste groups, giving ordinary Muslims, Dalits, and women no voice. Yet although there has been an effort to retrieve a few Dalit and women's writings over the last two decades,[29] the Muslim voice of the 1930s and 1940s still remains largely undiscovered.

When deconstructing the events of the Police Action, some of the earlier memoirs and autobiographical writings oppose the idea that the military invasion of 1948 was aimed totally at the Nizam. With a goal of understanding the "real" intentions of the Indian government, such narratives emphasize three specific political aspects: first, to study the larger implications of the Police Action from the perspective of Muslims; second, to examine the nationalist politics of Partition that isolated local Muslims in

Hyderabad state; and third and finally, to explore the major influence of the leftist-centered Telangana armed struggle throughout the state.[30] During my interviews, many interlocutors and political activists of the late 1940s told me that the Indian government was concerned more about the consequences of these two major political events than about the integration of Hyderabad state. To use the words of the activist Ashwaq Hussain, "first, the fear of the communists taking over the state, and then the fear of Muslims after the Partition had actually led to push the Police Action." Hussain said:

> The military invasion—*sainika durākramana*—was not about the Nizam. It was against the Muslims in the wake of the Partition and the rise of the historical Telangana armed rebellion. They were using the name of the Nizam and the princely state as an excuse. Most of my family and friends still call this an invasion—*durākramana*.[31]

Several writers who published their memoirs in the aftermath of the Police Action held a similar perspective. Fareed Mirza who resigned from the government service on July 15, 1948, protesting against, to use his own words, "the subversive activities of the Ittehadul Muslimeen Razakars and the then government's one-sided policy" documented his experiences as a member of the Central Relief Committee after the Police Action. Referring to the plight of various ordinary Muslims, Mirza noted:

> We were very much grieved to see that not only no attention is being paid to them but, on the other hand, seeing their pitiable plight, some officers of mean mentality are taking undue advantage of the helplessness of the widows. Inattentiveness prevails everywhere. Having shown with a heavy heart this sad state of affairs, we feel happy to state that almost at every place, where a lot of killing had taken place, many noble but illiterate Hindus risking their own lives, saved many individual Muslims and helped the widows (who had lost everything) with food, grains etc, for many days. In all the villages which we visited, we found that no government officer had taken any trouble to ask the Muslims about their sufferings after the Police Action and in what condition they were leading their lives.[32]

Throughout this narrative, Mirza presents his case speaking from the lens of an ordinary Muslim of the post-Police Action. At this point, it is also important to understand the dynamics of this mode of writing, namely, that these writers pursued it as an immediate necessity to articulate a Muslim voice. To begin with, the act of writing was not part of their profession, and they took to writing to represent a Muslim viewpoint against many historical and political writings that had pushed them to the periphery. In fact, they were trying to write something for the first time, and they all approached it from an extremely subjective angle. Although the late 1930s was known for the rise in print culture and journalism, none of these writers had ever tried writing a single article. For instance, Mohammed Hyder was an administrator in Osmanabad during the Police Action. As several accounts from this region show, Osmanabad was one of the worst-affected areas during and after the Police Action. During his jail time in 1949, Hyder had begun to fill notebooks about the day-to-day events, and these were later edited and published as his memoir *October Coup: A Memoir of the Struggle for Hyderabad*. Explaining the writing process of the book, the editor and Hyder's son Masood Hyder said:

> This memoir is an edited version of the account of his collectorship written by him in Osmanabad jail in July and August of 1949. His notebooks were typed up soon after his release in 1952, but not published at that time; presumably, he intended to first negotiate his professional future with the government. In 1960, rebuffed by the government, he put Osmanabad and everything connected with it behind him.[33]

Considered to be one of the earliest accounts of the Police Action, this memoir had become a major source in the recent debates about Hyderabad. During my conversations in 2010 and 2019, the freedom fighter Burgula Narasing Rao mentioned Hyder's work more than once. According to him:

> As an administrator, Hyder's skills in writing were extremely limited. However, these notebooks, later turned into a book, show his love and devotion to the Hyderabad state. When reading now, this memoir triggers my own past as a school kid. He was part of the government, me an activist. He was a Muslim, and me not being a Muslim does not make big difference when it comes to our emotional responses to Hyderabad.[34]

Burgula and many freedom fighters and activists of the late 1940s were intrigued by Hyder's narrative of the politics in Hyderabad. Many of them repeatedly mentioned his critique of the Congress's party-led politics. Despite his loyalty to Hyderabad state, Hyder was concerned more about the Hyderabadi Muslim community, and this memoir in many ways provides one of the earliest accounts of Muslim politics.

> The main political beneficiary of any process of democratization, the Hyderabad State Congress, though espousing the same aims as the Indian National Congress, had a past in which it had proved ineffectual and a future that was likely to be equally unpromising, as long as it continued to be so poorly led.... It had in the past made the wrong moves, such as initiating a civil disobedience movement in alliance with the Arya Samaj and the Hindu Mahasabha, parties less secular in outlook than the Congress.[35]

Discussing at length the politics of the Congress party, Arya Samaj, and the Hindu Mahasabha, Hyder's comments offer insights into their activities and contextualize the immediate politics of the Police Action. Although Hyder had numerous emotional moments in this writing, he was extremely conscious of the politics of different organizations both Muslim and Hindu. Towards the end of the memoir, he said:

> So much for myself. There is a larger question on which I must conclude: How can we best understand what took place between Hyderabad and India? The confrontation of 1947–48 is usually seen from the Indian point of view, and interpreted in terms of the aspirations of the Indian nationalist movement. I do not find this useful approach because, seen through that lens, the Hyderabad position appears perverse and illogical, suggesting a futile posture of defiance against the inevitable tide of history that favoured the emergence of a unified India. By now this is the popular interpretation, and the general impression persists that Hyderabad's negotiating position was unreasonable, and that in the end it became the victim of its own miscalculation.[36]

In his nuanced narratives of many events during the period between 1948 and 1949, Hyder emphasizes the rights of individuals and states. Hyder was clearly supporting the cause of Hyderabad state and was intent on developing a political argument to uphold his argument. Several activists who now oppose Hindutva terminology such as "liberation," "independence," and "integration" along with the dominance of the centralized power, tap into Hyder's earliest account and borrow an alternative terminology that allows the political situation of this period to re-assess the entire event. In addition, the translation of this memoir entered the public discourse at a time when even the Telangana Rashtra Samiti, the political party that led the Telangana separatist movement had subscribed to the Hindutva mission.[37] Burgula said:

> Political parties such as the Samiti were not exceptional in this case when it comes to the Muslim question. They openly called for the celebration of the Police Action as the "Telangana Independence Day." That shows the political manipulation of the majoritarian state. We need to study and understand empathetically how Muslims were actually engaging with the Police Action and the politics of their time. Hyder's book is an example.[38]

Amid the heated debates of 1998 to 2013, the translation of this memoir into Telugu further demonstrates its position in the Hyderabadi public sphere. This translation makes an intervention into the post-1998 Muslim politics in Hyderabad, particularly when the historical memory of the Nizam state and its political nature was back in the public eye in the wake of the Telangana separatist movement. In the process, there was an effort to redefine the politics of Hyderabad state and its developmental approach as regards arenas such as education and religious matters, most importantly Hindu–Muslim interactions. Whereas several narratives privilege an anti-Nizam stance, Hyder's memoir presents a ground-level approach by documenting positive aspects of the Nizam's rule.

Along with Hyder's memoir, several political and social activists also began to refer to another autobiographical work, this time that of Mir Laiq Ali (1903–1971), the prime minister of Hyderabad state during the Police Action (Figure C.4). In Chapter 1, in my discussion of the short fiction of Swamy, I recounted the fate of Dilawar, who decided to migrate to Pakistan. Like Dilawar, many Muslim officers of Hyderabad state had migrated to Pakistan. However, Mir Laiq Ali, being the prime minister during the Police Action, had an entirely different story.[39] According to the historian Narendra Luther:

> On 7 March 1950, the city woke up to a sensational day. The newspapers reported that Laiq Ali had escaped from the house arrest. All sorts

Figure C.4 Laiq Ali Khan

Source: Mohammed Ayub Ali Khan's private collection.

of stories were heard in the country about the manner of his escape. Immediately thereafter, all former ministers and others were transferred to the Central Jail.[40]

While several stories about his escape still make the rounds in the popular imagination in Hyderabad and Telangana, historians such as Omar Khalidi also returned to his political story. For the first time, Khalidi published a segment from the autobiography of Mir Laiq Ali in his volume *Hyderabad: After the Fall* in 1988. Khalidi described this work as "the only detailed account of the actual combat during that brief war."[41] When the same piece was translated into Telugu and published in the Telugu media in 2007 and later included in several publications, Laiq Ali's story became a springboard for several political discussions centered around the Muslim account of the Police Action.[42]

First published in Karachi in 1962, Laiq Ali's autobiography *The Tragedy of Hyderabad* was immediately banned by the government of India and was never allowed to be circulated there. Against the background of the post-1998 debates on the Police Action and the Hyderabad state, this was republished in 2011. During the launch of the book by the Deccan Archeological and Cultural Research Institute (DACRI) and the 1969 Telangana Movement Founder's Forum, the co-convenor, Kollu Chiranjeevi, said that the

Police Action was "not liberation but encroachment by the government on Hyderabad state."[43] The 2011 edition of this autobiography became a key source in re-writing the historiography of the Police Action and Hyderabad state. Writing about the process of this book, Laiq Ali said:

> The contents of this book were mostly scribbled during the days of my internment after the fall of Hyderabad and were among the few belongings with which I luckily escaped from the clutches of the Indian armies in occupation of the State. After my arrival in Pakistan the manuscript received some finishing touches and additions.[44]

It took almost nearly five decades to publish this book in India when a group of Telangana cultural historians had begun to excavate the archives of the Telangana awakening of the 1940s.[45] The editor of this team, Jitendra Babu, said:

> In the recent debates on the Police Action, Laiq Ali's book was instrumental in presenting a new evidence. This material also allows us to read the entire event in the wake of the Telangana resurgence thus helping us to see a more nuanced dimension of the inside story of the Police Action and the Hyderabad state.[46]

Similar to Hyder's memoir, so too Laiq Ali's autobiography highlights various aspects of the cause of Hyderabad, and the Telugu translation of this autobiography is particularly key in the wake of the Telangana movement.[47] Towards the conclusion of this book, Laiq Ali mentions how Muslims were persecuted during the Police Action on the "ground that almost every one of them was a member of the Razakars organization."[48] In this context, Laiq Ali was specifically talking about the fate of upper-class Muslims during the Police Action, which was indeed one of the central themes in the short fiction of Nelluri Kesava Swamy, which I have discussed in Chapter 1. Similarly, Chapter 2 discussed the political narratives that conflate Muslim identity with Razakar militarism.

Contesting the nationalist interpretations of the Police Action, Captain Lingala Pandu Ranga Reddy, who was a commander during the Police Action, published a personal historical essay entitled "September 17, 1948 Hyderabad Liberation Day: A Misnomer."[49] While pro-Hindutva organizations repeat stories of the liberation of Hyderabad, Reddy reveals that his General Commanding Officer openly instructed that "they were going to

Hyderabad to aid and assist Nizam against the depredations of Communists and Razakars."[50] In addition, Reddy also commented:

> However, motivated alien writers, settler-reporters, self-seeking politicians, rabid fundamentalists and half-baked historians who were ignoramus of Persian, Urdu and Arabic languages had twisted the truth to serve their end for obvious reasons. It was purely a military intervention and people had no role whatsoever in it.[51]

Whereas Reddy's essay presents the case from a military viewpoint, cultural historians such as Narendra Luther had simultaneously begun publishing personal essays—another prominent tool for retrieving the history of the Hyderabadi Muslims, particularly after the 1940s. As I have argued here, Luther's memoirs function more like a counter-memory given that the nationalist, secularist, and leftist narratives strategically erase or deliberately misread a Muslim dimension of the Police Action. Removing such lenses, Luther's memoir has captured the everyday life of the city through its portrayals of the key figures and events. Indeed, the initial writing strategy of this memoir, as Luther explains, was in the "first person by the City."[52] More than his career as an administrative officer, Hyderabadis remember Luther for his valuable memoirs later published in *Hyderabad: A Biography*; subsequently, some parts of this book were also translated into Telugu.[53] Along with an intimate association with the city, Luther's outlook, as articulated in these words, shows his conviction as a historian. Referring to the merger of Hyderabad state and the Andhra Pradesh governments, he said:

> It was a bad marriage from the outset. There used to be two lunch rooms at the secretariat for bureaucrats. One was for Hyderabadis and Urdu was spoken there. I remember going to the room for AP officials and they would say those fellows were lazy, only knew how to dress well, couldn't do any work, and then the Telangana ones would say these Huns had come, those fellows had no social graces, no courtesy and only talked about work and work. It was a really bad marriage and their hearts never met. I told that to the members of the Sri Krishna Commission.[54]

Luther's memoirs begin with the pre-modern history of Hyderabad and then revisit the times between the 1930s and 2004. For my argument here, his memoirs about the troubled decades of the 1930s and 1940s are relevant as they capably retrieve the history of a Muslim voice. He begins by describing how different events were happening at the same time. He documents this tense moment that includes events such as the formation of the Majlis-e-Ittehad-ul-Muslimeen (MIM), Bahadur Yar Jung's key speech on the birthday of Prophet Mohammad, the beginnings of the Razakar militarism, the first meeting of the Congress, and Swami Ramananda Tirtha's earliest phase of the Congress party activities. He said:

> Thus in 1938 and thereafter, there was politics all over. There were statements; there were agitations; there were bans and arrests; there were strikes and rustications; there were processions and slogans. There were also negotiations amongst the moderate elements and there were discussions between political leaders and officials of the government.[55]

Most such memoirs provide insight into understanding the contours of the new public sphere in Hyderabad state, what the historian Rama Sundari Mantena describes as "the surge of a civil societal activism."[56] Many sources in the Telugu public sphere emphasize the role of local libraries, publications, journalism, and cultural activism.[57] Within this new sphere of activism, Luther offers evidence for the participation of Muslim public figures and their discourses of dissent. He noted:

> Sir Mirza Ismail had said that in Hyderabad many Muslims had lost their heads. As time passed the number increased. But also, there were Muslims who were unhappy at the course of events, who believed that what was happening was wrong, whose heart came out in sympathy with the victims of the loot, arson, and rape committed by the razakars, and who felt that all this should stop.[58]

Luther's recollections about these personalities retrieve the untold history of Muslims of Hyderabad. In many ways, these memoirs also document a version of Muslim consciousness that was responding to new political systems, the religious environment, and cultural transformations that occurred between the 1940s and 1950s. By means of this activism, the Muslims of Hyderabad had overcome the post-Police Action times of anxiety and fear—a process that was very slow, but steady. In many ways, this phase also led to the narration of an exclusive and distinctive story of the Muslims of Hyderabad, as discussed in this book. Amidst the new debates after the 1998 turn of Hindutva and the significant level of new publications on the Police Action and Hyderabadi Muslims, now we need to turn our attention to the role of shared practices between Hindus and Muslims within this latest discourse.

HINDUS AND MUSLIMS OF HYDERABAD

Recent studies inform us about how ordinary Muslims of the premodern times, who had no role in state or religious authority, played a large part in the making of South Indian Islam.[59] Sebastian Prange argues that this version of Islam was shaped by the "reality of Muslims living within non-Muslim societies."[60] Nevertheless, these dynamics, I argue, become more complicated in the age of nationalism and modernity as the politics of the new nation-states in the post-1947 legitimized the othering of Muslims in various ways. The relationship between the Indian nation and the figure of a Muslim has been continuously in question, and this was further complicated during various conflicts such as the Babri mosque demolition of 1992, the Godhra riots of 2004, and the solidification of Islamophobia in the wake of the recent Hindutva politics. Amid these tension-ridden divisive politics, global religious politics after 9/11 also further deteriorated the status of Muslims, even in the remotest villages.

In *The Festival of Pīrs*, I argued that any "locally produced forms of Islam emphasize the embeddedness of local Islam in a pluralistic community of both Muslim and non-Muslim populations, as well as how Islam in a particular place is linked to processes at work in the larger Islamic world."[61] Continuing to maintain this argument, this book specifically focuses on the Police Action event to unpack the life stories of Hyderabadi Muslimness, which could be interpreted through either the lens of pluralism or the composite culture of Hyderabad and the recent upsurge of Telangana separatism. Despite many disruptions, this idea of Hyderabadi composite culture is deeply embedded in the constantly shifting dynamics of Muslims and Hindus. These interactions are now further complicated by the question: How do we understand these endlessly shifting interactions in the wake of changing political authorities and the religious conflicts that followed the state violence of the Police Action?

Acknowledging the urgency of discussing the complexity of Hindu–Muslim interactions, I will emphasize the connected discourses of these

Muslim pasts that pose new challenges in understanding the contemporary Hindu–Muslim dilemma that began with the Police Action. As in my previous work, this book likewise emphasizes that the Muslim question is not an exclusive or isolated discourse. While several questions and debates were a continuation of religious matters from before 1948, as many of my oral and written sources emphasize several key aspects of Hyderabadi politics underwent a major transformation after the Police Action. Due to the immediate political and governmental changes in the state of Hyderabad, the status of Muslims suffered a major setback. Whereas this process of minoritization was an outcome of the Partition and the related discourses, in the case of Hyderabad, the Police Action resulted in further deterioration of the Muslim situation. The literary historian Amir Mufti's 2007 work informs us about the process of minoritization as reflected in Urdu literature. His study focuses on various pressures, to use his words, "exerted on language, literature, culture, and identity in the process of becoming minoritized."[62]

Similarly, the process of minoritization of Muslims in the aftermath of the Police Action also had much deeper and broader consequences. Any debate about Muslims in Hyderabad or the current state of Telangana unavoidably recalls the event of the Police Action and the Partition as well. Several fictional and non-fictional narratives and oral accounts present the case of Muslim minoritization that had occurred at a fast pace between 1948 and 1956—which means until the formation of the Telugu linguistic state of Andhra Pradesh. Several of these sources lament the gradual erasure of Hindu–Muslim composite culture and multiple disruptions of the ethics of co-existence in Hyderabad. As mentioned before, Samala Sadasiva, a bilingual Telugu and Urdu writer who represents the pluralist ethos of the Hyderabadi *tehzeeb*, made provocative comments about the formation of the Telugu linguistic state. Those lengthy conversations with him ended in a simple sentence with complex implications when he said: "November 1, 1956 will be a black day in the history of Hyderabad and Telangana forever."[63] For many Telugu and Urdu writers of Hyderabad in the late 1940s and the early 1950s, this statement remained one of the dominant themes in their creative and critical works—and the key question in many discussions between Muslim and Hindu religious lives, along with the interactions between Urdu and Telugu cultural spheres. According to many of these writers, earlier there was no rigid partitioning of these spheres. Both of them still exist in a singular and undivided way, exemplifying the beauty of a pluralism embedded in the texture of ordinary everyday life. Nevertheless, when speaking about this pluralist texture of Hyderabad and Telangana, they never fail to document the disruptions and ruptures as well. In one of the interviews, Guduri Seetharam said:

> We know the dangers of overly romanticizing such notions in the present times where the Hindu nationalism on one hand, and a Muslim exclusivism on the other hand have become a social fact. We still lament the death of such an inclusive life style of the times before the Police Action.[64]

Although both Sadasiva and Seetharam were from the mufassil districts of the state of Hyderabad, their voices represent a shared sentiment which was ubiquitous among many Muslim and Hindu writers of the late 1940s. Even contemporary writers after the 1980s emphasize these dynamics between Muslims and Hindus, as a form of "minority literature"—a term that became key in the post-1980s identitarian turn in Telugu literature.[65] The new generation of Muslim writers who began to write extensively in this period identified themselves with the key concept of "minority literature" as opposed to the majoritarian Telugu literary sphere. Whereas the question of Muslimness has guided many of these Muslim writers and critics, the much-needed Hindu–Muslim dialogue, too, became a major theme. While many non-Muslim writers such as Swamy, Bhaskarabhatla, Kavi Raja Murthy, Sadasiva, and Dasarathi wrote about Muslims between 1940 and 1980, this turn to Muslims writing about Muslims was a new phenomenon in the Telugu literary sphere. To separate themselves from the dominant literary mode, this new generation of Muslim writers has begun to use an alternative term—"minority literature" or *Muslim vādam* (Muslimist writing). This aspect of claiming their status in the Telugu literature, I argue, is a defining step towards finding their agency and redefining the question of Muslim representation, where the voices of Muslims de-center the hegemonic narrative. All this effort, indeed, begins as the story that travels from an overly generalized setting to more specific Muslim neighborhoods which are called *mohalla* or *basti* in Urdu and Telugu. Although the journey into these interior landscapes and lifestyles of Muslims began with the writers of the late 1940s and 1950s, it reached its pinnacle in the late 1980s writings. To understand this shift, one needs to pay attention to the very idea of these Muslim neighborhoods and their role in the making of Muslim lives along with their interactions with Hindus, Dalits, and Christians.

NARRATING THE INSIDE STORIES OF MUSLIMS AND THEIR NEIGHBORHOODS

The idea of a localized sense of identity for Muslims has been one of the prominent themes in current research and also in public discourses for the last three decades in South Asian Islam and Islamic studies more broadly.[66] Offering a broader definition of such local Muslim spaces in north India, the historian Raisur Rahman observes that *qasba*s functioned as "the building blocks and microcosms of the larger Indian and global Islamic societies."[67] Vasudha Dalmia analyses the transformative nature of six different North Indian cities— Agra, Allahabad, Banaras, Delhi, Lahore, and Lucknow. Dalmia shows how "modernization took place at a greater and more discernible pace in cities than in the countryside."[68] Both of these works help us understand how alternative archives, such as fictional and non-fictional works, provide evidence of the changing dynamics of a city. Against these recently available tools, this book discusses the making of urban Muslim identity in the city of Hyderabad.

In addition, the history of Hyderabad as a capital city acquires a new dimension in the recent debates in light of the Telangana state separatist movement when the past and present of this city blended in an intriguing way.[69] Many Telangana activists returned to the medieval history of the Qutub Shahis of Golconda (1518–1687) which, as Leonard described, "has frequently been singled out as the best example of cultural synthesis in the Deccan."[70] The *Haidārābād Sirph Hamārā* ("Hyderabad belongs just to us") movement was one of the popular efforts to reclaim that entire history as a counterargument to the coastal Andhra dominance in the city.[71] Within these new debates, the Muslim question in the aftermath of the Police Action still remains a puzzle due to a lack of sufficient sources and historical evidence. Nevertheless, these debates in the Telangana context emphasize the urgency of recalling the Muslim question as related to the making of the *ṣahar* and its *mohallā*s.

Contemporary arguments about the identity of Hyderabad as a city deal with expansive networks of *mohallā*s, particularly in the old city of Hyderabad, known popularly as *purānā ṣahar* in Urdu and *pāta bastī* in Telugu. The patterns of these *mohallā*s have continually undergone major transformations as the political situations shift constantly. The sociologist Ratna Naidu has observed that the homogeneous pattern of the *mohallā*s was disturbed after the Police Action: "With the outmigration of Muslims from many areas and the fall in land and property values, the settlement pattern in the *mohallā*s also became more heterogeneous. Recently, however, this heterogeneity has been reversed due to the fear of communal violence."[72]

The defining features and individual perceptions of these *mohallā*s were likewise constantly changing. Yet, political and cultural activists such as Burgula Narasinga Rao had always resisted this idea of *purānā* and *pāta* for the old city as it privileges the rise of upper-class neighborhoods in the new city. They consistently argued that what the media projects as *a purānā ṣahar* ("old city" in Urdu) or *pāta bastī* ("old city" in Telugu) is the *asli* (real) Hyderabad. Whereas several Urdu, English, and Telugu literary figures describe the cosmopolitanism of these neighborhoods of the *asli* Hyderabad, the prose narratives written in Telugu in the aftermath of the Police Action provide a more detailed description of these *mohallā*s. In their fictional writings, both Swamy and Bhaskarabhatla offer what almost amounts to an ethnography of these changing configurations of Muslim and Hindu neighborhoods. In addition, the autobiographical works of Dasarathi and Sadasiva likewise focus on such aspects, with an emphasis on the sites of Urdu–Telugu bilingual public culture. Nevertheless, most Telugu narratives around this period use the idea of *ṣahar* or *bastī* as a broader category inclusive of the districts or mufassil areas in the state of Hyderabad. For them, *ṣahar* is an exclusive term that draws on diverse aspects of Hyderabadi culture. Their use of the words *cār sau sāl kā ṣahar* (the city of the four centuries) is a sign of their pride in its particular pluralist and unique cultural setting that represents the amalgamation of Muslim and Hindu practices. Writers such as Kavi Raja Murthy, Sadasiva, and Dasarathi also depict various moments of migration while highlighting how the culture of the *ṣahar* of Hyderabad had changed the rural and semi-urban *mohallā*s in the state of Telangana. Hence, any story about the *mohallā*s of the city is not confined to the city itself: it has also shaped everyday life even in the remotest villages of Telangana. Explaining this process, Burgula Narasinga Rao told me:

> What we now call *ṣahar* might not be the same as before the Police Action when the city was a citadel of elite groups. The real story of the *ṣahar* of Hyderabad began after the Action. Each *mohallā* turned into something, thus clearly distinguishing class and caste differences. Despite the longstanding legacy of the city as a pluralist *tehzeeb*, then when we were growing up, we can also see the transformation of each *mohallā*, most importantly, the dividing line between the old and new cities of Hyderabad and Secunderabad, too, had evolved into a different space with more Christian population.[73]

Like Burgula, many interlocutors of the Police Action narrate this categorical shift in the making of the city. As I elaborate in this book, we find testimonies for such changes in the portrayals of various fictional and non-fictional writings too. These narratives in many ways see the city through a critical lens, rather than—to use the words of anthropologists Magnus Marsden and Madeline Reeves—"romanticizing and over-exaggerating the innate capacity of such urban centers."[74] As evident from my sources from Hyderabad, I argue that the principles of co-existence or the grammar of conviviality demonstrate continuous transformations as time and place continue to evolve. As Marsden and Reeves observed, these dynamics also challenge the conventional binaries between the rural and the urban. At some point, as narrated in my sources, these differences blur and raise new concerns about the nature of an urban/rural Muslim identity and agency.

Based on this larger premise, this book has two connected specific goals: first, to explore how different themes of the question of Muslim belonging have reshaped everyday life in Hyderabad and Telangana after the Police Action; and second, to reconstruct broadly the history of the Telangana literary sphere that was produced before and after the Police Action, and more specifically to examine how writers engaged with each genre including fictional and non-fictional in response to the question of Muslim being and belongingness. Each chapter in this book focuses on one key theme that defined the identity of Muslims in Hyderabad as discussed in specific texts produced after the Police Action. Given that my primary sources are from and about Hyderabad state and the early Telangana political movements between 1940 and 1956 published in Telugu, the interventions made by such materials and their presence are vital for this work. At this point, we should also note that the essentialization of Telugu nationalism and the privileged historiography completely marginalized a diverse set of writings from Hyderabad state and Telangana between 1948 and 1956.[75] Against this background, in the next section, I will discuss a turn towards reconstructing Hyderabadi and Telangana literary history by various individuals and institutions.

BETWEEN MANY SILENCES AND A SELECTIVE AMNESIA

At the heart of this book lies a question about how we might characterize the long silence about the history of the Police Action and the role of

Muslims in the making of Hyderabad. At a broader level, as I discussed in the Introduction, we can say that there has been a silence in the mainstream or hegemonic historiography, but I argue that more properly, we might call it a selective amnesia that has been prevalent throughout the history of modern Hyderabad and Telangana. The politics of remembering, forgetting, and mentioning interfere with the articulations of the Police Action. For instance, the leftist histories of Hyderabad state, the Nizam's rule, and the Police Action privilege their version, which marginalizes the Muslim story, while the nationalist narrative continually presents a Nehruvian version and the Hindutva organizations highlight Sardar Patel's anti-Muslim perspective.

In the post-1998 debate on the Police Action, M. A. Moid identifies three categories of historiography by Muslims: Nizam apologetics, which speak about open-minded and liberal policies of the Nizam, the nostalgia that laments some beautiful past, and personal writings that "avoid traumatic history."[76] In addition, these observations, as mentioned by Moid, were still limited to Muslim historians and Urdu sources. However, as I demonstrated throughout this book, any version of the modern history of Hyderabad would be incomplete if we failed to examine oral histories and written sources in Telugu. Most historians have devoted their work to producing a single story of Hyderabad or Muslims. Unpacking some of these multiple dimensions of the history, my journey began with a simple question: Is there a single story of Hyderabadi or Telangana Muslims? On the surface, this question might sound like an extremely simple one, when in fact to begin such an exploration is highly complex and invites several challenges and political implications.

To begin with, we need to comprehend how the agency of Muslims works within the famous idea of a pluralist ethos of the Hyderabadi life—which is otherwise known as the Hyderabadi *tehzeeb* or the composite culture. Nevertheless, during the documentation of the oral histories and written sources, I have also realized that it is imperative to unpack multiple layers of such a pluralist story to comprehend the inner workings of the everyday life of Hyderabad. By unravelling this multi-layered narrative, we can return to an inter-connected question: How can we define and understand this pluralist ethos in the wake of the recent wave of Hindutva or a recent emphasis on the singular story of Muslim identity?

Thanks to the long history of the city of Hyderabad since its beginnings in the medieval times of the Qutub Shahi dynasty (AD 1512–1687), the city has been a treasure house of many stories and a matrix of many multi-cultural and religious dimensions. Due to their origins in Persian culture and language, the Qutub Shahi dynasty and the Golconda sultanate had promoted a distinctive repertoire of hybrid practices that blend both Islamic and Hindu elements along with global and local Islamic thought. In her 2020 work *Persianate Selves: Memories of Place and Origin Before Nationalism*, Mana Kia used the term Persian selfhood to define such a blend. She argued:

> The Muslim conquest and the Persian-speaking kings (migrants from Iran and Turan) are not the same…. The Persian-speaking migrants of Iran and Turan, also largely Muslim, stayed, intermarried, and made friends until they were not only migrants and their descendants but also locals. Memory and ongoing mobility defined the larger community.[77]

Along similar lines, the oral histories and written accounts in this book offer more evidence about how this idea of Persianate selfhood complicates the idiom of nationalism in a vernacular context. As discussed in Chapter 4, the literary and cultural work of Dasarathi and Sadasiva further show how the Telugu public sphere should be reconsidered from the perspective of a Persianate selfhood and the Urdu paradigms that defined political and cultural activism after the Police Action. Nevertheless, in recent efforts to construct a hegemonic singular story in the name of the linguistic state of Andhra Pradesh after the Police Action, nationalists suppressed most of the Persian- and Urdu-related historical aspects, in both political and linguistic narratives. The feeling of betrayal and the desire for separation has always been there at the heart of ordinary Telangana and Hyderabad citizens.

When it comes to this desire for a distinctive Hyderabadi and Telangana identity, both Hindu and Muslim narratives represent a liminal space that embraces both Hindu and Islamic dimensions. As explained in Chapters 1 and 4, several witnesses and activists openly claim that they inhabit a pluralistic setting in their everyday religious and social life. Throughout the book, I have attempted to unpack the ethics of this mutuality by providing evidence of a pluralist setting of the Hyderabadi *tehzeeb* from various non-Muslim narratives.[78] The evidence from oral histories and literary narratives reiterates that such an intense story is incomplete without the non-Muslim ("Hindu") narrativization of Muslim life in the post-Police Action times of Hyderabad and Telangana.

Towards the end of my fieldwork in Hyderabad in 2019, I met Ashwaq Hussain, whose life story speaks more about the other side of the trauma of the Police Action (Figure C.5). Ashwaq understands this intense moment

Figure C.5   Ashwaq Hussain
Source: Photo by Sajaya Kakarla.

as a new beginning for a version of Muslim activism. Seventy-five-year-old Hussain's story represents a progressive dimension of the Hyderabadi Muslim identity in the aftermath of the Police Action. Hussain's father Ghouse Ali Khan had migrated to the city of Hyderabad during the Police Action and remade his life from the scratch. Sharing his father's story, Ashwaq said:

> There was enormous level of disappointment, despair, frustration and anger. Yet, the new generation Muslims like my father were trying hard to build everything from the scratch. Unable to stand the atrocities of the military, my father left the village and sneaked into the old city, hiding in a truck. When he arrived in the old city, he became almost an activist for the poor, displaced and homeless Muslims.[79]

I met Ashwaq Hussain in January 2019 in the old city of Hyderabad, when I was still collecting oral and written history testimonials about the Police Action. One evening, I had arrived in his neighborhood of Musa Nagar in the old city when a couple of young Muslims arrived and dropped in at his house to share their latest experiences about some violence. From their conversation, I gathered that these young Muslims were still facing many violent injustices just because of their Muslimness.

Ashwaq was living with his son's family in a small two-bedroom house at the back of the local mosque. While I was interviewing him, he was surrounded by all his grandsons and daughters. As they witnessed the conversation, Ashwaq shared the life story of his father. During the Police Action, Ashwaq's father was a small farmer living in a nearby village of Ghatakeswar and known as a public figure as a kind-hearted person, and local Muslims and Hindus always needed his guidance in every matter. As the military was hunting down such public figures, particularly among the Muslim community, he left his village in the middle of the night and migrated to the city. Rather than being a victim of the fear factors—such as anti-Muslim discourses and hate speech—Ashwaq's story was defined more by his family's progressive outlook. When I met Ashwaq in 2019, we had an extensive conversation about his activism that resulted in finding homes for the displaced and uprooted Muslims in the old city. Collaborating with leftist activists such as K. Balagopal, Jeevan and Varghese, he started an organization named CHATRI (Campaign for Housing and Tenurial Rights).

Whereas Moid's essay analyzed how the new Muslim community focused on the key aspects of unity, education, and employment, activists such as Ashwaq advanced the same cause by taking up the issues of migration, displacement, and housing for the uprooted families in the old city. During one of our conversations, Ashwaq told me:

> Losing home is more than losing a face in the society. I see this painful face of loss and suffering whenever I remember my father. He was so brave and courageous. He never lost hope and he was always there with the Muslim community. Having experienced all kinds of trauma and loss after the Police Action, he taught us how to speak out and fight for the community.[80]

Ashwaq narrated many experiences to do with the Police Action and its impact on the local Muslims. The oral histories that he narrated made me revisit the stories of Nelluri Kesava Swamy (Chapter 1), and the novels of Bhaskarabhatla and Kavi Raja Murthy (Chapter 2). Reading the fictional work repeatedly and then relating them to oral histories was an intriguing experience for me. On the one hand, these oral and written narratives show the tensions between fictional and historical materials; more importantly, they unsettle almost every political narrative of the Police Action. Whereas the evidence I have presented from autobiographies, memoirs, and fictional work has its own value, oral histories such as Ashwaq's taught me more about selective amnesia as related to events such as Partition and the Police Action in Hyderabad state. Such oral histories made me realize once again that most memories and discourses disseminated by various political institutions fail to capture the everyday reality of a Muslim's life during and after the Police Action. These institutions conveniently "forgot" many aspects that do not serve their political mission. Their deliberate "selection" of incidents, personalities, and experiences represent a history that subscribes to their ideology.

In addition, the dominant narrative of the nation heavily affected the entire history by marginalizing other stories and communities, in this case, mostly a Muslim community and its story. In her 2013 work on the fictional writings of Sadat Hasan Manto, the historian Ayesha Jalal points out how her work is "intended to illustrate the extent to which the contours of the cultural nation, creatively and broadly construed, do not map neatly onto the limited boundaries of the political nation."[81] Whereas Jalal's observations are more about a literary personality, my work presents a case where that could be perceived as a broader base where everyday life, ordinary people, and their stories matter.

For Ashwaq, it was a battle on a daily basis until his last breath in 2021. Just like many writers and activists, Ashwaq fought for his right to speak about various aspects of the city, including the shared life world of Hyderabad and Telangana.[82] The case studies of oral histories presented in this book prove that any re-reading of a literary narrative is unfair and unjust if we fail to include and learn from oral histories.

Juxtaposing oral testimonials and written sources is not merely a methodological alternative; it also has theoretical implications for the major themes of Muslim narrativization. First of all, this kind of material raises a primary question about who is speaking for Muslims and what in particular they are speaking about. In the history of Hyderabadi or Telangana-based literary culture, Muslim writing is a fairly new phenomenon. Although there were Muslim writers and political activists, Muslim writing as a specific category emerged after the 1990s, which was the early phase of the Hindutva. Most of this Muslim writing emphasizing minority discourse, Muslimness, and local Islam was initially a response to Hindu nationalism, and the earliest Muslim articulations in Telugu were against the demolition of the Babri mosque on December 6, 1992. To capture the essence of this entire discourse, however, we need to understand the history of Muslim debates of the late 1930s and 1940s. Revisiting the political and cultural transformations during this period offers fresh insights into a debate about how Muslim narrativization within the Hyderabadi and Telangana literary culture originated and then circulated in various prose writings. Toward this goal, I have attempted to provide substantial evidence from the oral histories of the survivors and activists of the Police Action of 1948.

In a recent work, *Majoritarian State*, Angana Chatterjee, Thomas Blom Hansen and Christophe Jaffrelot discuss how the Hindutva dominant discourses silence or marginalize minority voices.[83] In the case of historical events such as Partition and the Police Action, as my witnesses explained, there has been an unparalleled silence or a selective amnesia even among the intellectuals and activists. Even several Muslim activists and victims were reluctant to speak about the Police Action. In Chapter 2, I introduced 75-year-old Razia Begum, the witness of the Police Action, who had a hard time recollecting the memories of the Police Action. Her memories of the late 1940s and early 1950s were confined to the historical Telangana armed rebellion, and later when we started talking about the Razakar militarism, she began to share more about the Police Action. The memory of her family's commitment to the Telangana movement and their "heroic" interactions with the movement had discouraged her from speaking about the Police Action. But her pain about conflating the Muslim identity with the Razakars made her share a few "undiscovered" moments of the Police Action. Similarly, most of my oral histories, either from Muslims or Hindus, speak about diverse themes of the Police Action including the rise of a new progressive Muslim, political activism, anti-Muslim sentiment, Urdu–Telugu language politics and gendered narratives. Looking back at the memory of the Police Action of 1948 in this way is not merely about retrieving historical memory, but also a key device in understanding the contemporary question of Muslim being and belonging and its future manifestations.

NOTES

1. Akeel Bilgrami, "Two Historic Deeds: The Common Muslim Has Done What Even Gandhi, Nehru, Ambedkar, or Azad Couldn't," *Outlook India*, February 17, 2020, https://www.outlookindia.com/ (accessed September 20, 2022).

2. I borrow this term "national problem" (*jātīya samasya*) from my interlocutors. For a recent discussion on this aspect, see Christophe Jaffrelot, *Modi's India: Hindu Nationalism and the Rise of Ethnic Democracy* (Princeton: Princeton University Press, 2021).

3. Manan Ahmed Asif, "Virulence of Hindutva," in *The Pandemic: Perspectives on Asia* (New York: Columbia University Press, 2020), 153–165.

4. Mitra Rastegar uses the idea of population racism that argues that "the figure of the tolerable or sympathetic Muslim—the patriot the liberal, the feminist—can appear to be an antiracist rejoinder to stereotypes of Muslims. However, representations of tolerable Muslims contribute to the racialization of all Muslims by reinforcing stereotypes as risk factors of a population." Mitra Rastegar, *Tolerance and Risk: How U. S. Liberalism Racializes Muslim* (Minneapolis: University of Minnesota Press, 2021), 12.

5. Jaffrelot, *Modi's India*, 6.

6. For an idea of various nationalist narratives, see K. M. Munshi, *The End of an Era: Hyderabad Memories* (Bombay: Bharatiya Vidya Bhavan, 1957); V. H. Desai, *Vande Mataram to Jana Gana Mana: Saga of Hyderabad Freedom Struggle* (Bombay: Bharatiya Vidya Bhavan, 1990); P. V. Kate, *Marathwada under the Nizams, 1724–1948* (Delhi: Mittal Publications, 1987); V. P. Menon, *The Story of the Integration of the Indian States* (New York: Longmans, Green and Co., 1955).

7. Interview with the author, Adilabad, India, 2007.

8. Swathi Sivanand discusses how the politics of territorial belonging redefined contemporary identities: "What the Hyderabad-Deccan Region Teaches Us about Belonging," *News Minute*, September 17, 2021, https://www.thenewsminute.com/article/what-hyderabad-deccan-region-teaches-us-about-belonging-155388 (accessed February 20, 2022).

9. N. Venugopal, *Lēci Nilicina Telangāṇa* (Hyderabad: Swechchaa Saahiti, 2000), 116–134.

10. Interview with the author, Karim Nagar, India, 2006.

11. Margrit Pernau, "Contested Emotion of Masculinity: The Court, the Street and the Negotiation Table in an Indian Princely State in the 20th Century," *Journal l'Homme* 32, no. 2 (2021).

12. Interview with the author, 2006.

13. Within the Telugu literary sphere, poets such as Dasarathi and Kavi Raja Murthy, too, mentioned in various ways about the accomplishments of Bahadur Yar Jung. For more, see Chapter 4.

14. Interview with the author, Karim Nagar, India, September 10, 2006.

15. Interview with the author, Karim Nagar, India, September 10, 2006.

16. Interview with Abdul Quddus Saheb, 2006.

17. Angana Chatterji, Thomas Blom Hansen, and Christophe Jaffrelot, eds., *Majoritarian State: How Hindu Nationalism Is Changing India?* (New York: Oxford University Press, 2019), 7.

18. For more on this side of discourses, see M. A. Moid, *Nizams Broadsheet* (Hyderabad: Anveshi, 2010).

19. *Hyderabad Question*, xi.

20. Vulli Dhanaraju, "The Telangana Movement (1946–1951): Folklore Perspective," *International Journal of Social Science Tomorrow* 1, no. 8 (2012): 1–7.

21. M. A. Seljouk, *Corpses* (London: Gerald Duckworth & Co. Ltd, 1966), 10.

22. *1948 September 17 Vidrōham* [1948 September 17, betrayal] (Communist Party of India [Marxist-Leninist] of Andhra Pradesh, 2010).

23. Purushotham, *From Raj to Republic*, 184.

24. Tadakamalla Vivek and Sangisetti Srinivas, *17 September 1948: Bhinna Dṛkkōṇālu* [Different perspectives on 17 September 1948] (Hyderabad: Telangana History Society, 2010).

25. M. A. Majid, "Mere Taboot Par Jashan" [Celebrations on my coffin] (Hyderabad: Taha Print Systems, 2014).

26. Majid's Urdu essay was later translated by M. A. Moid into English and published in Anveshi's Broadsheet on Nizam's rule and Muslims in 2010.

27. Majid, "Mere Taboot."

28. For more on Abdul Razzak Lari, see Luther, *Hyderabad*, 94–95.

29. Vasantha Kannabiran and Olga, *Mahiḷāvaraṇam* [Womanscape] (Hyderabad: Asmita Publications, 2001).

30. For an idea of how Partition impacted south India, see Nazia Akhtar, "Hyderabad, Partition, and Hindutva: Strategic Revisitings in Neelkanth's 'Durga' (2005)," in *Revisiting India's Partition*, ed. Amritjit Singh, Nalini Iyer and Rahul K. Gairola; and Nalini Iyer, "Partition's Other: The View from South India," in *Revisiting India's Partition*, ed. Singh, Iyer and Gairola, 305–342.

31. Interview with the author, Hyderabad, India, January 29, 2019.

32. Fareed Mirza, *Pre and Post Police Action in the Erstwhile Hyderabad: What I Saw, Felt and Did* (Hyderabad: Paramount Press, 1976), 47–48.

33. Mohammad Hyder, *October Coup: A Memoir of the Struggle for Hyderabad* (New Delhi: Roli Books, 2012).

34. Interview with the author, 2010 and 2019.

35. Hyder, *October Coup*, 3.

36. Ibid., 177.

37. For more on this take of the Telangana Rashtra Samiti, see Purushotham, "Destroying Hyderabad," 32; for an idea of how this political party was serving the Hindutva mission, see Kancha Ilaiah, "Contrary Theories," *Asian Age*, November 1, 2010.

38. Interview with the author, Hyderabad, India, January 26, 2019.

39. For a recent understanding of Mir Laiq Ali, see "The Captain Who Ensured the Sinking of Hyderabad Ship," *Siasat Daily*, September 17, 2021, https://www.siasat.com/mir-laiq-ali-the-captain-who-ensured-the-sinking-of-hyderabad-ship-2193573/ (accessed February 2, 2022).

40. Luther, *Hyderabad*, 302.

41. Khalidi, *Hyderabad*, xiii.

42. *Andhra Jyothi*, a Telugu newspaper, published about these aspects for four days starting on February 13, 2007.

43. *Siyasat Daily*, September 17, 2011.

44. Mir Laiq Ali, *Tragedy of Hyderabad* (Karachi: Pakistan Co-operative Book Society Ltd, 1962).

45. For an idea of the Telangana renaissance in the 1940s, see Mantena Rama Sundari, "Publicity, Civil Liberties, and Political Life in Princely Hyderabad," *Modern Asian Studies* 53, no. 4 (2019): 1248–1277.

46. Jithendra Babu, *Hyderabad Vishadam*, 18.

47. Enugu Narasimha Reddy, trans., *Haidarabād Viṣādaṁ* [Tragedy of Hyderabad] (Hyderabad: Pala Pitta Publications, 2016).

48. Laiq Ali, *Tragedy of Hyderabad*, xix.

49. Colonel Lingala Panduranga Reddy, *September 1948 Hyderabad Liberation Day: A Misnomer* (Hyderabad: Voice of Telangana, 2011).

50. Ibid., 4.

51. Ibid.

52. Luther, *Hyderabad*, x.

53. Luther's Hyderabad ran into two editions and the first edition was published in 1995, and the second edition in 2006. The Telugu translation of this book was published in 2017. Before this Telugu edition, his memoirs were also published in *Sakshi*, one of the largest circulated Telugu newspapers between 2014 and 2015. Punna Krishna Murthy, *Oka Hindūstānī ālāpana (Narēndra Lūthar tō Iṁṭarvyūlu)* (Hyderabad: Punna, 2017).

54. Narendra Luther, "Bureaucrat with a Difference," *Tryst with Dholpur House* (blog), January 22, 2021, https://chitramishra.wordpress.com/2021/

01/22/narendra-luther-bureaucrat-with-a-difference/ (accessed February 25, 2022).

55. Luther, *Hyderabad*, 232.

56. Rama Sundari Mantena, "The Andhra Movement, Hyderabad State, and the Historical Origins of the Telangana Demand: Public Life and Political Aspirations in India, 1900–56," *India Review* 13, no. 4 (2014): 337–357.

57. Jithendra Babu, *Telangānalō Caitanyaṁ*.

58. Luther, *Hyderabad*, 259.

59. Sebastian R. Prange, *Monsoon Islam: Trade and Faith on the Medieval Malabar Coast* (Cambridge: Cambridge University Press, 2018).

60. Prange, *Monsoon Islam*, 3.

61. Mohammad, *The Festival of Pirs*, 7.

62. Amir Mufti, *Enlightenment in the Colony: The Jewish Question and the Crisis of Postcolonial Culture* (Princeton, NJ: Princeton University Press, 2007).

63. Interview with the author (originally in Telugu), Adilabad, India, June 25, 2010.

64. Interview with the author, June 25, 2010.

65. This entire debate about the majority and minority resonates with what Amir Mufti discusses in his work *Englightenment in the Colony*. See in particular Mufti's mention about Gilles Deleuze and Feliz Guattari's *Kafka: Towards a Minor Literature* (1975). Mufti says: "In that milestone work, the authors suggest something like a definition of 'minor literature': 'it is … that which a minority constructs within a major language.' They thus link the de-territorializing impulse of minor literature to displacements in the mutural relationships of language, literature, culture, place, and people" (Mufti, *Englightenment in the Colony*, 12).

66. Raisur Rahman, *Locale, Everyday Islam, and Modernity: Qasbah Towns and Muslim Life in Colonial India* (New Delhi: Oxford University Press, 2015), 3.

67. Rahman, *Locale, Everyday Islam and Modernity*, 39.

68. Dalmia, *Fiction as History*, 2.

69. For more details, see Rama Melkote, *Hyderabad Yevaridi?* [Whose Hyderabad?] (Hyderabad: Hyderabad Forum for Telangana, 2009).

70. Leonard, *Hyderabad*, 233.

71. Some of these debates resonate with the *mulki* movement in Hyderabad. For an idea of the earliest phase of the *mulki* activism, see Syed Abid Hasan, *Whither Hyderabad?* (Hyderabad: Kavile Telangana Research and Referral Centre, 1935).

72. Ratna Naidu, *Old Cities, New Predicaments: A Study of Hyderabad* (New Delhi: Sage Publications, 1990), 138.

73. Interview with the author, Hyderabad, India, January 23, 2019.

74. Magnus Marsden and Madeline Reeves, "Marginal Hubs: On Conviviality Beyond the Urban Asia: Introduction," *Modern Asian Studies* 53, no. 3 (2019): 755–775.

75. Sangisetti Srinivas, *Dastram*; Kaluva Mallayya, Sadanand Sarada and Chandra, eds., *Telangana Kathalu* (Hyderabad: Visalandhra Publishing House, 2015); Mudiganti, *Telangāṇa Tolitaram Kathalu*, 2002.

76. Moid, *Nizams Broadsheet*, 5.

77. Mana Kia, *Persianate Selves: Memories of Place and Origin Before Nationalism* (Stanford: Stanford University Press, 2020), 16.

78. For a recent debate on the idea of the Hyderabadi *tehzeeb*, see Vara Vara Rao, *Tehjīb: Hiṁdūtva Phāsijaṁ Pai Laukika Viślēṣaṇa* [Tehzeeb: A secularist analysis on Hindutva's fascism] (Hyderabad: Viplava Rachayitala Sangham, 2021).

79. Interview with the author, Hyderabad, India, January 28, 2019.

80. Interview with the author, Hyderabad, India, January 28, 2019.

81. Ayesha Jalal, *The Pity of Partition: Manto's Life, Times, and Work Across the India–Pakistan Divide* (Princeton, NJ: Princeton University Press, 2013), 12.

82. In the process of writing about Hyderabad, the historian Karen Leonard's observations in which she once again returned to a literary narrative. Leonard said:

> Hyderabadis experienced traumatic changes after 1948 as India imposed a new regime. Some Hyderabadis migrated to the new state of Pakistan, created along with India in 1947, but Indian rule in Hyderabad meant such major readjustments that it was almost as though those who stayed had moved to a new place. Some Hyderabadis found the American Civil War novel, *Gone with the Wind*, evocative of the trauma. They likened old Hyderabad to the American South, some of them with nostalgic approval, others with disapproval. Rereading the novel, I found certain analogies, ones I will sweepingly overstate (as Hyderabadis often do) for effect. In both cases, there was a hereditary aristocracy, a society marked by hierarchies of race, class, national origin, and gender…. In both cases, one sees vanished worlds, diminished selves, and attempts to recapture those worlds in memory.

For more, see Leonard, *Hyderabad*, 25.

83. I borrow the term "majoritarian state" from Angana Chatterji, Thomas Blom Hansen, and Christophe Jaffrelot, eds., *Majoritarian State: How Hindu Nationalism is Changing India?* (New York: Oxford University Press, 2019). Particularly, Angana Chatterji's observations about the minoritization are relevant to my discussion. She notes: "In the context of India, the process of minoritisation is akin to that of racialisation in the global north, whereby 'racial', 'inferior', and 'anti-national' connotations have been ascribed to minorities, and manipulated to victimise them" (Chatterji, Hansen, and Jaffrelot, *Majoritarian State*, 405).

SELECT BIBLIOGRAPHY

DOCUMENTS AND REPORTS

1948 Septembar 17 Vidrōhaṁ [1948 September 17, betrayal]. Hyderabad: Marxist-Leninist Communist Party of India of the Andhra Pradesh, 2010.

Hyderabad Reborn: The First Six Months of Freedom (September 18, 1948–March 17, 1949). Hyderabad: Director of Information, 1949.

Imperial Gazetteer of India, 1909.

Operation Polo: The Police Action Against Hyderabad 1948. Delhi: Historical section, Ministry of Defence, 1972.

The Hyderabad Question before the United Nations. Documents and other materials prepared by the Hyderabad Delegation to the United Nations, Karachi, 1951.

White paper on Hyderabad. New Delhi: Government of India, 1948.

UNPUBLISHED SECONDARY SOURCES

Akhtar, Nazia. "From Nizam to Nizam: The Representation of Partition in Literary Narratives about Hyderabad, Deccan." Unpublished manuscript, University of Western Ontario, 2013.

Jha, Shefali. "Democracy on a Minor Note: The All India Majlies-E-Ittehadul Muslimeen and Its Hyderabadi Muslim Publics." Unpublished manuscript, University of Chicago, Chicago, 2017.

Reddy, Gautham. "An Empire of Literary Telugu: Remaking Language and Community in Colonial South India, 1812–1920." Unpublished manuscript, University of Chicago, 2020.

Roosa, John. "The Quandary of Qaum: Indian Nationalism in a Muslim State 1850–1948." Unpublished dissertation, University of Wisconsin-Madison, 1980.

Shah, Alison Mackenzie. "Constructing a Capital on the Edge of Empire: Urban Patronage and Politics in the Nizams' Hyderabad, 1750–1950." Unpublished manuscript, University of Pennsylvania, 2005.

Suneetha, Achyuta. "Telugu Nationalism and Police Action against Hyderabad: Notes on History, Historiography and Memory." Unpublished paper presented at the Berkshire conference on the History of Women 'Histories on the Edge' May 22–25, 2014.

NEWSPAPERS, BULLETINS, PERIODICALS AND SPECIAL ISSUES

ENGLISH

Asian Age
Economic and Political Weekly
India Review
The Frontline
The Hindu

TELUGU

Abhyudaya (Literary Monthly of the Progressive Writers' Association)
Andhra Jyōti (Daily and weekly)
Gōlkonḍa Kavula Saṁcika (1934)
Haryālī (Telugu Muslim writing special)
Kanzira Poetry Bulletin (1993)
Prajā Sāhiti (Literary monthly)
Sṛjana Ādhunika Sāhitya Vēdika
Sujāta: Telangāṇa Pratyēka Sancika (1951)
Svāti (Monthly)

Telugu Svatantra
Vārta (Daily newspaper)

HINDI AND URDU

Hans (Hindi monthly, August 2003)
The Siasat

TELUGU, URDU, AND HINDI PUBLISHED SOURCES

Angadala, Venkata Ramana Murthy. *Pinzaari: Mahā Vāggēyakāruḍu Ṣēk Nājar Āṭōbayōgraphī*. Hyderabad: Sauda Aruna Literature, 2001.
Ashokamitran. *Janta Nagarālu*. New Delhi: National Book Trust, 1985.
———. *The Eighteenth Parallel*. Translated by Gomathi Narayanan. Hyderabad: Orient Blackswan, 1993.
Ayodhya Rama Kavi, Adluri. *Haidarābādupai Pōlīsu Carya: Burra Katha* [Police Action of Hyderabad: Burra katha folk narrative]. Secunderabad: Konda Veerayya, 1948.
Bānō, Jīlāni. *Aiwane Ghazal*. Translated by B. Seetha Kumari. New Delhi: National Book Trust, 1998.
———. *Aiwan-e-Ghazal*. Translated by Zakia Mashahhadi. New Delhi: National Book Trust, 2016.
———. *Antā Nijamē Ceptā: Jīlāni Bānō Kathalu*. Translated by Mehak Hyderabadi. Hyderabad: Nava Chetana Publishing House, 2018.
———. *Bārish-i Sang*. Dihlī: Ejūkeshnal Pablishing Hā'ūs, Aḥmadābād, 2018.
———. *Das Pratinithi Kahānīyā*. New Delhi: Kitab Ghar Prakashan, 2007.
Chandar, Krishan. *Jab Khet Jāge*. Allahabad: Nafees Publication, 1967.
Gopala Krishna Rao, K. V. *Telugupai Udū Phāraśīka Prabhāvaṁ* [The influence of Urdu and Persian on Telugu]. Hyderabad: Andhra Pradesh Sahitya Academy, 1969.
Ḥusain, Sayyid Iḥtishām. *Urdū Adab Kī Tanqīdī Tārīkh*. Na'ī Dihlī: Taraqqī-yi Urdū Biyūro, 1988.
———. *Urdū Sāhitya Caritra*. Translated by Sadasiva. Hyderabad: Andhra Pradesh Sahitya Academy,1963.
Jithendra Babu, K., ed. *Jayanthi*. Special issue for Samala Sadasiva. Hyderabad: Visalandhra Publishing House, 2012.

———. *Telangāṇalō Caitanyaṁ Ragilcina Nizāṁ Rāṣṭrāndhra Mahāsabhalu.* Munagala: Sahitee Sadan, 2007.

Kandimalla, Sambasiva Rao. *Burra Kathā Pitāmaha Padmaśrī Ṣēk Nājar* [Padmasri Shaik Nazar, the father of Burra Katha]. Hyderabad: C. P. Brown Academy, 2009.

Kannabiran, Vasantha, and Olga. *Mahiḷāvaraṇaṁ* [Womanscape]. Secunderabad: Asmita Publications, 2001.

Krishna Murthy, Punna. *Oka Hindūstānī ālāpana (Narēndra Lūthar Tō Iṁṭarvyūlu). Hyderabad: Punna, 2017.

Krishnamacharya, Dasarathi. *Gālib Gītālu.* Vijayawada: Visalandhra Publishing House, 1962.

———. *Yātrā Smṛti.* Hyderabad: Literacy House, 2006.

Kulkarni, Khanderao. *Hyderabadu Ajnatha Charitra Putalu* [Pages from the secret history of Hyderabad]. Translated into Telugu by Nikhileshwar. Hyderabad: Navabharati, 1978.

Lalita, K. *Manaku Teliyani Mana Caritra: Telaṅgāṇā Raitāṅga Pōrāṭaṁlō Strīlu, Oka Sajīva Caritra.* Haidrābād: Strī Śakti Saṅghaṭana, 1986.

Lokeswar, Paravastu. *Nizāṁ Pai Nippulu Kuripincina Vīrulu* [The warriors who fought against the Nizam]. Hyderabad: Gandhi Prachuranalu, 2011.

Majid, M. A. *Mere Taboot Par Jashan* [Celebrations on my coffin]. Hyderabad: Taha Print Systems, 2014.

Mallayya, Kaluva, Sadanand Sarada, and Chandra, eds. *Telaṁgāṇa Kathalu.* Hyderabad: Visalandhra Publishing House, 2015.

Mazharuddin, Mohammad. *Zawal-e Hyderabad Aur Police Action.* Hyderabad: Rafeeq Printing Press, 1982.

Melkote, Rama, *Hyderabad Yevaridi?* [Whose Hyderabad?]. Hyderabad: Hyderabad Forum for Telangana, 2009.

Mohiuddin, Makhdoom. *Makhdūṃ Kavita.* Translated by Gajjela Mallāreḍḍi, Dāśarathi, Sī Nārāyaṇa Reḍḍī, Rāmbhaṭla Kṛṣṇamūrti, and Kaumudi. Vijayawada: Visalandhra Publishing House, 1970.

———. *Nizāṁlō Dōpiḍī Vidhānaṁ: Muslimla Kartavyaṁ* [Exploitative policies of the Nizam and the Muslim task]. Bejawada: Prajasakthi Prachuranalayam, 1947.

Moulvi Chirag Ali. *Adhunika Haidarabād Caritra: Sālār Jang Sanskaranalu.* Translated by Gajula Dayakar. Hyderabad: Adugu Jaadalu Publications, 2015.

Murthy. *Mai Gharīb Hu.* Hyderabad: Praja Sahitya Parishat, 1949; Hyderabad: Telangana Sahitya Academy, 2019.

Mutyam, K., and Sivalingam. *Kaṣṭāla Kolimi: Tyāgāla Śikharaṁ Sarvadēvabhaṭ la Rāmanāthaṁ Jīvitaṁ*. [The life story of Sarvadevabhatla Ramanatham]. Khammam: Rayala Subhash Chandra Bose Memorial Trust, 2021.

Narasayya, Lakshmi, and Tripuraneni Srinivas. *Cikkanavutunna Pāṭa: Daḷita Kavitvaṁ* [An intensifying song: Anthology of Dalit poetry]. Vijayawada: Kavitwam Prachuranalu, 1995.

Narasimha Reddy, Enugu, trans. *Haidarabād Viṣādaṁ* [Tragedy of Hyderabad]. Hyderabad: Pala Pitta Publications, 2016.

Narasinga Rao, Mandumula. *Yābhayi Saṁvatsarāla Haidarābādu* [Fifty years of Hyderabad]. Hyderabad: Mandumula Narasinga Rao Smaraka Samiti, 1977.

"Nelluru Kesavasamy Kathalu." *Andhra Bhoomi* (Telugu daily newspaper), March 22, 1999.

Olga. *Nīli Mēghālu: Strīvāda Kavitva Sankalanaṁ* [Blue clouds: An anthology of feminist poetry]. Hyderabad: Sweccha Prachuranalu, 1996.

———. *Sahita: Sāhitya Vyāsālu*. Hyderabad: Sweccha Prachurnalu, 2010.

Picchayya, Chadalavada. *Abhyudaya Sacitra Māsa Patrika*. Bezawada: Progressive Writers Association, 1946.

Pratap Reddy, Kandimalla. *Haidarābād Rāṣṭraṁ Bhāratadēśamlō Vilīnaṁ: Cāritraka Nēpathyaṁ*. Hyderabad: Nava Chetana Publishing House, 2017.

Ramaraju, Biruduraju, ed. *Qutub Sāhī Sultānulu – Āndhra Saṁskr̥ti* [The Qutub Shahi sultans and Andhra culture]. Hyderabad: Idaar-e-Adbiyate, 1962.

Rangacharya, Dasarathi. *Jīvana Yānaṁ* [The journey of life]. Hyderabad: Nava Chetana Publishing House, 2015.

———. *Jīvana Yānaṁ – Gaḍicina Gurtulu*. Hyderabad: Nava Chetana Publishing House, 2016.

Razvi, Jawad. *Haidarābād Saṁsthānamlō Rājakīya Caitanyaṁ: Vidyārthi-Yuvajanula Pātra*. Vijaywada: Visalandhra Publishing House, 1985.

Sadasiva. *Phārasī Kavula Prasakti* [Speaking of Farsi poets]. Hyderabad: Andhra Pradesh Sahitya Academy, 1975.

———. *Urdū Bhāṣā Kavitva Saundaryaṁ*. Hyderabad: Telugu University, 2004.

———. *Urdū Kavula Kavitā Sāmagri* [The poetic devices of Urdu poets]. Hyderabad: Andhra Pradesh Sahitya Academy, 1970.

Sajida, Zeenath. *Telugu Adab Ki Tāreef* [An appreciation of Telugu literature]. Hyderabad: Osmania University, 1960.

Seetharam, Guduri, ed. *Nelluri Kesava Swamy Kathalu*. New Delhi: National Book Trust, 2010.

Shajahana and Skybaba, eds. *Jaljala: Muslim Vāda Kavitwam* [The earthquake: Muslim-ist poetry]. Nalgonda: Neela Giri Sahiti, 1998.

Srinivas, K. *Telangāṇa Sāhitya Vikāsaṁ: Ādhunikata Vaipu Aḍugulu.* Hyderabad: Telangana Prachuranalu, 2015.

Srinivas, Sangisetti. *Dastraṁ: Telangāṇa Toli Taraṁ Kathala Sūci.* Hyderabad: Kavile Prachurana, 2004.

Sujatha Reddy, Mudiganti. *Bhāskarabhaṭla Kṣṇārāvu Racanalu: Kathalu, Navalalu.* Hyderabad: Visalandhra Publishing House, 2013.

———, ed. *Telangāṇa Tōlitaraṁ Kathalu.* Hyderabad: Rohanam Publications, 2002.

Sujatha Reddy, Mudiganti, and Sangisetti Srinivas, eds. *Toli Nāti Kathalu: Telangana Toli Tharam Kathalu, Rendo Bhaagam* [Stories from Telangana, 1910–1956]. Hyderabad: Navodaya, 2005.

Sundarayya, Puccalapalli. *Telangāṇā Pōrāṭamlō Strīlu.* Haidarābād: Prajāśakti Bukhaus, 1999.

Sunkara, Satyanarayana, and Vasireddi. *Mā Bhūmi: Nāṭakaṁ.* Vijayawada: Visalandhra Publishing House, 1957.

Syamala, Gogu. *Nalla Poddu: Daḷita Strīla Sāhityaṁ 1921–2003.* Hyderabad: Hyderabad Book Trust, 2003.

Tadakamalla, Vivek. *Telangāṇa Caritra: Punarnirmāṇaṁ* [The reconstruction of Telangana history]. Hyderabad: Telangana History Society, 2010.

Tadakamalla, Vivek, and Sangisetti Srinivas. *17 Seṗṭembar 1948: Bhinna Dṛkkōṇ ālu* [Different perspectives on September 17, 1948]. Hyderabad: Telangana History Society, 2010.

Vara Vara Rao. *Tehjīb: Hindūtva Phāsijaṁ Pai Laukika Viślēṣaṇa* [Tehzeeb: A secularist analysis on Hindutva's fascism]. Hyderabad: Viplava Rachayitala Sangham, 2021.

———. *Telangāṇā Vimōcanōdyamaṁ: Telugu Navala—Samāja Sāhitya Sambandhālu, Oka Viślēṣaṇa* [The emancipation of Telangana: The novel—The interactions between society and literature, an analysis]. Hyderabad: Sweccha Prachuranalu, 1983.

Venugopal, N., trans. *Talapula Tōva: Kaiphī Ājmītō Artha Śatābdi* [The path of many memories: Half a century with Kaifi Azmi]. Hyderabad: Veekshanam Publications, 2016.

ENGLISH SOURCES

Adhikari, G. D. *What Is Happening in Hyderabad?* Bombay: V. M. Kaul, 1949.

Ahmed, Shahab. *What Is Islam? The Importance of Being Islamic.* Princeton, NJ: Princeton University Press, 2016.

Alam, Javeed. "Inter-Community Life in Hyderabad: Reconfigurations." *Deccan Studies* 6, no. 2 (2008): 23–24.

Alam, Muzaffar. *Languages of Political Islam: India, 1200–1800.* Chicago: University of Chicago Press, 2004.

Alavi, Seema. *Muslim Cosmopolitanism in the Age of Empire.* Cambridge: Harvard University Press, 2015.

Ali, Agha Shahid. *The Country without a Post-Office.* New York: W. W. Norton, 1997.

Ali, Ahmed. *Twilight in Delhi.* New York: New Directions, 1994 (1940).

Ali, Mir Laiq. *Tragedy of Hyderabad.* Karachi: Pakistan Co-operative Book Society Ltd, 1962.

Akhtar, Nazia. *Bibi's Room: Hyderabadi Women and Twentieth-Century Urdu Prose.* Hyderabad: Orient BlackSwan, 2022.

Amin, Shahid. *Event, Memory and Metaphor: Chauri Chaura 1922–1992.* Berkeley: University of California Press, 1995.

Anjaneyulu, D. "Impact of Socialist Ideology on Telugu Literature between the Wars." In *Socialism in India*, edited by B. R. Nanda, 244–260. New York: Barnes and Noble, 1972.

Anjaria, Ulka, ed. *A History of the Indian Novel in English.* Cambridge: Cambridge University Press, 2015.

Appadurai, Arjun. *Modernity at Large: Cultural Dimensions of Globalization.* Minneapolis: University of Minnesota Press, 1996.

Azam, Kousar J., ed. *Languages and Literary Cultures in Hyderabad.* London; New York: Routledge, 2018.

Aziz, Qutubuddin. *The Murder of a State.* Karachi: Islamic Media Publication, 1993.

Badran, Margot. *Feminism in Islam: Religious and Secular Convergences.* Oxford: OneWorld, 2009.

Bānō, Jīlānī. *A Hail of Stones.* New Delhi: Sterling Publishers, 1996.

Bawa, V. K. *The Last Nizam: The Life and Times of Mir Osman Ali Khan.* New Delhi: Viking Penguin India, 1992.

———. *The Nizam between Mughals and British: Hyderabad under Salar Jung I.* New Delhi: S. Chand, 1986.

Beverley, Eric. *Hyderabad, British India, and the World: Muslim Networks and Minor Sovereignty c. 1850–1950.* Cambridge: Cambridge University Press, 2015.

Bhukya, Bhangya. *History of Modern Telangana.* Hyderabad: Orient Blackswan, 2017.

Bigelow, Anna. *Sharing the Sacred: Practicing Pluralism in North India*. New York: Oxford University Press, 2010.

Brueck, Laura R. *Writing Resistance: The Rhetorical Imagination of Hindi Literature*. New York: Columbia University Press, 2014.

Chakraborty, Chakrabarti, and Al-Wazedi Umme, ed. *Postcolonial Urban Outcasts: City Margins in South Asian Literature*. New York: Routledge, 2017.

Chatterjee, Partha. *The Nation and its Fragments: Colonial and Postcolonial Histories*. Princeton, NJ: Princeton University Press, 1993.

Chatterji, Angana, Thomas Blom Hansen, and Christophe Jaffrelot, eds. *Majoritarian State: How Hindu Nationalism Is Changing India?* New York: Oxford University Press, 2019.

Cohen, Benjamin. *In the Club: Associational Life in Colonial South Asia*. UK: Manchester University Press, 2015.

———. "Modernizing the Urban Environment: The Musi River Flood of 1908 in Hyderabad, India." *Environment and History* 17, no. 3 (2011): 409–432.

Cook, David. *Understanding Jihad*. Oakland, CA: University of California Press, 2015.

Copland, Ian. "Communalism in Princely India: The Case of Hyderabad, 1930–1940." *Modern Asian Studies* 22, no. 4 (1998): 783–814.

Dalmia, Vasudha. *Fiction as History: The Novel and the City in Modern North India*. New Delhi: Permanent Black, 2017.

Dandekar, Deepra, and Torsen Tschacher, eds. *Islam, Sufism and Everyday Politics of Belonging in South Asia*. New York: Routledge, 2010.

Daniel, E. Valentine. *Charred Lullabies*. Princeton, NJ: Princeton University Press, 1996.

Das, Chaity. *In the Land of Buried Tongues: Testimonies and Literary Narratives of the War of Liberation of Bangladesh*. New Delhi: Oxford University Press, 2017.

Datla, Kavita. *The Language of Secular Islam: Urdu Nationalism and Colonial India*. Honolulu: University of Hawaii Press, 2013.

Desai, Anita. *In Custody*. New York: Harper and Row Publishers, 1984.

Desai, V. H. *Vande Mataram to Jana Gana Mana: Saga of Hyderabad Freedom Struggle*. Bombay: Bharatiya Vidya Bhavan, 1990.

Devji, Faisal. *Muslim Zion: Pakistan as a Political Idea*. Cambridge, MA: Harvard University Press, 2013.

Dhanaraju, Vulli. "The Telangana Movement (1946–1951): Folklore Perspective." *International Journal of Social Science Tomorrow* 1, no. 8 (2012): 1–7.

Dharwadker, Vinay, and Stuart H. Blackburn. *The Collected Essays of A. K. Ramanujan*. New Delhi: Oxford University Press, 1999.

Dubrow, Jennifer. *Cosmopolitan Dreams: The Making of Modern Urdu Literary Culture in Colonial South Asia*. Honolulu: University of Hawaii Press, 2018.

Duderija, Adis. *The Imperatives of Progressive Islam*. New York: Routledge, 2017.

Eaton, Richard. *A Social History of the Deccan 1300–1761: Eight Indian Lives, Vol. 1*. Cambridge: Cambridge University Press, 2005.

Eickelman, Dale. *Knowledge and Power in Morocco: The Education of a Twentieth-Century Notable*. Princeton, NJ: Princeton University Press, 1985.

El-Edroos, Syed Ahmed, and L. R. Naik. *Hyderabad of "Seven Loaves."* Hyderabad: Laster Prints, 1994.

Farooqi, Mehr Afshan. "Literary Paradigms in the Conception of South Asian Muslim Identity." *Comparative Studies of South Asia, Africa and the Middle East* 32, no. 1 (2012): 183–194.

Faruqi, Munis D. "At Empire's End: Hyderabad and Eighteenth-Century India." *Modern Asian Studies* 43, no. 1 (2009): 5–43.

Fischel, Roy S. *Local States in an Imperial World: Identity, Society and Politics in the Early Modern Deccan*. Edinburgh: Edinburgh University Press, 2020.

Garcia, Mario T. *Literature as History: Autobiography, Testimonio, and the Novel in the Chicano and Latino Experience*. Tucson: University of Arizona Press, 2016.

Gilmartin, David. "Partition, Pakistan and South Asian History: In Search of a Narrative." *Journal of Asian Studies* 57, no. 4 (November 1998): 1068–1095.

Gottschalk, Peter, and Gabriel Greenberg. *Islamophobia: Making Muslims the Enemy*. Maryland: Rowman & Littlefield Publishers, Inc., 2007.

Gour, Raj Bahadur. *Glorious Telangana Armed Struggle*. New Delhi: Communist Party of India, 1973.

Guaba, K. L. *Hyderabad or India*. Delhi: Rajkamal Publications, 1948.

Hashmi, Syed Ali. *Hyderabad 1948: An Unavoidable Invasion*. New Delhi: Pharos Media and Publishing Private Limited, 2017.

Hai, Ambreen. "Adultery behind Purdah and the Politics of Indian Muslim Nationalism in Zeenuth Futehally's Zohra." *Modern Fiction Studies* 59, no. 2 (2013): 317–345.

Hasan, Mushirul, and Asaduddin, eds. *Image and Representation: Stories of Muslim Lives in India*. New Delhi: Oxford University Press, 2000.

———. *Legacy of a Divided Nation: India's Muslims Since Independence*. Boulder, CO: Westview Press, 1997.

Hasan, Syed Abid. *Whither Hyderabad?* Hyderabad: n.p., 1935.

Hasan, Zoya, and Ritu Menon, eds. *In a Minority: Essays on Muslim Women in India*. New Delhi: Oxford University Press, 2005.

Hodgson, Marshall. *The Venture of Islam: Conscience and History in a World Civilization*. Vol. 1. Chicago: University of Chicago Press, 1974.

Hussain, Iqbalunissa. *Changing India: A Muslim Woman Speaks*. Karachi: Oxford University Press, 2015 (1940).

Hussain, Khurram. *The Muslim Speaks*. London: Zed Books, 2020.

Hyder, Mohammad. *October Coup: A Memoir of the Struggle for Hyderabad*. New Delhi: Roli Books, 2012.

Hyder, Syed Akbar. *Reliving Karbala: Martyrdom in South Asian Memory*. New York: Oxford University Press, 2006.

———. "Up, Urdu's Progressive Wit: Sulaiman Khatib, Sarvar Danda, and the Subaltern Satirists Who Spoke." *Annual of Urdu Studies*, no. 20 (2005): 99–126.

"India: The Happy War." *Time*, September 20, 1948. https://content.time.com/time/subscriber/article/0,33009,780030,00.html. Accessed May 2, 2022.

Jaisi, Sidq. *The Nocturnal Court, Darbaare-e-Durbar: The Life of a Prince of Hyderabad*. New Delhi: Oxford University Press, 2004.

Jalal, Ayesha. *Self and Sovereignty: Individual and Community in South Asian Islam since 1850*. London: Routledge, 2000.

———. *The Pity of Partition: Manto's Life, Times, and Work Across the India–Pakisan Divide*. Princeton, NJ: Princeton University Press, 2013.

———. *The Sole Spokesman: Jinnah, The Muslim League, and the Demand for Pakistan*. Cambridge: Cambridge University Press, 1985.

Jalil, Rakshanda. *Liking Progress, Loving Change: A Literary History of the Progressive Writers' Movement in Urdu*. Delhi: Oxford University Press, 2014.

Jaffrelot, Christophe. *Modi's India: Hindu Nationalism and the Rise of Ethnic Democracy*. Princeton, NJ: Princeton University Press, 2021.

———. *The Hindu Nationalist Movement in India*. New York: Columbia University Press, 1998.

Joseph, Uma T. *Accession of Hyderabad: An Inside Story*. Delhi: Sundeep Prakashan, 2006.

Kabir, Ananya Jahanara. *Partition's Post-amnesias: 1947, 1971 and Modern South Asia*. New Delhi: Women Unlimited, 2013; Dhaka: University Press, 2014.

Kamrava, Mehran, ed. *The New Voices of Islam: Rethinking Politics and Modernity*. Berkeley: University of California Press, 2006.

Kate, P. V. *Marathwada under the Nizams, 1724–1948*. Delhi: Mittal Publications, 1987.

Kaviraj, Sudipta. *The Invention of Private Life: Literature and Ideas*. New York: Columbia University Press, 2015.

Khalidi, Omar, ed. *Hyderabad: After the Fall*. Kansas: Hyderabad Historical Society, 1988.

———. *Muslims in the Deccan: A Historical Survey*. New Delhi: Global Media Publications, 2006.

Khan, Bilquis Jahan. *A Song of Hyderabad: Memories of a World Gone By*. New York: Oxford University Press, 2010.

Khan, Maryam Wasif. *Who Is a Muslim? Orientalism and Literary Populisms*. New York: Fordham University Press, 2021.

Kia, Mana. *Persianate Selves: Memories of Place and Origin before Nationalism*. Stanford University Press, 2020.

Kidwai, Huma R. *The Hussaini Alam House*. New Delhi: Zuban, 2012.

Kidwai, Saleem. "Josh Malihabadi: 'There Will Never Be Another Like You'" [Urdu]. In *Same-Sex Love in India*, edited by R. Vanita and S. Kidwai, 274–282. New York: Palgrave Macmillan, 2000.

King, Christopher. *One Language, Two Scripts: The Hindi Movement in Nineteenth Century India*. Bombay: Oxford University Press, 1994.

Kosambi, Meera. *Gender, Culture and Performance: Marathi Theatre and Cinema before Independence*. London: Routledge, 2015.

Krishna, Yamini, and Swathi Shivanand. "BJP Made Gains in Hyderabad Using History as a Weapon: But How Accurate Is Its Version of the Past?" *Scroll*, January 21, 2021. https://scroll.in/article/983875/bjp-made-gains-in-hyderabad-usinghistory-as-a-weapon-but-how-accurate-is-its-version-of-the-past. Accessed July 21, 2022.

Kundalia, Nidhi Dugar. *The Lost Generation: Chronicling the Dying Professions*. Gurgaon: Random House Publishing, 2015.

Lalita, K., and Deepa Dhanraj. *Rupture, Loss and Living: Minority Women Speak about Post-Conflict Life*. Hyderabad: Orient Blackswan, 2016.

Lalita K., Vasantha Kannabiran, Rama Melkote, Uma Maheshwari, Susie Tharu, and Veena Shatrugna. *We Were Making History: Life Stories of Women in the Telangana People's Struggle*. New Delhi: Kali for Women, 1989.

Lambert-Hurley, Siobhan. *Elusive Lives: Gender, Autobiography, and the Self in Muslim South Asia*. Stanford, CA: Stanford University Press, 2018.

Lawrence, Bruce. *Shattering the Myth: Islam Beyond Violence*. Princeton, NJ: Princeton University Press, 1998.

Lawrence, Bruce, and Ali Altaf Mia. *The Bruce Lawrence Reader: Islam Beyond Borders*. Durham, NC: Duke University Press, 2020.

Lean, Nathan. *The Islamophobia Industry: How the Right Manufactures Fear of Muslims*. London: Pluto Press, 2012.

Leonard, Karen. *Hyderabad and Hyderabadis*. New Delhi: Manohar, 2014.

———. "Hyderabad: Mulki–Non-Mulki Conflict." In *People, Princes, and Paramount Power: Society and Politics in the Indian Princely States*, edited by Robin Jeffrey, 65–106. New Delhi: Oxford University Press, 1978.

———. "Reassessing Indirect Rule in Hyderabad: Rule, Ruler, or Sons-in-Law of the State?" *Modern Asian Studies* 37, no. 2 (2003): 363–379.

———. *Social History of an Indian Caste: The Kayasths of Hyderabad*. Berkeley: University of California Press, 1978.

Limbale, Sharan Kumar. *Towards an Aesthetic of Dalit Literature*. New Delhi: Orient Longman, 2014.

Lukens-Bull, R., and M. Woodward, eds. *Handbook of Contemporary Islam and Muslim Lives*. Cham: Springer, 2020.

Lunn, David, "Across the Divide: Looking for the Common Ground of Hindustani." *Modern Asian Studies* 52, no. 6 (2018): 2056–2079.

Luther, Narendra. *Hyderabad: A Biography*. New Delhi: Oxford University Press, 2006.

Mahmudabad, Ali Khan. *Poetry of Belonging: Muslim Imaginings of India, 1850–1950*. New Delhi: Oxford University Press, 2020.

Mani, Preetha. "An Aesthetics of Isolation: How Pudumaippittan Gave Pre-Eminence to the Tamil Short Story." *South Asia: Journal of South Asian Studies* 43, no. 5 (2020): 926–942.

Mansergh, Nicholas, ed. *The Transfer of Power*. Vol. 12. London: Her Majesty's Stationary Office, 1983.

Mantena, Rama Sundari. "Publicity, Civil Liberties, and Political Life in Princely Hyderabad." *Modern Asian Studies* 53, no. 4 (2019): 1248–1277.

———. "The Andhra Movement, Hyderabad State, and the Historical Origins of the Telangana Demand: Public Life and Political Aspirations in India, 1900–1956." *India Review* 13, no. 4 (2014): 337–357.

Marsden, Magnus, and Madeline Reeves. "Marginal Hubs: On Conviviality Beyond the Urban Asia: Introduction." *Modern Asian Studies* 53, no. 3 (2019): 755–775.

Masud, Khalid, Salvatore, and Bruinessen, eds. *Islam and Modernity: Key Issues and Debates*. Edinburgh: Edinburgh University Press, 2009.

Melkote, Rama, B. Pradeep, and B. Vijaya Kumar. *Living Those Times: Memoirs and Writings of Burgula Narsing Rao*. New Delhi: People's Publishing House, 2021.

Menon, V. P. *The Story of the Integration of the Indian States*. New York: Longmans, Green and Co., 1955.

Metcalf, Barbara. *Islamic Contestations: Essays on Muslims in India and Pakistan.* New York: Oxford University Press, 2004.

———. *Moral Conduct and Authority: The Place of Adab in South Asian Islam.* Berkeley: University of California Press, 1984.

Moghadam, V. M., ed. *Identity Politics and Women: Cultural Reassertions and Feminisms in International Perspective.* Boulder, CO: Westview Press, 1994.

Mohammad, Afsar. *Evenings with a Sufi* [Collection of poems from Telugu]. New Delhi: Red River Press, 2022.

———. *The Festival of Pīrs: Shared Devotion and Popular Islam in South India.* New York: Oxford University Press, 2013.

Mir, Ali, and Raza Mir. *The Anthems of Resistance: A Celebration of Progressive Urdu Poetry.* New Delhi: Roli Books, 2006.

Mirza, Fareed. *Pre and Post Police Action in the Erstwhile Hyderabad: What I Saw, Felt and Did.* Hyderabad: Paramount Press, 1976.

Misrahi-Barak, Judith, K. Satyanarayana, and Nicole Tiara, eds. *Dalit Text: Aesthetics and Politics Reimagined.* New York: Routledge, 2019.

Mitchell, Lisa. "Making the Local Foreign: Shared Language and History in Southern India." *Journal of Linguistic Anthropology* 16, no. 2 (December 2006): 229–248.

———. *Language, Emotion, and Politics in South India: The Making of a Mother Tongue.* Bloomington: Indiana University Press, 2009.

Mitchell, Timothy, ed. *Questions of Modernity.* Minneapolis: University of Minnesota Press, 2000.

Moghadam, V. M., ed. *Identity Politics and Women: Cultural Reassertions and Feminisms in International Perspective.* Boulder, CO: Westview Press, 1994.

Moid, M. A. "Muslim Perceptions and Responses in Post-Police Action Contexts in Hyderabad." *Deccan Studies* 6, no. 2 (2008): 234–255.

Moid, M. A., and A. Suneetha. "Rethinking Majlis' Politics: Pre-1948 Muslim Concerns in Hyderabad State." *Indian Economic and Social History Review* 55, no. 1 (2018): 29–52.

More, J. P. B. *Muslim Identity, Print Culture, and the Dravidian Factor in Tamil Nadu.* Hyderabad: Orient Longman, 2004.

Mufti, Amir. *Enlightenment in the Colony: The Jewish Question and the Crisis of Postcolonial Culture.* Princeton, NJ: Princeton University Press, 2007.

Munshi, K. M. *Report on the Razakars of Hyderabad.* Hyderabad: n.p., 1948.

———. *The End of an Era: Hyderabad Memories.* Bombay: Bharatiya Vidya Bhavan, 1957.

Muppidi, Himadeep. *Politics in Emotion: The Song of Telangana*. London; New York: Routledge, 2015.

Nag, Sajal, Tejimala Gurung, and Abhijit Choudhury, eds. *Making of the Indian Union: Merger of Princely States and Excluded Areas*. New Delhi: Akansha Publishing House, 2007.

Naidu, Ratna. *Old Cities, New Predicaments: A Study of Hyderabad*. New Delhi: Sage Publications, 1990.

Narayana, B. Kesava, ed. *Comprehensive History and Culture of Andhra Pradesh*. Vol. 8, *Modern Andhra and Hyderabad, AD 1858–1956*. Hyderabad: EMESCO Books, 2016.

Neelkanth, Kishorilal Vyas. *Razakar*. New Delhi: National Publishing House, 2005.

Nerlekar, Anjali. *Bombay Modern: Arun Kolatkar and Bilingual Literary Culture*. Illinois: Northwestern University Press, 2016.

Noor, Farha. "Negotiating Nostalgia: Progressive Women's Memoirs in Urdu." *South Asian History and Culture* 12, no. 4 (2021): 371–384.

Noorani, A. G. *The Destruction of Hyderabad*. New Delhi: Tulika Books, 2013.

Orsini, Francesca. "The Multilingual Local in World Literature." Comparative *Literature* 67, no. 1 (December 2015): 345–374.

———. *The Hindi Public Sphere (1920–1940): Language and Literature in the Age of Nationalism*. New Delhi: Oxford University Press, 2009.

Pandey, Gyanendra. *Remembering Partition: Violence, Nationalism, and History in India*. Cambridge: Cambridge University Press, 2010.

Panneeru, Ramesh. *Telangana Armed Struggle in Nalgonda District: A Case Study of Kadavendi Village, 1930–51 AD*. Hyderabad: Prajasakti Book House, 2010.

Pasco, Allan H. "Literature as Historical Archive." *New Literary History* 35, no. 3 (Summer 2004): 373–439.

Patel, Alka, and Karen Leonard, eds. *Indo-Muslim Cultures in Transition*. Leiden: Brill, 2012.

Patel, Eboo, Jennifer Howe Peace, and Noah J. Silverman, eds. *Interreligious/ Interfaith Studies: Defining a New Field*. Boston: Beacon Press, 2018.

Pavier, Barry. *The Telangana Movement, 1944–51*. Delhi: Vikas, 1981.

Pernau, Margrit. *Ashraf into Middle Classes: Muslims in Nineteenth-Century Delhi*. New Delhi: Oxford University Press, 2013.

———. "Contested Emotion of Masculinity: The Court, The Street and the Negotiation Table in an Indian Princely State in the 20th Century." *Journal l'Homme* 32, no. 2 (2021): 41–58.

———. *Emotions and Temporalities*. Cambridge: Cambridge University Press, 2021.

———. *Passing Patrimonialism: Politics and Political Culture in Hyderabad, 1911–1948*. New Delhi: Manohar, 2000.

———. "Schools for Muslim Girls: A Colonial or An Indigenous Project? A Case Study of Hyderabad." In *Perspectives of Mutual Encounters in South Asian History, 1760–1860*, edited by Jamal Malik, 263–276. *Social, Economic, and Political Studies of the Middle East and Asia*, Vol. 73. Leiden: Brill, 2000.

Petievich, Carla. "Gender Politics and the Urdu Ghazal: Exploratory Observations on Rekhta versus Rekhti." *Indian Economic and Social History Review* 38, no. 3 (2001): 223–248.

Pollock, Sheldon. *Literary Cultures in History: Reconstructions from South Asia*. Berkeley: University of California Press, 2003.

Powell, Avril, and Siobhan Lambert-Hurley, eds. *Rhetoric and Reality: Gender and the Colonial Experience in South Asia*. New Delhi: Oxford University Press, 2006.

Prange, Sebastian R. *Monsoon Islam: Trade and Faith on the Medieval Malabar Coast*. Cambridge: Cambridge University Press, 2018.

Purushotham, Sunil. "Federating the Raj: Hyderabad, Sovereign Kingship, and Partition." *Modern Asian Studies* 54 (January 2020): 157–198.

———. *From Raj to Republic: Sovereignty, Violence, and Democracy in India*. Stanford: Stanford University Press, 2021.

———. "Internal Violence: The 'Police Action' in Hyderabad." *Comparative Studies in Society and History* 57, no. 2 (April 2015): 435–466.

Qasmi, Ali Usman, and Megan Eaton Robb, eds. *Muslims against the Muslim League*. Cambridge: Cambridge University Press, 2017.

Rahman, Raisur. *Locale, Everyday Islam, and Modernity: Qasbah Towns and Muslim Life in Colonial India*. New Delhi: Oxford University Press, 2015.

Rahman, Tariq. *From Hindi to Urdu: A Social and Political History*. New Delhi: Orient BlackSwan Private Limited, 2011.

Rahmat Ali, Choudhry. *Osmanistan: The Fatherland of the Osman Nation*. Cambridge, UK: Osmanistan National Movement, 1946.

———. *The Millat and the Mission*. Cambridge, UK: National Movement, 1944.

Raj, Sheela. *Medievalism to Modernism: Socio-economic and Cultural History of Hyderabad 1869–1911*. Bombay: Popular Prakashan, 1987.

Rajyadhyaksha, Ashish. *Indian Cinema in the Time of Celluloid: From Bollywood to the Emergency*. Bloomington: Indiana University Press, 2009.

Ranga Reddy, K. V. *The Struggle and the Betrayal: The Telangana Story.* Hyderabad: Vignana Sarovara Prachuranalu, 2010.

Rao, Chandra Rajeswara. *The Historic Telangana Struggle: Some Useful Lessons from Its Rich Experience.* Delhi: Communist Party of India, 1971.

Rao, Devulapalli Venkateswara. *Telangana Armed Struggle and the Path of the Indian Revolution.* Calcutta: Proletarian Path Publications, 1974.

Rao, K. V. Narayana. *The Emergence of Andhra Pradesh.* Bombay: Popular Prakashan, 1973.

Rastegar, Mitra. *Tolerance and Risk: How U. S. Liberalism Racializes Muslim.* Minneapolis: University of Minnesota Press, 2021.

Ravikant and Tarun K. Saint, eds. *Translating Partition.* New Delhi: Katha, 2001.

Raychaudhuri, Anindya. *Narrating South Asian Partition: Oral History, Literature, Cinema.* New York: Oxford University Press, 2019.

Razvi, Jawad. *Political Awakening in Hyderabad: Role of Youth and Students 1938–1956.* Hyderabad: Visalandhra Publishing House, 1985.

Reddy, Arutla Ramachandra. *Telangana Struggle: Memoirs.* Translated by B. Narsing Rao. Delhi: People's Publishing House, 1984.

Reddy, Lingala Panduranga. *September 1948 Hyderabad Liberation Day: A Misnomer.* Hyderabad: Voice of Telangana, 2011.

Safi, Omid, ed. *Progressive Muslims: On Justice, Gender and Pluralism.* Oxford: OneWorld, 2003.

Saheb, S. A. A. "Dudekula Muslims of Andhra Pradesh: An Ethnographic Profile." *Economic and Political Weekly* 38, no. 46 (2003): 4908–4912.

Saikia, Yasmin, and M. Raisur Rahman. *The Cambridge Companion to Sayyid Ahmed Khan.* New Delhi: Cambridge University Press, 2019.

Saint, Tarun. *Witnessing Partition: Memory, History and Fiction.* London: Routledge, 2010.

Sarkar, Mahua. *Visible Histories, Disappearing Women: Producing Womanhood in Late Colonial Bengal.* Durham, NC: Duke University Press, 2008.

Sarkar, Tanika. "Semiotics of Terror: Muslim Children and Women in Hindu Rashtra." *Economic and Political Weekly* 47, no. 44 (2002): 2872–2876.

Schmitthener, Peter L. *Telugu Resurgence: C. P. Brown and Cultural Consolidation in Nineteenth-Century South India.* New Delhi: Manohar, 2001.

Seljouk, M. A. *Corpses.* London: Gerald Duckworth & Co Ltd, 1966.

Sherman, Taylor C. *Muslim Belonging in Secular India: Negotiating Citizenship in Postcolonial Hyderabad.* Cambridge: Cambridge University Press, 2015.

Sherwani, H. K. *History of Medieval Deccan (1298–1724).* Hyderabad: Government of Andhra Pradesh, 1973.

Singh, Amritjit, Nalini Iyer, and Rahul K. Gairola, eds. *Revisiting India's Partition: New Essays on Memory, Culture, and Politics.* New York: Lexington Books, 2016.

Singhavi, Snehal, trans. *Angaray.* New Delhi: Penguin India, 2018.

Sundarayya, P. *An Autobiography.* Edited and translated by Atlury Murali. Delhi: National Book Trust, 2009.

———. *Telangana People's Struggle and Its Lessons.* Calcutta: Communist Party of India (Marxist), 1972.

Taneja, Anand Vivek. *Jinnealogy: Time, Islam and Ecological Thought in the Medieval Ruins of Delhi.* Stanford: Stanford University Press, 2017.

Tharu, Susie, and Lalitha. *Women Writing in India: 600 BC to the Present.* New York: Feminist Press at the City University of New York, 1990.

Thirumali, Inukonda. *Against Dora and Nizam: People's Movement in Telangana.* New Delhi: Kanishka Publishers, 2003.

Tirtha, Swami Ramananda. *Memoirs of the Hyderabad Freedom Struggle.* New Delhi: Popular Prakashan, 1967.

Thomson, Mike. "Hyderabad 1948: India's Hidden Massacre." September 24, 2013. https://www.bbc.com/news/magazine-24159594. Accessed September 23, 2021.

Truschke, Audrey. *Aurangzeb: The Life and Legacy of India's Most Controversial King.* Stanford: Stanford University Press, 2017.

Tschacher, Torsten. "Can 'Om' Be an Islamic Term?" *South Asian History and Culture* 5, no. 2 (April 2014): 195–211.

Venkat, Dhulipala. *Creating a New Medina: State Power, Islam and the Quest of Pakistan in Late Colonial North India.* Delhi: Cambridge University Press, 2015.

Yamini Krishna, C. "Language and Cinema: Schisms in the Representation of Hyderabad." *South Asia: Journal of South Asian Studies* 44, no.6 (2021): 1027–1040.

Yazdani, Zubaida, and Mary Chrystal. *The Seventh Nizam: The Fallen Empire.* Cambridge: Cambridge University Press, 1985.

Waheed, Sarah Fatima. *Hidden Histories of Pakistan: Censorship, Literature, and Secular Nationalism in Late Colonial India.* Cambridge: Cambridge University Press, 2021.

———. "After Hyderabad's 1948 Annexation: Muslim Belonging and Histories of the Long Partition." *Asian Affairs* 53, no. 2 (2022). DOI: 10.1080/030683 74.2022.2076488.

Wilson, Jon. "How Modernity Arrived to Godavari?" *Modern Asian Studies* 51 (March 2017): 399–431.

Zamindar, Vazira Fazila-Yacoobali. *The Long Partition and the Making of Modern South Asia: Refugees, Boundaries, Histories.* New York: Columbia University Press, 2007.

Zia, Ather. *Resisting Disappearance: Military Occupation and Women's Activism in Kashmir.* Seattle: University of Washington Press, 2019.

INDEX